ARCHWAY
Life Before Dreams

by

Archie E. Anderson

Edited & captioned for the Terrian Journals Collection by

Donald Murray Anderson

ARCHWAY: Six Year Book of Dreams: Volume One

A Mythbreaker Book

2015 Edition

ISBN 978-1-987850-17-8

For information address: mythbreaker@mail.com

(a writer's autobiography and writings,
edited by Donald Murray Anderson)

Introduction

Archway: Life Before Dreams is a collection of writings by Archie E. Anderson arranged in chronological order, when possible, or, when not possible, under writing genre rubric.

This volume is an incomplete autobiography, covering a variety of youthful living experiences beyond the writings preceding, during, and following Archway: Six Year Book of Dreams.

Since AEA's life takes place before, after, and, in a more restricted sense, during the six years of mainly dreaming about life outside of war, life itself always comes before dreams.

Archway: Life Before Dreams expresses itself here in anecdotal, diary, essay, and fiction writing forms.

The story begins with the author's later-in-life, long-term memories of his childhood and ends with the actual diary notes and some expanded writing of his twenties.

In between are the surviving writings of his twenties, thirties, and forties.

His prose after Archway: Six Year Book of Dreams are mostly fictional. He writes little about himself in his prose. Exceptions include some of the dialogue in his stories, as well as "Unlimited" and speeches of his forties.

Almost all of his poetry is excluded because it is already published in Archway: Lifetime Rhyme and other volumes,

Nevertheless, a volume of Archie's writings cannot be complete without some poems, ones not filed with those appearing in his books of poetry.

His poetry often relates personal experiences, life events, and many of the people he encounters along the way.

The almost complete and comprehensive collection of Archie E. Anderson's fictional, thoughtful, and commercial prose appears here in one volume for the first time.

His plays, stories, essays, speeches, and humour are also found in this collection.

There are some gaps, due to forever lost pages. Whenever possible, those gaps are filled thanks to the author.

In one story with lost pages, "Conquest of Size", the editor adds a few words of continuity that are derived from the author's summary of his story when he originally writes it.

To a certain extent, all writings in this volume reflect their times and ways of thinking contemporary to those times, although there are some hints of progress too.

These hints reflect the author, who has a unique perspective coming from his personal unorthodoxy - his vegetarianism since childhood.

The few editorial alterations here include replacing "man" with "people" or "humanity"; changing "he" to "s/he" in general statements; and changing archaic measures to the worldwide metric system used by 96+% of humanity.

In other respects, the writings of this volume remain largely in their original form, as they are throughout the Archway series in the Terrian Journals collection.

AEA

Young Life Story

1. "Archie"
2. 1917
3. Stories of Childhood
4. Academic Outcomes
5. Exploring A Five+ Year Diary: Age 20 to 24

Assorted Writings

1. India & East
2. Essays & Issues
3. Journalism
4. Sports
5. Various Stories
6. Crime Stories
7. Science Fiction Stories
8. Plays
9. Continuity and Radio Scripts
10. Speeches
11. More poetry
12. Notes on scraps of paper
13. An Epilogue of Guesswork

Appendices

I. Five+ Year diary entries
II. Life (an extended diary)
III. 1944-1945

“Archie”

Archie McEachern

Archie’s father, WRJ Anderson, often tells the story of why he and his spouse ME Anderson name this particular child “Archie”.

WRJ says he has a swimming mishap during his youth and his friend Archie McEachern saves his life.

Unfortunately, the two Archies never meet. McEachern is killed in the 1914-1918 war.

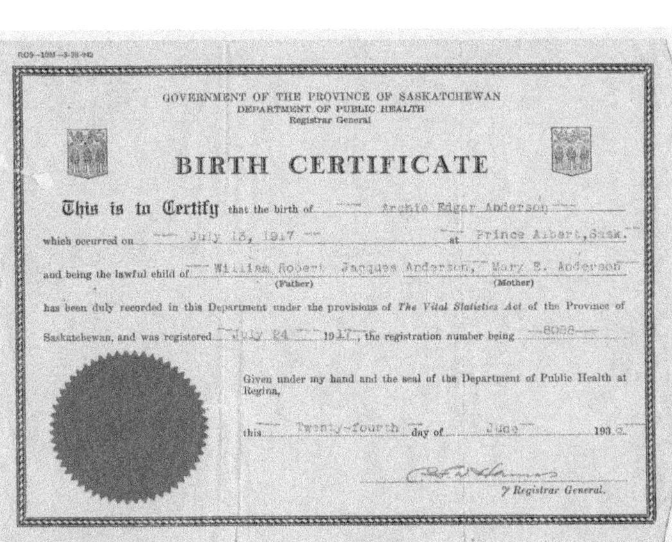

RO9—10M—3-28-940

GOVERNMENT OF THE PROVINCE OF SASKATCHEWAN
DEPARTMENT OF PUBLIC HEALTH
Registrar General

BIRTH CERTIFICATE

This is to Certify that the birth of Archie Edgar Anderson

which occurred on July 13, 1917 at Prince Albert, Sask.

and being the lawful child of William Robert Jacques Anderson, (Father) Mary E. Anderson (Mother)

has been duly recorded in this Department under the provisions of *The Vital Statistics Act* of the Province of Saskatchewan, and was registered July 24 1917, the registration number being 8088

Given under my hand and the seal of the Department of Public Health at Regina,

this Twenty-fourth day of June 193[illegible]

Registrar General.

1917

The year Archie E. Anderson is born, Wilfred Laurier is still a member of parliament and The National Hockey League is founded.

Canada celebrates its 50th birthday twelve days before Archie's birth.

Archie is born five years after The Titanic sinks off the coast of Newfoundland and Labrador.

He is born only three years after a far more deadly marine disaster, the sinking of The Empress of Ireland in the St. Lawrence River.

He is born in the final year of "the war to end all war". People in uniforms are gassed and slaughtered.

That was long before war became eternal under the warlords ruling the country south of Canada.

The Halifax Explosion occurs four months after Archie is born. It's the largest unnatural explosion in history before the atomic bombing of Hiroshima.

The UK invades Baghdad the year Archie is born too, but the U.K. is defeated, as are two modern empires attempting the same conquest.

Archie is born the year of the Russian Revolution, when a mass uprising topples a tyrannical monarchical dictatorship.

The year after Archie is born, 21 million people around the world die in a pandemic called the Spanish Flu. About 50,000 of the deaths are in Canada.

Archie's childhood passes in a happy age of fast living and partying, but not in his home town and family.

He is born into a family which grows to have seven children who lack the financial means to live fast or party.

In the idyllic setting of small town Saskatchewan, they can only enjoy simple pleasures while his family struggles to survive a great economic depression.

But Archie's parents are gifted in child rearing.

He and Lorne, one of his older brothers, are permitted to declare themselves vegetarians when they are only six years old.

So these brothers are very young pioneers in a brand new lifestyle in the “western” world.

They’re eating all the right things long before it becomes a popular fad or almost an act of religious sect devotion in the “western” world.

Archie and Lorne accidentally align themselves with the dietary behaviours that are part of the wisdom of the more ancient and advanced “eastern” civilizations.

Archie and Lorne are vegetarians long before “western” scientists and doctors discover that the brothers’ eating habits are the healthiest ones for anyone who wants to live long and well.

When Archie is only five years old, Banting and Best isolate insulin. When he’s only 11 years old, penicillin is discovered.

A baby born seven days before Archie, in Wainwright, Alberta will grow up to become Archie’s spouse of nearly 73 years.

STORIES OF CHILDHOOD

Mary's fifth

It all started for me in Prince Albert, Friday 13, 1917. It did take a year to finish WWI but I managed that and probably cut my first tooth at the same time.

Since I was the fifth to appear there was no record kept.

Cameron and Heap

Early memories are of visits to Cameron and Heap, a wholesale grocer where my father was the shipper.

He also augmented his wages by tending the furnace on weekends.

He would often take me with him and I was allowed to roam through the boxes and bales of food. In those days, groceries were packaged in large containers.

I explored the mountains of huge sacks of brown sugar. The smell of brown sugar still reminds me of those mysterious adventures.

Then there was the thrill of riding the freight elevator. I was allowed to help activate it by pulling a cord which evoked a hum and we were sliding upward toward new adventures.

One area on the second floor was a private locked room. I did manage to peak one day and was rewarded by the sight of endless rows of shelves containing chocolate bars and fancy boxes of candy.

Occasionally, my father would bring home some of those goodies, usually broken packages that could not be sold to the retailers.

Since dental care was not a priority, I am lucky still to have the majority of my teeth.

The elevator almost spelt the end for my father. One day he stepped on to an elevator that wasn't there. Somehow the security gate had not closed.

Miraculously, my father survived, probably because he landed on his feet. It resulted in one leg being permanently shorter than the other.

He was compensated by having his hospital bills paid and received full pay while he was recovering.

Had such an accident happened in the present there would have been a large settlement which could have made a considerable difference in the family's life style.

A chore

There is a faint memory of the chore I would perform before I reached school age. I was given the privilege of taking my father's lunch to him.

On one particular day I arrived at the warehouse only to find the large doors where I usually entered were locked.

Not realizing I could enter by the front door, I stood for an eternity, trying to keeps from crying until my father finally checked and rescued me.

My mother said I should have been called Alex and cited a story to show what she meant.

When I was pre-school age, I was asked to do something by the time-honoured method of saying' "I bet you a nickle you can't do so and so."

Apparently I replied, "I'll bet you a dime I am not going to try."

I have no knowledge of this of course.

Special diet

There was a fruit warehouse near the grocery warehouse where my father worked. As a result we always had stalks of bananas and cases of oranges in our basement.

In those days this must have been unusual as most families did not put as much emphasis on fresh fruit and vegetables.

Bread sharing

My father would sometimes bring home some doubtful items. One thing I remember is the huge round of cheese which sat in our basement until my mother finally ordered it removed.

The smell became too much for her. Some fanciers of strong cheese would be appalled by such waste.

As with many homes in those days, despite the fact we had at least one cat on hand at all times, we had mice from time to time.

My mother often kept spare loaves of bread on a shelf above the basement steps. One day she reached for a loaf and was amazed at its lightness.

The mice had hollowed it out, leaving only the outside crust. As with many families, our bread was home made. It was usually placed in a warm place to rise.

In one instance, our cat found a warm, soft bed which turned out to be a fresh batch of bread. That was the end of that pan of bread.

Bulk milk

Milk was delivered in large milk cans and each customer would have their own jugs. The milkman had measuring cups which he used to ladle out the amount each customer ordered.

When I first saw milk in bottles I could scarcely grasp the

idea of milk in bottles being the same as the bulk milk we bought.

It is interesting when one thinks that today's bulk foods were known many years ago. So much for progress.

Pen wagons

P.A. lived in the shadow of the federal penitentiary. We were always reminded of its presence by the passing of horse-drawn wagons manned by prisoners, winter and summer.

They hauled wood or other things. Hard labour was more than a word.

I never visited the penitentiary until years later with my parents who knew the warden. That visit in itself was an interesting experience.

Winter

In winter we wore wrap-around moccasins and rubbers. I have little memory of the cold, but have been told the temperature would drop to -60°C.

My father said it took a ton of coal a week to heat our house, which isn't surprising when you consider the lack of insulation which was the norm in those days.

Gordon saves us

One incident I vaguely remember. It was a cold winter morning and the kitchen stove was well-stocked, too well as it turned out.

The wood box beside the stove caught fire.

Gordon, the eldest was having his breakfast. Without hesitating, he turned on the tap at the sink, placed his hand over it and squirted water to douse the flames.

Father's brew

The kitchen stove had many uses, from heating our bath water to helping to make things cosy for home brew which my father sometimes made.

Failures were recorded, usually in the middle of the night when exploding bottles disturbed our sleep.

Waterway

Behind our house there was a low-lying area which flooded in the spring, providing a great spot for rafting and falling in from time to time.

Down towards the river there was a reservoir which we would explore but treated it with respect, at least I did as I could not swim.

Climbing stacks

Far more interesting was the pile of cordwood which the powerhouse used for fuel.

It was a great adventure to climb among the stacks, probably dangerous too but we never seemed to have any problem.

Streamings

Sometimes in summer we would wander down to the river below the powerhouse which provided an ideal spot for the minnows.

We would catch a few and put them in bottles until we either tired of the sport or the fish died.

The river was always an attraction, summer and winter. Some of the boys would dig for clams but I usually looked for petrified wood.

Out in the cold

In winter there was great scope for skiing and snowshoeing, especially along the frozen river.

Older brothers and sisters would toboggan on the hills beyond the flats where we lived. Before I reached the age to join in it was too late as the toboggan was smashed in an encounter with a tree.

No one was hurt but there was no money for replacement.

Carnival

A winter carnival was the big event. I remember the people trying to catch a greased pig, and the dogsled races. The races carried on for a week.

Each day's position for the racers was carefully marked and then they continued the next day from the same positions.

At the focal point of the winter carnival was a toboggan slide which was considered too dangerous for me.

I can't remember how old I was at the time, but I was allowed to snowshoe along the river with older brothers and sisters.

One event was when a man would skate down the toboggan slide.

Swimming

In summer there was swimming in the river at a marked off area. I could not swim at that time but wade in and even ducked under but not too often as I opened my eyes under water and could see nothing but the grey wall of the muddy Saskatchewan.

Brother Jim was a great diver and won medals for platform diving.

I don't know if he ever did or not, but some of the older boys would dive off the nearby railway bridge and swim down to the swimming pool.

I imagine there were some mishaps but can't remember any fatalities.

Walks

Sundays were often the time for family walks. We would walk a few kilometres.

It seemed a long way at the time but I discovered on a return trip in later years that it was no more than a couple of kilometres.

The destination was the Little Red River, an exciting place as there were big sand dunes to climb and a wonderful swing bridge.

Strangely enough, the sand hills seemed just as high when I returned at age 76.

Five corn

The government had a unique way of introducing the large nickels to replace the tiny five cent pieces in circulation when I was a child.

We learnt that if you bought a bag of popcorn you would find a big nickel in each bag. This carried on for some time until we grew tired of free popcorn.

Pasture eyes

Another memory is of the pasture land which was just beyond our house. There were usually several cows pastured there. It was fenced.

Apparently it was difficult at times and the only way I could be frightened was by threatening me with the horned cows.

I became afraid to pass by the pasture alone and it was not until I reached my teens that I was able to overcome my fear.

The manner in which I did so was through a cattle show at the Edmonton Exhibition. Boys were needed to lead cattle in front of the grandstand for judging.

As a free ticket to the fairgrounds was the reward, I applied.

Fortunately, my charge was a small jersey cow, but I did have misgivings about those horns.*

[Archie writes the whole story in the late 1930s. It is reproduced here as “Cowed” in the Various Stories section.]

Cook encounters

Several doors away from us there was a Métis family, by the name of Cook. Edna played with the children and actually picked up their accent.

Such words as kivers for covers and flewer for flour, to name but a few, soon were incorporated into her vocabulary.

My experience with one member of the Cook family was less friendly.
I would sometimes go to the local rink with friends to listen to the band which played for the skaters on weekend evenings.

The temperature was such that you could see your breath. We would blow out water vapour, which we thought was steam, and pretend we were smoking.

One night an older Cook boy spotted us and accused us of smoking. We denied any such thing but he promised to tell our fathers.

My father never said anything to me at that time. After all, he had started smoking at a very early age. He always said he was seven years old.

However, many years later he asked me if I had been smoking that night. I later did try that weed but never did acquire the habit.

Strangely enough, what put me off smoking was the example of older brothers smoking. It was such a messy affair, and I never did start.

Marvellous skater

Besides skating and hockey, the local rink had figure skaters and others performing from time to time. One night there was a one-legged skater.

We did not have the price of admission but managed to speak through an open glassless window.

Once the skater was started by a push he performed marvellously. I have always been reminded of that skill when watching two-legged skaters who in some cases did not do any better.

Road apples

A winter sport many young boys indulged in was playing hockey on the snow-covered frozen roads.

Lacking a puck the next best thing was a "road apple" (frozen horse manure which was round and hard).

Step party

When the two oldest brothers, Gordon and Jim reached the party age, my mother would throw parties for many of the boys and girls from their school.

I was too young to stay up but remember the excitement of the young people talking and laughing as they gathered together for games and fun.

Not wishing to miss anything, I would sit on the stairs and sometimes edge down to hear what was going on.

My mother said I would often be found asleep on the stairs from where I had to be carried to bed.

Boilerless bath

A big event was when one of the bedrooms was converted to a bathroom with a real tub.

This was a welcome change from the boiler on the stove routine which was fine for small children but soon became awkward and embarrassing as we started to outgrow the boiler.

Electric washer

Another memorable event, at least for my mother, was the acquiring of an electric washing machine.

It was no more than the old hand-operated type run by a motor but it must have greatly simplified the chore of weekly washing for a family of nine.

Macauley

We lived close to Macauley School, probably too close, as we were among the last to arrive each morning.

One episode I remember was when the principal told us one day in assembly that a new Canadian had brought his children to school for the first day and called him Mr. Macauley.

It was considered a great joke, probably embarrassing the children, that is if they knew enough English at the time.

Barn dance

Some things are not so innocent.

There was the case of some of the older boys and girls being caught in the midst of nude dancing in a nearby barn. In those days it seemed to be a matter for school discipline.

Most of those I knew thought it was funny, although none could see themselves in such a situation.

Kathleen

Our next door neighbours were called Deans. There were two girls, one Helen and the other, my age, Kathleen. She was my first girl friend.

After the end of June, our family moved to the Norwood district, corner of 95th Street and 115th Avenue, a large four bedroom house. (Edmonton)

I suspect that it was a matter of economics as the first house rental was probably ten dollars a month more than the $25 we paid on 95th Street.

I did meet Kathleen twice at the East End Swimming Pool. The first time I developed a shyness which did not allow me to acknowledge her.

The second and last time, we did wander around the zoo after swimming. She then lived in the Highlands which in those days was one of the better districts and was a bit remote.

Crockett

Many summer days were spent at the swimming pool. We would go when the pool opened and take our lunch. The admission was five cents.

One holidays the price was ten cents, which led us to avoid such days. However, on one occasion, one of the fellow had only five cents.

At that time the Crockett family seemed to run all such city athletic places. The oldest member of the family was in charge. He seemed ancient to us.

He took us to one side and said he would let us all in for five cents but we mustn't tell anyone.

That left some of us with an extra nickel to spend on our favourite toffee bar, Neilson's I think, which came in sections which we could break off and share.

I later was in the same classroom as his niece Ada, who was also sports minded.

I remember one class Christmas party when we exchanged gifts. Ada had drawn my name and I received a brand new puck.

I made good use of it but was disappointed as it was scarcely the gift a boy would expect from a girl.

I later played tennis with her cousin Ken who was a natural athlete, like most of the Crocketts.

Hockey

Hockey was the big thing and many backyards were flooded for rinks. Our yard was one of those used.

As we grew old enough to have some money of our own, a group of us were able to scrape up enough money to pay my parents for the extra water we used.

It was in such cramped quarters that many young hockey players honed their skills, especially in stick-handling.

Frozen toes were the accepted part of the game as we often became so engrossed with the game that we forgot or ignored the warning signs.

We soon learned that the traditional method of rubbing affected toes with snow was wrong.

The quickest and best way to thaw out was to plunge our feet into the hottest water we could stand. There was some pain but the relief came quickly with no after-effects.

Street car

We usually rode the streetcar and the price was ten tickets for 25¢. Sometime, when riding back from the pool, a group would get on together.

Some without the necessary ticket would hold their hand over the ticket box and hope the conductor would not notice.

I am sure the conductor knew, but he seldom called any back to pay the fare. Since times were hard, most understood and took no action.

Adversity seems to bring out the best in some.

Exhibition

The annual exhibition was a big event in most children's' lives. There was one free day for all school children and midway rides were five cents each.

It is surprising how much fun most could have for less than a dollar.

As we grew older, some of us would try to sneak in over the fence when the man patrolling was far enough away for us to outrun him and mingle with the crowd.

On one occasion brother Wally was along with several others. We saw our chance and all scrambled over and away.

Wally, who at that time was on the plump side, couldn't run fast enough and was caught.

However, a short time later on the midway we met him.

He explained that the fellow who caught him had been talked into releasing him by one of the men from one of the nearby horse barns.

Also, I suspect the sight of Wally crying influenced the stable worker as he handed Wally fifty cents, a most generous gift in those days.

We valued the exhibition as younger boys and girls to the extent that we would always visit the free places first.

We'd go to the barns to see the prize cows, horses, pigs, and sheep.

Then we'd see the manufacturer's building where there were always free samples of ice cream and other delights.

Then and only then we hurried to the midway for the thrills of the rides and perhaps a sideshow.

The decisions were many and we carefully calculated where and how to spend our few nickles.

One ride we always had to experience was the Ferris wheel, the closest approach to a space trip we could imagine, especially when the giant wheel would pause as our chair was at the very top.

Then it was back to earth again, but the thrill lingered on.

One of the main sideshows always featured a magician who would have a young woman climb into a small box.

We wondered how she could possibly fit into such a small space.

Then, with the lid closed, he would proceed to push swords through the box.

At this point, he would open the lid and invite people to view the miracle.

I always regretted I never did discover the secret as I could never manage the extra ten cents charged to look.

Plant

Some distance from our home there was an old gravel processing plant which was perfect for climbing and exploring.

We climbed to the top and peeked down at the chutes located at the bottom of each hopper.

Some of the more adventurous among us would climb down inside and slide out through the chute, a drop of nearly two metres.

I was content to climb the endless belt that conveyed gravel to the top.

Dog

(Archie, Lorne, & "Dog")

We had a dog, of which I have no memory. It apparently guarded me from everyone.

Its only problem was with fire crackers and thunder storms. Both noises sent him to cover under a bed.

School

Children started school at the age of six. There was a kindergarten type class for the first year. I recall our teacher writing something on the blackboard.

Those who could understand what she wrote were promoted to the first grade. I never did discover what the magic words were.

However, since I was in love with my teacher, I didn't really care. I think her name was Miss Pollock.

Being just below the middle in the group of seven children I was seldom bothered and could, to a degree, go my own way.

Edmonton partnership

A great change in all our lives came when my father had an offer to move to Edmonton and become a partner in a grocery store owned by an ex-employee of Cameron and Heap.

However, the owner, Everett Dean found conditions were deteriorating as the Great Depression was about to begin.

He did hire my father as deliveryman for awhile but even this soon turned out to be more than the business could support.

But as it turned out, Edmonton eventually offered more opportunities than Prince Albert where many existed only by such menial jobs as hauling wood or working at the ice house.

In my own case, it worked out reasonably well.

Prior to moving to Edmonton brother Lorne and I were outfitted with long pants as it was assumed the "big city" school boys would not deign to wear the shorts as affected by P.A. boys.

Of course when we appeared at Macauley School we were the only two wearing long trousers. So much for city sophistication.

The train trip to Edmonton via Saskatoon was quite an adventure.

It was the first such experience for the family, although our parents had come by train from Ontario at the turn of the century.

We arrived in Edmonton on April 1, 1927. We did experience a few April Fool's tricks too.

First the spring snow and then my father's disappointment over the lowering of his expectations for a partnership with Everett Dean.

As the Depression deepened, there were other setbacks.

...During those years both Archie and brother Lorne were interested in studying science at university, but their parents only had the money to send the older boy, Lorne.

ACADEMIC OUTCOMES

Among Archie's papers there are no records of his first five years of schooling. However, Grade 6 to senior secondary school report cards are among his papers.

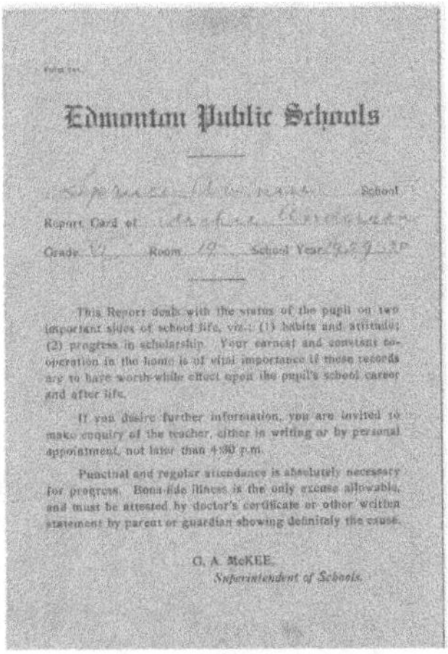

Here are some samples of those cards:

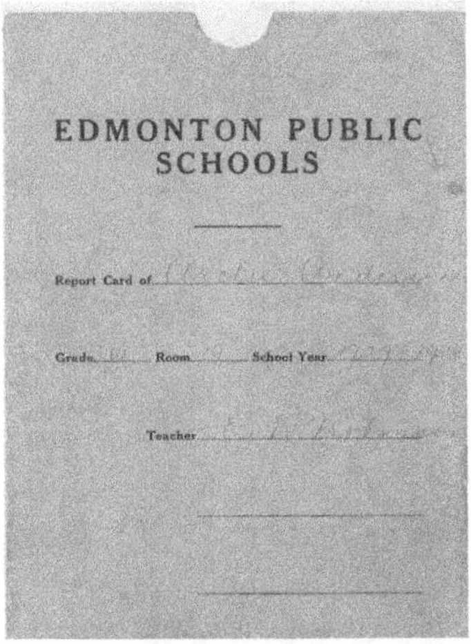

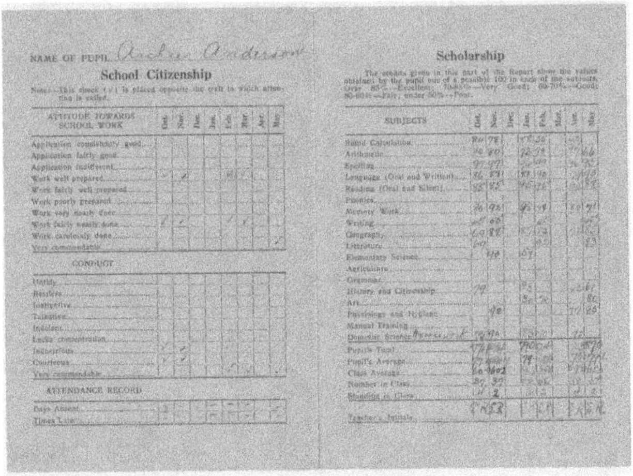

Form 181

Edmonton Public Schools

Spruce Avenue School

Report Card of E. Anderson

Grade VII Room 2 School Year 1932-33

This Report deals with the status of the pupil on two important sides of school life, viz.: (1) habits and attitude; (2) progress in scholarship. Your earnest and constant co-operation in the home is of vital importance if these records are to have worth-while effect upon the pupil's school career and after life.

If you desire further information, you are invited to make enquiry of the teacher, either in writing or by personal appointment, not later than 4.30 p.m.

Punctual and regular attendance is absolutely necessary for progress. Bona-fide illness is the only excuse allowable, and must be attested by doctor's certificate or other written statement by parent or guardian showing definitely the cause.

G. A. McKEE,
Superintendent of Schools.

Teacher's Remarks

October Speaks for self
November
December
January
February
March
April
May

Parent's or Guardian's Remarks

October
November
December
January
February
March
April
May

Parent's or Guardian's Signatures

October Mrs. W. Anderson
November Mrs. W. Anderson
December Mrs. W. Anderson
January
February
March
April
May

NAME OF PUPIL E. Anderson

School Citizenship

Note.—The check (✓) is placed opposite the trait to which attention is called.

ATTITUDE TOWARDS SCHOOL WORK	Oct.	Nov.	Dec.	Jan.	Feb.	Mar.	Apr.	May
Application consistently good								
Application fairly good								
Application indifferent								
Work well prepared								
Work fairly well prepared								
Work poorly prepared								
Work very neatly done								
Work fairly neatly done								
Work carelessly done								
Very commendable								
CONDUCT								
Untidy								
Restless								
Inattentive								
Talkative								
Indolent								
Lacks concentration								
Industrious								
Courteous								
Very commendable								
ATTENDANCE RECORD								
Days Absent	0	0	0	0	0	0	0	0
Times Late	0	0	0	0	0	0	0	0

Scholarship

The credits given in this part of the Report show the values obtained by the pupil out of a possible 100 in each of the subjects. Over 85%—Excellent; 70-85%—Very Good; 60-70%—Good; 50-60%—Fair; under 50%—Poor.

SUBJECTS	Oct.	Nov.	Dec.	Jan.	Feb.	Mar.	Apr.	May
Rapid Calculation	[illegible]		[illegible]			86		[illegible]
Arithmetic	[illegible]		[illegible]			100		[illegible]
Spelling	[illegible]		[illegible]			67		[illegible]
Language (Oral and Written)	[illegible]					84		77
Reading (Oral and Silent)								
Phonics								
Memory Work								
Writing	[illegible]		62			65		
Geography	[illegible]		[illegible]			92		[illegible]
Literature	[illegible]		[illegible]			95		91
Elementary Science								
Agriculture								
Grammar	[illegible]		[illegible]			91		77
History and Citizenship	[illegible]		[illegible]			88		[illegible]
Art	[illegible]		[illegible]			70		[illegible]
Physiology and Hygiene	[illegible]		[illegible]			[illegible]		[illegible]
Manual Training	[illegible]		[illegible]			66		67
Domestic Science								
Pupil's Total	[illegible]		[illegible]			[illegible]		[illegible]
Pupil's Average	[illegible]		[illegible]			[illegible]		[illegible]
Class Average	[illegible]		[illegible]			[illegible]		70.6
Number in Class	[illegible]		[illegible]			30		[illegible]
Standing in Class	2		2			3		2
Teacher's Initials	[illegible]		[illegible]			[illegible]		[illegible]

Archie Anderson

A credit is a mark of 50% or more.

	1st Unit	2nd Unit	3rd Unit	4th Unit	Class Av'ge	REMARKS
Composition	[illegible]					
Literature	[illegible]					
Hist. English Lit.						
History	[illegible]					
Geography						
Arithmetic						
Algebra	[illegible]					
Geometry						
Trigonometry						
Physics						
Chemistry						
Agriculture						
General Science	[illegible]					
Latin						
French						
German						
Art						

(1) Number of **subjects** taken by student is [illegible]

Number of **credits** obtained by student is [illegible]

(2) This student's estimate of **homestudy** is [illegible] minutes per week. The average amount of homestudy performed by successful students is 600 minutes per week.

(3) Number of days absent [illegible]

(4) Remarks—

[illegible signature]

Classroom Teacher.

N.B.—Parents are requested to keep this report for future reference.

This is a report of the standing obtained by

Archie Anderson

A credit is a mark of 50% or more.

	1st Unit	2nd Unit	3rd Unit	4th Unit	Class Aver.	REMARKS
Composition	B					
Literature	A					
The English Language						
History	A					
Geography						
Arithmetic						
Algebra	[illegible]					
Geometry	[illegible]					
Trigonometry						
Physics						
Chemistry						
Agriculture						
General Science						
Latin						
French	B					
German						
Art						

(1) Number of subjects taken by student is [illegible]

Number of credits obtained by student is [illegible]

(2) The student's estimate of homestudy is [illegible] minutes per week. The average amount of homestudy performed by successful students is 600 minutes per week.

(3) Number of days absent [illegible]

(4) Remarks:

[illegible]

Classroom Teacher

N.B.—Parents are requested to keep this report for future reference.

HIGH SCHOOL RECORD OF

HIGH SCHOOL RECORD OF [illegible]

Year [illegible]	Gr.	Gr.	Cr.	Year [illegible]	Gr.	Gr.	Cr.	Year	Gr.	Gr.	Cr.
[illegible]				[illegible]				[illegible]			

Typed by

Checked by

Credits Obtained

Total Credits

High School Diploma

Deputy Minister

Archie continues his education well into his 50s, taking secondary school courses and a finite mathematics course.

He is obliged to take the secondary school courses because all provincial education ministries in Canada do not recognize each other as having equal standards and during Archie's studies there is no apparent graduate equivalency test.

So Archie has to take one course at a time, while working full time and having a family and social life.

It is challenging, but he receives first class marks for all his course work, in spite of the provincialism and the demands of his routine daily life.

Five+ Year Diary: age 20-25

(Note: The entries of this diary are included as an appendix to Life Before Dreams.)

In a tiny five year diary with little space for each day of each year, Archie hints at his memorable daily events, places, and people.

The years recorded are sometimes 1937 to 1941 and sometimes 1938 to 1942. All of 1937, 1941, & 1942 are not recorded in this diary.

This diary thus almost covers more than five years.

Thus 1938 supplants it in later months of the year. Some dates in 1942 are blank, but blank spaces are very exceptional in this diary.

It has as many words as Archie can fit in the tiny space available.

He records his time of awakening and going to bed too.

He frequently mentions wanting to write; his submissions to writing contests, including the first prize he wins; and his problems concentrating on actually writing.

When available, this writing is added where it is mentioned in the diary. This provides only the chronological context. The inspiration for the writing is not specifically explained.

There is mention of weather, sports, reading, movies, family, friends, work, and four years of a seven year war.

Sometimes there is some minor commentary about people, places, and events too. But it has to be short and concise due to the writing space available in the diary.

In the first days of the diary, there is more often this is a record of the passing of a series of days devoted largely to employment.

Such days are predictably routine, uneventful, uninspiring, and unproductive in terms of both writing and personal fulfillment.

Archie gets up regularly, at either 7:10 or more often 7:15. He leaves work between 5:30 and 5:40 five days a week and at 12:30 one day per week.

Sometimes he has to return to work in the evening too.

He goes to and from work mainly by streetcar and sometimes by bicycle or in someone's car.

In the evening he bowls regularly, plays basketball, sometimes plays snooker, swims, occasionally plays Bingo, and rarely baseball, volleyball, golf, gymnastics, and ping pong.

Most of these activities seem to be held at the YMCA, which Archie always calls by its abbreviation: Y.

He is also interested in drama clubs and goes to some plays. He goes to the movies regularly. He buys and reads books and comics too.

He attends a meeting at which he and other people make

speeches. He also takes part in debates.

He usually goes to bed between 11:00 and 12:45, and at 1:00 a.m. Days off are usually, but not always the latest nights.

Life beyond employment is restricted largely to the one and a half days out of seven set aside for rest, recovery, and recreation.

On the $1^{1/2}$ days he gets up around midday, reads, goes to a movie, bowls, and sees a local league hockey game until the end of the season.

On other days off he goes on a long bicycle ride.

This is in 1937 and continues until the spring of 1938.

Then tennis and walking home Phylis and Hazel become Archie's main activities, with the exception of a few days in Jasper during the summer, as recorded in Archway: Six Year Book of Dreams.

He returns to more varied activities in autumn.

On the last day of 1938 and the third day of 1939, Archie begins adding writing in the business shorthand symbols of the time.

Unfortunately, his shorthand book(s) are discarded in 2015, making the task of decoding the shorthand more challenging. It may be more fun to guess.

Diary entries are expanded in two ways. One is through

dated memos included on the pages in the diary after December 31.

Diary entries are also expanded by adding entries from "Life", an extended version of writing about some days in 1937 and 1938.

Some highlights of the five year diary are shown in bold type face.

Highlighting is generally limited to mention of writing and the personal implications of the world war unfolding overseas.

Although Archie reads H.G. Wells' Outline of History and the Toronto Star, his diary entries make no mention of his impressions or opinions of war or the war overseas.

Archie also mentions voting in the Canadian referendum on conscription, but provides no hint of his thinking or voting decision.

Perhaps his views on war, the war of his times, and conscription are expressed only in conversations with people close to him, but not put in the diary.

Perhaps war times do not encourage people to think freely about war or to express careful thinking about it, particularly not critical thinking.

But Archie does comment in writing in his speech and essays of wartime, "Youth Fight Back", "What of prevention", and "Youth Takes Over".

Archie is also a conscientious objector who voluntarily joins the military in support of Canada. He participates in arms training and practice even though he will kill no one.

The last two years of the diary overlap and fill in some of the missing details of Archway: Six Year Book of Dreams.

The five year plus diary and "Life" are included, in full, as Appendices 1 and 2 of Life Before Dreams.

Two years of longer diary writings, during the final year of the 5+ year diary and after it, are lost on a train in India. Diary entries continue in Appendix 3: 1944-1945.

In these final diary writings of the era, Archie's activities become mostly sedentary. Ironically, this is during his years of wartime military service.

ASSORTED WRITINGS

Editors Note:

This is a collection of the surviving writings of Archie E. Anderson that are not included in Archway: Five Year Book of Dreams and Archway: Lifetime Rhyme.

Unlike previous Archway volumes, most of the writings in Archway: Life Before Dreams are stories, plays, essays, speeches, commentary, radio continuity, etc.

Not every item in this collection includes the date of writing because many of the manuscripts show no date.

However, it is sometimes possible to determine the approximate dates of writing because of the content or context.

Some writing also include the author's street address, giving another clue as to the time of writing.

According to Hazel Anderson, some of the writings mentioned in Archie's five year plus diary and elsewhere may have disappeared during wartime, when Archie's desk was left unattended and became part of a play area for his very young nephews and nieces during his years of absence.

Other writings were created by Archie in the first years following wartime and much later.

When it is possible to specify the dates of writing, they are indicated.

However, since all of the writings are not easily placed in their correct time context, they are instead ordered by genre in this collection.

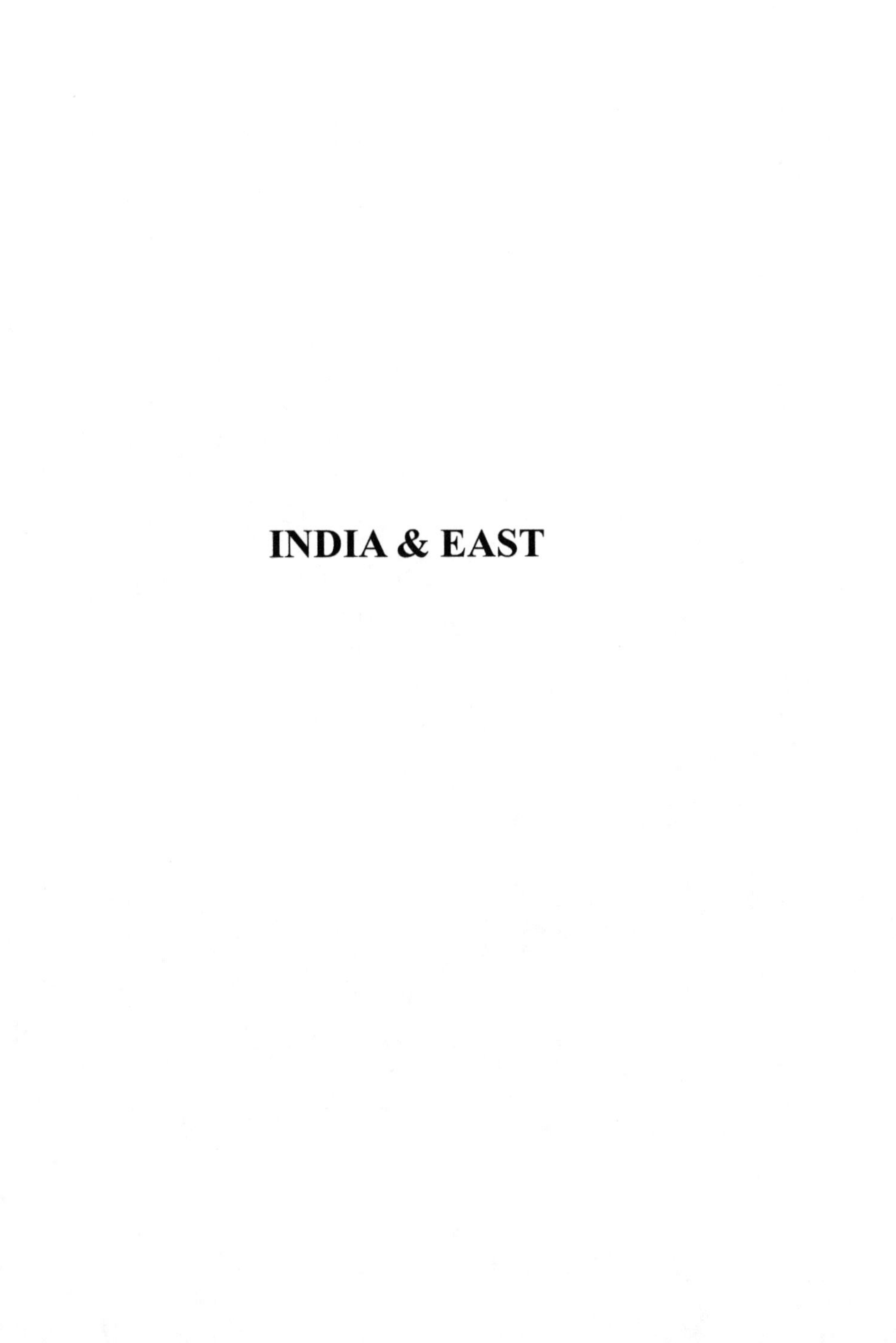

INDIA & EAST

THOUGHTS ON INDIA (1944)

[Although this typed item is identified, on the last page, as "letter 242 June 25, 1944" it is not filed with or folded to fit into the envelop sent from India containing letter 242. That letter is about an encounter with a fortune teller in Calcutta. In contrast, this typed item is more like Archie's telling of India's fortune.]

From where I sit, on the doorsteps of our room, I could be in the middle of the jungle. (There is an open balcony which permits roof top views.)

Thick green foliage reaches in hummocks and valley in every direction with the occasional palm rubbernecking above it all.

Daylight is doling out the final ration while night softly draws its velvet cloak over everything.

Countless insects send out their one note messages to whomever cares to receive.

Top heavy bats hurry by as if dashing ahead to meet the darkness half way. This must be their main airway.

Restless trees fidget and point listless fingers at the ghost of a breeze.

It is as if nature were trying to find a comfortable position before definitely settling for the night.

A silver slice in its own misty fleece cushion, crescent promise of greater beauty to come makes a lovely scar in the grey veiled blue which holds, as if loath to relinquish its grasp, the dying embers of another day.

Unlike the caressing farewell of northern days, here the light persists only as a flickering candle which is by-passed and outnumbered but feebly thrusts against the overwhelming powers of darkness.

On such nights as this, the lucent splinter of mood softens the blow by offering a contrast of light and shadow.

It sets out a pin-point array of star sentinels to guard the grey fringed dome against the return of the blazing monarch.

But, the forces of darkness press close, reaching to the very gates of the sky.

If I'm not careful I'll convince myself that this country has something. That may be, but I am certain that an unpleasant odour can be found somewhere.

Still, most people condemn before they try to understand. Despite the many disagreeable features, this part of India is fascinating.

Even as I hold my nose or fight back a feeling of disgust, I strain my eyes and ears in search of reasons where chaos and filth appear the sole rulers.

I am positive that a correct approach could lift the people from the slime and build a structure to make the world stand in respectful salute.

It's as if I were standing on a garbage heap but knew it

concealed uncountable riches of jewels and uncut gems.

The bright eyes and cheerfulness of inhabitants of this premiere nuisance ground of the East is the clue to hidden treasure.

Show them where to dig and there is no doubt of the wealth they'll surely unearth.

[Reference to Premier Mossadegh of Iran indicates that the following item is written between 1951 and 1953.]

MANY CAME TO TALK

There are three versions of this writing. One is short. In the other two, the paragraphs are in a different order but the same. One is missing from the two longer versions and is shown here in parenthesis.

(Many inferiors came before
And all had their day
But when a successor swept the world
They soon did fade away.)

Travel to the land of rice
And find someone of note
Who holds the key to much
That we could freely quote.

Power here to stir the millions
Rich or poor .. young and old
Crowned heads are faintly seen
But religion has a greater hold.

Strength in doubt, it would appear
Often weakening with a tear.
But then there comes a firm command
And a nation takes it's stand.

The word went out from East to West
And all the world did gain.
Though used by some for just a jest
A better purpose will remain.

Cave dwellers left no record,
Inscribed upon their painted wall.
The Pharaohs had a better way,

But Far East led them all.

Though words and pictures through the air
Have won their share of fame
It's recognized that this great pair
Needed our subject to play the game.

When Eastern Ancients found it
As their records show
The basic product was to stay
Two thousand years or so.

The presses roar and word goes out
And all who wish may read
Now separate the words you've read
From just one VITAL need.

Search among our forests vast
But not for any lumber
Think of something ground to pulp
And you've almost got my number.

[The editor knows of only one poem that Archie explains after writing it. The explanation follows.]

Could be Confucius. There is doubt on some sayings attributed to him. Religion based on his precepts in Far East. Many 'Confucius Says' jokes.

Could still be Confucius who was of royal descent but brought up in poverty by his mother. Other possibilities, Gandhi or the Aga Khan..

Premier Mossadegh of Iran. Always fainting and crying.

Some of his rulings have upset many people, especially in connection with the recent oil crisis.

Could be one of several people ... Nero, Alexander the Great ... Caeser ... Hitler Stalin.

Lord Beaverbrook. The boy in the street could refer to his newspaper interests, the reference being to a newsboy, of course.

Conference table could also mean the United Nations or any of the many prominent figures who attend meetings.

Should start suspecting answer is not person. Embalming science of Egyptians ... manufacture of gunpowder by Chinese. The art of writing. Probably other objects would fit, too.

Further the thought of writing, or art in the form of pictures on cave walls. Could be a book, or books too. Might even be ink.

Still points to books. Also newspapers.

Besides ink and newsprint, might be the alphabet.

Should be fairly obvious. Most people know what use is made of pulpwood. PAPER.

ESSAYS
&
ISSUES

MEMORIALS

[Editor's Note: "Memorials" is the original and full version of "Worthwhile Memorials" that is abbreviated, published, and later reproduced in Archway: Six Year Book of Dreams.

The short version is first published in 1939, the year that Archie turns 22.

"Memorials" provides context and explains the inspiration for the writing. It is also a more explicit and hard-hitting appeal for action.

Archie conducts an informal survey of the reactions of some of the people around him to this writing. The survey results are included here, following this "Memorials".]

Quite frequently I pass the Cenotaph by Dominion Motors. It was erected in honour of the dead. What a strange way to honour them.

A far better way would be to use money collected for that purpose, in the name of the person or persons we wish to pay tribute, to help the living in some material way.

Say John Smith had done some great deed and we feel that his memory should be perpetuated in some manner.

We look about us and see that a new school or hospital is needed.

Since Smith was a worthwhile man, how could we show our appreciation better than by helping some worthwhile cause in his name.

Memorials in the form of blocks of stone are a throw-back to ancient times. They are a form of idolatry.

Beautiful stone monuments are of little comfort to people with empty stomachs.

Pay ten thousand dollars for a useless slab of stone while many wallow in dwellings that a good farmer would not even expect his animals to live in.

As long as we continue to foolishly squander money on monuments when there are so many useful things we could be doing, we will keep muddling on to world-wide bankruptcy.

Let's snap out of our stone age memorial attitude and use a little intelligence. Buildings, roads, trust funds, and countless other things are in great demand.

This condition could be alleviated considerably if we used memorial money for these purposes.

I say down with memorials of useless stones and up some benefit for the living who, after all, are important.

Let's have three hundred and sixty-five Christmases a year. We'll have an extra one on leap-year of course. Seriously though, our present system of helping the less fortunate individuals only once a year is rather absurd.

How do you expect them to live the remainder of the year?

Another thing about our present Christmases is that they have been commercialized by National business houses.

Christmas is just a good advertisement for business.

Of course the spirit of Christmas can only be expressed by buying gifts for others – the more expensive the better – for the stores.

By elimination of this commercial aspect we would move a step closer to better things.

People nowadays seem to have the idea that giving aid to others is something that merely takes place during the Christmas and should be cast aside for the remainder of the year.

Christmas is good for stimulating thoughtfulness in everyone but the spirit should be with us at all times. I am not referring to the spirit some of you might be thinking about.

It certainly would be a fine thing if we all made a Christmas Resolution, call it a New Year's Resolution if you wish, to treat every day as Christmas day as far as helping our neighbours is concerned.

Once we get more people to spread Christmas through the year we will also defeat cheap commercialization of what was once a significant holiday.

Archie's survey on Memorials:

Should Memorials Be Erected and Why?

Jack Dodds: (Archie's best friend)

Yes. They tend to preserve in the memories of [people] certain noble virtues displayed by past heroes.

In this day and age the inspiration given to [people] by remembrance of former heroic feats, etc. tends to and indeed does spur [us] on to greater things which benefit the world as a whole.

Practically every great [person] noted for improving the culture etc. Of the world was in childhood inspired by the memory of some past historic figure.

The cost to build these memorials is on the whole small and in the main financed by fairly well-off people to whom the amount expended may be listed as a small luxury.

Lorne Anderson: (Archie's brother)

Yes. Such erection projects provide additional employment opportunities. No. Capital is expended without prospect of a tangible return.

Yes. When the purpose served is a worthy one, and is truly served thereby.

No. When the purpose is to glorify the memory of those

whose life's work is the slaughtering of their fellow human beings.

Yes. Opportunity is provided for the exercise of aesthetic abilities of sculptors and architects, etc.

No. The so-called "noble virtues" which are said to have been displayed by past heroes are "virtues" examples of which can be found in characteristic examples of the actions of many of the lower animals. Y

Yes. The mere beauty of some memorials is capable of giving intense pleasure to those who behold them.

No. It is a waste of the materials that go into the building of such structures.

Mary E. Anderson: (Archie's mother)

No and yes. No if it is from a monument for an unimportant person. (Unimportant in the sense that he made no particular improvement in the cultural or material wealth of people as a whole.)

[There is only one surviving typed page of this survey. There may have been others since the "yes" part of Mary's answer seems to be missing.]

FLANDERS FIELDS OF 1938
OR
WHY NOT ADVERTISE

[Archie writes this item in 1938, the year Archie turns 21. His name and address are typed at the top of the page, indicating it is a submission for publication or a writing contest. This item is a satirical adaptation of the famous poem written by Dr. John McCrae, who is killed during the 1914-1917 war. In 1938, Europe is on the brink of starting a second world war, perhaps inspiring Archie's implied anti-war and commercialism cynicism. Ironically, he will write advertising copy for radio after his own war service. In 1938, war propaganda is about to sell war to its participants and victims again. A quarter century later, when the editor discovers this poem, (as a child), and finds it funny, he suggests it should be read publicly. Archie rejects the idea, saying that it is likely to offend war veterans, which is not his intention in 1938.]

In Flanders fields the poppies grow

(It's fertilized with NU-SOILS-BEST
Which as you know leads all the rest!)

Between the crosses, row on row

(These crosses are so trim and neat.
Smith Brothers' work cannot be beat!)

That mark our place: and in the sky
The larks still bravely singing, fly

(Dick's Bird Seed helps their voices' tone.
For quality it stands alone!)

Scarce heard amid the guns below.

(If you intend to hunt this fall,
Get TRU-SHOT GUNS, the best of all!)

We are the Dead. Short days ago
We lived, felt dawn, saw sunset glow,

(You also can be always fit.
The KEEP-WELL PILLS will do their bit!)

Loved, and were loved, and now we lie
In Flanders Fields.

(When you decide to buy that ring,
An ICE-ROCK DIAMOND's just the thing!)

Take up our quarrel with the foe:

(Drink BIG-BOY'S SOUP to make you strong
And beat that man who did you wrong.)

To you from falling hands we throw

The Torch: be yours to hold it high!

(A GLO-BRIGHT LAMP in use tonight
Will make your home both clear and bright!)

If ye break faith with us who die

We shall not sleep, though poppies grow
In Flanders fields.

(Take SANDMAN PILLS: your off to sleep.
The cost to you is very cheap.)

UNLIMITED

[This is no doubt inspired by Archie's encounter's with Hazel's brother Philip, who Archie complains about in his five+ year diary a number of times.]

Babblers are Public Nuisance Number One. They talk and talk but never say anything.

I meet them at work, at home, on the street, and on the streetcar. They always have a representative lying in wait for me. Can I never escape?

Their slogan is "Don't Use One Word If A Hundred Will Do."

A true babbler never stops talking under any circumstances.

Public speakers usually talk on some particular subject. Babblers just corner their victim and talk on.

If I am ever so indiscreet as to comment on the weather, business conditions, or any other subject of general interest in front of a babbler, the monologue begins.

No babbler can take a hint. I grind my teeth, fidget, and finally try to make a quiet exit.

The babbler never seems to notice my boredom and he follows me if I try to leave.

I often try to break up with babbler's endless flow. It's useless.

Occasionally I manage to interject a word or two but the babbler pays no attention.

Babblers should be forced to listen to recordings of their own voices repeating the same thing over and over again.

Rid me of this pestilence and leave me in your debt forever. To gag all babblers would be too humane.

EDMONTON

[There is no title for this item.]

It sprawls out in an undecided way.

Portions of the country poke through to make the city look patchy. These gaps make Edmonton so indefinite.

One minute you are in the city then without warning you find yourself in the country. No, you are in the city. A strip of country has merely visited you.

To be or not to be. Edmonton cannot make up its mind.

Streets start together. They begin to crowd and finally manage to squeeze three or four of their number out of existence.

Now you have a street; now you have not. Bring on the padded cell.

Edmonton should make another attempt. It is in a hopeless muddle. The planning of Edmonton must have been done at night.

A dizzy collection of indecision is the result.

I give you Edmonton. If you know it you will not accept it even as a gift.

YOUTH REIGNS

Youth reigns supreme today
Yet victory is defeat
Young throw out yesterday
Yet no plan to compete

Yesterday fell far short
Yield of now oh so sparse
Youth eager to abort
Yet building is a farce

Youth takes impatient stand
Yearning to construct anew
Yet first before command
Youth must to self be true

YOUTH FIGHTS BACK

"The youth of today hold out their hands and take the general attitude that the world owes them a living," shout the pessimists and defeatists who take care to see only the gloomy side.

Look more closely at our youth, you critics who hold forth no hope. Those hands held out are clenched. Youth is fighting.

They fight not because they think the world owes them a living but because it is their just belief that the world owes them the opportunity to make a living.

That opportunity is being denied them now.

Who can say that they enjoy walking the streets, sponging on their parents, if they are fortunate to have homes, and seeing those things which are denied them in abundance everywhere?

Meanwhile, others of their number spend many extra hours but are not receiving remuneration proportionately larger for this additional work.

Frankly, youth is bewildered.

Why should youth suffer such a situation when they are in no way responsible for its inception?

Youth challenges the present set-up and demands that something be done.

Also, they are willing to aid in anything which will help us out of our present predicament. Will the world let them down?

Politicians continue to quibble among themselves, seeking to ignore the seriousness of what is happening to our youth.

Surely they realize that their indifference is jeopardizing our future and the future of democracy.

Youth is willing, in fact eager to assist in the herculean task of bringing order out of the chaos we are embroiled in today.

They are vitally interested in world events and carefully inspect new ideas and schemes that offer hope for the future.

The "isms" rouse their curiosity, the unemployed youngsters being especially interested.

Dictatorial states offer things the democracies are denying them. All are put to work. What if there are certain restrictions and drawbacks?

True, the danger of these, "One Person Countries" is apparent, yet youth are impetuous and may turn from democracy if action is not soon forthcoming.

Food looks good to a starving person even if the stipulations for obtaining it are severe.

Organizations such as the Y.M.C.A. do their part in guiding youth but that is not enough.

Governments, who after all are in a position to help, should be shown by concerted action of the people that now is the time to call a halt.

If petty differences are forgotten a solution will be reached in a surprisingly short length of time.

Then democracy will be made workable and youth will come into their own. This will give youth back the opportunities they do not possess now.

That is all they ask.

WHAT OF PREVENTION

[Reference to how long the war has gone on, to date of writing, indicates this writing is from 1940.]

Another country had been ravished by its powerful neighbour.

Immediately, subscription lists were circulated, tag days instituted, new relief organizations sprang up, and established welfare institutions took action.

This noble work of reconstruction was lauded by everyone. How wonderful to assist the unfortunate and innocent sufferers from denuded nations.

Praiseworthy action indeed, but for relieving conditions which could have been avoided.

Why must the peoples of the world spend so much time repairing when they would make greater and more lasting gains if they would only seek to prevent.

We have developed our various sciences for cure with little, and for the most part, no thought of prevention.

Dental surgery, medicine, to name but two, clearly demonstrate our inability to cope with situations as they commence.

True, we have made marvellous progress in many fields but how pitiful and insignificant these advances become when they are placed beside a list of things which we could not or did not try to prevent.

The present conflict involving nearly every nation of the world is blamed on one man.

We drop matches in the forest and ten when the fire sweeps forward in a furious conflagration we cry out that the wind is at fault.

With great vigour and conviction we stop the fire but only after untold damage has been done. Then, we begin over again.

No one thinks or bothers about prevention.

The predicament becomes more serious yearly. It is not so improbable to think of what might happen in the not too distant future.

Suppose we encounter a plague, man-made or otherwise, which we are unable to stop or for which we can find no remedy.

How long will our puny bulwarks of civilization withstand any such severe onslaught?

Today the warring nations of the world are rapidly dissipating their strength and wealth. At the present rate of expending, bankruptcy will soon be a serious threat.

Already European peoples are overburdened with taxation. The final straw is not a distant bugbear as we are generally led to believe.

Our financial structure cannot possibly stand the strain.

Let the scoffers explain why the war of a quarter of a century ago still remains unpaid for and may never be settled.

More money has been spent in this latest war which has run little more than a full year than has ever been paid out before.

All our present troubles can be traced to lack of foresight.

We could easily have prevented the majority of mix-ups in which we have become involved.

Think of the unnatural division of land through marking out friction-provoking borders at Versailles.

How simply could this have been avoided had the Allies established a group to adjust the boundaries from time to time until the best possible arrangement was obtained?

War occupies much of our attention these days but it is not the only example of our failure to prevent.

Look at the advanced mechanical stage we have reached. Yet observe how inadequate is our management.

A machine replacing ten people is brought into operation.

Instead of all the people having much shorter hours of employment a few work the same length of time while the remainder are idle.

This state is caused by individual control of inventions which rightly belong to everyone.

Similarly, centralized control of Finance has upset our present monetary system.

Perfection is admittedly the ultimate aim of humanity.

Progress is retarded since we are forever engaged in removing some evil or deterrent which exists simply because we would not take measures of prevention when they would have been more successful.

People live too much in the past. We keep referring to past occurrences which are not a satisfactory guide.

Before there can be much hope for betterment of our position in the world, people must become contemporary.

Such phenomenal advances have been made in the form of inventions that people's minds have been unable to keep pace.

We are trying to apply rules which have become useless and outmoded.

While improving material things we have neglected ourselves.

Our position is similar to that of a small child in control of a munitions factory.

If we do not begin to readjust ourselves soon we will never be able to gain control and chaos will eventually sweep us from the earth.

Again, the sceptics sneer and discard the idea as

preposterous. Those who go further than the surface, however, see the signs of warning.

Our present state is as far from the past as the wheelbarrow is from the aeroplane. Inventions of the last decade have changed the entire world as we know it.

Many of our unemployed will never find a place in industry again. Something must be done. Will we wait until it is too late or will we for once act in time?

It will be difficult to change the existing order. Countless factors must be considered. Tradition, customs, and usages are bromidic.

They have reached a venerable age and should no longer be considered as an adequate guide for the future.

Naturally, everything in connection with our building of civilization should not be pushed aside, but we must reorganize and strive to adapt our living to the new system which we must put into force if we ever hope to move forward.

The alarm has been sounded.

Intelligent watchers have noticed the ominous rumblings and know that we are approaching a point where ancient methods will not check our downward path.

A stumbling block, the principal one, is the fact that the very people in a position to expedite the change are not too anxious to assist.

After all, they are deriving benefits from the present setup and they refuse to look to tomorrow.

So far we have refused to seek a means of checking our troubles as they begin. There is still an opportunity left.

Re-alignment of values and adjustment of our system must come sooner or later. This first step is necessary if we wish to prevent a blackout of civilization.

EUROPEAN SPRING

Spring. Life begins with everything bursting forth into bloom. In Europe, however, big guns take the place of blossoms.

The citizens are digging trenches instead of gardens.

Is civilization about to be swept away?

Have we come this far only to be reduced to our former state of barbarity?

Must all our gains be lost through foolishness?

The picture is very bleak.

There is a faint glimmer of hope. That is education. People's minds patriotic conceptions have to be broadened.

We must break down these walls of narrow provincialism.

The word "Foreigner" could be changed to "Friend" if the proper method of tackling the situation were found.

The people of other nations have much in common with us.

Differences in language and customs are greatly exaggerated by individuals seeking power. After all, we are all human beings.

Opportunists, or to use a more recognizable term, dictators depend on their power which comes through their being able to secure results which they dupe the citizens into believing are good.

Dictators owe their very existence to the fact that the country which they gain control of was in desperate straights.

Where living conditions are bad, a strong boss who can organize the people is welcomed at first.

Removal of these self-appointed gods, then is one of the first most important steps.

To do this it is necessary to show the residents of these one-person estates how much better a democratic state can be.

That means setting our own house in order first. We must tackle the problems which confront us and remove them.

How can we hope to convince anyone that ours is a good state when conditions about us shout to the contrary?

While people starve and go without proper clothes or shelter in a land where stores are stacked high with goods we have actually less to offer than the dictators.

YOUTH TAKES OVER

LASTING PEACE! The words have become a mockery to our ears. A quarter of a century ago youth paid a terrible price for peace which they fondly believed would endure.

Today, we, the new youth, are fighting the same fight for the identical peace which many hoped had been secured when the first world war ended.

The price we must pay will be greater than any since humanity began its upward struggle.

We do not quibble nor seek to avoid our share of this conflict. It is not glory we desire but something infinitely more precious and substantial.

This time we shall have a lasting peace.

How often present-day speakers have declared that youth does not realize that democracy cannot be preserved in one struggle but that we might fight for it over and over again.

We refute such an unfair charge. Youth of today is far-seeing and desires to make a greater contribution towards the security of democracy than the youth of the First World War.

We see clearly that victory of arms is not enough.

When the last bomb has been dropped and the last gun fired in this war it will not be the end. Our real struggle will have but begun.

The facts are not hidden. We know the peace arranged after the first World War was a patch-work affair.

We know how the real or fancied wrongs of Versailles were used by an unscrupulous leader to further his own ambitions.

The realization that our present situation could have been avoided does not lessen our determination to push on and finish a disagreeable yet necessary job.

As we take our places in this new struggle, we do so with the conviction that this time there will be no half-measures. Peace will not be tossed aside again.

Our main thought now is of victory over force which we are sure will come. But our sight carries further than triumph in arms.

The mistakes of World War I shall not be repeated. Peace will come and shall be maintained. The past has gone but it is not forgotten. The future must be different.

When peace comes our fight will not end.

Rather, it will enter a new phase perhaps more important than the war itself. New blue-prints must be drafted for the entire world.

We shall not rest until a permanent settlement for the benefit of all is agreed upon.

Our arms shall be laid down only when we have secured certain lasting peace.

We are the youth, too, who did not answer the first call when the current war challenged with is roar of mechanized might.

In our hearts we hoped that right would prevail before too much damage had been done by the fanatic who was striving for world dominance.

This was a modern war. We conscientiously believed, and still do, that equipment, supplies, and munitions were the important factors.

Human power was a secondary consideration.

In ever-increasing numbers we are joining those who leapt to meet the Empire's* need when Hitler hurled his mighty challenge. (*U.K. Empire, collapsed after 1945)

The fight may be long and bitter but there is no turning back. Our fervour is no less than that of the more impetuous youth who had no second thoughts.

Our determination to see things through is the greater for having weighed and considered before acting.

We offer the best that is in us. Not for our country alone, nor for the Empire alone, but for humanity throughout the world. We cannot fail.

In the First World War many fought for the honour and the glory. Today we must fight for civilization and security from violence and barbarism.

The light of freedom must keep shining and we must stand

between that bright gleam and the obscure and frightful chaos of totalitarian dominance.

We are not professional speech-makers. As with all youth, past and present, we are concerned primarily with action.

This time it is not merely the action of adventure but action with a view to advancement. Advancement of world civilization and sooner fulfillment of the hope for lasting peace.

BOWS POLITELY

[Archie labels this one a speech and dates it January, 1940. It is mentioned in his five-year diary. It is a critique posing as praise.]

Europe bows politely and prepares to say "Merry Christmas" to the world.

How heart-warming to behold this land of the world's culture leading the parade of "Peace On Earth".

Why can't we residents of the discontented and warring North America follow the peaceful example of pacifist Europe.

They do not confine their benevolent activities to the Christmas season but spread their little deeds of kindliness throughout the year.

Let's turn our eyes for a moment upon the genial gentle people who might well by styled the instigator of the big-brother-to-weaker-nations policy which has been adopted.

Mussolini very generously took Ethiopia under his wing.

The fact that a great number of people got smothered in the process is incidental and beside the point.

Not to be outdone, the Japanese proceeded to civilize the poor ignorant Chinese.

Naturally they had to eliminate a few of the more stubborn resisters against their humanitarian movement, but it was done conscientiously and in the cause of world advancement.

These preliminary onslaughts, I mean brotherly gestures, were then followed, you will remember, by a minor family quarrel in Spain.

Italy and Germany could not bear to see this needless fighting.

So, true pacifists that they are, they quietly slipped in the back door, not wishing to receive any praise for their good work, for they are modestly unassuming, and proceeded to put things in order.

Of course they had to start from the beginning. It was useless to attempt to rearrange things so they simply had to more or less mop up the country first.

However, even after they began moving troops from the country when everything was settled, the two bashful gentlemen, Mussolini and Hitler refused to accept any credit whatsoever.

True, their ministrations resulted in the country being set back perhaps ten or fifteen years economically, but why bother worrying over such a trifling matter.

Next the spotlight came to rest on the most noble-hearted man in the world, Hitler.

Patiently, he chided Austria and then kindly yet firmly took charge of affairs.

Czechoslovakia became troublesome.

Hitler gently took command of the situation and soon had things under control, not to mention an inconsequential number of dead under the sod.

Those rascals in Poland began to fidget. That would not do.

In the midst of the charitable act of helping Poland at the expense of a few thousand lives, Hitler was surprised to hear ominous mutterings proceeding from the general direction of France and England.

Now the war-hounds of the world have been unleashed. In passing we might glance at Russia, now so busily engaged in assisting Finland.

WE THE PEN PUSHERS

[The Roundel is an RCAF newsletter published at the Bella Bella Camp where Archie was stationed after MacDonald, Manitoba, and before he was posted overseas. The Roundel was one of Archie's responsibilities. The writing item from that newspaper which is included here was not in Archie's files. It appears here only thanks to the efforts of Archivist McKenna at Canada's National Library and Archives in Ottawa, Ontario. McKenna's letter explains the writing following it here.]

Q7-23230

Dear Mr. Anderson,

I verified the contents of The Roundel for the period March to May 1942 and found only one article attributed to A. E. Anderson Cpl. "We the Pen Pushers", The Roundel (May 1942), page 17.

A copy of the issue title page and the article is attached to this e-mail. It appears that Mr. Archie Anderson served as an administrative clerk for the Station, and so it is probable that he was responsible for typing up not only the issues of The Roundel but also the daily Operations record books.

I hope this information is of use to you.

Sincerely,
Ilene McKenna
Archivist
Reference Services /Services de référence
Library and Archives Canada / Bibliothèque et Archives Canada

R.C.A.F. STATION

BELLA BELLA B.C.

Vol 1 No 2

Usually we are content to plod along, shoddy gibes that come our way with the acquired nonchalance of a long-suffering and eternally misunderstood trade.

But there is a limit and this it it.

We are tired of being dismissed with a casual "So you're a clerk, eh? Pretty soft." or something even more pointed, which only reflects the general misconception of our essential part in the scheme of things.

Of course we are not complaining, but a recent situation demonstrates the difficulties we sometimes face.

The kinks of a newly organized station were practically straightened out and the Orderly Room was about to slip into high gear when disaster struck, kicked and tossed us back for a heavy loss, groggy but still breathing.

Our staff of ten was whittled down by sickness; moved to bolster other sections; and postings; to a mere five.

Instead of folding up and shouting for help, we took up the slack, gritted our sound teeth (if any) and carried on as always. You get the idea – we hope.

But, looking on the bright side, there are some advantages. The shortage of typewriters is no longer a problem.

Simply by reducing the number of our staff, we overcame that handicap. We also have enough chairs to go around now – but there's no time to sit down. We can't win.

Besides our routine work, we act as an important bureau

(not through choice) for the entire station.

It is apparent that whenever anything is too much if a puzzle for anyone else to solve, we are JOE. And if anything goes wrong we invariably get the blame.

In case you are still wondering, we are merely trying to point out in a subtle way that we run the station.

Now there should be no further doubt as to where the nerve centre of the station is located.

(We will all be nervous wrecks if the present pace keeps up.)

We are prepared to fight it out to the last bottle of ink or final typewriter ribbon with any who dispute our claim to first honours.

1940s

[Impressions of a decade as it ends.]

We walked through the forest of history, hand in hand with Destiny. Yet we saw so little of the woods. Each of us was too interested in a few trees to grasp the full picture.

Historians may bring the proper perspective to the past decade after we are but memories, but we have a faint understanding of the greatness of our times even now.

The Forties started on a note of scepticism which has persisted to a greater or lesser degree to the present day.

The "phoney" war soon made a mockery of the security seeking. And the end of hostilities was but another phase in the uncertainty of the world.

It was a time of greatness and despair, when a war devoid of all chivalry and romance showed up incredible heroic fortitude and ingenuity of human beings in the rubble of their civilization.

Many fought with dispassionate gallantry for a way of life which had forsaken them during the Depression Years.

It was an age of paradox when the Great Event of Science, the Atom Bomb brought an uneasy Peace and more instability and unrest than the world has ever known.

WORK GETS

[This item is on a piece of paper all by itself with no apparent connection to any context of other writing.]

Work is something which most people do in hopes that some day they won't have to do anything.

But often they become so engrossed in work that they forget how to use leisure.

Since their objective was to secure unlimited leisure... their work has been for nothing... which is exactly what they get.

MUD

[A very brief story introduces this essay. The story is inspired by a true incident that happens during my childhood in Edmonton on 76th Street, in a vacant lot next to my parents' house. I'm less than six years old at the time. It's an event I always remember. I remember someone telling me to take off my boots, but I didn't want to get my feet muddy. Thus the intervention.]

Bill Smith was stuck in the mud. He had been trying out his new rubber bots and now he was in trouble. Instead of trying to extricate himself he began to shout for help.

Luckily, one of his companions did not lose his head but waded out to the mired boy.

In a few minutes this resourceful lad had shown his friend how to free his boots by tugging on their tops and lifting his feet at the same time.

There are many "Billy Smiths" in the world. Some are fortunate enough to be rescued by kind-hearted friends. Others receive no answer to their cries for aid.

They wallow about and sometimes stumble upon a method of overcoming the difficulties. Quite often, however, they simply throw up their hands and refuse to fight.

Our citizens seem to prone to listen sympathetically to doctrines of pessimistic defeatism.

They are told repeatedly that the cards have been stacked against them; that it is useless to struggle against the overwhelming odds that confront them at birth.

Besides, the government will look after them.

At least that is the attitude they are encouraged to adopt.

Conditions can never improve while people continue to look to others for assistance when they are in trouble.

If you hope for success you must be self-reliant. When you become mired down by seemingly insurmountable difficulties take things calmly.

Look about you and you will find a solution to your problem. Pull yourself out of the mud.

Archie's Attic

[This item is satirical. It appears to be an example of a regular column or opinion item for print media. It is also the only Archie's Attic in his files.

Unfortunately, the paper it is typed on has deteriorated and is now in taters.

This writing ends abruptly where the bottom of what is perhaps the final page has been torn away and has gone missing.]

Driving Tips

Hello there. I'm glad you took time to visit my attic. Things do get cluttered here at times, but it's never dull. There's always something or some person showing up with an interesting story.

Here's a little article for example, a child's steering wheel. This one is just a toy, but the trouble is that when some people get behind the wheel of a car they revert to children.

Incidentally, I have an arrangement with the young fellow who owns this steering wheel. He leaves the real steering wheel alone and I leave his alone.

Speaking of driving, though, have you ever noticed how a mild type of person is often converted into a raging monster when behind the wheel?

It's a case of – here I come, get out of the way or I'll run you down.

One of the most dangerous types is the driver who won't

give way. I had an encounter with this type a short time ago.

I was just about to pass when he sped up, but for a short stretch. Then he slowed down again. Then I tried to pass again and the same thing happened again.

I finally did get by, but do you know, I had to speed up to 70 km/hr to pass, and in a school zone at that.

Just imagine what a menace this type is – road hog and speeder.

One thing I can't understand is why the motorcycle cop gave me a ticket, even when I explained how the other driver was at fault.

But, let's get back to the purpose of today's visit to the attic.

You can realize by that little incident that I am well qualified to give some most valuable tips on safe and sane driving.

Actually, there are two reasons why I drive carefully and try to obey all traffic laws.

The most obvious is that I am of Scottish ancestry, which means that I don't like to throw money away on fines.

But, more important- a traffic ticket means less money for meal tickets.

You see, we budget my take home pay so closely that we

never spend more than a dollar and a quarter for every dollar I earn.

One of the most interesting things about driving is straddling the white line.

It gives a person a feeling of accomplishment; allows plenty of room on both sides of your car in case of emergency; and you can turn either right or left at the last moment without signalling or having to cut in front of anyone.

On the highway, of course, where there are two lanes only, it takes a bit more dodging cars coming from the other direction.

And, you get more kick out of this pastime when both lanes are full, seeing if you can force other cars off the road.

Now that the ghost patrol operates on our highways, it does restrict speeding activities but there's still plenty of scope for cutting in and out; passing on bends and hills; stopping suddenly after you get around a blind curve; and lots of other little schemes the really clever driver can work out.

Actually, city driving offers more scope because you have the pedestrians, or at least it's fun trying to get them.

One of the best places is when the car on the other lane stops at a crosswalk. That's you cue to hit the gas.

With average luck you can hit an unwary pedestrian as he or she steps from in front of the stopped car. Keep practicing. It takes time to get it down to perfection.

Sooner or later, when driving a car, you have to park. Angle parking can give a lot of laughs.

If the curb isn't too high, you can always run your car half way across the sidewalk. You might even hit someone in the process.

But, even the parking itself can be a challenge. Try to park at a different angle so that you take up the space of two or even three cars.

If that's not possible, park as close as possible to the car on your right. It's just possible that the driver can only unlock that car from the driver's side.

This will mean the driver will have to wait until you get back. Should you see the driver trying to get into the car, a good plan is to duck out of sight and wait until the driver gives up.

Parallel parking has its own thrills. You should try to park with the back wheels against the curb and the front wheels about 60-90 cm out.

This facilitates getting out of the parking spot. What does it matter if you do block off part of a traffic lane. After all, the streets are there for your convenience.

Here's another tip. When you see someone about to back into a parking spot and you're next in line, quickly pull up bumper to bumper and honk your horn.

There's always the chance that the other driver may panic and let you have it, I mean the parking space.

What happens next? Use your own discretion, but don't be fooled by meek-looking drivers. When the driver gets out of the car, that 's you cue to take off, not to stay and confer.

[Unfortunately, the writing ends abruptly at this point, due to a deteriorating and torn page. Only a few words, aded

However, over the years, Archie sometimes complains about drivers who honk at cars in front of them instantly when a traffic light changes from red to green.

Archie relates that one time, when he is the one getting honked at when a traffic light changes, he allows the honker to pass and then catches up at the next red light.

Archie honks as soon as the light turns green. The driver then turns and laughs, appreciating the lesson that Archie is teaching with a horn.

Perhaps this story is part of the missing ending of this writing item.

In the same vain as the preceding stories, Archie might write -

If you find yourself stuck waiting behind a car at a red light and the driver doesn't enter the intersection instantly after the light turns green, rev up your engine loudly and hold down the horn for a good long honk.

The driver in front might be so surprised that s/he will push down hard on the gas peddle, sending his/her vehicle dashing into the intersection and perhaps clipping the edge of straggling cars or knocking over a slow pedestrians.

Pedestrians & drivers

More pedestrians and all commuters walk more than they ride.

Nowadays, especially in this town, motorists walk more than pedestrians. To take an extreme case, people who live in a new subdivision spend most of their time walking.

For at least six months of the year he can't park anywhere near his house because of mud, which means several blocks walk each way morning and night.

Thus, unless the subdivision dweller can afford to use a parking meter or parking lot, he has to walk five or six blocks from where he parks.

If the driver can feed a meter, s/he can also get in a few kilometres of walking time. S/he walks back and forth to feed the meter.

It's good exercise, particularly if you work on the top floor of a building and keep missing elevators.

But the meters aren't there to encourage exercise. Their purpose is fundraising. The money put into a meter is used to buy more meters.

I saw a woman fretting over a meter as I passed. She was there again ten minutes later. I offered to help and discovered she was trying to get a refund for unexpired time.

There are advantages to parking in a lot. You can scrape up

against acquaintances.

Notes for pedestrians

Pedestrians can cross at an angle from the middle of the block to the corner. They can disregard the “wait” light. It’s just something installed by motorists to annoy walkers.

Dash out between parked cars.

Saunter to prevent motorists from making right turns.

Get off the bus and cross in front of it.

In a crowded crossing, don’t give way, plow right through.

FIVE YEAR REPORT

This is in the nature of a five year report.

November, 1956 we headed west with little more than a vague idea that the time had come to leave the half frozen rut for the balmy breezes of Vancouver Island.

We had to test whether opportunity was more a matter of dig-in than beggin'.

In a sense, our spirits followed the early pioneer as they struck towards the unknown.

Since the initial exhilaration of recovering some of summer's mildness had subsided, we settled down to rebuild and move towards a goal that had long evaded us.

Despite doleful predictions of no work nor prospects in Victoria, we "dug in" and found there was even a choice of jobs to fit our qualifications.

CANADA FIRST

It is time for Canadians to get their priorities straight. Narrow provincialism has no part in our modern world.

Nineteenth century thinking must be purged if we are to take our place as a vigorous nation of this age.

In fact, each day of delay increases the danger to our very existence as a national entity.

We are all equally to blame for the balkanization of this country.

In 1869 there was some excuse for the existence of opposing loyalties.

Now that we are literally side by side from coast to coast with instant communication and easy physical contact, it's time to bring our thinking up to date.

What's so different about the hopes and wishes of someone living in Vancouver to those of a person in Halifax, Ottawa, Montreal, or the smallest hamlet in Canada?

To read the report of any of our federal-provincial conferences one could be excused for thinking that each section of this nation is waging a cold war against the others.

The onus is upon one of our provincial leaders to rise above petty political considerations and set the pattern for a new Canadian patriotism.

To such an innovator, the rewards are unlimited.

The initial impetus must, of necessity, come from one of the so-called “have” provinces.

A premier, or representative need merely offer to assume a responsibility for a fair share of Canada’s needs, according to wealth of resources and industrial capability.

This tangible proof of Canadian citizenship responsibility could start a trend towards co-operative effort that might eventually sweep the world.

The astute statesman who does make such a move will run little risk of economic or political disaster.

Rather [s/]he will be applauded by Canadians from all sections of the country. It will mark the beginning of a new era in our country’s history.

The resulting reaction could well force many of the petty provincial-minded politicians from the scene.

It could herald the beginning of a new honesty in politics, attracting a higher calibre of candidate in future elections.

The premier who strikes the first blow must be prepared for possible defeat from entrenched interests.

Even if [s/]he does not succeed, others will be encouraged to follow.

Once the idea of sharing takes hold, the people will soon show their acceptance by supporting the idealists at the polls.

If our federal strength is to increase we must start thinking as Canadians first.

There is nothing wrong with pride in one's town or province, providing such pride is kept in perspective.

The strength of each community determines the ultimate strength of the nation only if the overall picture is kept firmly before us.

To survive as individual citizens, we must believe in our nation first.

Here is a direct challenge to political leaders from all levels to confirm their belief in a whole that is truly greater than the sum of its individual parts.

THE LAST, "LAST WORD"?

[This short item is from 14 January 1987. The context is precise.]

Worried about losing our cultural heritage? Concerned about free trade with the U.S.?

Forget it. The war is over. Of course there will be a few skirmishes, but the U.S. already has us in its pocket.

Regardless of free trade talks, schemes to retain our cultural heritage and keep our Canadian identity intact are a hopeless cause.

The war of words was lost long ago. It probably started with Sesame Street.

Ask any Grade One teacher about "Zee" instead of "Zed". A little thing, you say. Not really.

Imagine trying to change a tiny tot's mind when Big Bird has insisted on "Zee". Other TV programs make further inroads on the very structure of our society.

Adults are not immune - - take such words as "Zeenith". What happened to "Zenith"?

PANIC

[This item is dated June 21, 1995. The editor of this volume gives Archie his first P.C. about six months earlier. Archie is 77 years old.]

Panic? That's putting it mildly. For someone who started working when the only aid was a hand operated adding machine, P.C.'s offer a frightening challenge. It's as if a kite flier were put in charge of a Star Trek spaceship.

The jargon is incredible to one who learnt default was when the other team conceded without playing. Fonts were for christening babies, and icons were religious objects.

Paths were for getting around a park or garden. Of course there's a family association with motherboard and daughterboard.

And what about floppy disks that are quite rigid?

Most disconcerting is when the computer flashes "Retry Abort Fail". That leads to real panic as I fear, whatever I decide, the whole system will collapse or disappear in a puff of smoke.

I have made up my mind to boot the P.C. (When I first saw those letters I thought they might stand for Police Constable, or postcard.) and prepared if it should fight back or return the complement with a kick, or worse.

Whatever happens, I'll try to remember that the computer is an idiot, programmed by another idiot, to serve idiots such as I.

If the windows become too obscure I can always pull the plug and go back to my abacus and cryptic crossword puzzles.

JOURNALISM

SCHOOLING JOURNALISM

[This is an untitled work. April 17, 1938 appears in handwriting in the right-hand corner of page one. But the typed heading is "March Entry". This transcript is from a page with hand-written corrections.]

Last month when Robert Maynard Hutchins, President of the University of Chicago, broke into the headlines attacking schools of journalism, few people supported his views.

Those who heard President Hutchins passed the incident off lightly, saying it was apparent that he was attempting to ridicule the schools.

Some editors were prejudiced against these schools twenty years ago. President Hutchins' jibe might have been received joyfully then, but not today.

Editors know as much or maybe even more about the schools of journalism that President Hutchins, so they are not impressed by his statement.

Many of our present editors are graduates of journalism schools.

Others, who have had no such training, know that there is as valid a reason for training [people] for careers in journalism as there is for training [people] for careers in medicine and law.

WHAT IS NEWS?

[The six items which follow are written longhand in pencil on the back of a book of receipts for "193_", including some copies of actual receipts and some blank receipts that were never used.

The receipts are printed for Alan Burnside Harvey, Barrister, Solicitor, Notary of Edmonton, Alberta. This is Archie's youthful contribution to paper recycling.

Following these items about journalism, there is what appears to be a practice interview with "Dad", Archie's father WRJ. This item is dated June 12, 1937. Archie is 16 years old.

Following this interview there are three summaries of movie stories, all dated August 19 and 28, 1937. Archie is 17 years old. Two movie summaries end with the "30" traditionally used for ending news stories.

So the movie summaries are apparently news reporting practice.

The editor attributes all of these writings to Archie because they are handwritten in pencil and longhand, thus unlikely to be entirely others' words.]

1. Human conflict is news when conflicting interests come to a dramatic clash, creating an unusual effect and arresting the attention of people with sight or hearing.

2. Disaster is news because a flaw in machinery or carelessness of an operator sometimes causes an accident which is contrary to what ordinarily takes place.

3. It is unusual for nature to make some upheaval such as a tornado, earthquake, or volcanic eruption.

4. We are not expecting a storm coming out of season such as a snowstorm in mid-summer.

5. A great achievement is something unusual that is not done very often.

6. In a small town everyone is acquainted and a happening concerning a fellow towns[person] is news.

7.News is something of timely interest to a number of people. The best news is that which interests the greatest number of people.

8. Anything that happens to a well known individual is news since people are anxious to read about such persons.

9. In a small town where everyone is acquainted people are interested when they hear of someone breaking a leg.

10. Such a thing as a broken leg can assume national news interest when there are unusual circumstances connected with the accident.

11. If a trivial thing concerns a well known person, it is news in a big city.

12. Yes. Anything that is taking or putting money into the reader's pocket vitally interests him or her.

13. The Scopes trial concerned the issue of fundamental emotional appeal i.e. evolution vs. The Bible.

WHO? WHAT? WHEN? WHERE? WHY?

1. Who, what, when, where, why.

2. Sometimes one of the W's is more important than the

rest. It is, of course, placed first.

3. Who comes first when the news concerns some prominent figure.

4. What comes first when the happening is more important than any other factor.

5. Where comes first when the place it happened is unusual or well known.

6. When comes first if the time of year, day, week, or month is unusual.

7. Why comes first when the reason for a happening is unusual and is more interesting than any other factor.

[Editor's note: Archie makes no mention of "How?".]

NOSE FOR NEWS

1. Reporters curiosity and imagination impel him[/her] to look beneath the surface facts.

2. The elements of "nose for news" are curiosity to look beneath surface facts, imagination to consider what might have happened and reasoning to determine what did happen.

3. Many people do not notice many things. A person who observes sees things which others miss.

4. Yes, quite often.

5. Address sometimes affects the value of news by the fact of its location, e.g. the burning of a house in itself may not be of much interest but if the people living in that house are high in society or otherwise prominent the news interest is greatly increased.

6. Knowledge of a town helps a reporter because he knows the news sources and also can tell by the location of news whether it can be developed into more important news by the fact of its location.

7. It pays to search to the end as there may be something overlooked which might have great news value.

8. A trained reporter reasons automatically because [s/]he has trained him[/her]self to reason out things until reasoning has become a habit.

9. Initiative is the base of a reporter's curiosity and it carries him on to the end.

10. Curiosity when carried too far that it violates sensibilities is a bad thing. Decent curiosity is all that should exist.

11. If a reporter finds an assignment distasteful the only proper thing to to is resign.

12. Imagination enables a reporter to consider every angle and ferret out the truth separating the essential from the unessential.

13. Imagination cannot be used in connection with facts. The reporter must ask [her/]himself "Is it true?", not

"Might it be true?"

14. News value is tested by asking oneself a) Has it been published before? b) Are the persons involved important or known to the public? c) Is it unusual? d) Is property or wealth involved? e) Is the locality within the range of his[her] newspaper's community interest? f) Is it of general interest? g) Has it a personal appeal to many? g) Has it any special appeal which warrants its publication even though the foregoing elements of a good story may be absent?

15. People are mainly interested in something which has just happened or is happening hence news is only good for possibly twenty four hours unless more news is made each day. Yesterday's story is no good today.

16. "Yesterday" gives the reader the impression that the news is old. Readers want up-to-the-minute news.

17. Well-known names or institutions are valuable in a story because the reader usually has some association with the institution or name mentioned.

18. A reporter must be very observant and be able to pick out happenings which do not usually take place.

19. Destruction of property is loss of wealth. The reader appreciates news of property as [s/]he could also lose property.

20. A happening in a locality known throughout the world will have more new value than an identical event in some obscure place.

21. [S]/he relies on his/[her] common sense and knowledge of the town.

22. Something which touches people's fundamental emotions has human interest. Funny, tragic, or pathetic events have human interest.

23. Different classes enjoy different types of news.

24. Personal appeal of news to readers comes when they can associate themselves with the persons or places in the news.

25. Items which are odd have special appeal, e.g. commercial aviator goes for aeroplane ride for vacation.

26. Yes, e.g. people helping apparent beggar who turns out to be a millionaire.

SOURCE OF NEWS

1. Cultivation of friends in different walks of life helps because these friends are willing to tip off reporter friends as a favour. e.g. police department, fire department, all courts, railway stations, sports grounds, radio stations, government in times of session, City Hall, hospitals, theatre conventions, churches, aviation fields, morgue, jails, prisons, railway & steamship offices, industrial plants, clubs, financial institutions, schools & colleges, health department, undertakers, local news, telegraph (out of town), cable (other continents), city & suburbs, news from all parts of the country, foreign news, local staff of reporters, local news associations, and correspondents' news tips.

2. A reporter should hide his[her] identity when a disclosure would mean [s/]he would get no news.

3. The reporter must know the sources of local news.

TRADITIONS & ETHICS OF THE REPORTER

1. The reporter's first tradition is respect for confidence.

2. Do as the editor says. If you are unable to agree it is best to resign.

3. Yes. No personal feelings should enter into account.

4. Practice self-detachment so you will be able to observe clearly. Letting oneself become lost in the scene or events destroys clear vision.

5. A truth put in such a way as to give the wrong impression is in effect a falsehood.

6. The key to a reporter's ethics is – Obtain first the truth – all the truth you can get and make sure it is true, then so write your story that your words and phrases will convey to the reader an accurate picture of what happened.

A half truth may be the most mendacious of lies. A truth bluntly stated, without the attending circumstances or influences which give it is correct significance may be utterly misleading!

7. A libel suit may follow an inaccurate reporting of news which will result in the reporting losing his[/her] position.

PREPARATION OF COPY

1. On one side all.

2. In the upper left hand corner of the first sheet to show the story's source.

3. If you receive the story by telephone from another reporter you write [her/]his name after yours, e.g. "Jones from Smith" to show story's source.

4. Begin about [13 cm] from the top of the first page to make room for slugs to be inserted by copy desk.

5. Writing should always be double-spaced at least to make reading easier for the copy desk and linotyper, also to leave room for corrections and slugs.

6. At the bottom of each page but the last write "more" to show there is more to come.

7. "30" in a newspaper office means the end of the report.

8. To indicate continuation of a paragraph from one sheet to the next, draw a line from the last word to the lower right hand corner.

9. Don't crowds lines at the bottom of the sheet. Start a fresh page.

10. Do not divide words between two lines. If there is not enough room for all the word on one line, put the word on the next line.

11. "Slugging" your copy is the identifying name given by the city editor to your copy, e.g. if "bomb" is the slug it is indicated as follows "bomb" "bomb2" etc.

12. Write only one story on a sheet.

13. "Slugs" are ringed to show they are not to be printed.

14. Fold the paper in two with writing outward. This is so that a person can see that it at a glance. One with the writing inward may get lost. Paper to be destroyed should be crumpled.

INTERVIEW WITH "DAD":

SECOND HAND CARS

"The public is gradually being educated to the fact that second-hand cars are merely a bill of expense." according to Mr. WRJ Anderson.

"One must have parts replaced frequently and oil and gasoline bills are higher than those for new cars."

"Automobile companies could almost afford to give the used cars away, the revenue obtained from selling parts is so large."

Mr. Anderson said he thought that if a person bought a used car for personal use the cost of upkeep would far out-weigh its convenience.

"All cars which are more than seven or eight years old should be destroyed. Parliament should pass a law making such destruction of old cars compulsory."

SPORTS

SPEAKING OF TENNIS

Tennis in 7 hard lessons

We submit these suggestions to would-be tennis enthusiasts knowing that following them to the letter the beginner will soon be able to hold [his/her own on any ruby team].

1. Create an impression the first time on the court. Whether it is bad or good makes little difference.

This produces a following of fans, and this enthusiastic audience tends to inspire the novice.

Tricks such as jumping in the nets \, skiing on the shale, etc. never fail to impress.

2. Discourage would-be teachers. You become a good tennis player only by learning from the ground up; hence develop your own style right from the start.

Your style may be awkward but what difference does that make?

You may have trouble placing your shots inside the opponent's court, but they can't expect perfection the first five years!

3. If you can work it (on the sly preferably) arrange your sets so that you can play singles most of the time.

If the courts are crowded, it makes n difference; singles develop your game much better than doubles.

4. Never-never bring your own balls. This is your first year in tennis and old members should be sports enough to supply the balls.

Should you bring new balls the other members are apt to play you for a sucker and use yours instead of their own, which would be distinctly unfair.

5. Should you be unlucky enough to lose the set, grip the racket firmly in the right hand and with words especially adapted for the occasion toss it at the net.

This will not hurt your racquet but will have the effect of releasing pent-up emotions. It may hurt the net but then the club can afford it better than you.

Never throw your racket at the fence as this will prove disastrous to the thickness of your wallet.

6. If the game is going against you, start walloping the balls with all your might, regardless of the direction. This will scare your opponent and upset [his/her] game so that you can go on to win.

7. Don't let your opponents bulldoze you; if you think your ball was inside the tape, argue the point. Remember, every point counts.

Tennis began over four hundred years ago. Great advances have been made, resulting in today's scientific equipment and technique to aid the aspiring Tilden, Perry, or Alice Marble.

After four centuries of experience some players persist in

muddling along.

They decide to place tennis. At first they eagerly gobble up any and all tips that are available.

The season drifts along. Enthusiasm remains high but the beginner develops what he or she chooses to refer to as "My Style".

What matter if half the deliveries result in faults?

The ball does sizzle even when brought up short by the net.

Why bother keeping your eye on the ball?

You cannot miss all the time.

Maybe you wiggle your wrist on most shots. Results may not be satisfactory but that flick of the wrist looks so professional.

You forget the follow-through once the fundamentals have been mastered – almost.

A gloomy picture. Cheer up; things are not quite as bad as they seem. You the individual player, are the only one who can do anything about it.

Are you game? Let's go!

Watch the better players and notice how they meet each situation as it arises. Now, let's stroll over to the far court and watch some not so good tennisers.

Follow the play closely and you will see a remarkable number of things not to do.

You might, although never admitting it, see some of your own weaknesses displayed by these players.

Court vacant! Get out there and see what you have learnt. Tackle one fault at a time.

When you have strengthened that weak service, but not until it has definitely improved, work on another flaw.

You will find that as your playing improves your enjoyment becomes greater.

The satisfaction of being able to consistently turn in a good game will be a reward in itself.

Make up your mind to accomplish something this year.

Regardless of whether you win or lose, however, be a good sport at all times.

Could be Verse

To become first-rate,
You must concentrate.
Take your game apart;
That is where to start.

When success you find
Please keep this in mind:
You can't always win.
If you lose, just grin.

Men stoop not to cabbages;
All talk is now of kings.
Let's turn away from monarchs
And speak of other things.

In these days of summer,
When our outdoor sports we play.
Tennis fiends at Eastwood
Play into the dusk each day.

You know stars in tennis
Whom the fans praise long and loud.
But what of the hero
Now unhonoured in the crowd?

Though he plays at tennis,
For him there has been no fame.
That he should be unknown
Is at least a crying shame.

He started out with hope;
But alas his hopes were dashed.
Each game he played was deuce
As he ever downward crashed.

We should seek out this man;
To neglect him is a sin.
H played six games to deuce --
Lost six love and still could GRIN!

In our last edition
I had a little bit.
From my rhyme they dropped a line,
Perhaps to make it fit.

But this time I have a scheme
To hold them for awhile.
On this page a missing line
Will only make me smile.

Keep your eye upon the ball
'Til racquet hits it square;
Otherwise you'll merely hit
A vacant piece of air.

If you play behind the tape
Or else up by the net;
Mid-court is, you soon will find,
Never the place to get.

To burn your service over
Is very good indeed.
But in the court to place it
Is very pressing need.

"Push" is all right for a door,
But tennis is the thing.
And like our modern music
Goes better if you swing.

When waiting for that service
You should relax your grip.
But grasp your racquet firmly
When at the ball you whip.

Wait a moment for the ball
Until it gets to you;
Otherwise your shot may fly
Above a cloud or two.

Many books tell of this game
And they are helpful too.
But what happens on the court
Depends alone on you.

SKATING MADE EASY

Everyone should know how to skate.

There is the possibility that one will make up some cold morning to find the water pipe burst causing the rink to be formed in the basement.

A knowledge of skating would make it possible to skate around the basement and perhaps make a fire in the furnace.

Under such circumstances, however, the plumber would be the only one to make a profit despite the fact that the householder would own a private rink.

Think though, how such a happening would be an absolute loss to the non-skater. This is just one of the blessings that skating offers.

Some people are born skaters but most of us are just born. If the born skaters do read this even they may learn a great deal.

Most important of course is to secure a pair of skates before trying to learn. Without skates difficulties would most surely arise.

Care should be taken to avoid cheap skates unless you intended to pay the bill anyway.

Ice is an important item too. Summer is not a good time to start skating.

It is practically impossible to make a summer rink using ice cubes from the refrigerator although one would be able to get the "feel" of the ice.

A great deal depends upon the manner in which the novice begins. To slide boldly out on to the ice at first is to court disaster. One must be cautious.

Choose something to support yourself with until confidence is gained. An old chair is a good thing to use or perhaps a friend.

BOXING REPORTS

[This item has no title.]

A long while after the bulk of the gathering had departed, with only a few very loyal boxing spectators left to witness two unknown fighters have it out in a belated preliminary, sportswriters were pouncing away at their typewriters and wire operators were clicking their telegraph keys with the news that Tommy Farr had managed to stay 15 rounds with the champion Joe Louis on August 29 in their celebrated boxing show at the Yankee Stadium in New York.

Every well-known sporting writer in the East practically was on hand but each one was what might be termed the proverbial needle in the haystack among the estimated 300 reporters present.

Quite a liberal sprinkling of English newspaper correspondents were on hand, as well as foreign press association reporters, giving the ring event an air of internationalism.

When the main fight was over and Louis had given what the consensus of opinion agreed was one of his poorest exhibitions, sporting columnists broke out with reams of copy explaining their pre-flight enthusiasm for the champion and making an analysis of his awful showing.

Western Union made an estimate that pretty close to 200,000 words of press stuff went out from the stadium the night of the big fight and that an additional 25,000 words were sent over the seas by foreign correspondents seated at the ring side.

Boxers get punchy.
Wrestlers get paunchy.

Influence of wrestling in my life:
Every time I remove my shirt,
my five-year old starts wrestling me.

CONCESSION VIEW OF WRESTLING

[Archie is so poorly paid as a writer at a broadcasting company in Edmonton that he and his spouse (Hazel) have to moonlight as concession workers selling junk food and drinks at the concessions counter of a local sports arena in the evenings. Thus he sees many sports events, enabling him to write this item about wrestling in response to a newspaper column.]

During the years of reading your bits of writing I've been entertained and at times amused. In Saturday's Edmonton Journal, I ran across your observations on wrestling both on and off TV.

Before we go any further ... let's establish some facts. I have not in the past, nor do I expect in the future, to become a wrestling fan.

However, I have viewed a fair share of professional mat wrestlers during the past eight or nine years. There is a weekly card in town and I work on the concessions.

In other words, I get paid whether I watch the bruising blubber or not.

Their antics did fool me, for the first five minutes or so, but when I saw a wrestler stand up under six or seven apparently vicious rabbit punches, the whole thing became obvious.

From this point on, you and I differ, if what you write can be taken as your conviction, whether you take a humorous vein or not.

I was puzzled. Here was a group of perhaps 3,000 people

shouting their heads off at something which was clearly phoney.

There had to be a reason. Since I'm the type that must get down to the whys of everything, I started to study the situation.

The answer didn't burst upon me. I didn't leap from my shower bath and gallop down the street in a bath towel or less, shouting my knowledge to whoever would listen.

To begin with, our police are a bit sensitive about partly clad or near nude people dashing around the city. It might be that we are so near to B.C. and their Doukobors, that they are out to nip the spread of such tactics in the bud, or buff.

But in the final analysis, the height of the wrestling season is in mid-winter and I have no desire to become a frozen discoverer.

As I said, it was a gradual process, but an elderly woman gave me a final clue. She attended all matches and seemed more the type you see at elite concerts.

One night I went to have a look to see how soon we might be having an intermission.

You see, certain wrestlers work so close to schedule you can often tell by their particular hold or manoeuvre how soon the bout will end.

Through a lull in the general shouting and screaming I heard a shrill piercing voice going on something in this fashion, “Kill the dirty bum! Twist his head off! Gouge his eyes out!”

You guessed it. It was the old woman.

The remaining parts of my wrestling jig-saw fell into place.

Probably not more than half a dozen people in any wrestling crowd, which includes the short-sighted mentioned in your column, actually believe that wrestlers hurt each other or even seriously try.

You see, in this modern world, a person seldom yields to the urge to do physical violence. But the desire is often there.

It’s so simple to get someone to go through the motions while you shout and scream your head off. Nobody cares how much noise you make.

In fact, the fellow in the next seat is too busy doing the same to bother with you.

That’s why I no longer jeer at wrestling fans. They’ve found the safety valve that we all need in these days of high-pressure living.

I’m certain that anyone who attends wrestling matches regularly will never heave to worry about a nervous breakdown or even more serious ailment.

An interesting note in that connection is that each week one or two bus loads of men from a provincial home for the mentally ill come to the wrestling matches.

For all I know, it might be part of the therapy treatment.

Most of the time, our local newspaper, radio, and TV sports announcers merely report the weekly bouts and let it go at that. However, several years ago, Gorgeous George came to Edmonton.

Now, I don't know whether it was because ticket sales hadn't been too good or what, but the sports writers got passes from somewhere and they turned out in force.

For the next week, sports writers gave all wrestlers in general and Gorgeous George in particular a terrific word lashing.

Then, as far as they were concerned, that was the end of the matter. Even in sports you can just get so much out of a subject.

Little did they know what havoc they had wrought. Crowds fell off and former fans talked disdainfully of the fake wrestling racket.

But there was a wistfulness in their voices, and they spoke in the tones of people when they discuss the merits of a dear friend who had died.

Of course, most of the followers of wrestling finally did straggle back, but who can say how many even now lie twisted and warped, racked with mental anguish because their main safety-valve was plugged up.

To give one specific example –

I had a barber who would dash from work, it was usually seven before he'd swept up for the night, each Tuesday and never missed a wrestling match if he was able to walk.

I liked this barber. He was always cheerful, never let anything upset him, and he also did a fine job of hair-cutting.

Then came the Gorgeous George fiasco.

My barber turned into a surly, scissor-snapping crank. His work remained the same, but you could see his heart wasn't in it.

He slowed down to the point where he had to get an assistant.

Like most men, I hated the thought of losing my barber and having to look for a new one. So it was up to me to repair at least some of the damage.

He knew that I worked at the concessions so it wasn't difficult to get an opening.

One night, a wrestler accidentally pushed his opponent too hard. The fellow toppled out of the ring and broke a leg.

As it happened, I needed a haircut, so, instead of putting it off until my wife started making pointed remarks about violins, I saw my barber the next day.

Cautiously, I skimmed the bait towards him. "Leo the Cat showed them he wasn't fooling last night." I wriggled the rod and he almost pulled the line from my hand.

“You mean, someone really got hurt?” He tried to keep the eagerness from his voice.

“I’ll say. The Cat broke Smiling Boy’s leg. Doctor said it was a compound fracture.” I started to reel him in.

“They can’t say that was a fake.” He started to grin and a far away gleam came to his eyes.

“I saw his leg and there was no fooling about it.” I raised my gaff and gave him the full treatment.

“You know, a fellow can get a lot of fun out of watching wrestling. That is, it’s good for laughs, and they do have their rough moments. Why some of those guys have cauliflower ears. It takes more than a tap to do that.”

The barber was well and truly landed.

“I guess you’re right. And, being behind the scenes like your are, you get to know a few things the sports writers miss.”

I let it rest there. He finished cutting my hear in half the time he had been taking since the slow down, and it was one of the slickest job I’d ever had.

Even my wife was impressed.

The following week, as I was standing by the concession counter at the wrestling (right you are) the barber came up to me.

His eyes sparkled and he seemed to have grown younger.

“They’re really roughing it up tonight.” He leaned over the counter, and said in a hoarse whisper, “Of course I know they’re not getting very badly hurt, but I sure am enjoying it. I’ve shouted so much I won’t be able to talk for a week.”

The barber seldom mentions wrestling these days, but I can tell by the way he works, his tone of voice, that he’s enjoying life and the wrestling matches.

Who cares what the sports writers say?

I know you must fill your column, but isn’t it frightening to see what a few thoughtless words can lead to?

To come out flatly against something is fine, but to ridicule what might be someone’s shrine, why there’s no telling what it might do to a person.

It could even destroy a nation.

By the way, I’m a radio continuity writer, and you can take that into account on the barber story, although it is essentially true.

You might be interested to know, although I don’t read comic books, except to my son, I do read the daily comics in your local paper.

Which leads to one of the reasons I read your column.

My wife and I have the habit of reading the comics together. I read much faster and at one time I’d sit and fidget while she finished the page.

Then, they put your column in one corner of the first page of the comics. I started to read it as a filler and now I can't stop.

Maybe it's just like the wrestling, sort of a habit one acquires.

VARIOUS STORIES

COWED

[This true story of overcoming childhood fear is written in the late 1930s, seven or eight years after the event described.]

"You better be good or the cow will get you," warned mother during my pre-school years.

At fourteen I still feared the monster, especially the long-horned variety. Boy fashion, however, I kept this weakness secret.

One morning a pal brought what he believed to be good news.

We were to lead cattle in the annual livestock parade. Our reward would be free tickets to the grandstand show performance of the Exhibition.

To decline under any pretext was out of the question.

The day of the parade found me sadly wending my way towards what I felt was my doom.

I was introduced to a sharp-pronged beast who, I learned, was of nervous temperament and needed a firm hand.

Only last week she had almost put a boy's eye out. No need for me to worry about that.

Hugging close to my charge to avoid her death-dealing horns, I did manage to reach the grandstand in front of which the parade was to take place.

Disdainfully, the cow brought her hoof down on my foot.

Finally, I staggered weakly back to the stable.

Although I now realize how harmless cows are, I will always remember that first encounter.

TRAMP'S LUCK

[the tale of Cheerful Bo]

The shabby dressed figure trudged wearily along the railway track. Far ahead the dim forms of large buildings slowly took shape.

The tired tramp finally sat down to ease his burning feet. His shoes were on their last legs or at least they were on their last feet.

The soles were barely clinging to the tops. One heel was missing and the other was worn down to the sole.

The weary wanderer gazed sadly down at his feet.

"Well, these shoes should last me another ten years, at least," he observed brightly, the next moment showing the true trend of his meditations as he angrily flipped the loose and well-worn sole of his better-shod foot.

But, with a flash of his one-time professional wit, he continued, "These aren't so hot although they sure make my feet feel plenty warm."

He rose reluctantly, pulled his threadbare coat tighter around his body, and thrust his hands deep into his pockets.

"I could do with some new clothes too," he mused, ruefully surveying the tattered remnants.

"These are almost worn out. They're so thin that if I joined a nudist colony I wouldn't have to take them off."

They were extremely disreputable looking; a disgrace to even a tramp.

The pants hung in ragged ruins. A huge, untidy patch flapped from one knee. The seat exhibited a large, sharply contrasting patch of brilliant green.

His coat, if one could call it a coat, was practically indescribable. It was a buttonless, ragged, shapeless cloth. The sleeves were both out at the elbows.

A safety-pin did service as a button.

To put it mildly, the coat had undergone a great change since leaving its original owner.

After a careful scrutiny, any reasonable individual would readily admit that it might have once been some sort of wearing apparel.

"Cheerful Bo", for such was the name he had earned by his happy-go-lucky manner, was not living up to his name.

He could hardly be blamed for being despondent under the circumstances.

A forcible ejection from a fast-moving freight-train, especially if it is [24 kilometres] from the nearest town, does not tend to bring a happy smile to any person's face.

He had been put out in more ways than one and he felt more than mildly bitter towards all brakemen.

As he walked, his anger quickly slipped away. Soon he

was swinging briskly along, expertly whistling various song hits of the season.

The distance between himself and the city gradually diminished. The sun, which had been peeping over the horizon when he started, rose higher and higher.

Another hour would see him in the city.

Cheerful increased his pace. Once he reached the city he would no doubt be able to get food from some kind person. With luck he might also secure an old suit of clothes.

He was passing a railway crossing when a small leather object caught his eye. He pounced upon it.

The wallet seemed lined with money. Fifty dollars! It was like a gift from heaven. He could scarcely believe his good fortune.

"I hope it isn't a dream," he breathed.

It did not take him long to realize that the money actually existed. Putting it carefully into his one good pocket, he strode jubilantly on his way.

Upon entering the city limits he moved warily. Many year's experience taught him to avoid meeting a police officer if possible.

They had the annoying habit of popping up unexpectedly from nowhere. He did not wish to encounter one, at least not until he had spent the money.

Then it wouldn't matter so much.

Cheerful Bo threaded his way through back lanes and side streets. If he could find a small second-hand clothing store he would be able to make himself more presentable.

A parcel at the foot of an ash-can attracted his attention. Investigation showed it to contain a pair of shoes, slightly worn it is true but in far better condition than his own.

They fitted perfectly.

Luck was running his way. First the money and now a pair of shoes. He tossed his discarded foot-wear aside.

A broad grin spread over his face. Cheerful Bo was living up to his name now.

He emerged from one alley and was about to enter another when a muffled sob reached his ear. He stopped and looked around.

A poorly dressed woman stood in the shade of a dilapidated building. She was weeping softly, endeavouring to conceal her grief.

"What's the matter?" he gently inquired.

His kind, sympathetic tone moved her. It invited her to confide in him.

"I shouldn't talk this way to a stranger," she commenced, "but I must speak to someone. I'm unable to pay the rent and tomorrow I'll be turned out."

"Now, now," Cheerful soothed. "Cheer up. Perhaps I can help you. How much money do you need?"

"I'm afraid that you can't help me," she replied. "I need fifty dollars."

Cheerful dug down into his pocket and produced the money.

"Here," he said, "Take this."

She gasped with astonishment.

"Why, I--- I---" she began.

"Forget it," he muttered and started to move away.

He had gone a few steps down the nearby alley when a heavy hand descended upon his shoulder.

"You better come along with me," growled the police officer. "I'll put you away where you won't be able to panhandle for a long while."

Cheerful meekly allowed himself to be led away. He'd get a free meal if nothing else, he optimistically assured himself.

FRIENDS

Reggie Mather stared at the shabby figure.

"Well hello there, Jim!" he cried.

"Hello Reggie," Jim Wilson acknowledged, running his eyes over the other's well-tailored clothes and highly-polished shoes.

"You seem to have done well over in China."

"Yes, I am the firm's Hong Kong agent. I am on vacation just now. How are you getting along?"

"I manage to get by all right," Jim assured him, rubbing his hand across a stubble-covered chin.

Reggie held out his hand.

"I have to run along. See you before I leave."

Jim gazed wonderingly after his departing friend and then down at the ten-dollar bill in his right hand.

"I certainly must look the part," he mused.

A wave of his hand brought the limousine to his side.

From beneath a mass of fishing equipment, he ordered, "Home, Jeffries."

FOR SALE

He didn't feel like a man who had just inherited half a million dollars, but he did have the money.

John Prentiss ran a gnarled hand through wiry grey locks that were always undecided whether to lie down or stand upright.

Money without Matilda was as pointless as a head with no body.

The house was quieter than usual this morning, since the painters and decorators had left.

He had allowed them to complete the job simply to have it finished. There was no point in stopping with so little remaining to be done.

Of course it would not have altered the sale value one way or the other these days.

Matilda had looked forward to their golden wedding anniversary with such girlish enthusiasm. But fate trumped ruthlessly and irrevocably.

She had tumbled down the stairs so easily that it appeared as slow motion to his agonized gaze.

Helplessly, he had watched her strike the bottom and lie still.

As he waited for the eggs to boil, he recalled their wedding breakfast.

Matilda hadn't burnt the toast, but the eggs had been far too liquid to rate the generous term of soft boiled. He had teased her about it for weeks.

Topping one of the eggs, he grinned in spite of himself. It was solid.

The tingle of the telephone cut through his thoughts. It probably was another would-be buyer.

There had been so many anxious to move in when they heard he was leaving. Yet, he couldn't leave the old house to just anyone who came along.

Funny how the ringing always reminded him of the night when Jim had called long distance.

He was so excited about getting home on first leave that he forgot the difference in time. They had many laughs over that early morning awakening.

Jim had always found life such a happy adventure.

Later, the official notification from the War Office had seemed a grotesque joke perpetuated by the devil.

Outwardly, Matilda had remained bright and cheerful, but John knew that a part of herself had gone with Jim.

"Hello."

The brisk young voice from the other end of the line was bubbling over with eagerness. "Mr. Prentiss? Have you sold your house yet?"

"No. Who is that calling?"

"I'm Bob Black. We, that is my wife and I, would like to see the house."

"Why, of course." John liked the young man's vibrant tone. The voice was as refreshing as a cold shower.

It somehow eased the numbing grief to know that there was much in life for some to exult over.

"You can come over this morning if you wish. Any time will suit me. Goodbye."

Turning towards the living room, he gazed musingly at the sun-gilded baby grand. Matilda had always treated it as something near sacred.

He could never forget the rapt look on her face that Christmas morning.

She just stood for awhile and stared at the answer to a prayer about which she had never dared even to think.

Cathy had followed her mother's love for music, soon learning to play and love the big piano. He hoped that Cathy would be happy with her English husband.

They had met during an air raid in London while she was with the ambulance corps. Ralph must be a real man. He could visit them for a few days on his travels.

There was no hurry now.

He couldn't possibly stay in the old house, where memories peeked from every corner. But, at least he would see that someone who would appreciate it would take over.

That was the smallest favour he could do for Matilda.

The Blacks arrived flushed and breathless, as if they had run all the way. John felt that they were two small children.

They stood by the open door as if waiting for permission to speak.

"Come in, you two." He led them directly to the living room. The girl stopped and stared.

"Oh, Bob, isn't is wonderful!"

"It sure is, Kay." He explained to the older man. "Kay can never get enough when it comes to pianos."

A dreamy expression came to John's eyes as he invited the girl. "Pleas play if you wish."

"Thank you." Her fingers gently caressed the keys and the music lifted John with it.

Matilda's spirit filled the room bringing back so many yesterdays, sorrowful, but sweet with the knowledge that they had lived countless happy hours together in the past.

The remainder of the tour was an anti-climax. Their constant happy exchange of glances told him that this was their dream house.

"We, that is...." Bob floundered.

"If it's a case of money," John came to his rescue, "A monthly rental basis would suit me fine."

After all, they were the right people, and he didn't need the money.

"As far as the furniture is concerned, we can include that if there is any of it that you can use."

They both started to talk at once, then stopped. They all laughed together.

"You don't know how much it means to us, Mr. Prentiss." Bob caught Kay's hand in his, and neither of them seemed to notice

"We hardly knew what we should do if we didn't get this house. It was our last chance. With two young children, it looked hopeless to rent."

John gruffly brushed aside their thanks. "Glad to be able to help. By the way, would you like to move in right away?"

"We wouldn't think of rushing you..." Kay began.

"Nonsense. I was leaving tonight, anyway."

After they left, John went to the telephone.

"Hotel Royal? I should like to reserve a room with bath for tonight. The name is John Prentiss. Thank you."

One night wouldn't hurt. He had planned to leave the next day in any event and everything was packed except for a small bag. He dialed another number.

"Hello, Bert. This is John Prentiss. Could you draw up the papers for the transfer of deed for the house this afternoon? No, it isn't exactly a cash deal.

"The Blacks don't know it yet, but this is their lucky day. What's that? Yes, it's the same family that was burnt out the other night. Goodbye, Bert."

Might just as well finish packing now, John thought as he started for the stairs. He sighed contentedly.

"Martha would be pleased."

He had just snapped the suitcase lid shut when the door bell summoned. They were waiting at the door, more out of breath than ever.

Bob was nervously nibbling his knuckles.

"We have a suggestion, Mr. Prentiss. I hope we aren't being disrespectful, but Kay had an ideas..."

"You belong with this house." Kay carried on as Bob faltered.

"I thought perhaps you didn't really want to wander around the world alone. Why not stay here with us?"

"I'd only be in the way." John tried hard to convince himself.

"We'd enjoy having you around." Bob assured him.

"Won't you please give it a trial?" Their manner reminded him of how Cathy and Jim once bullied and teased.

"Well, I suppose I could stay for a week and see." John knew that he would remain with Bob and Kay as long as they would have him.

FROM THE AIR

Bob peered anxiously along the crowded station platform vainly trying to pick out a familiar face.

Then a bright-eyed young woman forced her way through the mass of people to reach his side. With a click of his heels, Bob snapped smartly to attention.

"Pilot Rawley at your service, Miss er...Jones, if I remember correctly."

"Oh Bob, quit teasing." Her laugh tinkled musically through small creamy teeth.

"O.K. Mary. How's this?" For a few breathless moments she held on and didn't worry over broken bones.

At length he released her and held her at arm's length.

"So you're not a dream after all. Six months is a long time. Say, where's my father and mother?"

"I'm sorry, Bob, but they are out of town. They took a trip up to Crow Lake a few days ago."

"That's too bad. My leave will probably be over before they return. I don't suppose it would be much use wiring.

"It would probably be a week before they could get back from up there."

"Yes, especially since there is no road fit for automobile travel. I'll do my best to keep you entertained."

She started towards the station and Bob followed with his suitcase until they managed to struggle through to the comparative calm of the waiting room.

He turned questioningly towards her.

"Where from here?"

"Right this way. The gem studded chariot awaits your lordship's pleasure."

Outside he stopped and clutched her shoulder, staggering weakly to a standstill.

"Cinderella, I am overcome. These reports about women drivers are malicious lies, after all. Or..."

He pretended to carry out a careful check of the roadster's paint job, "Is that camouflaged wrinkle on the right rear fender?"

"You take charge, sir." She saluted mockingly. "If there are any serious breaks, knocks, abrasions, cylinders lost or missing, I stand ready to correct and adjust.

"Further, if you do not agree that your roadster is in far better shape than when I took over, dinner's on me."

"It's luck that I'm not hungry today." He climbed in beside her. "Nothing wrong so far. I might hold together for a few blocks."

"Thus begins your leave. I have everything lined up for your stay here. Sit tight Bob and we'll whirl through on schedule. Home, my good man. The Jones residence."

"Thanks, Mary. I wouldn't like to stay at my own home all by myself. You seem to have things figured out right."

Mary's parents met them at the doorstep. Everyone talked at once for the first hour or so. Later in the evening Bob turned to Mr. Hones as they stood alone in the living room.

"It is a shame that dad and mother can't be here."

"Yes, son, but we'll do our best to keep you happy. Now, what were we talking about.

"Oh yes, that day when Jim Preston and you got mixed up with those crooks down on the North Side. It certainly was funny to hear about how you boys got the best of them."

Up in his room Bob pondered over this strange action of his host. Why did they shy away from talk of his parents. Surely they weren't hiding something from him.

He'd try to have it out with them in the morning. After all he wasn't a child. Whatever was wrong, he should know about it.

Somehow, the next day and the ensuing days of his leave, Bob was carefully steered away from anything connected with his parents.

Several times he tried to bring up the subject directly but no one, not even Mary would say anything more than that his parents were at Crow Lake.

What could they be hiding?

He knew they wouldn't lie but they were holding something back.

And yet it didn't seem to be bad news as they were happy rather than sad when he tried to pump them regarding his parents.

"Look here, Mary." A day of his furlough remained. "Perhaps I could take you out, get you drunk and then solve this mystery."

"I'll be firm. You can't lead me astray. Villain, unhand me or I'll scream for help."

"Let's have a final fling before we go. I can't promise to keep from asking the same questions but you can bring along two bodyguards to keep me quiet."

"I feel quite capable of handling you and not letting out any secrets. Now, today calls for a visit to our old stamping grounds on Clear View Ridge. Just the two of us."

Up in the calm stillness of the big hill, they wandered and chased one another as they often had played together as children.

At last, flushed and breathless, they sat down to gaze out over the city.

"Well, I may not see our little town again for a long time so here's for a last long look."

He fondly tweaked her ear as she nestled at his side. Together they silently gazed out over the swiftly moving city whose sounds did not reach them.

"Yes, you'll soon be back up there." Mary pointed at a long plane high overhead. "But let's not think about that. We came here to enjoy ourselves.

"You have to work for your lunch. Help me unpack the food."

As dusk crept on they went back down the winding white road. Turning along the street toward Mary's home, Bob noticed a car drawing away from the curb.

"Isn't that in front of your house?" Bob pointed at the vanishing car. Must have been your other boyfriend. He arrived both too late and too early."

"We evidently forgot you were around, Bob." Her voice became more serious. "I wonder who it could be?"

"Patient my child. We'll soon find out. Shall I run the car up into the front room so that you can find out all there is to know, sooner?"

"All right smarty, you're just as curious as I."

The car had barely stopped when she leapt out and dashed up the front walk. "Come on, slowpoke. I am a way ahead of you."

Bob slid out from behind the wheel and sprinted after her. She was not in sight when he got inside. Instead, Mr. Jones stood waiting in the front hall.

"Bob – I, that is to say..." Mary's father shifted his feet and cleared his throat. "We have been hiding something from you. It's about your father and mother. They..."

"Is it anything serious? Please come directly to the point. I can take it."

"Well, come into the living room and I'll explain." He stood aside for Bob to enter. Bob took a few steps forward and gaped.

"Surprised, son?" His father came forward and his mother rose from the chesterfield to fling herself into his arms.

"You see," his father explained. "the message from Mr. Jones got through and we flew back this afternoon. There's an airport near Crow Lake, now ..."

DOUBLE TRIUMPH

[Although the story is probably entirely fiction, the location and circumstances are based in fact. This writing is a product of Archie's months in the remote R.C.A.F. base of Bella Bella (B.C.) in 1942, a few months after marrying Hazel.]

Walt Peterson slapped the typewriter carriage back across the machine and surveyed his work with a disgusted one sided droop of severely thin lips.

Jerking the offending paper from the grip of the platen, he crumpled it and aimed a shot in the general direction of the waste paper basket.

"Ah neitz! It'll do in the morning."

The office clock wagged its tail and pointed out that it was ten minutes after five. Walt raised his glasses clear to rub sleepy grey eyes.

"The mail boat will probably late as usual and not arrive until late tomorrow night." Walt spoke his thoughts aloud in the empty office.

Vicious white flecked wave mouths reached up to snap at the island's impassive rocky guardians.

Walt scarcely glanced at the ocean as he turned the key in Headquarters Orderly Room door.

Fragments if grey sky drapes sagged to hide nearby mountain peaks.

Rain had called a truce after days of almost steady downpour that seemed to have saturated the very rocks.

Surely the Air Force could have sent a single man to this isolated spot. When a fellow was married it was that much harder to take.

Besides, he should be near Jean, especially at a time such as this when she needed him more than ever. It wasn't fair to either of them.

His raincoat draped on one arm, Walt adjusted his wedge cap over a rebellious head of wiry black hair.

He walked hopefully over to the next building and entered a door which bore the Wireless Section sign.

"No, I'm afraid not, Peterson." The operator's negative head shake emphasized the words. "We don't appear to have a message for you today."

Walt mumbled his thanks and headed for the mess hall. Scrambling up the rock strewn path, he joined the inevitable line of waiting airmen.

He simply had to have some word from Jean now. Of course it might be merely a matter of hours before he heard but – He mentally curbed his wishful thinking.

He picked at the stew but soon pushed the half empty plate aside. After a few nibbles at a slice of raisin pie, Walt gave up and went outside.

Many of the men were strolling around in fatigue clothes,

enjoying the break after their long siege of dreary wetness.

A strenuous walk by the sea should do him some good. At least he'd be away from the noisy camp.

He stopped at the barracks to button a tunic over the fatigue sweater he was wearing.

One of the guards whom Walt knew cautioned as he passed the wharf, "Better not go too far, Walt. The tide's coming in and it'll soon be dark."

He punctuated the warning with his rifle butt. "Scrambling through trees when the rocks are covered isn't exactly child's play."

"I'm only going for a short walk." Walt half slid, half ran down the path to the unfriendly rock armoured beach. "I'll be back before the tide rises high enough to cause trouble."

Grim, blue black, water smoothed rocks took on grotesque forms as dusk pulled its shroud over the dying day.

In a few minutes the land jutted out to hide the wharf from view.

If anything went wrong and Jean was in trouble. Further supposition was suddenly postponed as his foot slipped on a water soaked log.

He wavered uncertainly but did not fall.

"That was almost too close." Walt retrieved his hat from where it lay in a jumble of rocks.

"Perhaps I should go back before I stumble again. My luck may not hold. With no one near, I would be in a tough spot."

His gaze carried out along a channel leading to the open sea. A flicker of light blinked. Walt paused.

Off-on-off-on-off. Then it stopped. Nor did it flash again although he watched and waited.

No answering signal came from the short stretch of shoreline that he was able to see. But there was a point of land a few [metres] away.

He could check that far in case there was something wrong. The way things were on the coast you never knew what might happen next.

No time to go for help. He would have to take a chance.

Carefully picking his way, Walt crept stealthily to where the shore changed direction.

A shadowy indistinct shape took form in the gloom. From it light blinked in a stream of dots and dashes. Walt edged closer.

Beneath his foot a rock skidded. Silence clattered away as the stone skipped across the rocks.

The signaller whirled and Walt squinted blindly in the full glare of the light's beam.

He sprang at the centre of the light, arms outflung. A

sharply probing flame roared, struck him and thrust one shoulder back.

Walt felt his hands close on the other man's clothes. He clung desperately, senses reeling.

Revolver and flashlight fell clanging, unheeded as the two men grappled savagely in the darkness.

They staggered briefly on the damp, uneven surface and reeled drunkenly to tumble in a confused heap together.

Walt set his teeth as he heard the gritting crunch of crushed bones. His adversary lay motionless, uttering no sound.

Walt's shoulder throbbed. His arm hung limp and useless. He struggled free and tried to stand up. The effort squeezed beads of sweat on to his forehead.

Searching fingers of water crept along his outstretched hand. He bent weekly on both knees.

Then he flopped helplessly to the ground, his body refusing to carry on the fight.

Myriads of coloured circles danced and twirled around him. His head seemed to be lifting from his shoulders. Then his entire world blacked out.

Water moistened his lips and water trickled down his throat. Walt spluttered and attempted to push aside the smothering blackness.

A hand gently forced him down.

He became aware of an open window. Sunlight poked sunbeams into his eyes that protested after that long stretch of darkness.

An unmistakable hospital odour tickled his nose.

The room gyrated crazily and stopped right side up. Gradually things took shape as the haze cleared.

Walt noticed someone beside the bed. The M.O. placed the partially emptied tumbler on the table by the bed as he spoke to his patient.

"Take it easy, Peterson." The doctor smiled pleasantly.

"You'll have to be careful with that shoulder for a while. Lucky for you that we arrived before the tide rose any higher. Your head was in the water."

"But was there –" Walt wrinkled his forehead and closed weary eyes. Why wouldn't that irritating buzzing stop.

"It was a submarine all right. The guard heard the shot and sent for help." The M.O. patted Walt's arm. "You did a fine piece of work."

Walt hardly comprehended, concentrating on his own problem.

"I only want to know if a telegram came for me."

"This must be what you mean." The medical officer unfolded the printed form. "I nearly forgot about it."

Walt reached for his glasses and managed to hold the telegram steady. The lines smoothed out of his brow as he read:

ITS A BOY BOTH DOING FINE
mother

AS I SAY

[The street address on this story indicates it is writing from between 1950 and 1956.]

Thinking about it afterwards brought beads of sweat to his forehead. Sixth sense, premonition, or whatever you care to call it, the fact is that he did turn just at the right instant.

To the casual onlooker, his spontaneous action must have seemed premeditated. All Jim knew was that he had to get there before the bus.

Countless confused thoughts milled about in his head but all were thrust aside in a desperate desire to save her.

She wavered undecidedly, lifted one foot from the curb and then began to tumble swiftly into the path of the speeding bus.

Jim Walters reached her side almost at a dead run and managed somehow to scoop her back to safety. For a moment she lay shuddering in his arms and then struggled free.

The bus driver hit the sidewalk at a run, but slowed down to an angry stride when he saw the woman standing on the sidewalk, unharmed.

He waved his arms agitatedly in all directions, his lips seeking to frame the words.

"Haven't you any sense?" he finally asked, filling in the blanks with gestures more clearly expressive than any expletives could have been.

Then, turning to Jim, "Lucky you were quick on the up-take, young fellow."

The woman had quickly regained her composure and was gazing unconcernedly at the gathering crowd.

"You probably think that I purposely fell in front of your bus," she observed rather absently as if her act had never really been more than a passing thought.

"Oh no," the bus driver reassured her in his most patient manner. "You know, I'll bet it was the gremlins that pushed you. Those naughty things. I know your type.

"First thing I know, you'll be trying to bum a free ride."

"Why not let me take care of her," Jim cut in, putting his hand on the driver's shoulder. "She doesn't seem to be feeling too good."

The bus driver shrugged his resignation and started back to his bus, "I've got a schedule to keep. The pleasure is all yours, Mister," he called back over one shoulder.

"Let's go somewhere and talk this over," Jim suggested as he took the woman's arm. She started to go with him as if it made no particular difference where she went.

"Say you two, what's going on here?" a police [officer] demanded, wading through the ebbing crowd.

Then, getting a full view of the woman, he snapped, "So

it's you again. Haven't you created enough trouble on my beat for one day?"

"It was an accident, officer," Jim attempted to explain. "She almost slipped in front of the bus, but I got there first."

"All day she's been trying to fall, or maybe jump, off bridges or get run over." the police [officer] declared.

"I've a good mind to lock you up in a nice safe room in our jail house, Ms."

"I'm sure everything will be all right now," Jim assured the man in blue. "I'll see that she stays out of trouble in future."

"This is the last time I'll be warning you, "the police [officer] reminded her. "One more break and there'll be no argument.

"Move along folks. Don't block the sidewalk. There's nothing to see."

Jim quickly led the woman away from the busy streets. They walked through the park in silence, neither attempting to start the conversation.

Seeing an empty bench, Jim steered his charge to the seat.

"There, that's more like it," Jim sighed as he leaned back and relaxed. "Now, would you mind explaining this foolishness?"

"Why should I tell you anything?" she asked with a faint spark of spirit.

"I did save your life," he reminded.

"Why didn't you just leave me alone? I didn't ask for help," she protested, her eyes flashing angrily.

"Hold it. If you're gong to be that way about it, I'll try paging another bus," Jim answered, vainly trying to bring even a shadow of a smile to her lips.

"I tried to nerve myself several times to jump today, and just as I succeeded, you had to spoil it with your interference," she accused.

"Far be it from me to spoil such good clean fun, but think of the mess it could make on a shiny bus, not to mention the street," Jim teased as he tried again to make her smile.

"You must have given that cop plenty of work, even before that finale I so rudely interrupted."

"He was only suspicious. I hadn't really attempted anything before. I tell you I hadn't," she insisted as Jim raised his eyebrows.

"That's all beside the point." Jim told her. "The world hasn't treated you that badly. Besides, only cowards take the easy way out."

"I didn't ask for a sermon. When the one you trust and love deserts at a crucial moment, there is nothing left to live for," she said with a listless droop of her body.

“Ridiculous,” Jim snapped in exasperation. “You’re not being fair to yourself or anyone else.”

“It isn’t my fault if someone else hasn’t the courage to stick it out either,” she complained. “I was willing to carry on, but there was no incentive.”

“To be alive is the important thing,” Jim said. “Think it over. You can’t change the past, but you can at least try harder in future.”

“Don’t preach. Everything is hopeless,” she replied.

“While you are still alive, hope is never dead,” Jim soothed.

“What’s the use, with even my husband against me?” she asked, a faint trace of hope tinging her voice.

Jim picked his words carefully as he answered her, “Perhaps you haven’t given him a chance to understand. There are two sides to every question, you know.”

She didn’t reply, but sat thoughtfully staring out across the green grass and brilliant flower beds.

Jim waited, not pressing his argument. He studied her face closely and then made his decision.

He rose quickly from the bench and strode swiftly along the path, without a backward glance, positive at last that he had convinced her.

The woman seemed so engrossed in her thoughts she

hardly seemed to notice and scarcely turned her head as he disappeared from sight.

Jim hesitated for a moment as he reached the street and then headed for the Fifth Street Bridge. There were a few people crossing as he approached.

He had the bridge practically to himself as he neared the middle. For several minutes he studied the swift current with its eddying whirlpools.

It wouldn't take long for the racing water to complete the job if a would-be jumper survived the fall.

With the greatest deliberation, Jim unbuttoned and removed his coat. Placing his hat on top, he bent down but straightened up.

No use bothering with his shoes.

He put one hand on the railing and turned sideways to crouch in a vaulting position. Slowly, tensely, he began to count: one, two, three, four, five...

"Jim!"

She ran the last few metres. He opened his arms and gathered her in.

"I'm so glad I arrived in time, darling," she gasped.

"It's all right, Mildred. I didn't really mean to jump," Jim confessed. "After I pulled you from in front of the bus I had to find some way to bring you to your senses."

SHE DRIFTED HOME

For Gertie, cars are out-of-date,
But aeroplanes she thinks are great.
She likes to sail up in the sky.
To date her up you have to fly.

Many an eve she takes a flight,
And often when the moon is bright
A boy-friend takes her for a twirl;
Air-conscious Gertie—What a girl!

Away up there she's never scared,
And what is more, she goes prepared.
Now, if her friend gets out of hand,
A parachute takes her to land.

HUNGRY CHILD

"But grandmother, I'm hungry." Eyes which seemed too large for the tiny head gazed upward with an appeal stronger and more eloquent than words.

"Hush child. We must be brave. Soon the British will come and then we shall be hungry no longer.

The words came slowly as if even they were rationed and scarce.

Her face showed no bitterness or hate, but there was a solemn mask which accentuated the pinched, angular, age-lined features.

It was as though her body had been robbed of sunshine and laughter, leaving only a gaunt, humourless frame.

Nearly four years had slowly and wearily dragged by since her daughter Marie had brought Jean, then but a month old, to this quiet corner.

Marie and her husband had gone cheerfully to the aid of France. The memory of those anxious months was still fresh in her mind.

Then, just before the humiliation of France, had come the news of their death. She had struggled on, but it was difficult for an old woman to keep two mouths fed.

"Look, my dear." Large, liquid eyes followed the pointing finger as the child clung close.

"They will come from over there, and up out of the sea, climbing cliffs such as these to drive the Germans from our land."

"Will they bring some chocolate, grandmother?" Jean remembered the small square of chocolate which the old lady had contrived to save.

In her childhood wisdom, she had only nibbled a bit each day until the treasure finally dwindled and was gone.

"Yes, and many more good things." For an instant the ancient eyes kindled as her mind conjured up visions of prosperous days her companion had never known.

"Will they come tomorrow?" persisted the infant, unable to imagine anything that could not be definitely set forth.

"Perhaps not tomorrow, but soon my dear. Already their guns rumble in the distance."

She drew herself erect, appearing to grow in stature as she glared scornfully yet half pityingly down at the town and its busy wharves far below their vantage point.

As if reciting a creed or a lesson well learnt, she continued.

"Then the true France shall rise and crush those filthy German swine underfoot until not one remains alive on our country's soil!"

All the vehemence of the long, weary, bitter years was behind the words though her manner retained a certain quiet defiance that comes from knowledge of ultimate victory.

Then she paused and became once more an ordinary old woman, a calmly patient expression hiding her emotions. “Come, we must get home before dark.”

They hurried down the slope to a little cottage nestling among the trees, well sheltered from the fury of winter winds which roared up from the ocean.

After the youngster had repeated her prayers and climbed into her little bed, the old woman returned to the living room.

She sank heavily into a soft, time-worn chair that embraced and swallowed her as the gathering gloom made her form blend with the chair’s bulk.

A deep sigh shivered through her wasted frame as she shook a greying head.

Why didn’t the Allies hurry? There was a limit beyond which no one could be expected to endure. That limit had been almost reached.

Those Germans were always finding new ways of squeezing a bit more from her.

First there had been the cow. Jean needed milk to build up that poor, thin little body. Not content, they now took most of her meagre crop of vegetables.

True, they paid for what they seized, but with money printed newspaper fashion as needed. None of the town folk would give full value for it, though there was little one could buy these days.

But brooding would not help matters. She picked her way through the darkened house to the inner room.

Pausing by the child's bed, she re-arranged the tumbled bed clothes. Bending low, she kissed the pale forehead.

"Poor child," she murmured, "Not even enough to eat."

Noiselessly undressing, she quickly slipped into bed and bell into a troubled sleep. At length, she stirred and then sat upright. Something was wrong.

She sensed it in the thinning grey shadows that clung to the corners reluctant to leave. Her eyes began to function properly and focus once more.

Her body suddenly stiffened with apprehension. Jean's bed was empty, blankets trailing on the floor.

"Jean, Jean!" She pulled a dress over her nightgown and fumbled with her shoes. No answer.

A draft of cold air swirled around her ankles.

The outside door swayed ominously in the early morning breeze.

Why had she forgotten to latch it? No time to ponder that now.

At a shambling trot, she set off for the cliff top.

In the first misty light of dawn, the rocky edge of land jutting to meet the sky appeared bare with no sign of life.

She slowed to a walk, breath coming in painful gasps, threatening to burst through her chest.

Silently she prayed that the child had not wandered too near the edge. Where could she be?

A slight movement caught her eye. Perhaps her eyes were playing tricks but – no, something was stirring.

It must be Jean. A few moments and her hopes were confirmed as she recognized a tousled head.

Jean, nightie carefully tucked under her, sat serenely contemplating the swelling ocean.

In her arms she clutched something which the old lady could not see. As she gazed she waved her tiny hand to an invisible someone, far out in the water.

The next instant she was gathered into her grandmother's arms.

"Grandmother was so worried, dear. You shouldn't have come out here in the cold and dark. It's not safe for a little girl."

"But grandmother, I met a nicest men with black faces. Were they the British?"

As if to answer, there came a deep rumble and the ground trembled.

From the town far below them an expanding grey smoke plume spread upwards, then slowly split, one part descending to leave a forlorn cloud swirling uncertainly.

Eager orange flames greedily enveloped the harbour.

For a moment, the old woman stood transfixed, the fire reflecting on a face which had become alive and eagerly expectant.

"Yes, child." There was a triumph in her voice. "This is only a visit, but they will be back."

Her gaunt body seemed to expand and glow in the light of the sun as it slowly crept above the horizon.

"All France knows they will come some day and that time is near!"

"The nice men told me these were chocolate." The child took a firmer grip on two sardine shaped tins labelled, "Emergency Rations."

COLD

[It's not clear whether this is the beginning of a story or a complete one. However, it is the same length as other items written for contests. The handwritten date is 1939.]

Jim swung down to the ground at Fort McMurray station. Frigid air thrust icy needles against his face.

He hunched his shoulders and tried to snuggle down inside a coat that had suddenly become a mere cheese cloth heavy shawl.

Everything seemed shrivelled and congealed by the penetrating chill. A few yards away a curtain of murky whiteness closed in.

Shivering plumes of smoke became rigid banners beneath winter's merciless grasp.

Brittle snow crunched complainingly underfoot.

Four layers of wool were a puny barrier as frosty barbs probed at Jim's shrinking feet.

Jim cautiously sampled the air. Its sharp blades pierced his nostrils and ripped at his lungs threatening to reduce him to a miserable heap of icicles.

His gasps jarred on the silence of that deathly white world.

The thermometer's blob of red waved a sliver of crimson beside the numeral "-50" as Jim shivered his way to the hotel.

SPECIAL BOOK

It looked the same as any other pocket dictionary but the moment he saw it, Jim knew there was something special about it.

In the first place, it was balanced on top of a fire hydrant.

That might happen to any dictionary, except for the fact that this particular one had only a single corner resting on the fire plug.

He didn't touch it immediately. This could be a trick of some sort.

A careful survey revealed no strings, mirrors, or sky hooks. Cautiously, he flicked the book. It spun slowly for a moment and then came to a rest, half open.

Jim leaned closer. Both pages exposed had the same words printed in large block capitals. Why, it couldn't be. The lettering was clear enough.

His own name, Jim Duncan, was the only printing on the two pages. As he grasped the book, it snapped tightly shut.

The first word of the title was obscured but Jim could make out the remainder fairly easily. It was some sort of a pocket dictionary all right. But how had his name ...

He struggled with the pages. They seemed glued together. That was strange. Could someone be playing a trick? Yet he was sure the book had been open.

Thrusting the book into his coat pocket, he hurried back to the hotel.

Several people stopped and stared after him. Jim was still puzzling that one out when the desk clerk put his finger on the trouble.

"I beg your pardon, sir..."

"What's the trouble?"

"That book, sir. Isn't that an unusual place to carry it."

"What book?" Jim noticed the slight weight on his shoulder. It was the dictionary again. How had it got there?

ANOTHER ANGLE

[On February 13, 1947, Archie submits this story to the Women's Canadian Club of Ontario Literary Competition (1946-1947). He uses the nom de plume "Plus One". The WCCO of that time probably saw women in the same way as they are depicted in this story. Although Archie is never in Italy in wartime, his feelings about returning literally to the old job after war may be parallel to those of the main character in this story.]

Bert Johnson gazed gloomily out of the front office window. The rain blurred street seemed a reflection of his own confusion.

What in the world did he want? It had all been so simple even up to a few months ago. Now, everything was a mess.

"Okay, Bert," the diminutive stenographer motioned toward the inner office, "Mr. Turner will see you now."

"Thanks, Peg. Keep your fingers crossed."

He hesitated for a moment in front of the door which announced in cold impersonal gilt that James J. Turner was the general manager.

Well, this looked like it. Old Turner certainly had taken his time. But then, he always had moved slowly and deliberately although relentlessly.

Bert could never quite forget that first carpet standing when he had been with the firm only a matter of weeks.

Of course he had been cleared of that stamp box trouble but the feeling of a hovering eagle had remained. Turner always made him feel like a paralyzed mouse, powerless to do anything but wait.

"Sit down, Johnson." The approach hadn't changed in eight years. James J. (Even among themselves the staff never used the bare initials. It was unthinkable) leaned back, a sneer playing at being a smile flitted across thin tight lips, ready to fly at the first crack of his whiplash tongue.

"I suppose you know why I sent for you, Johnson." The repeating of the surname was another cruel trick which he always used on his trained seals.

"I've been watching you for the last few months. You've lost the old fire. You did better when you first got out of the service.

We were ready to make allowances then, but you should be completely re-adjusted by now, Johnson."

"I'm sorry, but I feel so confused. Everything seems to go wrong these days. I can't concentrate on one thing for more than a few minutes at a time."

As the other man's voice droned through the same harangue which he had heard so often in the past few weeks, Bert felt his mind drifting back over the year since his discharge.

It had been so simple then. Return to civilian life would answer all questions. What if he hadn't really enjoyed selling stationary before the war?

Amid the filth and death of Italy it had been easy – too easy to call the correct play for ‘civy street’.

He had sold himself a bill of goods on the old job, all right. When nothing beyond the present moment was certain, even the future security of a job waiting had been something to which his mind could cling ...

“Much against my will, Johnson, because I think you have the necessary push if you get a grip on yourself, I’m practically forced to suspend you for two weeks. That’s all.”

Bert stumbled over himself as he hurried out. That hadn’t been too bad, but money was going to be a problem. Or at least more of a problem. And, how could he tell Molly?

Now she would insist on holding her job a bit longer. This would have to happen just when he had almost switched her around to seeing his side of the wife working question.

Might as well drop into Andy’s Garage for the rest of the afternoon. It would be better than sitting around home. Andy could always use an extra pair of hands.

Even if there wasn’t much doing, he could putter away on that engine idea. “Sure, Bert,” Andy had said. “Drop in whenever you feel like it. The things you can do to a motor are uncanny.”

“It’s just luck, Andy,” Bert protested. “I got so accustomed to patching engines with bits and pieces in Italy that now when I have the proper parts it makes every job a cinch.”

“Maybe, but I like your work, and you can use anything in

the shop at anytime. By the way, have you been working on that idea of yours lately?"

"No, but I'll have plenty of time for that, for the next two weeks at least."

He became so engrossed in a balky carburettor that he almost forgot to go home.. Andy finally reminded him.

"Better break it up, Bert. Your wife will wonder what happened. Here's something for your help this afternoon."

"But, I can't take money from you. I'm just an amateur having fun."

"That's a professional job from where I stand. Let's not start out like this. Either you let me pay you or it's no deal."

"O.K., if it will make you happy. Well, so long for now."

Molly reached the gate at the same time and they went in together. He waited until after the supper dishes had been put away.

"Molly, I have some bad news..."

"Don't tell me that old sourpuss had laid you off, hon."

"How did you know?"

"I could see it coming for weeks. But, don't let it worry you too much. You can do better than that silly stationery business. What about giving one of your engine ideas a try?"

"I did putter around at Andy's this afternoon, but there's no future in being an automobile mechanic."

"I wouldn't be too sure. Let's skip it for tonight. Aren't you the young man who promised to take me to the Roxy? I'll beat you getting ready."

Molly scrambled ahead of him to the bathroom but he managed to get his foot in the door.

"Take it easy, hon. Even basement suites aren't plentiful these days. Let's not tear this one apart."

"You aren't cheating fair. Still, I can spot you ten minutes easily and be waiting while you worry over the finish coat of your paint job."

At first Bert found it interesting to look after the suite while Molly worked. But, after the first week it palled. He began to hate himself.

What kind of a man was he to let his wife do all the work? The money angle bothered him most of all. Of course she always offered him her pay envelop but he felt that he had to consult her over the spending of every penny.

In desperation, he even applied for a civil service position. That was as far as it went. Of course there was the odd dollar to be picked up working around Andy's garage.

And, it was the work he enjoyed. Why couldn't he find something like that with a future attached?

Andy had gone over the sketches of Bert's new engine design with him. He tried to persuade Bert to submit the idea to one of the larger automobile manufacturers.

"I'm telling you, Bert, that's the cleverest design I've ever seen. Why not send it to Acme Motors or one of the other big companies?"

It's not that good. Why, I haven't ironed out all the bugs yet."
"Mind if I borrow this sketch? Perhaps I can make some suggestions once I've had time to study it in detail."

"Go ahead. You can keep that copy if you like. I have another one at home."

"I'll have to buzz bow, Andy. Turner is expecting me today."

"Good luck, Bert. Be seeing you."

Peggy met him with her usual cheery smile.

"Hello, Bert. You certainly picked the wrong day. Mr. Turner is positively ugly today."

"Thanks for the warning. No use putting off the evil hour. Is he busy?"

"No, go right in. I think he's expecting you."

"Well, Johnson?" His tone was one which he reserved for lectures during his most vicious moods. Bert squared his shoulders and braced himself for the blast.

“Have you anything fresh to add to our talk of two weeks ago? I hope your are prepared to settle down and take your job a little more seriously.”

“I have always tried to do my job well.” That wasn’t such a good start but Bert found that he no longer cared. The old man could be more civil.

He had no right to be nasty merely because something else had upset him.

“I don’t like your attitude, Johnson.”

“Look here, Mr. Turner.” Bert took his courage in both hands. “I’ve always done my best for the company. Perhaps I’m not the best salesperson you have, but I do work to the best of my ability.”

“Now, see here young man,” Turner bloomed purple and threatened to spatter the office with shocked mauve spots. “I consider your manner exceedingly rude and entirely uncalled for. You are hardly in a position to shout at me. I have a good mind to ...”

“I am not shouting. You think you can frighten everyone. You and your silly over-bearing manner. If you were going to extend my suspension, forget it. I don’t intend to work for you for one second longer.”

Bert sizzled for several blocks before the red haze began to clear. He stopped short and laughed. A woman passing at the moment glanced nervously over her shoulder and hurrie on and out of sight around the corner.

“I don’t think anyone could ever talk to old Turner that way, least of all me. That certainly did settle things, but permanently. Now I’ll have to find something else, and quick.

Andy immediately sensed that Bert was annoyed.

“What’s the matter. Didn’t you and Turner get together?”

“We got together, all right. Another five seconds and I’m sure I’d have taken him apart.

He made me so hot that I boiled over and out of my job.”
“That’s bad. But, you know I’ll be glad to have you around here. Of course it’ll just be spare time work at first.”

“Thanks Andy, but I’ve got my eye on something bigger.”

“O.K. Bert, but if you can’t find the right job for a while you can always fill in here.”

Molly was already at home when he arrived.

“What’s wrong, hon? Didn’t you do so good today?”

“Bad is the word for today’s news, but tragic – almost.”

“Why, what happened? Don’t tell me you punched old Turner in the nose.”

“Not quite, but I did walk out. He dusted the welcome off his mat for keeps as far as I’m concerned.”

“What say w have supper first and discuss it later.” She

could see the warning lights in his eyes. "There's no use getting upset all over again."

Later that evening as their favourite radio show came to an end, Molly turned to him.

"I hardly know how to tell you this, hon..."

"Oh, come now, dear. Don't tell me you lost your job, too."

"Nothing as simple as that. I saw Dr. Armstrong this afternoon. He..."

"You mean..."

"Yes, I'm going to have a baby."

"That does it."

"Oh, Bert."

"I'm sorry, sweet. Everything seems cockeyed these days. Of course I'm happy to know about the baby, but it certainly complicates matters."

"I'm sure everything will come right, eventually, dear. I'm sure you'll soon find yourself."

"I'd just as soon find a steady income."

"How about that engine plan you had?"

"I'm not so sure."

“Why not submit it. At least you would know one way or the other then.”

“All right, but please stop talking about it.”

“I was just trying to be helpful.”

“I’m tired of being pitied and having you treat me like a child. I feel like a little boy asking for a copper.”

“But hon., you know that any money we have is for both of us to use whenever we wish.”

“Please forgive me, dear. I hardly know what I’m saying tonight. What say we call it a day and try again tomorrow.”

“Yes, I know you’ll see things differently by daylight.”

“I’ll give it a try.”

Shortly after Molly left for work the next morning, the telephone tinkled.

“Hello, Bert.” It was Andy. “The mail just arrived...”

“Fine. So you call me up to tell me that the mail has arrived.”

“Hold it. Wait until you hear the rest.”

“I can hardly wait.”

“Remember that engine design of yours?”

"Don't tell me that someone offered you a million for it."

"No, not quite. If you'll just be quiet a moment I'll let you know what happened."

"Well, shoot. You mustn't keep me from my housework, you know."

"I sent a sketch of your engine to Acme Motors and there's an answer from them."

"Well, what do they say?"

"They can't use your design. However, they are interested in your work. I gave them your address and they say they'll get in touch with you direct."

"Oh. Thanks for calling, Andy. Pretty phrases won't pay the rent. If they really like my ideas, though, perhaps there is hope."

"I'm sure you've got the stuff, Bert. Your chance will come. Here's luck."

Bert took out his sketch and pored over it for the rest of the morning. Perhaps a slight modification might turn the trick.

He heard a step on the stairs. Who could that be? Molly had taken her lunch. He looked up to see that it was her after all.

"What's the trouble, Molly? Aren't you well?"

“I did a silly thing this morning. I almost fainted. It’s the first time that ever happened. Mr. Rogers insisted that I take the rest of the day off.”

“I should think so. It isn’t right for you to be working at all, especially now.”

“I’ll be all right after a few hours rest, hon.”

“Say.” Andy waved the papers he had been studying. “I nearly got some good news today.”

“Oh,? What was that?”

“Andy sent a copy of my design to Acme Motors. They couldn’t use it but they were interested.”

“I’m glad to hear that, hon. I know you’ll make good, and soon too.”

“Sooner would suit me better.”

Somebody else was coming down the stairs. Bert went along the hall and met a middle-aged man who carried a brief-case under one arm. He greeted Bert with a friendly smile.

“Are you Mr. Johnson?”

“Why, yes. I’m afraid I don’t know you.”

“My name is Peters, from Acme Motors. I came to talk to you in connection with that engine design of yours.”

"But, I thought you had rejected it."

"That's true, but we think you have possibilities. Acme Motors can use men with ideas. How would you like to work in our research laboratories?"

"Would I? Molly, come pinch me quick."

CRIME STORIES

CRIME

[This is an essay, not a work of fiction. But it introduces Archie's late 1930s' view of crime, helping to explain the content of his fiction crime writing.]

Many people would forget that "Crime does not pay." if they were not being continually reminded.

The newspapers do a great work by printing news of crime.

Suppression of crime news would remove our daily reminder of the unprofitableness of crime.

The result is fairly obvious. There would be a definite increase in crime if such a foolish move took place.

Who is silly enough to even contemplate suppressing crime news? Crime is a worldwide problem and the people pay the bill.

Are they not entitled to learn the details so that they might help to find a solution?

While we have the vial question of crime presented to us day by day through the newspapers we will continue to seek to eliminate crime.

When we are tempted ourselves, news of crime will show us the folly of crime.

Before suppressing crime news, let us consider the matter carefully.

EASY COME

A distant clock struck twice. The figure in the shadows straightened and softly opened the door. Once inside he slipped quietly into one of the rooms.

A beam of light flitted around, revealing the many rows of books. It stopped as a large picture on the opposite wall came into view.

The intruder carefully crossed the room, his feet making no noise on the thick pile carpet.

He tugged gently. The picture swung forward, disclosing a neat little wall safe. Swiftly, his nimble fingers began caressing the dial. Minutes passed.

With a grunt of satisfaction he opened the safe. Reaching inside, he drew out a flat, black case. He extracted the diamond necklace. Its glittering brilliance dazzled him.

"What beauties!" he gasped.

"Very pretty, isn't it?"

He snapped off the light and darted towards the door. Too late! The darkness was thrust abruptly aside.

They blinked at each other in silence. The younger man slowly raised his hands as his stout captor made a threatening gesture with a wicked-looking automatic.

"I'll have that necklace if you don't mind. Put it on the table. Move slowly and you better not do anything rash.

This gun has no safety catch.

“There, that’s right. Now you may keep your hands down but don’t try to make a break. I might not like it.”

“So you thought you could get away with it?” He passed a hand over his shiny bald head as he surveyed the downcast young fellow, noting the shabby clothes and cracked shoes.

“I was a fool, I know, but I had to get money somehow. This way looked easy. I didn’t expect to find you or anyone else here.”

“How did you know where the safe was and the combination?”

“Why .. I am a safe expert. I helped put this one in when I was learning the trade.

“The company I worked for folded up during the depression. I haven’t worked for over four years.”

The fat man gazed thoughtfully at the other man.

“Listen, Buddy,” he spoke slowly as if still considering the matter as he talked. “I’m going to give you a break. Perhaps you don’t deserve it.

“I’ll have to take that chance. I’ll accept your story at its face value. No one else is here tonight. Lucky for you that I, rather than some other person, caught you.”

“I... I,” began the young man.

"Forget it," growled his benefactor.

"Here," putting a hand beneath his dressing gown, "take this." He pressed a bill into the other's hand.

The fat man waited until he was certain he was alone.

Satisfied, he scooped up the necklace, removed the dressing gown and stood fully dressed.

"I can make better use of these than he can," he muttered.

Pausing just long enough to retrieve his hat from behind a bookcase, he switched off the light and silently left the house.

"Beefy" Maxwell mounted the creaking stairs of the gloomy rooming house and eased his ponderous bulk through the first door as he reached the second story.

The shrivelled up, sharp featured occupant of the room, interrupted in his game of solitaire, looked up through a dense cloud of smoke.

He laid down the cards, his cruel, beady eyes darting in all directions yet keeping the newcomer always under observation.

"Hiyah, Beefy," he greeted. "Any luck?"

"You know me, Weazel. It was too simple. I let him do the work, then I stepped in to collect the sparklers. He certainly did fall for my line.

"He thought I was old man Mortimer. He had a hard-luck story to tell me so I pretended I was a kind-hearted old gent and told the poor sap to scram.

He patted the bundle he carried under his arm.

"This dressing gown came in handy. That was the easiest job I ever did."

"The Weazel" squirmed impatiently.

"Let me take a squint at them," he urged.

"Beefy" passed over the jewels. His friend examined the diamond necklace carefully.

"Why... why..., you've been gypped," he managed to splutter. These are worthless!"

"The dirty low-down snake must have switched them," shrieked "Beefy", his face taking on a vivid purple hue as he strove to express his feelings.

"What a sucker I was. I let that baby-faced punk fool me."

Tom Preston grinned triumphantly. His companion set the empty glass back on the table. The tiny room was crowded although it contained only the one small table and two old chairs.

"Well, Joe, I certainly showed that fat guy a trick or two tonight. He'll be hot under the collar when he discovers that I slipped him a handful of glass.

“I’m glad I took that necklace along to put in the place of the real one.

“That dressing gown didn’t fool me for one minute. He was glad to get rid of me with such little trouble. I know he didn’t believe the yarn I spun.”

Joe Herman shrugged. He fingered a crackling bill.

“He pawned off this bum ten bucks on you, didn’t he? He’s not too dumb.”

“Yeah, but you couldn’t expect him to hand out a good one.”

Tom held up the necklace for inspection.

“Not bad, eh?”

Joe did not reply immediately. For some minutes the necklace was given a careful scrutiny.

His small, piggy eyes suddenly popped angrily open and threatened to jump from their sockets. A snort of disgust exploded from between his thick, coarse lips.

“These are no good. A window pane would make better diamonds.”

Tom stared stupidly at the necklace. Who was a fool now? Savage rage enveloped him. The necklace went hurtling to the floor.

George Mortimer sat up, yawning and stretching. Nine o'clock. His wife appeared at the cabin door.

"Good morning, George," she greeted. "You seem to have recovered from last night's performance."

"The sea's calm this morning. There's scarcely a ripple. The yacht is certainly riding very smoothly."

"Good morning," he replied, flattening down his few remaining hairs. "You would insist on my playing the part of the villain. I am glad that the weather is god, though."

"I've been worrying about my necklace," she confided.

"But you are doing so needlessly, Jean," he assured her.

"I meant to tell you before that I put it in the bank the day we left. The necklace in the safe at home is that duplicate I had made."

PLANNED JUSTICE

Night again. Tony Locenti peered cautiously out on the night life of the city. Fresh air was what he needed. He too his coat off the bed.

Slender fingers ran through his shiny black hair as he turned to the other occupant of the room.

"Guess I'll take a stroll. You stick around and don't get any more of those funny ideas about turning me over to the flat feet.

I might get really rough next time."

"Let's forget that," Mae Flagg placed a hand gingerly on the angry red welt marring her pretty yet crime-hardened face.

"I must have lost my head. This

he broke off and stared hard at his coat. "What's the idea? Are these green buttons your happy thought?"

"They look pretty good to me and they do go well with your coat." She lit a fresh cigarette and sauntered back to her easy chair.

"Be careful. Some smart copper might spot you." Her words seemed to challenge rather than caution.

"Not a chance," he sneered, buttoning his coat. "I'll avoid the bright lights. I'd have to walk into the police station before they'd even notice me. Lock the door after me."

He slipped out into the hall and down the back stairs.

Tony crept stealthily through the back gate into the deserted alley. It felt good to be outside. The last time was just before things began to happen.

That was nearly a month ago. In a few more weeks he could take the fifty grand and blow. He laughed softly to himself.

Mae thought she was going to be cut in on the dough. What a sap she was.

Acting on an impulse, Tony turned down a dimly lit thoroughfare and strode briskly along.

The boys would be surprised if not pleased to see him.

Of course the cops would not think of looking for him at Joe's. He glided silently down a flight of stairs and paused before a massive steel door.

Response to his know was immediate. Two eyes flickered in recognition from a narrow slit. The door shut quickly on his heels as he entered.

"Hi, Pete," Tony smirked. "Surprised? Thought I'd drop in on your boys."

"Aren't you taking a chance with the boys in blue still interested in you?" [Pete replied.]

"They're too dumb to think of looking for me in the city. I bet they think I skipped out of the state."

Tony did not remove his coat but moved in the direction of a door marked “Private”. “The boss around?”

“Yeh, he’s in but feeling rather grouchy tonight.” [Pete cautioned.]

“I’ll see if I can cheer him up a little.” Locenti did not bother to knock. Joe Primer’s pig-like eyes blinked up through the smoky haze.

“Hello Tony,” he grunted, shifting his ponderous bulk which ever threatened to flatten the sturdy armchair he overflowed.

He chewed vigorously at a stubby cigar. “What’s on your mind?”

“Nothing. Just dropped in to say hello. How’s tricks?”

“Could be better. Say, it would be embarrassing if the cops paid a social call while you were here. Sorry you have to run off so soon.”

“I’ll go.” Tony’s black eyes flashed dangerously. “A nice way to treat a friend. Why not tell them I’ve been here? They might cut you in on the reward.”

“That’s not a bad idea.” Joe dismissed Tony with a disdainful wave of the hand. “Don’t trip on the stairs as you go out. Good night.”

Tony sailed out under full steam. He walked a block before he cooled off sufficiently to think even half coherently.

The rat! Imagine that good for nothing scum treating him like that. Why he had more brains than Primer's whole mob combined.

Someday he would fix that guy for good. His sharp features fairly glowed with hate. They couldn't treat him like that and get away with it.

A car cruised slowly by. Nearby a street light flashed momentarily on brass buttons and uniforms.

Somebody must have tipped off the cops. Had Primer squealed? No time to puzzle over that. He had to ditch those coppers.

Ducking into a lane, he sprinted through the darkness. He emerged on a side street. A theatre sign a short distance away attracted his attention.

No police car in sight. He shoved a bill at the girl. "One, sister." He hurried inside.

AN usher appeared out of the gloom. Why did the kid stare at him like that?

That wasn't possible. Neither the police nor the newspapers had his picture.

Tony waited a few minutes after the usher withdrew then he moved across to the other side of the theatre.

On the screen guns blazed as gangsters fought it out with the law. Dumb guys who didn't use their heads enough.

It would take a smart bunch of bulls to pick up Tony Locenti. Only mugs got caught. That reminded him of the usher's curious gaze.

An exit shone redly near at hand.

As he started towards the door an usher approached, the same one who had shown him to his seat.

"Excuse me, sir. Are you the gentleman I ushered in a short while ago?"

"What if I am." Tony's fingers tightened on his gun.

"Well, you forgot your change."

Tony stuffed the money into his overcoat pocket. He waited until the boy had gone.

Outside the theatre he breathed easier for a moment. Then he stopped. How had the kid known him again in the dark?

And that had been after he had changed his position, too. That was queer.

He had better not go direct to the hideout. If he walked around for awhile first he might be able to tell whether or not he was being tailed.

Satisfied, after an hour of twisting and turning down many sideways and alleys, Tony headed back.

This meant that he could not attempt to leave town for at least another month. Well, he could wait.

That was the trouble with most men in his position. They did not have enough patience. He was clever, though.

No use sticking his head out. He was safe enough. Another month and they would practically forget him.

Mae would get a kick out of the story he had to tell.

Also, during time he had to lie low he would be able to plan how to square things with Joe.

Tony neared the gate at the rear of the block, feeling his way in the darkness.

"Put up your hands, Locenti," a voice grated from behind that wall of unrelieved blackness. "Don't try to move. I've got you covered."

Tony leapt sideways and groped for his gun. The stillness retreated before the din as two guns spat fire.

Tony Locenti crumbled and fell forward.

The other man bent down to turn over the fallen figure. Three luminous spots glowed up at him.

"That girl was clever. He never suspected that his coat buttons were covered with phosphorous paint."

ON THE SPOT

The phone rang sharply.

Joe removed the cigar from his mouth and lifted the receiver.

“Hello.” he drawled.

“Hello Joe.” The soft, silky voice lingered lovingly over the words. “Don’t you remember me?”

“No! Why should I?” Joe snapped, “I’ve no time for guessing at names with every fool that happens to ring up. Who are you and what do you want?”

“Now, now, little boy, don’t get angry. You don’t seem to recognize my voice so I’ll refresh your memory. I’m the little playmate you had shipped down the river. Yes, I’m Jimmy the Dope.

Joe stiffened and almost dropped the receiver in his surprise.

The voice continued, “There’s nothing to be frightened about. I couldn’t hurt you over the telephone even if I wanted to.”

“No, I haven’t broken out of the big-house,” he went on. “I was such a good little boy that the warden let me out early and gave me a big shiny nickel.”

“See here,” broke in Joe. “What do you want? Money?”

The man at the other end of the line dropped his light, bantering manner.

“You know I don’t want your dirty money,” he grated.

“All I’m going to do is pay you a visit. Maybe it isn’t your birthday but I’m bringing you a beautiful little present. No, don’t guess. I’ll tell you. A wonderful little sub-machine gun.”

“By the way,” he added, “You better make out your will. Accidents are so likely to happen now-a-days. One can never tell.”

“Well, I’ll be seeing you.”

For a full minute Joe sat starring dazedly at the telephone, too stunned to move. Finally he roused himself and replaced the receiver.

Jimmy the Dope was out.

Five years ago Jimmy the Dope had become troublesome. Consequently, Joe had him framed and put out of the way. Now he was free.

Joe, a coward at heart, was badly frightened. [He panicked and ducked out the back alley.] So far he had not been observed.

He quickly reached the street and hailed a passing taxi. Changing from this one to another he used every trick he knew to throw off any possible shadowers.

Half an hour later he was satisfied.

He dismissed the taxi and entered a small restaurant which he occasionally patronized. Soon he was enjoying a perfectly cooked meal. Joe certainly knew his restaurants.

The meal finished, he pushed back his chair and lit a cigar. A full stomach made a much braver man of him.

He left the restaurant in a happy, almost jaunty mood.

"I guess I'll take in a show," he decided. "I'm in no danger yet. "

He strolled leisurely down the street to a small theatre. A surprise awaited him inside. The picture was on which tended to destroy his peace of mind.

It was a gangster picture. One gangster was being trailed by a man he had framed.

When it reached the point where pursuer and pursued met face to face he could stand it no longer. He left hurriedly.

As he walked on his way he kept looking furtively around half expecting to see his enemy appear out of thin air. Before he had gone a block he was a bundle of nerves.

"I shouldn't have gone to that show," he muttered. "Maybe I'm [nuts]." Joe cursed his foolishness and continued on his way.

The place where he was going to hide was not far away. In a short while he would be safe.

Rat-tat-tat.

This time there could be no mistake. Jimmy the Dope was out to get him. He must reach some safe spot at once.

He started running, looking back over his shoulder at the time time.

A slight bump on the side walk made him stumble, stagger, and fall. His head struck the side of a hydrant with a sickening thud.

With a convulsive shudder he collapsed into a crumpled, unnatural heap.

People began to gather around; gazing horror-stricken at the limp figure.

High above their heads a pneumatic-riveter clattered monotonously on.

THE LIGHT CHANGES

[Diary entries indicates this writing is completed on March 18, 1940.]

Jim Lertz squinted behind thick lenses.

“So, Mack,” His voice slid over the words. “You boys are in trouble, need help.”

“Yeah,” Mack Stevenson admitted. “This stuff is hot. My men are watched. The cops know I’m shoving dope from my warehouse.

They’re waiting to jump me if I try to move this last shipment. You could do the job. It’ll be easy for you.”

Lertz carefully removed his spectacles.

With a large silk handkerchief he polished each glass thoroughly, ignoring his slim, dark visitor. No change touched his face.

“Maybe – I haven’t forgotten the time you, ah, tried to get me out of a jam.”

Stevenson flushed darkly.

“Can’t we forget that. It wasn’t really my fault. Besides, you’ll be well paid.”

“How much do I get?”

“Ten ‘G’s’. I won’t make anything myself but I have to unload quickly.”

“Yeah, I know. You’ll lose money.. perhaps. How soon do you want me to pick up the stuff?”

“Six tonight. The streets will be crowded then, which will give us a better chance. Two of my boys will make a dash first to draw off any watchers

“All you have to do is drive down behind my place. I’ll help you put the stuff in your car.”

“Wait a minute. How are you going to be sure everything will work out all right? I can’t afford a slip-up.”

“Simple enough, Jim. Here’s the plan of action, giving the exact time for each move.” He shoved a typewritten sheet across the desk.

“Just memorize this, and don’t forget to burn that paper. Here, set your watch with mine. See you later, Jim.”

Lertz slowly read the printed information after the other man had left. His pudgy finger speared one of a row of buttons.

A shrivelled individual popped up from nowhere in particular.

“Snipe, find out if Mack Stevenson’s warehouse is being watched. Tell the others to come here. I don’t like the look of this.

“If Mack dropped a dime into a blindman’s cup there’d be a string attached.”

Lights were shining through a film of dusk at Jim Lertz' car approached the docks. He drove directly to Mack's. Two men lounged along the pavement nearby.

From the alley came the throbbing hum of a starting engine.

A sleek black sedan leaped from the gloom, swept past him.

Almost simultaneously, another car appeared, picked up the two watchers and was gone.

Scarcely glancing in the direction taken by the two cars, Lertz steered down the murky alley.

Stevenson stood in the shadows near the loading platform. His shoulders hunched, both hands were thrust in his coat pockets.

A brown, paper-covered, oblong package lay at his feet. Lertz cautiously slipped from his seat to join the other man.

"O.K. Mack, let's get this loaded."

He bent down, left hand outstretched to reach the parcel. Stevenson took a step forward.

Sensing the danger, Lertz twisted sideways as an orange streak spurted past his shoulder.

He leaped back, automatic growling its muffled rebuttal. Stevenson bowed a silent acknowledgement and slumped beside the package.

"You rat." Lertz bent over the crumpled figure. He straightened, fingering a sheaf of bills. "Now we're both paid in full."

Quickly he heaved the package on to the back seat. This would simplify delivery to his own gang.

Unhurried, he cruised around until the hands of his watch shone at seven. Time to move. They'd be waiting.

He turned up Second Avenue and soon reached the heart of the city.

A green light beckoned as he neared the corner. At the middle of the intersection he became aware of the other car. It hurtled towards him.

"Fool," he screamed, clutching frantically at the wheel. The oncoming vehicle struck squarely, bringing blank nothingness.

A uniformed figure pushed through the crowd.

"Stand back, this is no peep show. Move along." He peered where a man knelt beside the body. "Is he badly hurt?"

"Dead, broken neck. Probably never knew what hit him."

"He cut through the red light. My car sideswiped him. He didn't have a chance."

The police [officer] turned to the crowd, shoving the people before him. "There's nothing more to see. Quit blocking traffic."

Stragglers scattered as a squad car slammed to a halt beside the battered remains of Lertz's car.

The patrol [officer] explained. "Fellow tried to beat the light. Killed outright."

"Why," the newcomer gasped, "that's Lertz, big-time gambler."

The plain-clothes [officer] glimpsed the tattered parcel on the ground. "What's this?" Then, ripping the paper from one corner, "Whew! So that's where it went."

He examined the dead man's gun. "He probably used this on Stevenson."

Pocketing the weapon, he helped the patrol [officer] place the battered bundle of dope into the car. "Keep the people moving, Day. I'll make a separate report."

The two detectives discussed the case as they drove back to the station. "What puzzles me, Bob, is why Lertz was so careless. You know his reputation for cautiousness.

"Why, we never could put the finger on him for so much as parking too long. Funny that he should miss a traffic light."

"Perhaps he lost his head, Sam. It has happened to other mighty cool men."

"But Bob, you know that Jim Lertz never had anything

resembling nerves. Anyway, you could hardly find a more careful driver.

"No, that accident doesn't ring true. I'd stake my reputation on it that he didn't know he was crashing the red light."

Patrol [officer] Day left the call box after making his report. A new cafe sign took on a new significance as he neared the corner again.

A man in the doorway nodded guardedly as Day stopped.

"This is your place, isn't it, Stevenson?"

"What if it is?"

"That sign will have to be moved. It's too low and too near the road."

"All right, but I don't see what difference it makes. A man can't even hang a sign where he wants to these days."

Day warned, as he turned to go. "You can't have it on until it's moved."

"Okay, I was getting ready for a funeral anyway." He stamped inside to turn off the light.

The police [officer] gazed thoughtfully at the offending sign. A green blob winked beneath the words:

"GREEN DOT CAFE"

JUSTICE

They were about to capture Sam Pearson, Public Enemy Number One. The two detectives could make good use of the one thousand dollar reward.

The trail had let to an old warehouse on the waterfront. Bob Rexton paused, his hand on the door.

"You take the side door. I'll go in here. Be careful, he's a deadly shot."

"I'll take no chances," Jack Miller answered him. "But we might have to shoot it out with him."

Cautiously, Bob pushed open the door. Nothing happened. H surveyed the dim interior. A door standing slightly ajar caught his eye. On tip-toe he advanced.

With a quick motion he kicked it open.

Face to face with Pearson.

A shot shattered the silence. Jack Miller ran swiftly across the warehouse.

Bob Rexton stood motionless above the dead gangster.

"Are you all right, Bob?" Jack anxiously inquired.

"I...I," began Bob.

"Where did he get you."

Bob's reply was a hoarse whisper.

"I killed my own son."

MISTER IN STREET

[It's not clear whether this is the beginning of a story that has long since disappeared or whether this is a complete story.]

He carefully checked each pocket with a definite finality... even to the lining of his coat. Nothing there.

And yet the parcel couldn't disappear without him knowing.

"What could have happened to it? I'm sure it was in the breast pocket of my jacket."

"Looking for something, mister?"

"Why, I..." John sensed the other's interest was more than casual. "Guess I was thinking out loud."

"That's a bad habit, buddy, especially these days when everybody is so jumpy. You might say something that would be dangerous...especially here with so many odd characters drifting around."

"I don't see what business it is..."

"Now don't get nasty, mister. Perhaps I'm a little brownie sent by your fairy godmother to help poor little you."

Too late, John realized the other man's intent. The street was deserted... no chance of any help... nor was there a handy doorway.

He stood poised on the curb and then noticed a car had slid

up beside them. With a shrug he turned and said, “Your trick.”

“Now you’re being sensible.”

Two men hustled from the waiting car... quickly forced him into the back seat and they were on their way. No one spoke as they sped out of the city.

FRUIT SALAD

Of course the solution must be oranges and grapefruit. And why not?

Ada Small began a quick and systematic re-arrangement of the window display in Dad Forrester's Store.

The man browsing through the array of magazines glanced across the store but continued his reading. Let him look. She had nothing to lose.

Her thoughts continued to short-circuit on the same line as deft fingers worked on the fruit design.

Why did Dad have to be so stubborn? He could have avoided trouble.

At least he couldn't be feeling overjoyed about everything now, watching one of the gang work on the wall safe in the back room.

Apparently they hadn't been able to pry the secret of the combination from him. But, even that was hardly a good argument for being so stubborn.

Dad's stand had never varied when she begged him not to keep such a large sum in the store vault.

"No banker is going to use my money. This safe will never let me down and it won't do any swindling either." he had said.

This evening certainly gave her the right to employ a

vigorous “I told you so.” At the moment she would gladly trade that small satisfaction for a big police [officer].

Was it really tonight that Bob, the veteran cop on the beat had returned her wave as he started on his rounds?

Events had crowded after each other so rapidly that she still half-hoped the nightmare might end with the ringing of her alarm.

Everything, from where the crooks sat, moved as smoothly as a well-plotted movie thriller.

Four men drifted silently through the doorway. Three of them whisked Dad Forrester away to the back room. The fourth lingered.

“Take it easy, sister. As long as you don’t get excited, nothing will happen.”

He hadn’t bothered her further, but she felt his veiled scrutiny wherever she moved.

A melodramatic touch was added each time a customer entered. Thrusting one hand deep into his coat pocket, he would gaze at her with an inquiring lift of eyebrow.

A chance customer had started the idea simmering. While making a purchase, she exclaimed, “My these oranges are lovely. They are nearly as large as the grapefruit.”

There, the window was almost ready. The hands on the wall clock indicated fifteen minutes before midnight. Just in time.

Bob would be passing the store within the next few minutes. She put the last orange in place and stepped back to survey the fruit combination.

For an instant, she forgot about her captor.

As she studied the effect, the man put down his magazine and moved towards her.

She forced herself to appear casual as she turned to walk deliberately across to the cash register.

He followed her to the other side of the store. She waited but he glared in silence before revealing his thoughts.

“Take a friendly tip from a guy with an itchy finger. I know the flatfoot is due to stroll back this way about this time. Lift a finger and you’ll be waving at angels.”

Bob slowed his pace and grinned broadly as he gave Ada a friendly one finger salute.

She lifted one corner of her mouth but the intended smile congealed into an uncertain grimace.

Desperately, she tried to hold his eyes as if the plea for help might be sent to him by telepathic suggestion.

He glanced down at the window display. The next instant he had gone. Ada’s guard returned to his reading.

Did Bob understand? Surely he would return. But there had been no flicker of understanding. Slowly she began to tidy the store and prepare for closing.

The man made no attempt to collect the evening's take. After all, why should he bother with such small pickings. Ada began to sweep the floor.

Poor Dad would never fully recover from this disaster.

And to think that only a few weeks had separated him from his dream of many years – a little place in the country.

Now it seemed that the old struggle must begin all over again. What chance was there for retirement with his life savings gone?

Her misery deepened as one of the men hurried from the rear of the building. He muttered a few words to her guard and the two of them turned as if to rejoin the others.

She had failed. Dad wouldn't blame her but she had let him down. They had opened the safe, of that there could be no doubt.

Soon they would be leaving with the money. Why hadn't she taken a chance and tried to warn Bob?

Remembering his charge, her guard turned back with a final warning.

"Just a reminder, sister. Don't try to be too clever when..."

There was a confused scuffling and the sound of raised voices from the rear. As they fumbled for their automatics, the front door was thrust open.

The store seemed filled with blue uniforms.

Ada finally managed to pick out Bob from the crowd. He grinned down at her as she gaped and tried to say something but couldn't even voice a hello.

Did you really thing I had deserted you, lass?"

"I thought that you had missed my message in the oranges and grapefruit." She pointed to the letters H E L P formed by the fruit arrangement.

He frowned and shook his head, blankly uncomprehending the lettered design.

"What has the fruit to do with it? I became suspicious when you didn't return my wave. It was the first time that had ever happened.

I knew something was wrong. Besides," He bent down to whisper his confidence, "I never could tell the difference in colour between oranges and grapefruit.

SCIENCE FICTION STORIES

TRANSPARENT MIRRORS

[The date is not shown, but this manuscript is typed on the back of a dated letter, indicating Archie is about 26. It's a form letter from Archie's pre-war employer, a glass company called Pilkington Brothers (Canada) Ltd. (Toronto) Archie has the shaving-mirror described at the outset of this story, even now. Perhaps he bought it from "Pilks".]

The idea first struck him when he bought the shaving-mirror.

One side was ordinary flat glass but the reverse was concave, giving an enlarged view of any part of the face he cared to examine.

That in itself was not fatal but it did start the thoughts whirling.

His brother Joe kidded him about it, "What's the trouble, Ben? Surely you don't think you're beautiful."

"I've been thinking. This mirror has possibilities." Ben replied thoughtfully.

"Not for you, with your face." Joe shot back.

"Wise guy. Did you ever read "Alice Through The Looking Glass." Ben went on.

In a more serious tone Joe replies, "Years ago. Say, are you feeling all right?"

"Of course, silly boy. What I'm trying to get at is that there is more to this than shows on the surface." Ben continues in his thoughtful demeanour.

"Hurry and get it over with." Joe stifled a yawn. Squeeze yourself through the mirror and I'll keep watch to see that no one breaks it and spoils the fun."

"I might prove that you are the silly one if you stick around. Did you ever read the story of the [person] who discovered the secret of a giant observatory reflector?" Ben lectured.

"Listen, I'm beyond the fairy story age, and you are a big boy now too. Better stay out of the sun." Joe shakes his head and wanders away, leaving Ben pondering.

Thus the matter stood for several weeks.

Ben had almost forgotten it altogether. Almost, that is, until he happened to glance into a display window at Manson's Departmental Store.

The words did not register immediately. Ben turned back and looked again. Why hadn't he thought of it before? The sign read, "Transparent Mirrors"

A sales-clerk explained to the impatient Ben, "The glass has an extremely thin film of silvering on one side, which allow part of the light to pass through.

"By regulating the light from one side you have clear vision one way and a mirror the other.

"You must only remember to have the bright light shining on the side which you wish to appear as a mirror."

"I understand. Le me have that smallest one." Ben replied.

"If it's for your front door, don't forget that you must always have the stronger light outside to get the desired effect." the clerk added.

"Yes, yes, I know. Please, I'm in a hurry." Ben snapped. He snatched the mirror from the clerk and hurried outside. Now, if it would only work, he thought.

Ben half ran the last few meters home. The afternoon dragged. After making a pretense of eating, he quickly excused himself and made his way to his room.

Carefully closing the door, he proceeded to set the shaving glass at the head of the bed, held in place by a pillow. Now for the transparent mirror.

Propping it up with several books, Ben set it at an angle so that the light from his reading lamp would reflect off the shaving mirror so as to strike the transparent mirror at right angles.

He then took up a position directly behind the transparent mirror and gazed fixedly. He saw nothing but a cloudy image of his own face.

He tried brighter lights but still there was a fuzzy dimness about the reflection. Perhaps it was sunlight that was needed.

He carefully put the mirrors aside. Maybe it would be sunny tomorrow.

The weather sulked until the weekend. Sunday turned out perfect and Ben was soon up and making final preparations.

He would have to wait until the afternoon for the sun to shine directly through the window,

He sat in front of the mirror reading as he waited. A beam glanced from the shaving mirror. He peered intently. Nothing happened.

Ben changes the angle slightly. The brilliance of the reflection dazzled him.

As he strove to get a clear view, a dizziness swept over him as alternating light and dark patches flashed before him.

The sun must have moved along. But, something was wrong. Everything seemed oddly twisted. What in the world could it be?

Vainly he tried to concentrate before utter blackness took over.

As memory drifted slowly back, the pieces began to fit slowly into place. It was night now. Who was that on his bed?

Why no, it couldn't be... and yet... Ben could see himself, (or was it?) lying in bed asleep. This was the craziest nightmare yet.

But, he knew he wasn't dreaming.

There was no way of telling how long he waited before daring to look back.

A grey nothingness stretched its infinite ripples of blank

space into the void.

He tried to move forward but was brought up short by a hard glassy substance. Glass. A scream rose to his lips but no sound cam forth.

Trapped in the mirror. What a fool he had been.

Dawn finally crept grudgingly under the grey curtain of night. The mirror background took on a rosy hue which gradually faded into blue.

Ben discovere he could move unrestricted. The movement seemed effortless as his body appeared to flow in all directions. What a marvellous sensation.

Perhaps this wasn't going to be so bad. There came a sudden crushing sensation as if somebody or thing had squeezed him into a small cylinder.

That was his own face staring intently at him. The image pressed closer. His own reflection leered evilly.

"You don't like it, eh?" Now he was sure he must be crazy. A talking mirror. Only he was inside looking out.

"Need proof? Try this for size."

The face went through a series of grimaces. Each change was like a slap on the face as his muscles twisted and contorted as if pulled by invisible hot wires.

"Do you get the idea?" You've pushed me around enough. Now it's my turn. You were silly enough to get too curious.

You'll pay for it." Ben's mirror image gloated.

Ben's mouth moved but no sound came forth.

The sun crept slowly higher. Then the light was eclipsed by a black night that crushed him into nothingness. What now?

This must be more new devilry. The mirror must have been covered or turned over. He hung in vacantness and waited.

From time to time the other self brought back the light to continue more torture by face twisting and changing mixed with taunts and jeers.

[No further pages of this writing appear to exist. But there is no indication that this is the final page. There is no # symbol indicating The End. But this story appears to be complete in the same sense as other writings of this genre.]

NO BLOTTER

[There is no date on this story.]

"Mr. Scripp will see you now, Mr. Wells." The pert little stenographer opens the door marked "Private" and ushers the apologetically meek visitor into the office of the general manager, Super Links Limited.

Wells coughs gently as he stands just inside the door, waiting for the other man to notice him.

The executive finally deigns to look at his inoffensive appearing visitor. Behind their horn-rimmed defense, Wells' eyes peek timidly at Scripp.

"Have a seat, Mr. Bells." Scripp waves a hand. "I understand you have a new process which you think will interest my company. My time is valuable so be brief."

"My name is Wells." With this gentle correction, he reaches into his coat pocket and carefully withdraws a small bottle of ink.

"There's enough ink in this container to supply your needs in blue-black for a year."

"Please, Mr. Wells, I told you I'm too busy to listen to anything but business."

"But this is business. The fluid in this bottle is actually countless tiny organisms which feed on any dead organic matter."

Scripp slides softly from his chair. "Excuse me, Mr. Wells," he soothes. "I suddenly remembered that I have forgotten to tell my stenographer about an appointment."

He's back almost immediately. His face shines with nervous good humour. Seating himself carefully on one edge of his chair he purrs.

"Your idea seems to be extraordinarily good. Why, we will be able to revolutionize the ink industry."

"Of course, Mr. Scripp, I would not want my discovery to be used to the detriment of other companies."

"Certainly not. But tell me more about this ink." Scripp looks longingly at the door.

Wells unstoppers the small bottle. Its contents bubble darkly.

"It has to be handled carefully in this state. I'll demonstrate how quickly it can multiply."

"Perhaps you would prefer to make the test in one of the laboratories where my chemists can watch the results." Scripp fidgets nervously.

"This is just a simple test. Afterwards, if you are still interested, your own people can check with their own experiments."

The scientist turns in his chair as the door is unceremoniously banged open. Two police officers crowd into view.

Eyeing Scripps visitor, they step to his side.

“That’s the man!” Scripp stands up and well back. “He came in here with a crazy story. You had better lock him up where he can’t bother people.”

“Certainly, Mr. Scripp. We’ll take good care of him.”

“Gentlemen,” Wells protests. “Please give me a chance to prove my point. He reaches for the bottle of ink.

“Oh no you don’t.” A police officer grabs his shoulder as Wells’ fingers touch the bottle. It slides from his grasp and sends a thin trickle of the inky fluid across Scripp’s large, glass-topped desk.

Scripp snatches up a sheaf of paper just in time.

“I must remove that.” Wells struggles unsuccessfully to free himself as the two police officers drag him from the room.

As they practically carry him through the outer office and outside to a waiting squad car, Wells cries out, “Please let me warn him before it gets out of control.”

“Sit down! We’re going to take you to a nice clean jail.” the police officer says as he pushes Wells into the car.

Scripp lays a blotter on top of the ink on his desk cover. He watches as the fluid soaks right through to darken the white oblong paper.

As he draws another blotter from a drawer he watches the first one becoming a sodden mass.

"That's peculiar. There didn't seem to be that much ink there."

Then the first blotter disappears completely. One moment it's there and the next there is only a larger pool of ink.

Three more blotters rapidly vanish into the dark liquid. One edge of the pool laps at a dictionary on one corner of the desk.

Scripp reaches across to save it. But before he can touch it, the book slides into inky dampness. He staggers to his feet. The desk top is almost completely black with ink.

Frantically, he buzzes fro his stenographer.

"Ms. Cooper, get someone to clean up this mess." She rushes into the office, only to halt motionless and stare at the sea of ink.

"Well, don't just stand there. Hurry! Stop it before it runs onto the carpet!" Scripp cries out in panic.

A few moments later, the building janitor is sticking his head around the edge of the office door. Seeing the pool of darkness he advances with a handful of rags.

Carefully, he begins to mop up the ink. A clean strip of desk appears. Then he notices the rags in his hands are changing from cotton to inky fluid.

It ripples toward the edge of Scripp's desk. With a sudden surge the black pool descends upon the floor. As it cascades, both the janitor and Scripp withdraw from its path.

Instead of merely a few drops of ink falling to the floor, the entire blot moves across the desk and rolls to the carpet.

Taking a jelly-fish form, the mass heads for the door. Behind it, a strip of floor shows barely where the ink creature passes.

“It’s alive!.” the janitor points a shaking hand at the sloppy shape as it rolls out of sight.

[No further pages of this writing appear to exist. But there is no indication that this is the final page. There is no # symbol indicating The End. But this story appears to be complete in the same sense as other writings of this genre.]

COLD & HOT

[This is only the beginning of a story, leaving the reader wondering where it's going to go next. It's like a movie trailer without the film.]

Bob Price didn't see anything for a moment as he stepped into his basha from the glare of the midday tropical sun.

The heap in the corner of the hut stirred and there came a whisper of a moan. He was at the young Indian man's side in a moment. It was Kanti.

"What happened?" Bob demanded.

Kanti turned a swollen face towards Bob's face but no sound came.

Kanti struggled to speak but the words were swallowed in an agonized spasm as his fixtures contorted and then relaxed into an ominous smoothness.

Bob gathered up the meagre bundle that was Kanti and ran across the compound to the doctor's quarters.

Dr. Thomson straightened and turned to Bob. "He's dead enough, but frankly I'm puzzled."

It wasn't such a surprise, Bob felt that it was bound to happen sooner or later. He said, half wondering half musing, "Then he wasn't beaten to death?"

"Hardly," Thomson replied as he waved a hand at the body. "He was badly bruised, but nothing serious."

"Any ideas, Doc?" Bob queried.

"This may sound fantastic, but he shows all the symptoms of having frozen to death." Thomson stated this in a matter-of-fact tone.

"Take it easy. This heat is bad, I know, but get a grip on yourself." Bob consoled.

"I tell you, I'd stake my professional reputation on it. But it doesn't make sense." The doctor wiped the beads of sweat from his brow.

"Let's sit down and talk this over, Sam."

SATAN'S CHICK

[The date on the original manuscript is April 2, 1947.]

The hard boiled egg ticked again. Steve let it slide from the spoon back into the saucepan. Then it happened.

A crimson beak forced the shell outward and the egg exploded to reveal a blood-red chick.

He started back as it hopped up over the pen's edge to settle comfortably in the middle of the open gas flame.

This certainly called for some deep thought, and fresh air.

Steve Jenks clutched at his hat and stumbled towards the door, not daring the briefest backward glance. Things like this just couldn't happen.

But, he had seen it with his own eyes. Perhaps he had been living alone too long.

He wandered aimlessly through the park, pondering on the appearance of the peculiar old woman who had persuaded him to buy the eggs.

What if the other five turned out the same?

She had been so old and wizened – almost as if ...

A cloud of steam blossomed upward. As the saucepan clattered to the floor, the chicken shot out and sprang into the open oven.

For a moment he did little more than stare foolishly from his scorched glove to the empty pan. Then, he noticed the chick calmly preening itself, at the same time making a noise like a miniature fire siren.

No use getting excited. At least the bird was friendly. It hopped up on his foot and pecked inquisitively at his pant cuff.

Steve noticed an acrid scent of burning cloth. He hurriedly tipped the chick back to the floor.

A slightly scorched streak appeared on his pant leg and another on the linoleum where the chick had rolled before regaining its feet.

"Whew! You're too hot to handle. Let's see what can be done to keep the place from burning to the ground."

Scooping up the chick on an egg turner, Steve deposited it in the fireplace below the gas radiant. It hopped up to the burner and thrust its beak deep into the flame.

"The phoenix certainly had nothing on this bird." Steve muttered.

"I guess I'll just have to let it be until I can figure out some angle. Lucky it isn't dangerous, much, that is."

Days began to drift by as Steve kept puzzling over his peculiar problem. The fiery hen was no trouble so long as the gas was turned up.

But, whenever he turned the jet too low for the fowl's

comfort it would ruffle up its feathers and turn on its siren chirp which would swell louder and louder until Steve had to increase the heat or have the whole neighbourhood pounding at his door.

At first he didn't connect the stories of blazing meteors with his fire-bird.

Then came the series of mysterious fires. One morning Steve noticed a scorched patch on the open sill of his window.

Picking up the morning paper, he carefully read the latest accounts of meteors and fires.

Link Meteors With Mysterious Fires

> The latest theory which has been advanced regarding the current epidemic of fires is that these are being caused by the large meteors seen in recent nights.
>
> Apparently each fire has occurred immediately following the appearance of one of the meteors.
>
> One scientist has been quoted as saying that the so-called meteors are really missiles from another planet...

Steve thrust the paper aside and began to pace the floor. Perhaps if he turned the gas out that would settle his flame-eater.

It was worth a try. Th chicken pecked at his hand as he reached towards the radiant.

Although he pulled back quickly, there was an angry red

mark across his hand where the hen's beak had grazed it.

He shook his fist at the feathery fire-ball but it merely glowed more redly than ever and gave forth with a muted siren shriek.

That, obviously, wasn't the answer. But what did one do with a red hot hen? If he went for assistance they'd laugh at him and probably lock him up as insane.

No, this needed a different approach.

Closing the window might help. He slept peacefully that night but the papers brought yet another account of fire and meteor.

Maybe that scientist was right after all and his freak guest was blameless.

Steve had almost begun to believe that his chicken was not guilty. The true explanation came one restless night.

That night he had found sleep extremely difficult. After tossing and turning between nightmares in which flaming giant chickens pursued him, Steve switched on the light and reached for his slippers.

For a moment he blinked around the room. Gradually his eyes began to focus properly. The chicken was not in the room.

Why hadn't he thought of the chimney?

This was his chance to turn off the gas before the bird

returned. There, perhaps that would make a difference.

Now to wait for the return of the fire foul. Steve settled in an easy chair and waited.

Light was beginning to riddle the night when Steve heard a fluttering in the chimney. He shook off his drowsiness and leaned forward.

The flaming bird dropped down to the radiant. Did he imagine it or was it a duller red than usual? It seemed more like a glowing coal than a flaming torch.

Finding the flame extinguished, the bird began to rustle features with the noise of crackling wood.

Steve remembered the fire extinguisher which had just been placed in the hall. A chemical might fix the chicken.

He twisted the door handle and sprinted to the head of the stairs. In a moment he was back in front of the open door of his room. A wall of flame barred his path.

Emptying the extinguisher into the inferno, he tossed the useless container aside and raced to warn the other occupants.

As the crowd watched the fire, a man beside Steve pointed at the peak of the flames.

“Look, what’s that?”

A shaft of fire broke loose and hurtled skyward. It was son swallowed by the blackness. Steve stumbled away from the burning building.

It was several days before he found another room. He purposely chose a section of town as remote as possible from that disastrous spot.

Anyway, he had got rid of the fire bird.

Extra work kept him later than usual that day. Groping uncertainly in the dark, he finally found the light switch inside the door of his room. Then he noticed.

“I must be tired. I’m just imagining the darn hen is back.”

But he knew there was no mistake. Carefully he closed the door and hurried outside.

Several drinks later, sufficient of his courage had returned to allow him to go back to face the fiery menace.

“Huh,” he told himself. “Why should I let a hot fowl keep me out of my room?”

Still, he cautiously opened the door and peered through the gloom for a moment before daring to enter. He switched on the light. The bird was gone. Would it be back?

Slowly he began to pack. What was the use of fighting this thing?

It must have supernatural powers or it could never have traced him to this place. Perhaps if he left town it would let him go.

Dawn was just lifting night's lid when Steve slipped into the street. Was it his imagination or did something flash across the sky?

It was so fleeting he couldn't be sure.

Later, at the station, he noticed a red glow in the sky. That bird had been busy again. Maybe it was too busy to notice that he had left town.

At least there was a hope that he had seen the last of that strange bird.

The train trip was uneventful except for the roof fire. It started from live cinders out of the engine stack, so the conductor told him.

Steve wondered. Surely there was some solution.

It was dusk when Steve swung down at the small seaport town. The more water the better. Even that fire bug would find the Atlantic too wet, he hoped.

He found a room overlooking the waterfront and carefully closed the window. Fortunately, there was no fireplace to worry over.

Steve tossed his coat over a chair and lay down on the bed.

It was hard to tell how long he had slept but he was wide awake in an instant. At first he didn't know what had disturbed him.

As he lay quietly in the darkened room he became aware

that something was watching him. Rolling on to one elbow, he looked towards the window.

He sprang from the bed and pulled the blind before he turned on the light.

It was a matter of time, now. Framed in the window he had seen the fiery bird, larger and brighter than ever.

Perhaps he should make a dash for the water. No, it would overtake him before he had gone more than a few [metres]. Better to sit and wait.

Three cigarettes later it started. It began in hail storm cadence. The darn thing couldn't be so clever after all.

Instead of breaking the window, it was trying to peck a hole in the roof. It was some comfort to know that the thing was not too intelligent.

The pecking rose to a thunderous clatter and Steve could imagine the whole town being aroused.

A splintering crack and he knew the bird had broken through. Inaction should soon be at an end.

Seconds quickly matured into minutes and there was no further sound.

He started to relax slightly when he realized what was happening. A rustling crackle brought sudden confirmation of his fears.

The wily fowl was going to burn him out again, maybe.

Steve reached for his coat and hurried outside. He had barely reached the street when events slipped into high gear.

A ball of fire shot from the roof and descended upon him with siren opened full.

He twisted sideways to escape the searing fame, and felt the hot breeze of the avenging bird beat upon his body.

While the hen waved uncertainly in the gutter, throwing up clouds of steam from where a puddle had been, he sprinted for a nearby house.

He tugged at the door handle. Nothing happened. The fire bird, after a warning shriek of its siren, began a flapping run towards him.

Steve turned from the door and fled blindly down the street. He had to find shelter, but quick.

The increasing heat told him that his pursuer was rapidly overtaking him.

Ah, there was a door that might be the right one. He twisted the door knob. The door held fast. No time to try anywhere else.

Steve put his shoulder to the door. He could sense rather than see the flame red chicken speeding closer.

Was his mind playing tricks or had the thing really grown to the size of an ostrich?

A red-hot beak poked savagely at him. Steve summoned a final desperate strength and felt the door give.

He tumbled into the darkness and as he fell there was a fleeting glimpse of a crimson beak transfixed to the door.

Someone brushed against him in the corridor as he scrambled up.

He didn't wait to investigate but fled away from the winged monstrosity, searching for a way out and escape from the livid horror.

A patch of light loomed up. He turned to one side and felt a door knob. The key was in the lock. In an instant he was outside with the smell of the sea strong in his nostrils.

His second step met empty air. There was nothing to fill his clutching hands.

The next moment he struck the yielding ocean and went down deep in the cool welcome water. No fire could follow him here.

Steve struggled with his shoes and then he remembered the pen knife he always carried. The going was easier with his shoes gone.

He shrugged off his coat and undid his belt. Now a chill began to set in.

He floated for awhile. A strong current seemed to be carrying him out to sea. Looking back at the town, he could see half the village waving angry flame banners.

There's no way of telling how long he had been in the water but his legs were becoming numb. His swimming became little more than an ineffectual dog paddle.

Burning would have been quicker. Out of the frying pan all right, but it was a wet grave.

This must be it. Now he was imagining he could see lights. Not steady lights, but flickering beams that bobbed up and down.

Surely he was getting delirious. Soon he must slip down into those cold depths. It wasn't such a bad death.

Those lights were real. Steve fought against the lethargy that clutched him tighter and ever tighter.

Oblivion began to thrust its wall before his eyes.

But here was something solid. He reached out towards the bulk and felt slippery wood. From a long way off he heard a voice which seemed to come out of the sky.

"Ahoy, there."

Steve felt himself moving up and up to meet an enveloping brilliance. A fiery bird expanded to fill the entire world and seemed to sear Steve's very soul.

He screamed and pounded his fists against the flaming horror. It dissolved into a soft glow of setting sun.

Someone was bending over him.

“Had quite a turn, didn’t you?”

The pungent odour of tar was not unpleasant. Steve tried to sit up but settled down again just in time to keep his head from bursting into countless fragments.

Memory abruptly thrust the confusion aside.

“The fire bird? Where is it?”

“Take it easy. You soaked up more than your share of water last night.”

The speaker steadied down from a billowy ghost to a sweater clad sailor. Through the open porthole Steve caught a glimpse of sky and water.

Surely the bird was left behind for good this time.

He gulped the hot soup offered and fell back into a dreamless sleep.

The sun was shining again when he opened his eyes. The sailor had gone.

Steve didn’t risk telling the captain any part of the fantastic adventure. Better let things take a natural course.

They assumed he had fallen from a small craft and took his word when he assured them he wouldn’t be missed.

Short-handed as they were, the captain didn’t begrudge the food and quarters in exchange for the dubious help of a land-lubber.

As the days drifted by, Steve became more and more contented with his odd job position. The crew were kind enough, too.

Late one afternoon, the cook pointed to the horizon. Steve followed the direction of the pointing finger but could detect nothing more than the sky and water of former days.

"Land in sight." His companion enlightened him. "We should dock sometime tomorrow."

"It'll be a relief to have things steady underfoot again." Steve turned to go below. "This up and down existence never gives my stomach a chance to settle properly."

He crawled into his bunk earlier than usual this night, eager to bring the next day sooner. A few days more should be interesting.

If that bird was waiting.... All that was in the past.

It must have been hours later but Steve felt that his head had barely touched the pillow. Something must have disturbed him but he wasn't sure.

He was about to turn back to sleep again when he noticed the glow. There were no lights on in the cabin but a bright beam shone through the porthole.

Hurriedly, apprehension mounting, he dressed. Up on deck he found most of the crew had already assembled.

They were all watching a brilliant object which grew nearer and larger as they stared. No, it couldn't be.

“A shooting star.” One of the sailors offered his opinion when he noticed Steve had come on deck.

“It’s headed straight for us.” Another argued.

“Break out the lifeboats.” The captain was taking no chances.

As the siren sound came to his ears, Steve knew that this must be the finale. He scrambled after the others who were already seated in the lifeboats, waiting for further orders.

The night had taken on a reddish brilliance, brighter than any day. The air become intolerably warm and sticky.

The boats were in the water now and the men were rowing away from the doomed ship. The flaming sphere seemed to cover the whole sky.

Steve screamed and flung himself to the bottom of the lifeboat. The heat grew to a suffocating intensity.

The others dropped their oars and cowered beneath the vengeful fire as it made a final spurt and blotted out their world.

Steve felt his eardrums pound in frenzy as the sound of a million sirens threatened to tear the nerves from his flesh.

Water bubbled and boiled, sending the small craft bobbing and plunging.

A hissing, shrieking took the place of the siren and Steve was swallowed in a blood-red welter of unconsciousness.

His mind pried feebly at the curtain. One corner lifted and he sensed rather than saw his rescuer.

“This one seems to be alive.” The man bent over Steve and the words came clearer. “He’s the only one the meteor spared.”

Steve grinned and fell back into a dark world of forgetfulness.

CONQUEST OF SIZE

[Reading like fantastic science fiction today, this tale of imagined times past recounts the experiences of inventive scientists who make an alarming accidental discovery.

While attempting to create a new technology, something they call a "television machine", they find out that their world is in peril.

Will anyone believe them before it is too late?

Can anyone do anything to stop the impending disaster before it overwhelms them and all that they know?

Unfortunately, several pages of this story have gone missing over the years since Archie penned them.

Fortunately, this gap can be filled with part of a summary of the entire story which Archie writes and which does survive..

For this purpose, a fictional editorial note quotes directly from Archie's summary and explains that the more detailed account of the story is destroyed during the chaotic events described.

Like many historical records and relics of the story's fictional time context, the detailed account is lost in all the confusion.

Fictional historians living in 2014, many years following the fictional story, can only speculate about the details of missing records of events lost in the fictional times.]

"We must unite before we can hope to succeed. Calling all..." The voice died away.

Paul turned to the older man, switching off the radio as he did so. "What do you make of it? That is the only thing I can get since I put in those new tubes I was telling you about."

Tom Jackson ran his fingers through his grey-flecked hair. “It is a puzzle, Paul. We’ve checked all possible sources with no luck.”

“There must be some answer.” Paul Roberts stretched his full [183 cm] of smoothly muscled body and yawned sleepily as he peered out of the laboratory window.

“Perhaps..., but no, the idea is too fantastic.”

“Do you mean you think that this set is picking up broadcasts from another planet?”

“Well,” Paul admitted, “I can’s see where else those speeches could come from. The talk about White Marchers and the Red Warriors doesn’t seem to belong to this world.”

“You may have stumbled on something of that sort. I know the whole thing sounds rather impossible but after all, think of the early explorers.”

“The new and strange people and lands they encountered were possibly more bewildering to them than this mystery confronting us.”

“I suppose you’re right, even though it does not explain the fact that the voices are English with no trace of accent.”

Paul glanced at his watch. “Say, it’s getting late. Half-past twelve. I still have some work to do on the new television machine.”

“You better get some sleep first,” Tom advised. “That research will keep until tomorrow.”

Together they crossed the darkened grounds where the gloom was alleviated slightly by a gigantic neon sign which flashed six stories above their heads to tell the world about Acme Super Radios.

They passed in silence through the gate of a small picket fence surrounding a cosy bungalow that snuggled in one corner of the factory yard.

"Evidently Billie didn't bother waiting up tonight." Tom switched on the hall light.

"I don't blame her." Paul was already in their bedroom and half-undressed. Soon Tom had joined him and they both concentrated on sleep.

Grotesque monsters pursued Paul as he tried to arrive at some solution to the puzzle. A huge bat-like mass descended and grasped him by the shoulders.

He fought to shake it off.

"Wake up, you can't sleep all day." Billie laughed down at him, her brown eyes twinkling mischievously.

"Good morning Billie," Paul yawned. "You just arrived in time. A nightmare had almost caught up with me."

Seated at the breakfast table, Paul dreamily studied the edge of his plate. What did his discoveries mean? The idea of invasion from another world was fantastic and yet...

"Still asleep, Paul?"

“I’m sorry, Billie, I was thinking about the experiment.”

“You and dad have practically lived at the plant for weeks. I think I’ll drop in on your two tonight and listen to your voices from nowhere.”

Tom Jackson playfully tousled his daughter’s glossy black locks.

“You’re not exactly a stranger at the company hangar. I wouldn’t be surprised if you sprouted wings one of these days.”

The two men left Billie cleaning up the breakfast dishes as they went to work in the Acme Research Laboratories.

Paul could scarcely contain himself as he waited for the day to end.

Immediately after supper he was back at the laboratory where he was soon joined by Tom. They set to work on the strange machine. More messages.

Nothing definite this time. Merely garbled bits of speech.

“Soon we shall begin the conquest of size,” a voice cut through the jumble. “The first test will be carried out in a short while.”

“Here I am.” Billie burst into the room. “Are you two listening to anything? I can’t hear a thing.” She started to cross the room but paused halfway.

“Why.. that’s queer. I couldn’t hear a word until I got here, then it suddenly began."

Paul sprang to his feet and strode to the far side of the room. "That's right. No sound reaches me here." He walked back towards the set.

"Right here the voice becomes quite loud as if someone had just turned on the set."

The result was the same regardless of the direction from which they approached the radio.

At a distance of [4.5 metres] the set could not be heard.

"I think I can explain this apparent mystery," Tom Jackson smiled. "Both of you close your eyes and listen. Notice anything strange?"

"There's something odd about the sound," Paul puzzled. "It seems to come from somewhere close to my ears. I can almost imagine the sound is inside my head."

"I have the seem feeling." Billie's brow wrinkled in perplexity. It is as if someone were sitting inside me talking."

"Exactly. That is because you are not hearing anything. What we took for sound is actually thought-waves." Tom snapped off the power.

"This machine is interpreting what appears to be telepathic messages from some intelligent being. There too is the reason the broadcast seemed to be in English."

“Phew!” Paul anxiously faced Tom. “Then it must be from another planet.”

“That seems to be the most plausible explanation.” Tom shook his head bewilderdly.

“But who will believe us?” Billie worried. “Everyone will think we are crazy.”

“We will have to keep in touch with them,” Tom asserted. “If we can collect enough information perhaps we will be able to get someone to listen.

“But even then the invaders might have weapons against which we would be powerless.”

“I don’t suppose there is any real danger tonight,” Billie interposed. “You two come along with me. It’s terribly late.”

The next day and for many days after both Paul and Tom gave all their spare time to the mysterious radio signals.

They could make no progress beyond establishing the fact that the invaders were faced with an obstacle which was preventing the invasion.

References were continually being made to the difficulty of size. Clearly, they were too small to successfully carry out their conquest.

However, reports of experiments kept coming through to the two men. Evidently the unknown enemy was nearing a solution to that problem.

Occasionally confident mention was made of the closeness of the time when humanity would be exterminated forever.

Paul sat silently before the machine. Messages of what seemed to be routine business were being broadcast.

"The consolidation of the main groups has now been accomplished.

"Experiments are progressing satisfactorily and preparations are going forward for another AGENT NUMBER FOURTEEN REPORTING."

The thunderous interruption brought Paul to his feet. He cut down the volume with a twist of the wrist.

"I am in enemy territory. My present position is the great research laboratory approximately twenty marches from headquarters.

"I will make out my detailed report when I return."

Tom appeared in the doorway.

"What was that, Paul? I could hear the noise in the next room."

Paul bent over the sill of the open window. A small object occupied his attention. He turned towards the older man.

"Ants! It can't be." He gazed bewilderdly at the radio and then back to the window sill.

"You mean that's where the messages are coming from?"

Paul scooped up the insect in a convenient tumbler. He twisted the volume control and waited.

“I have fallen into enemy hands. They have trapped me. I will report developments from time to time.”

Tom brushed the moisture from his forehead.

“But think what this means. Consider how many ants there are. If they all join together and discover how to make themselves larger...”

Paul shut off the set. The two men stared thoughtfully at each other. Finally Paul spoke.

“We have to get proof. That’s the only way we can get people to believe us. What should we do first?”

“You collect a few ants, Paul. I’ll see if I can get some of the scientists to come here and help us. Luckily, the national meeting is being held here.”

“All right, I’ll have everything ready in a couple of hours.”

The sun had sunk low in the west before Tom returned. Six men accompanied him. Paul recognized several as the most prominent scientists of the continent.

Prieston, a small dark individual with a sinister squint, acted as spokes[person].

“What is this astonishing thing you two have discovered? We are busy people. You are fortunate to have this much of our time. Our fellow scientists are even now waiting for our return.

Tom quickly explained their experiment and their deductions. The other men appeared sceptical when Paul brought out several bottles containing different species of ants.

The two men showed the scientists all that they had discovered. Their scepticism lessened. Only Prieston remained unconvinced.

“How do we know this is not a hoax; a publicity stunt your company is staging? We’ll have to have more proof than this.”
“This is no time to quibble,” protested Tom. “We want your help. If something is not done immediately it will be too late.

“Please believe us. These ants are almost ready to act. Now we can probably prevent them. Once they have made themselves larger we will be helpless.

Billie charged into the room, dressed in flying togs, a newspaper under one arm

“Are you two coming for supper? You’ll have...”

She became aware that other people were in the room and became suddenly confused, a pretty flush spreading over her face.

“Gentlemen, you will have to excuse my daughter. Sh is so impetuous.” Tom took the paper from her, glancing casually at the headlines.

“Won’t you please give me a chance to prove the assertions I have made? I know...” His mouth fell open.

He rubbed his eyes and read the lines again. Wordless, he handed the paper to Prieston.

The latter scanned it for a few moments.

“Incredible!”

The others crowded around. Paul took the paper and read aloud.

Ant Monster Attacks Lonely Farm House.

> Samuel Morris, farmer of the Upper Heights district stumbled into the city this afternoon with a fantastic story of how what he declared was an ant as large as a dog attacked his farmhouse, killing his livestock, breaking the horses necks as if they had been made of straw.
>
> Local authorities are investigating this ant story but they point out that Morris may have been mistaken as the monster raided the farm early in the morning when the light was poor.

“Mr. Jackson,” Prieston stretched out his hand. “I am sorry I misjudged you. You can count on my help from now on.”

“Thank you,” Jackson gazed questioningly at the others. “We must seek a means of destroying them before they begin to march. This laboratory is at your disposal.”

Prieston paused on the way to the door.

“We will have to organize the entire world if we hope to

succeed. Petty differences will have to be forgotten or everyone will perish. I'll do my utmost."

The other scientists added their assurance of aid and the plant owners agreed to give Tom and Paul all the assistance possible.

Soon the group of scientists had established the approximate location of the main ant headquarters but it was too well-trodden to unearth immediately.

Day and night they worked, too, seeking a weapon for destroying the ant monsters which already were carrying out raids in isolated points.

The public, as usual, took the mater as a hoax or publicity stunt. Whoever heard of ants as large as St. Bernard dogs?

Radio comedians poured out a stream of jibes and bombarded the public with satirical skits.

The people laughed off every effort the scientists made to make them realize the seriousness of the situation.

One morning several weeks after they had enlisted the aid of the scientists, Paul and Billie were seated at the breakfast table.

Tom stamped into the room, waving the newspaper.

"Their still calling it a joke. It'll soon be too late to help anyone. Why can't they wake up and see how near we are to annihilation."

“There, there, dad,” Billie soothed. “You know how people suspect everything these days when radio advertising is so cleverly presented.

“They’ll believe us if we keep pounding.”

“Billie’s right, Tom.” Paul fiddled absently with the radio control knob. If we keep talking the public will finally be convinced.

“Perhaps we will find the place where the ants are carrying out their enlarging experiments.”

The music of a dance orchestra which was coming from the loudspeaker stopped...”We interrupt this broadcast to make a special announcement.

“Carvel, a village of approximately one hundred and fifty, located [32 kilometres] west of this city, has just been completely depopulated by horrible ant creatures as large as horses.

“A motorist has just arrived here with the news. He barely escaped destruction from these monster insects which he declared travelled at a speed of [40 km/hr].

“Further details are not yet available but the authorities are investigating immediately.

“Please stay tuned to this station for any new developments which may come to us from time to time.”

“We must act now!” Tom was through the front door almost before he had finished the words. Paul hurried behind and they entered the laboratory together.

"What do you intend to do, Tom?"

"Remember that electrical repelling force that we were working on last week? We must perfect it. That is our only hope of salvation.

"Any known weapons will be useless against these armoured insects.

"Think how strongly protected they are if they have gained proportionately with their increase in size."

Later the scientists joined Tom and Paul. Tom explained things briefly and they all fell silently to work. At noon Billie brought them food and also a tragic announcement.

"These ants are advancing rapidly. Our guns have very little effect on them. They city is being evacuated."

Tom turned to the assembled scientists.

"I think we can get immediate results from the force machine if we are able to secure enough power. The question is where?"

Paul thoughtfully stroked his chin. A grin of satisfaction spread slowly across his face.

"What about that new power project the government has just completed on Big River?"

There was a chorused assent. Nothing would serve their

purpose better. The site was situated high in the hills which would make is easier to protect.

"We have no time to approach the authorities. We'll have to reason with the people in charge of the plant." Jackson turned to his daughter.

"Can you get a plane, Billie?"

"I think so, father."

"Let's go then. You go with her, Paul. I'll stay and help assemble things." He faced the others. "We'll have to work fast.

"If we build a small machine it should protect us if the ants get here before we can move."

Paul dashed after Billie who was already seated in the roadster with the engine running. At the airdrome they found empty hangars gaping at them.

Billie looked hopelessly at Paul....

[EDITOR'S NOTE: Here the story is interrupted by a gap of nine missing pages. So here is what they could say:

In all the ensuing worldwide chaos it is not surprising that many written accounts of human life are destroyed, eliminating scientific historic records which we only recently begin to piece together by finding and interviewing a few of the now elderly survivors.

With the hindsight of today, it is obvious that the situation of those times past became worse and then dire. Awful events overtook the world.

When the written story continues in the final surviving pages, we find Paul and Billie at the Big River power plant.

Here is a summary of what happens after they find empty hangars at the aerodrome:

Paul and Billie finally manage to secure a plane and Billie pilots it to the plant. However, they find the ants have control of the plant and one has been left guarding it.

Paul and Billie manage to kill the insect by dropping a large boulder on it from a cliff.

Unable to operate the machinery at the plant, they are startled by the sudden appearance of Angus McPherson, who escaped when the ants took control.

With his help a wall of force is tested and found to be workable.

While Billie returns for the other scientists, Paul and McPherson build a wall to encircle the power plant.

The ants attack but the wall of force throws them back. The details for erecting electrical force walls is passed on to the rest of the world.

Lack of power causes many cities to fall before long.

After Billie returns with the scientists they hear shocking news.]

...a radio in the main hall of the plant drew their attention.

The announcer's voice, pitched high with excitement, poured out details of the march of the ants.

"The seemingly invincible monster ants continue to advance. Here in New York plans are going forward for defence.

"Hundreds of cities have already fallen. The great need is for more electrical power.

"Mr. Jackson's electric wall requires much more electricity than most cities can supply.

"Here is a flash from London ...The Prime Minister today stated that in most parts of that country people consider the ant scare is merely a giant hoax.

"However, other European envoys are speeding to the U.S. by plane. That is all the news we have at present. Keep tuned to this station for further developments."

"What fools they must be." Tom threw up his hands. "By the time they decide to move in Europe it will be too late.

"The defences in this country are weak. They might not be able to hold out very long."

At that moment, Prieston hurried up to them. He had been supervising the building of a larger converter set.

"We've sighted a small group of ants. Lucky that set is completed."

“Where’s McPherson? Paul wanted to know. “Tell him to switch on the power.”

The whole group, numbering about seventy-five, gathered outside to watch. The huge dynamos slowly gathered speed.

Finally the switch controlling the converter was thrown over. Across a jumble of rocks the nightmare troop of gigantic insects advanced.

Sighting the humans, they broke into a quick trot, their many legs carrying them smoothly and swiftly forward.

One of the insects plunged ahead of his fellows. His feelers suddenly bent in two, there was a crashing purple discharge and the shrivelled remains lay writhing and twitching among the rocks.

Its companions paused and cautiously approached the fallen ant. There was a hurried brushing of feelers in consultation.

Baffled by their repulsion, they finally withdrew carrying the dead ant with them.

The defenders of the plant burst into jubilant talk. Those monsters would not be able to reach them here. Tom Jackson waved them to silence.

“That was a minor victory. We can’t expect them to gather around so that we can electrocute them one by one.

“Everyone will have to set to work and see if we can find

some way of striking back. Otherwise, the human race is doomed.

"Our position will not always be secure. There are many problems which we shall encounter before long."

Silently the crowd dispersed and Tom took Billie and Paul by the arm as they went back into the main living quarters.

"We must find a solution," he declared. "And quickly, too, if we hope to save anything."

Paul said nothing. His mind was working furiously. Could they possibly turn the wall of force into a weapon? For the time being he decided to remain silent.

No use building up the others' hopes. After all, there would quite likely be no way of converting the force into an offensive weapon.

The wall was, he knew, only a lining up of the molecules so as to form an impenetrable wall of matter. There was actually no force exerted to be used as an agent of destruction.

Time dragged slowly. Reports filtered in, becoming fewer as one stronghold after another fell before the ferocious onslaught of the ants.

Paul spent many hours working on the electrical wall.

He succeeded in making the wall more resistant but made no headway at all in his search for a means of converting it into an offensive weapon.

The nations of Europe finally took warning and began to prepare for the time when the ants would attack them.

However, their efforts were not coordinated as each distrusted the other. Then the ants mastered the controls of ocean liners.

Great numbers crossed to Europe and began their march of destruction.

Some of the larger cities held out for a short time while but industrialized Europe soon began to starve from lack of supplies from other parts of the world.

Meanwhile, repeated attempts were made to overcome the little band of people with Tom Jackson.

One particular thrust was to be long remembered by everyone. The attack began one morning as dawn broke.

Wave after wave of the fearless insects hurled themselves at the invisible wall. At first they were tossed back in shattered heaps.

Gradually, the pile of dead ants grew. Higher and higher it reached as the monstrous creatures came on in an endless stream.

The crackle and roar of contact became louder until the defenders had to shout to be heard.

"Say, Tom," Paul screamed at the scientist standing beside him, "what are they trying to do? Surely this mass suicide will gain them nothing?"

“I’m not so sure of that, Paul.” Tom pointed at the mounting stack of electrocuted ants.

“If they can build high enough they’ll be able to form a bridge over our protecting wall. Something will have to be done.”

“Perhaps we could throw a wall of force over the top for a roof.” Paul eagerly suggested.

“At least we can try.” Tom conceded.

They set to work stringing wires to carry the current. Feverishly they fastened insulators and rigged temporary poles.

As they worked the ants kept advancing and building. Anxiously the [defenders] glanced at the ever-growing pile of insects.

Angus McPherson increased the output but this had no great effect although the greater power shrivelled the ants and slowed down the rapidly growing stack.

Tom wrapped a wire around a final insulator. The ants had nearly reached the top of the wall.

At last Tom Jackson was satisfied. He signalled to McPherson. The other man pushed a switch. At that moment the ants were at the top of the wall.

One sprung forward. Something seemed to catch it in mid-air, twist it grotesquely and hurl the shuddering remains back.

Realizing they had been outguessed, the insects retreated to consider.

Apparently they decided against further sacrifice for in a few minutes they had gone, taking their dead with them.

"Whew!" Paul mopped his brow. "That was close. We made in just in time."

"This means we will have to post guards," Tome declared.

"They might think up some new scheme. Say, Paul, what became of that receiver with which you first contacted the ants?"

"I put it somewhere," Paul explained. "Do you mean we shall be able to learn their plans through using it?"

"And why not?" Tom pointed out. "We will be able to read their minds and forestall any new schemes."

Billie came up to Paul and Tom. "It's lucky you have me around to look after your things. I brought your ant radio along after you had left it behind."

"Lead me to it, Billie," Paul caught her playfully by the shoulders. She led him into one of the buildings they had used as a laboratory in their search for a weapon to combat the gigantic ants.

"Here it is, tucked away in a corner." She dragged the set out. "I hope it wasn't damaged during its journey here."

"I'll hook it up and see." Paul found the cord and plugged

into a wall socket. They stood waiting for the machine to warm up.

"Final victory is near," the loudspeaker carried the thought waves. "Only a few isolated forces are holding out but these will soon be destroyed."

The broadcast cut off abruptly as if the report had been completed.

"We must have caught the tail-end of that," Bill said. "Think what that means!"

"Our future isn't exactly one to be envied," admitted Paul. "But we'll give a good account for ourselves before we're beaten."

He stared unseeingly at the thought-carrying radio. "And why can't I," he muttered. "It certainly won't hurt for me to try."

Billie gazed strangely at him. "What are you talking about? What are you going to try?"

"I have an idea that may work." Paul told her. "It might happen to be what I was looking for ever since I started. Sorry I can't tell you now, Billie.

"It wouldn't be fair to build up everyone's hopes only to disappoint them."

"Please tell me," she coaxed. "I might be able to help you."

"All I can tell you right now is that it has something to do with the tube that made this machine possible and the wall force apparatus."

Paul wanted to start immediately but Billie insisted he have a good night's sleep first.

"I can make you rest now," she told him, "but once you become interested in the plan I'll not be able to tear you away.

"Don't argue with me. After you've slept you can work but not until."

Reluctantly he allowed himself to be led back to the sleeping quarters.

The following days were busy ones for Paul. He lived in the little workshop scarcely stopping for food. Once he fell asleep in the midst of his work.

They put him to bed but after a few hours sleep he insisted on going back to work.

"You'll kill yourself." Tom argued. "At least you could let us help you."

Paul brushed the offer aside. "When I have everything lined up it will be time enough.

"You have a great deal to do yourself to keep everything in shape and prevent the ants from breaking through."

Tom turned away and left Paul alone. Although he would

not admit it, Paul was making little headway in his experiment.

He had built a small sending set using the new tube and the electrical force equipment.

In the front of the machine he had a funnel shaped device for the purpose of directing the force rays.

His success was limited. He had managed to concentrate enough power to bum paper and wood held directly in front of the device.

Surely there was some way of stepping up the power of his ray machine. He made changes and adjustments but with no better results.

Finally he was forced to approach the others for assistance. It seemed, however, that the difficulties could not be overcome.

"I think I know what your trouble is," Tom said one evening several weeks after they had decided to leave the experiment for the time being.

"I'm not sure, though, so let us three go down to the workshop and see if I'm right."

"What have you in mind?" Paul queried. "We tried almost everything we could think of but there were not worthwhile results."

"We'll try it first. You'll have to be patient until I make the test. If I'm wrong we can forget it."

"You're as bad as Paul, father," Billie protested. "Why can't you tell us first?"

"It'll be much better to show you," Tom Jackson countered. "Here we are. Surely you can wait a few minutes. The attempt will not take long."

The scientist led the way into the building and walked over to the ray machine. He knelt behind it for a few moments. At length he straightened up and stepped back.

"We're ready to try our luck," he declared. Stand behind the machine in case I have found the answer."

He plugged in and turned on the switch. Nothing happened. Attempting to appear casual he shrugged his shoulders and turned his back to the machine.

"My hunch must have been wrong." He put his hand on Paul's shoulder. "Oh well, we can try again. Possibly it is just.."

"Look!" Billie's hand shook as she pointed to the far side of the room.

They all gazed dumbfounded at a wall which wavered and silently settled in a heap of fine powder to the floor.

A gaping hole showed blankly where the plastered wall had been. Tom was the first to move. He snapped off the set.

"It must have taken time to warm up. I had forgotten about that." He told Paul and Billie.

"But what did you do?" Paul asked.

"I thought a great deal about your experiment before I realized what the trouble was.

"You see, the machine you built and the electrical force apparatus were radically different.

"The electrical force built up a field of molecules which remained more or less stationary to build an impenetrable barrier.

"On the other hand, your machine sped up the action of the molecules and caused them to flow outwards.

"This flow of controlled atoms bombarded any solid matter in its path and forced the atoms of the bombarded matter to fly apart to break down into a powder as that we see on the floor beside that hold in the wall."

"I understand it now," Paul cut in, "The natural result of combining the two was similar to the action which would take place if an irresistible force met an immovable body."

"Exactly," Tom Jackson agreed. "One negated the other."

"As you no doubt realize now, I merely disconnected the section containing the electrical force apparatus."

"Will it work the same way on the ants?" Billie asked.

"It should," Tome answered. "We can make a test and see."

Early the next morning they carried the machine outside

and set it up inside the wall of force. A curious member of an ant patrol strayed near.

Jackson signalled to McPherson. The wall barrier was shut off. The barrel of the ray machine was trained on the oncoming insect.

Then it happened. One moment the monster insect loomed ferociously. The next and there was nothing save a small heap of reddish powder.

The besieged party cheered and crowded around the three. Jackson held up his hands. "Our work has just begun," he declared. "We will have to carry the fight to these monstrous insects until no ant remains alive.

"After that we shall rebuild the world and civilization."

Paul slipped an arm around Billie as he murmured, "We will try to build better than those before have done."

THE STINKER

[Unfortunately, there is only one surviving page of this typed story.]

It didn't seem possible, that after nearly two decades, he was the only person on earth who could save humanity from such a peculiar fate.

And yet, all scientists had agreed, he was their only hope. Why, back in 1960, the idea would have been too fantastic to even consider.

Ben remembered that summer in 1960 when the first break-through came. At first it had seemed no more than an entertaining scientific stunt.

But then, as the possibilities of science's great discovery became more apparent, people had demanded that the United Nations make the greatest use of this new gift to benefit all humanity.

A few voices had been raised in cautious protest. They were laughed into silence.

The monster they had all helped to create, had appeared as a boon at first. Slowly, insidiously, it spread around the world, until all the countries had been engulfed.

Then there was that fateful day, October 2nd, 1967, when the final step was taken.

A system of worldwide dissemination brought that must be the ultimate answer, or least, so they thought. Slowly, realization of what had happened to sift through.

Of course, Ben Stoner didn't remember too much of the early days of the so-called refinement, and it wasn't until about a year later that it began to affect his life.

There was that first incident after he had finished a strenuous work-out at the gym. He thought the other people were staring at him in a rather odd manner.

As is the way with teenagers, he didn't give it another thought until the following week, in the gym locker room. He had a delayed double-take.

Of course, whey hadn't he realized before what made him different from the others...

PLAYS

PURELY PERSPECTIVE

[This play is typed with some lines of dialogue crossed out and others added on separate pages in handwriting in pencil.]

Characters:

Julia Bradley – a spoilt girl
Dennis Harlow – her fiancé
Sylvester – a tramp who has seen better days

Setting:

Park bench at rear of MacDonald Hotel overlooking the Saskatchewan River. As curtain rises, Sylvester is discovered sleeping on bench. Off stage we hear music and laughter from the hotel. Sylvester snores. Enter Julia in a temper, also an evening dress. She is tearing her handkerchief.

JULIA: (Flouncing in and looking off left) Oh, oh, oh, oh! (Stamps foot) India of all places. He can go to – India.

SYLVESTER: (waking up) India? What's that about India? (He yawns, stretches, and sits up)

JULIA: It's Dennis – He wants me to go to India, and I (gives a double-take) who turned up your volume?

SYLVESTER: (yawning) I assure you (yawning) I was under the impression that you had spoken to me about India. A most remarkable place, India.

JULIA: How do you know?

SYLVESTER: How do you suppose I know? Do I strike you as the type who spends his time poring over travel books. I have most definitely been around.

JULIA: All right, I can see that you have been (sniffs) around, but India – Dirt, disease, beggars, and child marriages.

SYLVESTER: (mimicking) Rajahs, riches, pachyderms, and dusky maidens.

JULIA: If everything is so wonderful in India, what are you doing here?

SYLVESTER: Ah my child, your youth speaks so naively. Let me put it this way, 'Breathes there a soul so dead, who never' --

JULIA: Oh, nuts. I learnt all that in school. There must be some bad things you could say about India.

SYLVESTER: But why should I find fault with that magic realm, that teeming massive land of mystery, charm, and grotesque contrasts.

JULIA: (impatiently) All right, let's not go over that again. You're a dreamer like all men, an impractical dreamer. You never plan ahead – (slight pause) I wonder if --

SYLVESTER: What's troubling you now?

JULIA: Nothing, I was thinking.

SYLVESTER: A most commendable pastime.

JULIA: (disregarding his remark) I was wondering if you – (She breaks off and goes over to the terrace entrance to see if Dennis is coming and then hurries back to Sylvester) What I had in mind was, that is, how would you like to earn a few dollars?

SYLVESTER: The only lucre I found to be filthy is that soiled by toil and perspiration.

JULIA: (digging into her purse) Your tongue is what I need.

SYLVESTER: I'm afraid that would be most inconvenient. It happens to be fastened tightly inside my mouth. In the middle with both ends loose.

JULIA: (impatiently)You know what I mean.

SYLVESTER: It becomes clearer by the second.

JULIA: If you don't hurry, Dennis will be here. He always chases after me when we quarrel.

SYLVESTER: I wonder why.

JULIA: That's not funny. Do you want to earn five dollars?

SYLVESTER: You must be plentiful endowed with worldly things. But, let's approach this matter cautiously. Exactly what is the service required inn exchange for such a trifling sum?

JULIA: It's easy. You don't even have to lie.

SYLVESTER: I am relieved to hear that. A person of my

integrity can't be too careful, you know.

JULIA: Cut the chatter & pay attention.

SYLVESTER: My mind stands open and ready for the gems of wisdom you appear ready to scatter.

JULIA: Here's my problem. Dennis wants me to go to India with him.

SYLVESTER: And Dennis is ---

JULIA: My fiancé.

SYLVESTER: Please accept my warmest congratulations.

JULIA: Shut up and listen!

SYLVESTER: But surely, in view of the acute shortage of men, you are most fortunate.

JULIA: (angrily) It isn't that way at all! Do you want that money or not. (looks anxiously at entrance)

SYLVESTER: It is practically spent. Very well. I am ready to assist as far as my capabilities permit.

JULIA: (sits on bench) Come here, Mr., that is --

SYLVESTER: Sylvester Handury-Thorton (bows) in full, but Sylvester is adequate. (He comes over to the bench and leans over the back towards her. She gives him the five dollar bill.)

JULIA: I want to hear some <u>bad</u> things about India.

SYLVESTER: Now that I reconsider, there are certain inconveniences in that far eastern country.

JULIA: Let's have facts.
SYLVESTER: There's always the heat. I remember Chitters ---

JULIA: Chitters?

SYLVESTER: Sorry. That is how we travellers usually refer to Chittagong. During the monsoons it's positively ghastly, not so much from heat as humidity.

When the thermostat hovers around 37.7°C, with the humidity registering 97%, --

JULIA: That's good. Anything else?

SYLVESTER: Insects abound.

JULIA: Now we're getting somewhere. I hate spiders.

SYLVESTER: One has to be careful to shake the sheets at night to ensure that no centipede lurks in the folds.

JULIA: Anything else?

SYLVESTER: The bazaars often reek with filth and stench to turn the strongest stomach. Of course you understand that I am deliberately selecting the least desirable facets.

JULIA: It would take many good features to offset the

horrible things you've mentioned.

SYLVESTER: I assure you that it is not wise to discount the good --

JULIA: Are you going to help me or not?

SYLVESTER: I assure you that you shall have cause to be ever grateful for my assistance this evening.

JULIA: I'd better get my five dollars worth.

SYLVESTER: Must you be so mercenary?

JULIA: You accepted my money. Let's get on with the preparation. I want you to pretend that you don't know me.

SYLVESTER: That will not be pretense as our acquaintance has not passed the cursory stage.

JULIA: There you go again.. Shut up while I explain. I'll bring up the question of India with Dennis and that will be your cue to cut in. All you have to do is enlarge on the bad points I mention.

SYLVESTER: As simple as that. I've been pondering this problem. Do you think it is wise to deceive your future husband?

JULIA: It's for his own good. He has an offer right here in Edmonton.

SYLVESTER: The same type of employment that is offered in India, no doubt.

JULIA: Of course not. This is a steady, respectable position, not a silly roving engineer's job.

SYLVESTER: Let him be respectable by all means.

JULIA: It's none of your business, but I love Dennis too much to have him throw his life away in those horrible uncivilized parts of the world.

SYLVESTER: I'm glad to know that you have his interests at heart, but don't forget that security has more interpretations than the one most immediately discernible.

JULIA: You're as bad as Dennis. I didn't pay for a sermon. Do you understand what you must do?

SYLVESTER: Ah yes. Your plan is clear enough. I shall be guided by your interests.

JULIA: That's better --- (She looks toward the entrance) Someone's coming. You go over there out of the way and remember what I told you.

SYLVESTER: You may rest assured that I shall not forget.

(Sylvester wanders up stage left as Dennis enters. Dennis crosses to Julia's side without seeing Sylvester)

DENNIS: Oh, there you are. I wondered where you'd gone.

JULIA: (coolly) You certainly didn't put yourself out searching for me. I've been sitting here for at least fifteen minutes.

DENNIS: (teasing) Are you sure it wasn't fourteen minutes, fifty-nine seconds?

JULIA: Whether I sat here a minute or a year I wouldn't change my mind about India.

DENNIS: Do we have to go over that again?

JULIA: Everything is settled as far as I'm concerned.

DENNIS: You mean you want to sit here and rot as we live from hand to mouth.

JULIA: You're exaggerating. Whatever happens we'll have each other and our friends.

DENNIS: That's comforting.

JULIA: Can't you see how foolish it is to dash off to a foreign country where nothing is certain?

DENNIS: Five hundred dollars a month, over and above expenses, is worth a few sacrifices. Besides, it isn't as if we'll be away for long. Five years isn't a lifetime.

JULIA: If only it would end after five years, but you know that it will be only the beginning. The next move will be China, Africa, or South America.

You'll never want to settle down. Oh why did you ever join the Air Force? Before the war you were quite satisfied with Edmonton.

DENNIS: But I've seen so much since 1939. Security is no

more than a state of mind. It doesn't depend on your location.

Money in the bank is no use if there's no contentment. I've seen babies playing in the dust in native villages who had more security than maharajahs seated on shaky mounds of riches.

JULIA: India has gone to your head. I wish you'd never sen the place. I'm sure it's a terrible country.

DENNIS: It's not just about India or my short time there. After the first atomic bomb dropped, many people started to realize their concept of security had been all wrong.

Some of us didn't need that much of a shock.

JULIA: A steady job and a home of our own is quite enough for me.

DENNIS: Why are you so much against India?

JULIA: There is nothing good in India and you'd admit it yourself if you weren't so stubborn.

DENNIS: Just because I spent a short time there, under adverse conditions, doesn't prove it hasn't got its good points.

JULIA: If you go to India, you'll go alone.

DENNIS: But, Julia... (noticing Sylvester)...

SYLVESTER: I beg your pardon but I couldn't help

overhearing your conversation about India. I happen to have an extensive knowledge of that country.

DENNIS: (looking at him up and down, takes a good-humoured attitude) You certainly have that well-travelled look.

There's a thought. How's about flipping this fellow instead of a coin to decide whether or not to go to India?

SYLVESTER: I beg your pardon?

JULIA: Don't mind Dennis. He'd flip a coin at his own funeral.

DENNIS: How would you like to sit in on this argument?

SYLVESTER: I wouldn't want to intrude.

JULIA: Maybe you could help us decide.

DENNIS: What good would that do? You said your mind was made up.

JULIA: Let's hear what this man has to say. If he can give enough good points I might change my mind.

DENNIS: Are you willing to accept what he says, good or bad?

JULIA: If he has been to India, I'll bet he's seen the seedy side of things.

DENNIS: All right, I'm ready to take a chance.

JULIA: Then, it's all settled.

DENNIS: If this gentleman is agreeable. What do you say Mr.---

SYLVESTER: Just call me Sylvester. A few more details would assist.

DENNIS: Briefly, this is it. I have an offer to go to India on an engineering project if I sign up for five years. The pay is $500 a month.

SYLVESTER: I see. Perhaps your finacée would like to ask a few questions.

JULIA: Quite a few. Isn't the climate terrible with the heat and the monsoons?

SYLVESTER: December and January bring a wine like flavour to the air that invigorates to such....

JULIA: But surely the monsoons are frightful.

SYLVESTER: ON the plains, yes. But you can always escape to the hills ---- Darjeeling, Shillong, or even up to Srinagar in the Kashmir.

Cool crisp nights and fresh warm days.

JULIA: (taken aback) But I thought you said .... that is, I mean....

DENNIS: What's the matter, Julia? You're all excited...

JULIA: I'm not excited. (turning to Sylvester, she almost shouts) Here's something you can't turn around – filth, dirt, and beggars.

SYLVESTER: The streets of Segunderbad in the native state of Hyderabad shine spotless and they could safely be used for a table.

In all the state of Hyderabad there are no beggars, and scarcely a ragged dhoti.

JULIA: Your just making fun of us. How can you say such things after....

DENNIS: (getting suspicious) After what?

SYLVESTER: Your finacée is probably distraught at the thought of having to keep her promise to go to India.

I haven't told about the fruit yet, the succulent juiciness of pomelo, or Burmese oranges, the unforgettable flavour of fresh pineapple and the smooth sweetness of sugar plantains.

JULIA: Shut up! Why don't you go away?

SYLVESTER: I wouldn't think of intruding.

DENNIS: There's no need to blame him, Julia.

JULIA: That's what you think.

SYLVESTER: Perhaps I should leave. But before I go, here's your $5.

DENNIS: What's going on here?

JULIA: Why, he, I... that is, we ...

DENNIS: Julia, how could you do such a thing? So you wanted to be fair?

JULIA: (half-defiantly) I wanted you to stay here with me. It ... it seemed like a good idea at the time.

[Editor's note: Handwritten pages indicate that Julia becomes angry and leaves. Dennis wants to chase after her, but Sylvester stops him. The play ends abruptly, with no apparent ending. Any further dialogue has apparently been lost. The editor has thus added the following lines of dialogue, which represent a plausible and logical conclusion given the apparent incompatibility of the characters' ways of thinking. They would have a better chance of "living happily ever after" with this ending too.]

DENNIS: I think you were right in the first place.

JULIA: About India?

DENNIS: Yes. You were right when you said that if I go to India, I will go alone. Goodbye Julia.

CLUB CHIPS

[A draft of a complaint letter to Woodward's Department Store is on the backside of the final page of a carbon copy of this very short play. The letter is dated. Archie is 30 years old. The play is untitled.]

Characters

Martha Smith, [homemaker in early forties]
John Smith, her husband around the same age.
Betty, their eight year old daughter

Setting

The scene is a kitchen with table on one side, to the audience's left and a stove on the other side. A doorway to the other parts of the house is in the centre with a clock above it. There is a cupboard near the table.

Martha is busy setting the table as the curtain rises and is attending to various items of breakfast. She glances at the clock several times as she bustles between stove and table. Finally, with a snort of impatience, she crosses to the inside door.

MARTHA: John! Are you coming to breakfast? You're fifteen minutes late already.

(John enters, buttoning his shirt as he comes. Shoes are on but untied while tie hangs over one shoulder.)

JOHN: Plenty of time.

MARTHA: (Emphasizing points with egg turner) Wipe that shaving soap off your ear. Must you always come to the table half-dressed?

JOHN: What does it matter. Are you expecting royalty? You're too fussy.

MARTHA: I'm always cleaning after you. Can't you take a little care?

(The both sit down.)

JOHN: Pass the sugar, please. (He glances at the paper.) Hmm. Quite a storm they had down south.

MARTHA: Never mind that paper. (John puts down the paper and sighs) What I want to know is, what time did you get in last night?

JOHN: Why, uh, it couldn't have been much after twelve.

MARTHA: I heard the hall clock strike three.

JOHN: Maybe it's wrong again.

A clock is heard striking.

MARTHA: Well?

JOHN: (Rising from his chair) I didn't realize it was so late. I should be ....

MARTHA: That's not what I meant.

(Their eight year old daughter comes in rubbing her eyes.)

BETTY: I can't find my shoes.

MARTHA: You're as bad as your father. Here, let me fix your hair.

(John quickly slips away to the next room, but first he slides something under Martha's plate unobserved by the other two.)

BETTY: Ow, you're pulling my hair.

MARTHA: Stand still, or I'll never get these tangles out... There, that's better. You'll find your shoes where I put them, in their proper place.

(John re-enters wearing coat and carrying hat. He tries to SNEAK OUT unobserved. Betty turns on her way back to the bedroom and sees him.)

BETTY: Goodbye, daddy.

MARTHA: Oh, so you thought you'd get away. We haven't settled that little matter yet.

JOHN: But, dear, I'm late now.

MARTHA: I don't care. It won't take you a minute to explain last night's carousing.

JOHN: But, I tell you, it was just the regular club meeting. (He puts his hand on the door-knob. There is a knock. He opens the door and speaks to someone outside.) Just a moment. (turns back to Martha) How much milk do you want?

MARTHA: Two litres.

JOHN: (to milk delivery person) Yes, two quarts will do. (He starts to leave.)

MARTHA: It must have been some meeting. (Betty comes back in and hands her mother a poker chip.)

BETTY: What's this, mommy?

MARTHA: John!

(John comes back into the room.)

JOHN: I tell you, I'm going to be late, and ....

MARTHA: Do you always use poker chips at club meetings? (She waves it at him.)

JOHN: Well, we had a friendly game.

BETTY: Mommy, what's a poker chip?

MARTHA: Never mind, child. (to John) How much did you lose?

JOHN: Why, I didn't exactly... (He stops and listens and then stares out the partly-opened door.) There's Jones now. He said he'd give me a lift.

MARTHA: But, I ...

JOHN: Sorry, I have to run. (He quickly exits.)

MARTHA: That man.

BETTY: What is a poker chip?

MARTHA: Hush, child. You wouldn't understand. Sit down and eat your breakfast.

(Martha begins to clear the dishes. She lifts her plate and sees the money left by her husband.)

BETTY: Where'd you get all the money, mommy?

MARTHA (counting) Two hundred dollars. Why, he ...

BETTY: Is that money for poker chips?

MARTHA: Not exactly.

THE LAST GENIE

[The surviving pages of this play end abruptly. Unfortunately the story of the play now remains a mystery.]

Characters

Don Grant: About 33, cynical and overly materialistic.

Genie: Sentimentalist. Majestically wistful. Proud bearing with air of one who has seen better days and commanded respect.

Ms. Morris: Don's landlady

Setting

Modernistic, severely stream-lined den. Desk on audience's left, slightly left and downstage of the centre. Easy chair and foot stool to audience's right and well upstage. Bookcase against right wall and downstage, well filled. Several books between bookends on desk. Pen set and bottle of ink on desk. Lamp on desk and floor lamp by easy chair.

(Don Grant is seated at desk writing. Mrs. Morris taps gently and enters. She is dressed for the street and carries a book under one arm.)

MS. MORRIS: Good evening, Mr. Grant. I hope I'm not disturbing you.

DON: 'Evening. No, not at all. I'm trying to figure out

where all the money goes.

MS. MORRIS: Isn't is a fright how the prices are climbing? Why, a body can scarcely pay for food and clothing these days.

DON: It is vicious. Me, I'll settle for a million dollars.

MS. MORRIS: (Holding out her book.) You should read this book that I'm returning to the library.

DON: Oh, what is it?

MS. MORRIS: Arabian Nights. There's a fellow called Jenny, I don't know why that's his name. He comes out of a lamp and makes all sorts of wonderful things happen.

DON: You mean the Genie. (sneeringly) That's kids stuff.

MS. MORRIS: Maybe, but it does a body good to dream now and then.

DON: You're welcome to your dreams. I'll keep my eyes open. The boss doesn't pay for sleeping on the job.

MS. MORRIS: Maybe you'll understand when you're my age. (Moving towards the door.) Well, I must be going. I just dropped in to ask you to watch for callers while I'm out. I shouldn't be gone long.

DON: O.K. Ms. Morris. (Teasing) If the Genie calls shall I have him wait?

MS. MORRIS: Why, I ... (She turns back for an instant and

then realizes he is joking.) Go 'way with you. Always joshing a body. (Half to herself as she leaves room.) Even a Genie might find it hard to supply all the money you seem to want.

DON: She's certainly a sentimental old woman. Too good-hearted for her own good. (He whistles softly as he rises and crosses to the bookcase. While he is choosing a book, an old man with flowing beard, bent back and crooked staff hobbles in and seats himself in the easy chair. Don strolls back to his desk, leafing through the book he has selected. He's about to sit down when the old man coughs gently. Don turns around and almost drops the book in surprise.)

DON: Who... what... which circus did you escape from?

GENIE: (Slowly and majestically.) I am the last Genie.

DON: Sure, sure, and I'm Little Red Riding Hood, or is it Goldilocks.

GENIE: You jest with the brashness of inexperienced youth.

DON: Listen, wise guy. I've been around enough to be able to pick a phoney. Who sent you? Was it Joe, or Pete maybe?

GENIE: (Sighs.) It has always been the same from time immemorial. People are always ready to scoff. I suppose you require some proof?

DON: Sure, but that should be easy for you. (Holding out his hand.) Here, grandpa, fill that with shekels.

GENIE: (Shaking his head sadly.) Just as I feared. You humans have no sense of values. Each time I hope it will be different, but it never is. Now, if you were to ask me to fill the room with flowers...

DON: Wouldn't that be nice.

GENIE: I remember once when a young girl did ask for flowers and my hopes were high... but she wanted them to have golden petals. If I could only be permitted a bit of advance preparation.

DON: Well, do I get the money?

GENIE: My son, I could fill this room with gold and gems. To what avail. Your troubles would merely multiply.

DON: Start multiplying, brother.

GENIE: Unfortunately, it is not so simple. We must conform with the procedure and custom of the age. Now, if you would like to win a contest...

DON: Are you sure you aren't from one of the quiz programmes. I know one fellow, a friend of mine, who had to dress like Father Time and go around borrowing watches. The idea was that they would give him ten dollars on this programme for every one he collected. But, I still don't get your angle.

GENIE: Angle? I'm afraid I don't follow you.

DON: (Suspiciously.) Say, you haven't got a hidden mike or some recording device? I've heard of them doing that and then playing it over the air.

GENIE: Mike is friend of yours?

DON: This has gone far enough. You're acting too dumb to be natural. I'm reasonable. Either you produce or hit the road.

GENIE: I... ah ... I presume you mean that you want proof. Very well, but I must warn you beforehand that should you be displeased at the result after a wish has been granted you shall immediately forfeit not only that wish but any others which you may have made.

DON: Fair enough. Let's go. Here's an easy one to start with. I would like a car and to make it easier, I won't even specify the make.

GENIE: That is easily arranged.

DON: I suppose all I have to do now is walk outside and drive it away?

GENIE: Don't be impatient. These things must take a natural course.

DON: I'm waiting, but not very long. I'll give you exactly five minutes.

GENIE: That won't be necessary.

(A knock is heard as he speaks.)

DON: I suppose that is someone delivering it now?

GENIE: Open the door and see.

QUIET EVENING

[Editor's note: another version of this play is called "A social sip" and is written when Archie is in his early thirties.]

Good evening, I should like to present, Quiet Evening, a modern comedy. We are about to spend a quiet evening at the home of Madge and Sidney Peters.

Theirs is an average living room with an easy chair on one side of the room and a chesterfield opposite with a coffee table handy.

That just about completes the picture except for two striking examples of surrealist art, and when I say striking I mean just that.

These people fortunate enough to be struck blind by the first glimpse are indeed the lucky ones.

Before introducing the characters, you should be told that the credit for casting this play can be given to the Understudy Group.

Now, the characters. But suppose we let them speak for themselves:

Sidney Peters, thirtyish... read by Art Glazer

His wife, Madge... read by Eleanore Bowerman

Brother Tom, in his twenties... read by Ed Patterson

Isabelle Turner, Tom's current heart throb... read by Al Halhead

Lastly, a persistent drunk... read by Les Pilcher

Characters

Sidney Peters: in his middle thirties, overly fastidious, doesn't smoke, drink, or swear and does not condone such actions.

Madge Peters, his wife, about the same age as Sidney, normally fairly easy-going.

Tom Peters, Sidney's brother who does just about everything to make up for his brother. Is three or four years younger.

Isabelle Turner, Tom's girlfriend, in her late twenties. Slightly on the dizzy blonde side.

Drunk, well saturated.

Mr. Townsend, Sidney's boss, on the stuffed shirt side.

Setting

The Peters' living room, comfortably furnished with easy chair on audience's right, chesterfield on the left with coffee table in front of it and slightly downstage.

The door from outside is upstage middle. Door to other parts of house to audience's right and upstage. One picture on wall above chesterfield and one above easy chair.

Pictures surrealist, the brighter the better.

(Sidney is sitting in easy chair doing a crossword puzzle. He leans back puzzling over a clue. He writes something and erases it. Glancing back to the door, he calls to Madge.)

SIDNEY: Oh, Madge... what is a six letter word meaning slang for a small bottle of liquor? The first letter is “M” and the last “Y”.

MADGE: (Entering with a brown paper wrapped bottle in one hand.) Why, a mickey, of course.

SIDNEY: Yeh, that’s right. I couldn’t quite tag it.

(Madge sets the parcel on the coffee table but Sidney is too absorbed in his puzzle to notice what she is doing. His arm pushes one of the antimacassars out of place and she re-arranges it.)

MADGE: You’re always wrinkling these.

SIDNEY: Why do you insist on so many doodads? (He carefully moves an antimacassar and eyes it critically.) There, that was half a [millimetre out of place].

MADGE: You big tease. I think the antimacassars add a touch.

SIDNEY: That touched look, no doubt. (He rises as he speaks.) Speaking of Ponoka [*], did someone forget their nightmare? [*mental institution in Alberta, Canada]

MADGE: I don’t know what you mean.

SIDNEY: I mean that fugitive from a frustrated rainbow. (He crosses to the chesterfield and removes the picture, turning it to the wall.)

MADGE: Sidney, don't be like that. I think it has something.

SIDNEY: (Coming back to the easy chair and giving the other picture similar treatment.) I hope it isn't catching. The painter must have got caught in a revolving door. If that's art, I'll take his brother.

MADGE: (Lightly.) You're never wrong, are you honey? But, I love you.

SIDNEY: Mighty decent of you. I'll make a note to remember you in my will.

MADGE: You have a will too, WILL that is. No one will change it in a hurry.

SIDNEY: Now, I'm not that hard. Some day we'll build a rumpus room in the basement and you...

MADGE: Yes, I know, you'll let me cover the walls, ceiling, and floor with brilliant pictures.

(Madge rumples Sidney's hair as he settles back in the easy chair and they laugh together.)

SIDNEY: And don't get anything as sombre as those things.

MADGE: Oh, those dull sketches. You know, you can be wonderful when you put your mind to it.

SIDNEY: How nice. Shall we page Mr. Hyde?

MADGE: Silly, I mean, why can't you always be a good sport.

SIDNEY: So now I push old women off streetcars.

MADGE: It's not that bad, hon. But, I remember the day when you clowned and got a kick out of everything. Why... you... (She glances toward the coffee table.) ... even remember how you kept the gang roaring at parties. And, you didn't mind their bottle-tipping either.

SIDNEY: Kid stuff. I've smartened up about fire water.

MADGE: Drink in moderation is ...

SIDNEY: Let's not turn on that record again. I'm not in an arguing mood. (He picks up his crossword.) Now, let me see, where was I? Ah, yes, Mickey. (A sudden thought seems to strike him and he looks across at the coffee table.) That parcel. Madge, is that a crock?

MADGE: I thought ... you know how Tom and Isabelle are ... a little sip isn't going to...

SIDNEY: (Crushes paper and stands up.) I thought we settled that – our house is dry.

MADGE: But Sidney, this is just a drop to liven up the Cokes. I know how you feel since your father ...

SIDNEY: Never mind my father. There's no such thing as a little drink. Look at the parties Tom and Isabelle are always having... stupid brawls. If my brother and his girlfriend want to carouse let them go somewhere else.

MADGE: That's not fair. It isn't like you to be so narrow. What's the matter? Why this sudden concern for elbow benders?

SIDNEY: I never subscribed to Alcoholics Anonymous and I don't intend to send them any new customers.

MADGE: You've got the wrong slant. I won't touch it if that will help, and I'll water down a [soda pop] for you, sweetheart.

SIDNEY: Most amusing, but that's not the point. Think of my position. You know how Mr. Townsend is thumbs down on jungle juice; not that I'd let that influence me one way or the other. But he's always calling around here at odd times. Imagine his reaction if he happened along tonight.

MADGE: That hypocrite. He shakes a warning finger with one hand and reaches for a flask with the other.

SIDNEY: You're not being fair. He sets a fine example at work.

MADGE: A, "Do as I say," policy is all right, but he doesn't have to be so sanctimonious.

SIDNEY: Maybe he doesn't follow his own preaching but is <u>is</u> my boss.

MADGE: He can't possibly object to private entertaining.

I'll promise to keep you from staggering outside.

SIDNEY: No doubt you'll hide the evidence under the chesterfield if necessary.

MADGE: Or, behind those lovely pictures. (She puts her arm on his shoulder.) Please don't spoil the evening. Relax and act human while Tome and Isabelle are here. They won't stay long because of the dance.

SIDNEY: Long enough to get half-cut. (He flops back into the easy chair and smooths out the paper.) Better forget the gin.

MADGE: Rum.

SIDNEY: Whatever it is... It's all the same, poisonous stuff. Alcohol is out.

(Sidney starts to work the crossword again.)

MADGE: (Sitting on the arm of his chair.) Let's grow up. If there's a hiccough tonight you can blame indigestion.

SIDNEY: Why argue. This would be the thin edge. And, I don't appreciate Tom's efforts to spike every glass I fill.

MADGE: He just teases.

SIDNEY: I'm not so sure.

MADGE: Like it or not, I'm treating tonight. Why not be a good sport?

SIDNEY: Madge, put that bottle away.

MADGE: Don't treat me like a child... and don't shout.

SIDNEY: I'm not shouting. I'm trying to tell you that there'll be no booze parties in this house.

MADGE: You're impossible. Why can't you be yourself again? We had such fun at Tony's in the old days. You were always clowning and enjoying life. What's gone wrong? You've changed Sidney.

SIDNEY: If anyone has changed, it's you. We are mature people, you know, not adolescents.

MADGE: My how quickly you've grown up, junior.

SIDNEY: Don't be infantile.

MADGE: You're the childish one. (Setting the bottle firmly on the table.) Do what you like. The bottle stays.

SIDNEY: Now who's being unreasonable? Can't you struggle along with [soda pop] for one night?

MADGE: Imagine how Tom and Isabelle will razz.

SIDNEY: Why should they? I never was a lost weekend specialist.

MADGE: I'm not going to drench the house with alcohol. Why not unbend? I don't make a habit of drowning our friends in joy juice.

SIDNEY: Don't be ridiculous. I'm doing it for your own good. No need to act so silly.

MADGE: I merely want to entertain the kids.

SIDNEY: That doesn't call for tonsil antifreeze.

MADGE: You are the most stubborn person I've ever known.

SIDNEY: I'm stubborn? What does that make you?

MADGE: Why can't we have some hard stuff? It won't hurt anyone.

SIDNEY: There'll be no tipping in this house. That's final.

MADGE: Final for you. I have some say in this matter.

SIDNEY: You've already said too much. Why waste breath.

MADGE: You're so smug and so right about everything. Don't you feel sorry for us ordinary humans?

SIDNEY: Now, now, don't get excited. Think things over. You'll see that I'm right.

MADGE: Of course you're right... right out of this world, you... you... starched store dummy. I've taken enough of your bossing. I resign.

SIDNEY: Resign? I don't get it.

MADGE: Just what I say. I'm through.

SIDNEY: Madge, please calm down. Don't get hysterical. You are in the wrong.

MADGE: Hysterical am I? In the wrong, eh? You're just too perfect. No one could measure up to your standards. I don't intend to try any longer. You can struggle on alone.

SIDNEY: You're being unreasonable. Why, I've a good mind to take... (there is a knock on the door) Oh.. that must be Tom and Isabelle, I'll ...

(Tom and Isabelle breeze in without immediately discerning the chill atmosphere.)

TOM: Hello you two, what's the good word tonight?

ISABELLE: Hi, kids. (She notices the pictures that Sid took down.) Did your pictures fall down? It's bad luck, you know.

SIDNEY: (Strained.) Hello, folks. Excuse me, there's something I must do. (He quickly exits.)

MADGE: (Forced gaiety.) Take the weight off.

TOM: Did he dash off to raid the wine cellar? (He looks closely at Madge.) Maybe it wasn't funny. Say, what's with you, something wrong?

MADGE: Everything's wrong. Oh, Tom I can't stand it any longer.

ISABELLE: Headache dear?

TOM: What's the complaint?
MADGE: It's Sidney. We... quarrelled I'm leaving him.

TOM: It can't be that serious. Everybody argues now and then.

ISABELLE: Even Tom and I, don't we dear?

TOM: Cut it Izzy, this is serious. What's the trouble, Madge? Tell Uncle Tome everything.

MADGE: This started it. (She shows them the bottle.) You know how he is.

TOM: A good shot of panther milk might thaw him out. My brother is a stuffed shirt at times.

MADGE: He used to be all right, but lately ...

ISABELLE: He has such a wonderful wave in his hair.

TOM: Don't mind her, Madge. We'll work out something.

MADGE: It's gone too far for that. (She crosses to the easy chair while Tom and Isabelle take the chesterfield.) Everything's a mess.

TOM: (Picking up the bottle and removing the stopper.) If I thought it would do any good, I'd pour this down the sink.

MADGE: No, I wouldn't want you to do that. If he has to be so narrow-minded...

ISABELLE: We don't want to come between you and Sid. You're such a wonderful couple. I'll bet you still love him.

MADGE: Can't you see it's no use. (She notices that Sidney has appeared in the doorway with an armful of [soda pop]. Sidney carries them to the coffee table and then sits on the chesterfield. Three is an awkward silence.) Oh, Izzy, I've something to show you.

ISABELLE: (Rising and taking Madge's arm.) Goody, and I've something to tell you. It was while I waited in the beauty parlour this afternoon. Two women sitting beside me were talking ... (The last part of their speech is lost as they leave the room.)

TOM: (Waving a hand at the [soda pop].) What, no mint juleps.

SIDNEY: Not a chance.

TOM: Don't take it so hard. I'll lend you my permit.

SIDNEY: You're so helpful.

TOM: Any time, just lift a finger and I'll do the pouring.

SIDNEY: When do you go on the radio?

TOM: As soon as I get a sponsor.

SIDNEY: With your wit, I'm surprised people aren't beating a path to your door.

TOM: That would help keep down the weeds. Say, how

are things at the office?

SIDNEY: Booming. We can hardly keep up with orders.
TOM: That's good. Townsend still running Sunday School classes between binges?

SIDNEY: He's not that bad.

TOM: No? When did he change?

SIDNEY: He treats me well.

TOM: Sure, but look at the work you do.

SIDNEY: I enjoy it.

TOM: Man bites dog no longer news with you making a new headline, Man enjoys work.

SIDNEY: You want to try it some day. You might be surprised.

TOM: Never touch the stuff. Which reminds me. What's eating you? Madge is a good kid, and here you treat her...

SIDNEY: Now you preach to me. Since when did I appoint you my personal advisor?

TOM: Okay, okay. I was just trying to be helpful. (He picks up a bottle of [soda pop] and holds it to the light.) Hmm. This is potent dope.

SIDNEY: Better for you than that mouth wash you gargle.

TOM: The prospect of straight [soda pop] makes me dizzy. Let's dilute them.

SIDNEY: Very funny. You should be on the... (there is a loud knock.) Who can that be?

(Sidney crosses to open the door. A man staggers in and clutches at him. Sidney draws back but cannot disengage himself.)

DRUNK: (Quickly.) Say, Mister, does old Jonesy live here?

SIDNEY: Of course not. I'm afraid you'll have to leave.

DRUNK: (Thickly.) Don't be afraid. You can stay if you like. Glad to have you around.

SIDNEY: (Patiently.) You've made a mistake. There's no Mr. Jones here.

DRUNK: (Belligerently.) No? What did you do with him? If you've hurt old Jonesy, I'll...

SIDNEY: No one has hurt Mr. Jones. We don't even know him.

DRUNK: What? You don't know Jonesy? Everybody knows old Jonesy.

SIDNEY: Let's talk this over outside.

DRUNK: 'Sa good idea. Stuffy in here anyhow. Need some fresh air.

(They exit. Tom picks up one of the bottles and removes the top. He drinks part of the [soda pop] and refills it from the bottle of rum. Sidney starts to come back into the room, sees what is happening and tiptoes out again. Tom completes the job and forces the cap back on the [soda pop] bottle. Sidney makes a noise as he re-enters looking backward as he does so.)

TOM: I hope he didn't contaminate you.

SIDNEY: Hardly.

TOM: How'd you shake him so quickly?

SIDNEY: He wandered off of his own accord.

TOM: He's my idea of a happy man.

SIDNEY: If liquid paralysis is the key to happiness, I'd rather be sad.

TOM: Come now, don't you ever feel the urge to let yourself go and get stinky?

SIDNEY: What a revolting thought.

TOM: You didn't answer my question.

SIDNEY: The idea is absurd.

TOM: You may be a dry stick most of the time, but I'll bet you'd like to kick up your heels...

SIDNEY: Ridiculous. Wishful thinking on your part.

You'd sure like to get me woozy.

TOM: I'd give a lot to see you reeling. Do you good.

SIDNEY: Don't try anything. (He picks up the spiked drink.) I'm thirsty.

TOM: Take it easy. That's stronger than water, you know.

SIDNEY: Don't worry. Say, where are my glasses?

TOM: I'll get them. Save your strength. You might need it. (Tom exits.)

SIDNEY: (to himself) I'll show them. (He sets the doctored bottle down and picks up another one.) They'll get a silly display but I'll have the last laugh.

(He leans back in the chesterfield and closes his eyes. Tom comes back with the glasses and gals.)

ISABELLE: Poor Sidney must be asleep.

TOM: The mere proximity of our vile concoction was too much for him.

(Opening his eyes and stretching.) I was only relaxing, my way.

MADGE: (Sitting in easy chair while Tom and Isabelle sit beside Sidney on the chesterfield.) You be butler, Tom, and use the opener.

(play ending cut due to amazon total page limit.)

CONTINUITY
AND RADIO SCRIPTS

Commercial writings

During his thirties, Archie writes for radio at a private commercial broadcasting company in Edmonton (Alberta).

He creates scripts and comes up with ideas for new programming too.

Some of the writings reproduced in this section are designed to meld advertising with music shows.

Only a few representative samples of the hundreds of pages of radio continuity scripts that are broadcast. He keeps then on file for a lifetime.

For the most part, these writings are sponsors' advertising messages that are used for introducing songs on popular music shows such as "Hit Parade" and other broadcasts.

By way of introduction to this section, the letter offering this writing job to Archie is reproduced here.

This is the beginning of what Archie says, in a speech much later, are his five years of writing continuity for a broadcasting company in Edmonton, Alberta. (1949-1955)

Only at this time in his life does Archie get paid for writing and hear his work published on a daily basis, on the radio.

It is all writing for commercial purposes and so not categorized as "creative writing".

Archie also comes up with ideas for radio shows and does some research too, as shown in correspondence about music included here.

Unfortunately, Archie's abilities are not encouraged or fully appreciated by his employer.

Archie and his wife have to moonlight, selling hot dogs and other junk food at the concessions stands of Edmonton's hockey arena at night to get by financially.

One can only imagine and speculate about what might have happened if the broadcasting company had encouraged, fully recognized, and made use of Archie's broad creative writing experience,

The broadcasting company could have benefited greatly when it expanded into television.

Instead, Archie and his family moves away and he returns to his work in the field of accounting and finally purchasing.

Although Archie writes some articles, speeches, and many poems in his leisure time after leaving Edmonton, he abandons fiction writing altogether.

Although his poetry writing abilities are greatly appreciated by the people around him at work and play, the larger society misses out entirely on discovering Archie's full potential as a writer during his peak prime years and times.

Archie will have to await the advent of new publishing technology to finally see all of his work together in print. He is then in his nineties and the twilight of his life.

Sunwapta Broadcasting Company, Limited

PHONE 22101

109 CPR BUILDING
EDMONTON.
ALBERTA

November 21, 1949.

Mr. A. E. Anderson,
12345 - 76 Street,
EDMONTON, Alberta.

Dear Mr. Anderson:

We wish to confirm our understanding of arrangements completed by telephone with regard to your future employment at CFRN as a continuity writer. We will expect you on November 28th and should there be any material or information which you would like to have beforehand, please feel free to call around.

We remain,

Yours sincerely,

SUNWAPTA BROADCASTING CO. LTD.

George A. Duffield

G. A. Duffield,
Broadcast Manager.

GAD/im

Clippings from newspaper ad

THE EDMONTON JOURNAL, SATURDAY, OCTOBER 30, 1954

MEET THE STAFF OF CFRN-RADIO

CHRONICLE OF 20 YEARS

PRODUCTION AND CONTINUITY — *Writers and production staff plan new programs and top entertainment for the listeners. Back row — Helen Ramsey, Continuity Editor; Jim Findley, production; Leo McKinnon, writer; George Kidd, production. Front row — Archie Anderson and Margaret Tanner, writers.*

1260 On Your Dial

CONTINUITY'S TEN DEMANDMENTS

ONE. Thou shalt not be sick for any reason

(In case of death... please circulate a memo to all concerned... at least 24 hours before the impending event.)

TWO. Thou shalt not use words of more than one syllable

(Special instructions to announcers should be typed in red and suitable excuse decided upon before the writer involved is accused of causing the announcer to read the copy his own way.)

THREE. Thou shalt not take more than the time allotted for coffee

(When you do stay out more than two hours .. please leave a forwarding address in case any memos in current circulation reach your desk.)

FOUR. Thou shalt not use too many original ideas

(The general rule for re-typing a card is when the point is reached where pencilled changes take up more than three-quarters of any spot or flash .. including, of course, the sponsors name.)

FIVE. Thou shalt have no system

(This is purely a device for perpetuating your job. There is a danger that, should the department become too "systemized" .. someone might discover that the work could be done easily by one writer and an armful of cards...

(unlikely of course, but possible...)

SIX. Thou shalt not refuse any "last minute" demands from salespeople

(It is felt that any new account can be aired within ten minutes of the time that the writer is notified. All the information required is the Sponsor's Name .. and business (e.g. clothes .. cars soap) .. The fact that the salesperson knew all about the account and starting date a week in advance is irrelevant and immaterial and cannot be considered as a valid "out" for the writer)

SEVEN. Thou shalt not cross out errors

(If there isn't time to erase or re-type just let the copy go "as is". This is one sure way of becoming popular with announcers, and it makes life generally more interesting.)

EIGHT. Thou shalt not belittle the stipend

(Although it is quite true that ditch-diggers and garbage-collectors do get bigger wages .. they do not get the same satisfaction from their work. Besides, if you were paid more ... you'd only spend the money foolishly on frivolous items such as food and rent.)

NINE. Thou shalt not make carbon copies of carded formats

(It makes the operator's copy SO messy. Also, it has been calculated that owing to the fact that the red portion of the typewriter is used most extensively in typing formats, that it is actually less expensive to type two originals. In other words, the saving on carbon paper over typewriter ribbon ink is more than enough to offset the extra time lost by the writer.)

TEN. Thous shalt not be sick for any reason

(This is repeated to stress the fact that nothing .. BUT NOTHING .. is more important than being at work (in the office that is) .. even if you do arrive one or two hours late every morning.)

NOTE: The order of the DEMANDMENTS given above is not meant to imply that NUMBER ONE is more important than, say NUMBER FIVE. Each writer is required to consider each one (Demandment that is) of paramount importance as it affects his or her day to day existence.

Samples

[These items are from a single piece of paper. The may be rough drafts for commercial messages, typed with corrections in Archie's handwriting and numbers over some words which may indicate how many seconds it takes to read up to that word. Time is money in commercial radio of the era.]

Wanted: ten thousand pair of feet, assorted sizes. Morgan's Shoe Emporium will supply shoes for all those and more during this week's half price sale.

Let's enjoy these fresh Fall days but remember the old gentleman with the deep freeze breath and hoarfrost beard is sharpening his icicles.

Have your car winterized by Kelly Motors today and laugh at the sagging mercury this year.

Kelly Motors have an experienced staff who will give your car prompt attention to ensure comfortable winter driving.

Don't wait until the last minute. See Kelly Motors, corner of Third and Jasper today.

If you're looking for a spot as romantic as a harvest moon, this is your lucky night. Wind up your jalopy and head along the Calgary highway to Joe's Dine & Dance spot, only a few minutes drive from the city limits.

You can drift and dream to the dulcet strains of Dave Dawe's orchestra or sit one out by the crackling logs of a friendly fireplace.

And as for food, mmm, mmm. Whether it's a full course meal or a tasty sandwich, Joe has the answer.

It's a date. Remember, just follow the Calgary highway. Joe's Dine & Dance will take over from there.

LET'S TRACE THE MUSIC

THEME: .. ISLE OF MAY

ANN: Let's trace the music.. from low to high .. and some in-between. The main aim is to enjoy good music and to bring a fuller appreciation of music generally to all who care to listen.

The process of lifting bits and pieces from classical and operatic numbers .. has a long history .. but no constructive purpose has ever controlled it.

Perhaps .. by reversing things .. we'll open new doors .. and expand our musical knowledge easily and pleasantly.

We'll start with our theme .. which you may have recognized as a once-popular tune .. Isle of May ..

ISLE OF MAY .. ESTABLISH AND THEN FADE FOR ..

ANN: Now, we lift our sights .. and discover that Tchaikovsky has a priority claim. His title may not be nearly as glamorous .. but let's listen to .. Quartet Number One in D Major ..

QUARTET NUMBER ONE IN D MAJOR

ANN: In some cases, it is surprising how little change takes place .. in this particular case .. even the original name is retained ..

MARTHA .. ESTABLISH AND THEN FADE..

ANN: That was, of course .. Martha .. which was like so before it got the “treatment” ...

MOODY'S SHAVER SHOP – YESTERDAY ONLY
Release Time: 9:00 a.m. Date: Jan 3/53

[Note: The script is introducing recorded music and the sponsor.]

ANN: Time for all you shavers.. big and small.. to get in the mood with the king of the close-shavers.. TED MOODY .. with his YESTERDAY ONLY SHOW.

#3122 ... IN THE MOOD .. HOLD 15 SECS
FADE SLOWLY AND OUT FOR:

ANN: Right about now .. most of us could do with a big helping of last summer's holiday .. with pay, of course. It would come in handy for resting up after all the excitement of the past two weeks. At least we can produce a summery atmosphere .. by simply waving our magic wand of music ... which transports us to past seasons. This time, we find ourselves in a canoe .... but, careful, you know how these things are ..... watch out .....

#7917 ... TIPPY CANOODLE CANOE

ANN: Of course your husband wouldn't expect you to kiss a cactus. Even the idea may sound silly but, how about that bristly beard left by your man's broken-down face scraper. The solution is as simple as calling at MOODY'S SHAVER SHOP .. on 101A Avenue .. next door to the Safeway Store.

ANN: TED MOODY can show you all the top makes of

electric shavers .. and explain the finer points of each. He's quite reasonable when you bring up the matter of a trade-in, too. If you can't talk that fellow of yours into calling around .. grab his old face-cropper and head for MOODY'S SHAVER SHOP. When your husband learns how well you did with the allowance on the beat-up shaver .. and when he tries that new electric shaver .. he'll love you more than ever. .....

Some people plan holidays so that they can get away from it all .. which brings up this suggestion .. If I Had You On A Desert Island ...

#7722 ...IF I HAD YOU ON A DESERT ISLAND...

(Script ending cut due to amazon total page limit.)

DISCONTENTED STREETCAR

ANNOUNCER: Attention all streetcars. Do you suffer from worn trolleys, flattened wheels, and sagging springs? You do? Then, listen to the story of the disconnected, I mean discontented Streetcar. And here is Ethelred, the streetcar, to tell you his experience.

(TROLLEY SONG UP STRONG DOWN AND OUT)

STREETCAR: You folks are lucky. You pay your fare and that's it. We streetcars can't even choose our passengers. I have an itchy wheel too, and .... but, let's go back to the beginning. It all began when the workers turned me over to the conductor.

WORKER: Okay Bill, she's all ready for testing.

CONDUCTOR: Say, it sure is a beaut. Here goes.

(SOUNDS OF STREETCAR STARTING UP AND GRADUALLY GATHERING SPEED" FADE INTO BACKGROUND)

STREETCAR: I'll never forget that thrilling tingle when the current brought my first kilowatt of life. We raced along the track, stopping for no one. This was for me. I could travel on and on forever.

(FEW BARS OF TROLLEY SONG AND OUT ABRUPTLY)

The next day they put me on a regular run. The stop, start, stop, start nearly drove me mad.

(BRING IN SOUND OF STREETCAR RUNNING JERKILY. SUSTAIN FOR MOMENT AND THEN OUT.)

And the people

(MURMUR OF CROWD. SUSTAIN FOR MOMENT AND THEN FADE INTO BACKGROUND)

They pushed, crowded, and shoved. Oh, my shiny paint, my bulging sides.

CONDUCTOR: Step back in the car. (LOUDER) Back in the car, p-l-l=ease.

STREETCAR: Children pawed me with sticky, grimy fingers. The brats.

WOMAN: Johnny, take your dirty fingers off the back of that seat. Don't scrape your feet on the walls. Quit fidgetting.

STREETCAR: I hated the man in the smoker most (CHOKING COUGH) Whew. I never seemed to be able to shake that stale smoke odour. (BRING IN SOUND OF STREETCAR SLOWLY AND FAD

BEHIND) I wanted to travel. What did I get? The same routine day after day. There I was, following tracks instead of making them; flattening my wheels and wearing down my weakening springs. And, for what? (SOUND OF STREETCAR COMING TO SQUEAKING HALT. HOWLING WIND UP AND DOWN BEHIND) The High Level Bridge frightened me squeaky. I never could stand heights. The wind would tear and push at me. I was glad to reach the other side, any side. (WIND OUT) I did want to travel, but no mountains, thanks.

(SOUND OF PNEUMATIC DRILL UP AND SUSTAIN FOR MOMENT AND OUT)

Then they built the 101st Street subway. My splitting top. It wasn't deep enough and I had to be the one to get stuck. And, the conductor didn't improve my spirits as he held me up to ridicule.

CONDUCTOR: Wouldn't that kill you. The darn thing's stuck. Now we'll have to cut the top off this car. I'll be .....

STREETCAR: At least I had a rest while they remodelled my roof. But, how the other cars rattled and squeaked at me. And, my beautiful shape.... I felt that middle-aged spread had descended. The worker finally gave me the okay

WORKER: Well, she's all set to go again .... Take 'er away Pete.

CONDUCTOR: I hope they measure all the cars before they dig anther subway. Of all the stupid...

STREETCAR: Worse was to follow. Just as I was settling down to take the daily rounds in my stride ...

WOMAN: Conductor! Conductor! The car's on fire. (CONFUSED SCRAMBLING AS PEOPLE LEAVE CAR)

STREETCAR: It had started from a short-circuit under my floor.... so they said. If you ask me, it was one of those smokers. They never did butt out their cigarettes properly. (SICKBED MUSIC SOFT AND LOW SUSTAIN FOR MOMENT AND OUT) I was horribly burned and wavered between life and scrapheap for weeks. Finally, I was patched and re-painted – an amateurish job – ready for more drudgery. (SOUND OF STREETCAR SLOW AND UNCERTAIN AS IF INVALID. HOLD FOR MOMENT AND THEN CUT)

WOMAN: Wooden seats... First thing you know they'll make us all stand. I have a good mind to complain to the mayor.

STREETCAR: Yes, it was true. They had to replace my

old seats with wooden slates. But, (BITTER LAUGH) I did enjoy seeing the people squirm. That would teach them. Let them suffer for a change. But, I still had other troubles. No more smoking, (except when someone sneaked a few puffs) but....

FIRST VOICE: Chew Goody Gum.. It's delicious.

SECOND VOICE: Harvey Hams are best.

THIRD VOICE: Help yourself to health with...
(AD LIB MIXTURE OF VOICES REPEATING SLOGANS OVER AND OVER)

STREETCAR: (SCREAMING) Stop! Stop! (CUT VOICES) You guessed it. Those corny commercials pursued relentlessly. Sometimes there were no passengers to annoy me but the ads clung to my sides at all times. Some displays of ladies' intimate wear made me hang my trolley in embarrassment. The humiliation of it. And then there was the gossip.....

FIRST PERSON: Did you hear about Mrs. Jones?

SECOND PERSON: Yes. Wasn't it terrible. And for her to be so brazen about it. Why, just the other day ....

STREETCAR: I tell you, it was sickening. Every board,

every bolt, and every corner of me ached to get away from such a dreary, disgusting routine. Most people get one day off a week. They let me stay in the car barns only when I was ailing. A greasy, dull, drafty old place. I soon got to have those short respites. The newer streetcars would sniff at my shabbiness. That was bearable, but when the trolley buses began to invade the city I writhed with anger.

TROLLEY BUS: Your days are numbered, old time. We trolley buses will soon replace all you ancients.

STREETCAR: We are more reliable than you upstarts.

TROLLEY BUS: Huh. You stick to those rusty old tracks, but we wander where we please on the road.

STREETCAR: And off the road, too. You're a reckless crowd. Not even you know where you might go next.

TROLLEY BUS: We know where you will go... straight to the scrap heap.

STREETCAR: At least you never saw a streetcar with a flat

TROLLEY BUS: Very funny... So long old crock. (SOUND OF TOOTING, STARTING UP AND

DRIVING AWAY)

STREETCAR: What was the use? Those youngsters thought they knew everything. (TROLLEY SONG SLOWLY AND DELIBERATELY AS IF STREETCAR THINKING. SUDDEN CHANGE TO QUICK TEMPO AND OUT) I had it! Why hadn't I thought of that before? The idea was perfect. I waited for my opportunity. It came sooner than I expected. One raw fall night when we started on the last round, I began to coax the conductor. (BRING IN SOUND OF WHEELS ON TRACK AND HOLD BEHIND) He needed a little encouragement. (STREETCAR VOICE ON FILTER AND TO RHYTHM OF WHEELS) Come on, let's go faster, come on faster, come on faster...

CONDUCTOR: Even the car seems to know this is the last round.... Say, its wheels can almost talk.

STREETCAR: (CONTINUE FILTER AND RHYTHMIC CHANT FOR CAR) I can talk, sure I can. Make it faster, make it faster, make it faster....

CONDUCTOR: I guess it won't hurt to open it up a little. The sooner I get home the better.... A bit more should be safe. This old bus is sure rolling now.... Hey, I can't seem to slow down.... Got to stick with the car....

STREETCAR: (OFF FILTER) Faster and faster I sped while the poor conductor struggled in vain. Served him right. I passed the administration building and raced down the hill towards the High Level Bridge. My wheels sang in triumph as we sped down the incline and neared the corner. (BRING UP SOUND OF STREETCAR AND SPEED FASTER AND FASTER TO THUNDEROUS PEAK. REVERBERATING CRASH. SOUND OF SHATTERING GLASS AND MINGLED SCREAMS FOLLOWED BY BRIEF SILENCE) My broken trolley. My shattered panes. I didn't care, though. It didn't matter what happened to me now. They wouldn't be able to push me around any more. What a glorious way to die. My name would make headlines ... But, I soon found out, this was not quite the end after all. (TROLLEY SONG IN SOFT AND LOW GRADUALLY UP TO STRONG AND OUT) Yes, those clever workers again...

FIRST WORKER: I never thought this old crock would run again, but there you are, all in order and ready to go...

CONDUCTOR: For my money, it's an improvement over the original.

STREETCAR: When they started to work over my poor numb parts, I was puzzled at first. Hey, what did they think they were doing? They quickly tore out the remains of my seats. Good riddance. What in the world... There were days of sawing and hammering in my middle. It gradually became clearer....

WOMAN: I want Treasure Island for my little boy.

LIBRARIAN: Certainly, here it is.

WOMAN: There was a book by Faith Baldwin that I wanted ..... it doesn't seem to be here.

LIBRARIAN: Give me the title and I'll see if I can bring it for you next week.

WOMAN: Thank you. Come now, Johnny, we mustn't keep other people waiting .... Why, Mrs. Jones, so glad to see you. Did I ever tell you...

LIBRARIAN: Move along, please .... Make room for others ... Yes, what would you like?

MAN: Could I put this poster up here?

LIBRARIAN: I'm sorry, sir ... no advertising allowed on this car .... Excuse me, but you'll have to put out that cigarette..... That's all for today, folks. We'll be back at the same time next week.

STREETCAR: It's wonderful. No smoking, no commercials, brats must behave..... But, that's not all. Now I am able to visit far away lands ....thrilling adventures are mine for the taking .... knowledge is spread before me. You see. I am a veritable storehouse of knowledge and entertainment. And, those people who do climb my steps can't be passengers. I never thought there could be such perfect happiness for a broken-down streetcar. And, why shouldn't I take it easy after 65 long, weary years. My blue and gold sides set me apart from common streetcars and upstart trolley buses. Yes, I'm spending my declining years as a travelling representative of The Edmonton Public Library.

KINDNESS FREE

Good morning, everyone.. isn't it a wonderful day. Why, if it weren't for the sub-zero temperatures, the ice, and the snow.. the weather would be perfect.

In fact, it looked so nice out this morning... I was tempted to just leave it out and go back to sleep, But, here I am ... and there you are .. I hope.

It's terrible the way motorists speed around the city .. like the case I ran across today.

When I was driving down here this morning, the car in front of me persisted in burning up the road.

And, do you know .. I had to do 70 km per hour or better before I could pass him. They really should do something about it..

That's like an experience I had with a young woman I know.. when the car ran out of gas .. whoops, sorry, wrong story.

This woman was driving me through town one day, during the rush hour.

Now, as a rule .. when I'm a passenger ... I stick strictly to passengering and never a word of instruction or criticism.

But, after several near misses I had to protest .. Wasn't that a bit too close .. you nearly hit that other car. She merely smiled and sweetly put me straight.

“There isn’t a thing to worry about ... see I have a safety stick on the windshield.”

Oh, brother.

Since we are tangled up in cars and driving .. here’s something else I’d like to tell you ..

I often wonder if too many people these days have lost the true sense of values .. but let’s take it from the beginning.

One night, my wife and I were getting into our car after dumping our young fellow at Gramma’s .. when we saw a man juggling two large bags of groceries.

He was trying to hold them and get something out of his pocket at the same time. One bag slipped .. he made a desperate grab .. it split open and the road was full of groceries.

We helped him pick up the pieces ... discovered he was a stranger and couldn’t find the right address which was one street over.

It was a simple matter to dump stranger and groceries in the car and whip him around to the right house. We were feeling mighty good about the whole affair .. you know how it is when you can help someone like that .. when crash, boom ..

Just as we turned back to the car, he reaches into his pocket and says ... “How much do I owe you?”

That incident recalls the saucy little “chicos” in India.

Many of these children were professional beggars, whining for backsheesh.

One routine that really tickled me, went like this .. “Nay momma, nay papa .. nay sister .. nay brother .. nay khana .. backsheesh sahib!”

On the whole, though ... the people of India are a remarkable happy crew .. probably because they can’t miss things they’ve never had.

TO TICKLE YOUR FANCY

ANNOUNCER. Here's a light subject which should tickle you. Don't get the wrong idea. This is not a humorous tale, but......(SPEECH TRAILS OFF INTO LAUGHTER)

JOEY. Look at those men, Red.

RED. I see them, Joey. They're just loading a truck.

JOEY. Yeh, I know, but that's Mr. Greenberg's warehouse, and he went away for the weekend.

RED. Maybe he gave them the key.

JOEY. Let's sneak over there ..... I bet they're crooks.

RED. We'd better wait. They might catch us.

JOEY. Well, if you're scared...........

RED. I'm not scared. We're late for our swimming lessons and ....

JOEY. We can swim any time. Come on if you're coming.

RED. Okay. I'll follow you.

(SOFT STALKING MUSIC)

JOEY. (WHISPERING) We can watch through the cracks in this box. Look, they're carrying big bundles of something.

RED. Gosh those bundles must be light. See, that man is carrying one under each arm.

JOEY. I was right. They are crooks. See, they busted the lock.

RED. Yeh. Let's run for the cops.

JOEY. Too late for that. They're getting into the truck. I'm going to follow them.

(SOUND OF RUNNING, TRUCK STARTING AND PULLING AWAY)

RED. Joey, wait, I can't keep ..... Gosh. Joey climbed right on the truck. I'd better get help.

(SOUND OF TRUCK IN AND UNDER)

SLIM. Well, Fingers, wasn't that simple? Nobody saw us and Greenberg won't be back 'til Monday.

FINGERS. All right so far, Slim, but I won't be happy until we can ditch these feathers.

SLIM. (LAUGHING) I'd like to see the cops' faces when they discover someone stole a [tonne] of feathers.

FINGERS. Yeh. It'll tickle them, too .... I mean if they

discover why.

SLIM. You sure were a dope.

FINGERS. You know it couldn't be helped.

SLIM. Pretty sloppy work on your part.

FINGERS. Forget it, can't you. We've got the stuff now haven't we.

SLIM. Sure. What's a few million feathers more or less. And, don't forget, I traced them.

FINGERS. Okay, okay. You've had your say .....Here's the the place.

(TRUCK SLOWS DOWN)

SLIM. I'll open the door.

(TRUCK MOVES INTO BUILDING AND ENGINE IS SHUT OFF)

FINGERS. Now for the feather counting. Don't scatter them too much.

SLIM. We'll try this one first.

(SOUND OF TRUCK BEING RIPPED OPEN)

FINGERS. I can't feel anything in this one. How about... (MUFFLED SNEEZE FROM JOEY) Hey, what was that? All right you. Come out with your hands up.

JOEY. I didn't do anything Mister. (SCRAMBLE AND THUD AS JOEY CLIMBS OUT AND JUMPS TO FLOOR)

FINGERS. Why, it's just a kid.

JOEY. I'm 13 .... almost.

SLIM. Cut it. What are you snooping around for?

JOEY. (AFTER A SLIGHT PAUSE) We ... we were playing a game. I hid in your truck. It moved away before I could jump out.

SLIM. Yeh? You don't expect us to believe that. We can't take any chances with this brat. Let's put him out of the way for awhile.

JOEY. (TEARFULLY) I tell you, I wasn't doing nothing.

SLIM. We can tie him with this rope for the time being Quit snivelling, you.

JOEY. (BRAVELY) There's something in my eyes.

FINGERS. We've waited enough time. I'll hold him while you do the tying.

JOEY. Ouch, you're hurting my arms.

SLIM. Shut up or I'll stuff this rag down your throat.

FINGERS. There, that should hold him.

JOEY. I'm telling you, I don't......

SLIM. Button up or I'll ....

JOEY. (ANXIOUSLY) I'll be quiet.

FINGERS. Leave the kid alone. We've got work to do.

(SOUND OF SACK BEING RIPPED OPEN)

SLIM. (BLOWING FEATHERS) Whew. This is ticklish work.

FINGERS. (GRUNTING) Nothing in this one, either.

SLIM. I'll get another. (DRAGGING NOISE. SACK RIPPED OPEN)

FINGERS. We better strike soon.

SLIM. Another blank. This is getting..........

FINGERS. What's that? Take a squint outside, Slim. (SOUND OF CAR SLOWING DOWN OUTSIDE)

SLIM. The cops. I'll bet this punk tipped them off somehow.

JOEY. But, I didn't.... (SOUND OF BLOW AND GROAN)

SLIM. That fixes you.

FINGERS. Did you have to slug him?

SLIM. He might have warned them.

FINGERS. Yeh. Let's make a break for it.

SLIM. Sure. We'd better take the kid. (BREATHLESS FROM LIFTING JOEY TO BACK OF TRUCK) There, he'll be all right on the back where we found him.

FINGERS. Swing the doors and jump aboard.

(STARTING OF ENGINE, RAPID ACCELERATION AND GUNFIRE MINGLED WITH SHOUTS> AS SOUND OF ENGINE RECEDES ANOTHER STARTS UP AND FOLLOWS)

SLIM. (OVER SOUND OF ENGINE) We sure caught them flatfooted. Flatfoots flatfooted, get it?

FINGERS. Aw, cut that. We aren't away yet. This crate can't keep ahead for long. (SCREECHING OF TIRES AS SUDDEN CHANGE OF DIRECTION IS MADE) This lane looks about right.

SLIM. What's up? We've no time for garbage inspection.

FINGERS. Listen carefully. I'm going to swing the truck

sideways to block this narrow alley. We can ditch these bales in one of those warehouses. We'll slip through the cops' fingers so easy.

SLIM. They aren't in sight yet.

FINGERS. Get ready to grab some feathers. Leave the kid.

(TRUCK ENGINE SUDDENLY CUTS OUT. SOUND OF TWO MEN RUNNING GRADUALLY OUT)

JOEY. (GROANING SLIGHTLY) Where am I?

RED. Take is easy, Joey. The police are here.

POLICE
OFFICER. You're a smart kid. Dropping those feathers was clever.

JOEY. I thought they'd blow away.

POLICE
OFFICER. Too calm for that. You certainly dropped enough.

RED. We followed the trail easily. Feathers all over the road. Gee, this just like a detective story.

POLICE
OFFICER. Feeling better now, son?

JOEY. I'll be okay.

RED. How about that swim?

POLICE
OFFICER. Sure you're all right?

JOEY. Yeh. What happened to the crooks?

POLICE
OFFICER. Some of the boys chased them but they got away.

RED. Come on, Joey.

JOEY. Okay. Just a minute 'til I tell the officer something.

POLICE
OFFICER: What's bothering you?

JOEY: I'd like to tell you alone.

RED. That bump must have affected you. I'll go ahead.
(SOUND OF RED'S STEPS RECEDING.)

POLICE
OFFICER. Let's have it.

JOEY. As soon as I jumped on the truck (GRADUALLY FADE OUT VOICE FROM HERE) I noticed the feathers and I started to throw some ....

(SHORT MUSIC BRIDGE)

RED. Wasn't that a keen swim?

JOEY. Yeh.

RED. What's eating you, Joey?

JOEY. I was just thinking....

RED. Say, isn't that one of the two crooks who .....

SLIM. Bright boy. Get in the car, and don't argue.

RED. (SHAKY) What are you going to do to us?

(CAR STARTING UP FOR A MOMENT AND DOWN. HOLD UNDER)

SLIM. You're going for a nice long ride.

JOEY. You better let us go.

SLIM. Sure. Leave any time.

JOEY. You wouldn't do anything to ....

SLIM. Quiet. You talk too much.

FINGERS. Never mind those kids. See if we're being followed.

SLIM. Nothing in sight.

FINGERS. Good. Better blindfold the kids.

SLIM. Here, put this over Red's eyes. Tie it tighter.

JOEY. What are you going to do?

SLIM. Play blindman's bluff. You two are it. Quit wiggling. There, that should hold you.

FINGERS. Keep them out of sight.

SLIM. Get down you brats.

FINGERS. We'll soon find out what's (SOUND OF ENGINE UP AND OVER VOICE AND THEN OUT> MUSIC BRIDGE> SOUND OF DOOR OPENING)

SLIM. Get inside.

JOEY. It's dark in here.

FINGERS. Shut up.

SLIM. Tell us what you did with the stuff and we'll let you go.

JOEY. I, I don't know what you mean.

FINGERS. You're lying.

SLIM. Perhaps he'll talk if we do a bit of persuading.

FINGERS. No rough stuff.

SLIM. Sure. We'll play patty-cake.

FINGERS. Use your head. If we mess up these kids the cops'll turn on the heat.

SLIM. How can we make him talk?

FINGERS. I'll tie them up first. Hold that light steady.

SLIM. What's the idea?

FINGERS. That should hold them. A few hours in the dark may help your memory.

RED. Don't leave us alone.

SLIM. Talk to your friend. He might tell you his secret. (DOOR CLOSES)

JOEY. Don't be scared.

RED. (QUAVERY) I'm not...... It sure is dark. Do you think they'll torture us?

JOEY. (TRYING TO CONVINCE HIMSELF) N-o-o. They wouldn't dare.

RED. This is your fault. If you hadn't jumped on that truck....

JOEY. Don't be a baby. Let's try to get out of here.

RED. Sure. We could roll out, but the rope's too tight. It's cutting my hands.

JOEY. Say, that's an idea. I've got a knife in my

pocket.

RED. What good does that do?

JOEY. (IMPATIENTLY) Roll over beside me and I'll tell you.

RED. Why should...... Okay. I get it. Which pocket?

JOEY. Here..... That's right. Can you open it?

RED. I think so... Now, wait 'til I find the rope. (SCUFFLING NOISE AND HEAVY BREATHING)

JOEY. Ouch! You don't have to cut my hand.

RED. Sorry..... There. Did I get it that time?

JOEY. Let me have the knife. (MORE SCUFFLING)

RED. That's better. My hands were going to sleep.

JOEY. Try the door. Be careful. Those crooks might be outside. We don't want to get caught again. (SOUND OF DOOR BEING GENTLY RATTLED)

RED. It's locked. What'll we do now, Joey?

JOEY. Maybe there's another way out. You go along the wall that way and I'll go this way. (STUMBLING NOISE AND THUMP AS

RED FALLS)
What's that?

RED. I tripped......there's something soft and fluffy... just like feathers.

JOEY. Never mind... This must be a window that's boarded up .... a board's loose.

RED. Let me see. Perhaps we can climb out.

JOEY. Darn it. We can't get down that steep wall.

RED. Aw, what's the use. Why don't you tell them what they want to know?

JOEY. It wouldn't help.

RED. Why not?

JOEY. You wouldn't understand.... Say did you say there were feathers over there?

RED. It felt like feathers.

JOEY. It is feathers. Help me move these bundles (FADE OUT VOICE FROM HERE) and I'll show you what I ....
(SHORT MUSIC BRIDGE)

FINGERS. I wonder how the kids are feeling.

SLIM. If that kid won't talk, I'll .....

FINGERS. Take it easy. He'll be ready to blubber it out to

us.

SLIM. He'd better.

FINGERS. You'll see as soon as I get this door opened. (DOOR RATTLES AS THEY OPEN IT)

SLIM. All right you punks, are you ....Hey! They're gone....

FINGERS. Are you sure? Why, the little ......

(SOUND OF SCUFFLE AND MUFFLED SHOUTS. DOOR SLAMS)

RED. (GASPING AS THEY RUN) That was smart, JOEY. They won't get rid of those feathers in a hurry.

JOEY. Save your breath. They'll soon be after us

RED. Look, isn't that a cop?

JOEY. I think so .... It is........

POLICE OFFICER. Here now, what's the hurry?

JOEY. Two crooks....... they're after us.

POLICE OFFICER. Well, now, that's interesting. I suppose you two are secret service agents, or something.

JOEY. I tell you they had us tied up and ......

RED. They were going to torture us...

POLICE OFFICER. Were they, really? What do you want me to do, call Dick Tracy? That must be them coming now. What say we get their side of the story?

FINGERS. Thanks for stopping our boys, officer Kids sure take some handling these days.

JOEY. Don't listen to him, he's .....

FINGERS. He has a lively imagination. I suppose he pitched some yarn about us being crooks or some such fantastic story.

POLICE OFFICER. Why, yes, he did and his friend is quite excited too.

SLIM. Red always was high strung. It's the radio programmes the kids listen to these days.

POLICE OFFICER. Come along, lads. Go home with your fathers like good boys.

RED. Please don't let them take us away.

POLICE OFFICER. None of your fooling. Get along with you before I lose my patience.

JOEY. I tell you, they are crooks. See, he's got a gun.

SLIM. Let go of my pocket.

RED. Watch out he's going to shoot.

(SOUND OF SCUFFLE ND TWO RAPID SHOTS)

POLICE OFFICER. Nice work, lad. You threw him off balance by grabbing his legs.

JOEY. You sure got the other guy.

POLICE OFFICER. He won't be much trouble. Get up, you, and look after your pal. Don't try anything.

FINGERS. I know when I'm licked.

SLIM. I'm dying.

FINGERS. It looks like a shoulder wound to me.

POLICE OFFICER. Get moving, you two. We'll patch you up at the station.

RED. Gee!

JOEY. I hope there's a reward.

RED. Say, what were they after?

JOEY. Jewels.

RED. Real jewels?

JOEY. Of course. They hid them in the bundles of feathers.

RED. But, how..........

JOEY. When I was leaving that feather trail, I found jewels in one of the bundles.

The advent of television

[Archie's radio station employer expands into television. The following items are Archie's suggested words for introducing the new broadcasting medium venture.]

He: It's sure nice to sit back and relax and listen to the radio in the evening.

She: Yes, isn't it dear. And, just think, this fall we'll be able to watch television over C.F.R.N. You know, I was talking to Mrs. Jones today and she say they're going to get the biggest TV set possible, with the largest screen.

He: But wouldn't that be rather silly, since the screen should be in proportion to the size of your room for best viewing.

She: I don't see how that should be. We get better reception on this big radio in the loving room than on that tiny set in the kitchen.

He: Of course, but television is quite a bit different in a number of ways. Look at it this way. What happens when you sit in the front row at the show?

She: I remember the last time that happened. I had a stiff neck for a week and my eyes were sore for hours after.

He: That's just what I mean. When you buy a television set with a screen that's too big for your room, there's trouble ahead.

She: Yes, you're right. I see what you mean now. But, how is a person to be sure of the right size TV set to buy?

He: It's simple enough. Roughly speaking, the size of your TV screen should be about 5 cm for every 60 cm of length in your room.

She: Why, of course. I see how it works. In this room, for instance, since it's about 5 meters long, we'd get best results with about a 40 cm screen on your television set.

He: Exactly. You know, there's a lot more to this television business than most people realize.

Advantages of TV over radio

When you turn off the radio you may be missing something and yet you'll never know. On TV just close your eyes and listen. That way you'll know you're not missing a thing.

TV & children

You hear a lot of chatter about TV's ill effects on children, covering everything from eyes to morals.

About the most disturbing experience I've had is what happened one morning about daybreak.

I woke up to hear a rustling noise that I couldn't identify. Being unable to get my wife to investigate, I tiptoed cautiously into the hall.

Glancing through the bath room doorway I saw our five-year old vigorously brushing his teeth.

I asked him what was going on and he gave a disdainful snort. "Don't you watch TV Daddy? You're supposed to brush your teeth in the morning."

I crawled back under the covers.

Every evening when I get home I have to check to see who's on the welcoming committee. A Davey Crockett outfit is usually the tip-off, but sometimes it is merely a disguise for Wild Bill Hickok or the Range Rider.

Archie TV

[This item ends abruptly, indicating that either the remaining pages are lost or that this is the end of the sample.]

Hello there. I'm Archie Anderson, which may mean nothing to you. But believe me, it means quite a bit to me.

The reason you're watching me now is because of an idea.

You see, since you are new at this game of watching, I persuaded those who could do something about it to give a new face a chance.

Not that my face is new, as it is the same one issue to me quite a few winters ago ... not to mention a number of summers ago.

Of course, there has been some wear and tear which is to be expected in a model that has had steady use for so long. But, all this doesn't justify my being here.

The big reason you are in front of your TV set now is that you want to be entertained. And, since the greater part of this entertainment should be visual – if there is nothing for you to watch while I talk I might just as well be out of sight – like so.

To justify my face by itself in your picture tube, I would have to have some unusual feature, or perhaps a humorous or fascinating mannerism.

Failing this, I need a gimmick, such as this...

Before I tell you about this card, I want you to know that the entertainment I intend to provide comes under the heading of "Usable Information" .. notice I said "usable", not useful.

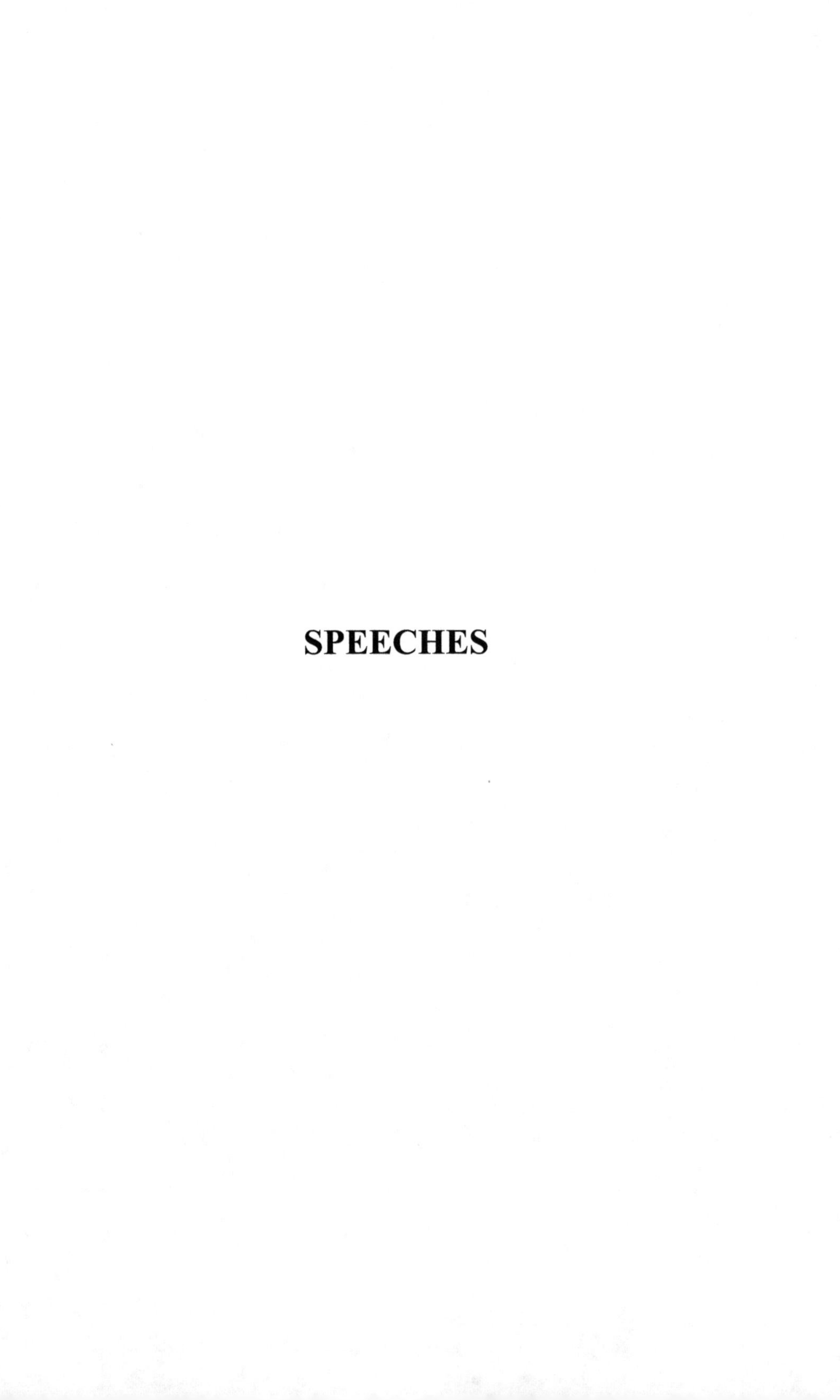

SPEECHES

ICE BREAKER

[This is the first of five handwritten speeches written and delivered by Archie. "Ice Breaker" is a humorous autobiography. It is a speech written by Archie to introduce himself to a Toastmasters group. Archie says that a Toastmasters gathering is not an ideal place to develop speech-making skills. This item is Archie's earliest surviving autobiographical account. It is dated November 24, 1960. Archie gives this speech in Victoria, B.C. Canada/]

Are you superstitious?

That may sound rather an odd way to begin a personal story, but you can judge as the tale unfolds.

Towards the end of World War I, a fifth child was born to the Anderson family in Prince Albert, Saskatchewan.

Although the name on the baptismal paper showed Archibald Ernest, it wasn't until almost a world war later the I discovered the vital statistics branch of the Government of Saskatchewan had registered me as Archie Edgar.

Which poses the question, Am I really me? If not, who am I? However, since there must be a starting point, let's say I was, I am, and go on from there.

Being just past the middle of a five boy, two girl family has certain advantages.

There's always someone handy to play or fight with and two or three to a bed is certainly cosy on a sub zero night such as is common in P.A. in winter.

In 27, the family edged westward and landed in Edmonton where the opportunities were greater for a larger family and the winters comparatively milder.

It did seem much warmer in Edmonton if only that instead of having weeks of [-29ºC] to [-40ºC] we had days of [-34ºC] to [-51ºC], with the odd break when the backwash of a Southern Alberta Chinook warmed the city briefly.

The Great Depression hit our family hard and I concentrated on the commercial side of education. After my final year I started in the office of a paint and glass wholesale company.

When war came, I was like many other young fellows, a bit dubious as to whether it was phony or not.

I joined a reserve artillery battery while trying to decide and then went to the R.C.A.F. Now this move had a great bearing on my life afterwards.

The Air Force started me out in the deep freeze of Brandon, Manitoba. Did I say it was a case of edging west from P.A.?

Perhaps this was a backing up for a running start. From deep freeze it was a short ski to the main locker at MacDonad, a base about [113 kilometres] from Winnipeg.

Thoroughly chilled after almost a year in Manitoba, even after a blistering summer, I got the nod to go west – some sill thing about Japanese submarines, or was it logs, lurking off the west coast.

Bella Bella was the spot where I landed, which in February was wonderful. The sun did struggle through one day in four months.

This may seem weird, but that started me wavering. Previously I had visited the coast in summer, liked it, but didn't realize how much until that mid-winter experience.

The next move carried me across Canada to Halifax and overseas. A few months in England and I was ready for more touring.

This time we backed up to South America to get a running start for the Far East. Three years in India – East Pakistan and I was heading back west once more.

Native bearers thought I was a White Hindu which gave me preferential treatment.

As with many others, settling down was not too easy. A second string in my bow had to tried. Writing had long been a hobby. Now it became a means of livelihood.

Five years writing continuity was an experience that showed me what really goes into the making of the much maligned commercial content of radio and TV.

The westward move was not an overnight thing, although the final decision was spur of the moment – almost.

Several visits to Victoria in summer whetted my appetite for more. Besides, we considered it cheaper to move out here rather than back and forth to visit my wife's folks.

Or was it that simple?

But back to that question about superstition. We arrived her with the equity from our Edmonton home, in November, 1956.

Investing in a duplex built up enough for the down payment on a home. Then we set out to work on plans for our "dream" home.

The duplex was sold on a rising market and we waited until this spring to build our present house.

In the space of 15 years we had parlayed a small a small down payment on V.L.A. [Veterans Land Act] to a 50% equity, or about ten times our original investment.

Add to this the fact that we came here on spec.

My wife took a job as well. The B.C. Hydro was on the way up when we arrived.

I caught the bottom rung and gained enough foothold in two years to remain while others were pruned in the retrenching process.

What does all this have to do with superstition?

Simply that I was born on Friday the thirteenth.

ARE BRAINS BEING TRADED FOR MACHINES?

[This second hand-written speech is dated February 6, 1961. A notation at the end Archie writes the time it takes him to deliver this speech. It is five minutes and ten seconds. Could a machine read it faster and better?]

To be more specific – Does automation mean that [people] will eventually sit back and need no more brain than that required to decide which button to press?

Or, as the more pessimistic among us are inclined to believe, have we created a Frankenstein-like monster that will eventually destroy us?

The only danger is that of being satisfied with push button thinking.

From the earliest days of [humanity's] climb from the dark corners of the caves to the present plateau of floodlit intelligence, we have dreamed up ways to improve our productive skills, tools, and machines.

You could say that automation is but the fulfillment of Aristotle's forecast 300 years B.C., of a time when every tool, when summoned or even of its own accord could do the work that befit it.

That last is the key to the differences between machine and human brain. Machines do the work that befits them. Human brains are not so restricted.

The human brain I refer to is more than the pink-grey jelly

that fills our skulls. Remember this –

No machine has the imagination that is to be found in even the least developed human brain.

The machine does not have emotions and sentiments, volition, hopes, aspirations, or take inventive excursions.

In other words, a machine can repeat the same operation several million times without variation but it cannot deviate from the role originally assigned.

And every machine must be started. No machine can fabricate something new, such as a sonnet, a code of laws, an aeroplane, or even another automatic machine.

Mental efficiency has been, is now, and so far as we know, will be in the future, the foundation of every other kind of efficiency.

Of course automatic machines have certain advantages over the human body and over machines that must have human attention.

Some do jobs that people could not do at all or so effectively.

For example, steering a ship, manipulating an atomic particle, directing a rock missile, or controlling rapid chemical reactions.

However, there are vital differences between the human brain and the most precise automatic machine.

A machine may work out the what if something goes wrong and signal the fact, but the "how" and the "why" of it are in humanity's province.

Automation is not new. In 1496 Leonardo da Vinci planned an ingenious machine for sharpening needles at the rate of 40,000 an hour.

The more we automate, the more important will the human brain become.

Machinery, no matter how intricate, will never replace humanity's specifically human qualities, our ability to think, to analyze, to balance and synthesize, to decide, and to act purposefully.

Of course, automatic machines must take over the drudgery of routine and the back breaking jobs, but we must conserve and train ourselves for operations requiring judgement and highly developed skills.

One thing you may be sure of in the uncertain world – the human brain will never become obsolete!

YOU GET THE TV PROGRAMMES YOU DESERVE

To go a step further, you are also responsible for the TV programmes which you do not watch.

By the way. This applies to the people who dismiss all TV as so much trash, the same people who either do not own sets or view the video offerings with a rather jaundiced eye.

You don't think this makes you to blame? That's where you're wrong.

Cast your mind back to the latest occasion when that knight of the Korny West started shooting holes in the living room atmosphere.

What did you do? Of course, you retaliated by shooting him down, either with a twist of the channel selector or the complete obliteration of a switch off.

This, you ask, is aiding and abetting? Absolutely.

You who look over the evening offerings and do not even turn on the set are equally to blame.

Let us revert to radio for a moment, where I had the opportunity to study listener reaction.

Listeners to the lower form of much and programmes as it were, have always been the most articulate and voluble.

These vociferous fans, though usually in the minority invariably dictate what it presented on radio and TV is no different.

After all, TV is little more than radio with a seeing eye camera.

As for you and I, whether we like or dislike a particular programme is usually our secret so far as those that can do anything about it are concerned.

So you see, by not fighting the supporters of corn, you are in effect joining them. After all, broadcast managers are not psychic.

They can judge what the listener wants only from what they are told.

Whether it's a good situation or not, TV is business and must operate at a profit. Naturally the people who pay the bills want a return on their investment, which is quite reasonable.

In the same position I'd take the same stand. Wouldn't you?

What's the solution? It's simple. Do you remember when flying saucers were in the news and the rash of cartoons that lampooned?

There was one in particular which pictured someone confronted by several creatures from outer space.

One of the creatures is speaking and says, "To heck with your leader. Take me to Marilyn Monroe."

Far be it from me to spoil anyone's fun, but we must ask to see their <u>leaders</u>.

In other words, whether it's a complaint or a commendation, the next time TV irks or pleases, rush to your nearest pen and paper.

Tell the TV station and the sponsor. Don't let it rest there. Stir up others who feel as you do. Let them know that you aren't sitting back while TV sinks to the lowest level.

You're doing something constructive.

When you come right down to it, television has the greatest potential as an entertainment and educational medium, but it must be put on the right channel now, while there is still time.

You take action and you'll not only get the TV programmes you deserve, but more important, the ones you want.

MAKE MINE VITAMIN "C"

[This healthy speech is dated March 13, 1961. It's timed at five minutes and thirteen seconds.]

We've heard a great deal about Vitamin "C" or ascorbic acid in recent years. However, its importance has been realized for many years.

When fresh fruit and vegetables were not available on long sea voyages, the British sailors were given lime juice to prevent scurvy.

This incidentally led to the name "lime juicers" and later "limeys".

But all this is aside from my purpose tonight. Everyone is vitamin conscious these days and we tend to overemphasize the value of concentrated doses of vitamins.

Near miracles are constantly being claimed by purveyors of vitamin tablets. Don't get the idea I'm in that category but I reiterate – Make mine vitamin "C".

Now I admit that ascorbic acid is no elixir nor panacea.

You may have read about athletes being fed extra doses of vitamin "C".

One instance with a football team where some took large quantities of ascorbic while others had none. Those taking vitamin "C" had fewer bruises and aches, and injuries healed much quicker.

Here is my personal experience. As long as I can remember I've had colds, from two to four a year.

My druggist happened to mention how he took vitamin "C" to lessen cold misery. I decided to make a test – twice a day.

When sore throat warned, I increased to as much as 1,000 milligrams a day. Result – no colds in over two years.

Probably get one now, but I still will make mine vitamin "C".

SOUNDS OF MY LIFE

[This final speech is undated.]

Listen! No I didn't drop a pin. One of the most important sounds of my life is that which I hear most imperfectly – my own voice.

If you have never heard yourself from the outside as it were, try it with a tape recording.

I have yet to hear any person who actually recognized their own voice or at least admitted it the first time a tape was played back to them.

But, to start at my beginning. The first sound probably went like this.

Then there was a steady progression, although I, in common with most, am scarcely in a position to document the first few years.

However, since I was one of a family of seven, I heard how younger ones were bombarded, from the first kitchy-koo on to – and the father bear said, "Who's been sleeping in my bed?

One sound which haunted me for years was the moo of a cow. But I have since got even with bossy by downing large quantities of milk.

The crunch of a shoe on snow in sub-zero weather, to the drowsy hum of insects in June, and the thunderous reports of summer electric storms – all added to my sound memory.

But it is such things as a barker's voice that really stay and conjure up pictures.

My sound life was broken into by a news series as World War II.

A thousand room mates at Manning Pool – the snorts, snores, and mumbles cut short as always by Reveille.

Even sound association had upsets – a Yiddish speaker with an English accent. I couldn't understand any of the English at first.

India with its multitude of noises, mostly voices – beggar routine stands out.

Noise of a plane – I still don't look directly up after being trained not to.

Boat fog horn sound effect – one reason I came to the coast.

Return to civy street – new words, sound of coffee break.

Consider how sounds affect you. One person's music is another person's noise. Rock and Roll by my son.

However, every person here has a sound in common – buzzer. [Speech time's up!]

MORE POETRY

Although Archway: Lifetime Rhyme contains most of the poetry Archie writes and files, the current volume includes a few more poems that are filed separately and presented here for the first time in the Archway series.

Tomorrow And Yesterday

'Tomorrow' and 'Tomorrow' we've all heard her say;
So how could we believe, this really is the day.
It isn't that her act won't set all to grieving,
But we've reached the point where, 'seeing is believing'.

And even when the time has come and gone again,
There'll be a doubt to plague us every now and then --
Did Grace intend to leave our tent and go away,
Or did our southern "Suburb" hog-tie her one day?

Path Parade Presents

A winding path of rusty clay,
Beat smooth by barefoot, flat and splay,
Clings close to slope of green clad hill,
Which seems a giant old and ill;
A sleepy mound with breeze for sigh
And misty cloud wrap from the sky.

Quaint cloak wrapt dolls come trudging down
The Khasi women head for town,
With dunce cap basket on each back
And head strap holding up the pack
Such loads they lift without a blink
Would make a circus strong man think.

Around a bend there comes in sight
A village huddle, wan and white
As crowd of dusty giant sheep,
Clutches close, pasture slanting steep,
The trail twists on, and cuts a way
Through nature's blooms, so bright and gay.

One colour scheme of flower crop
Persists from bottom to the top --
A thick tall leaf wall sets the scene,
For orange, yellow, red, and green,
As if a painter's random splash
Had picked out tints and hues to clash.

No bald pate top the tree clad heap;
But man cut strip allowed a peep
Across to terraced steps so great --
For mighty feet of human's fate,
While distant earth folds, misty blue,
Hold promise of an endless view.

Here reign the scented pine trees proud;
Free, undisturbed by local crowd,
So clean and fresh in lofty realm,
With nature's whims to take the helm
And steer above all human grime --
To drift, unchecked, an ageless time.

(October 17, 1944)

Peace Unlimited

Through valley of the war,
We Struggled in the dark
To reach a distant hill
Where hope had struck a spark.
In dullest of the gloom,
The blackest of the night,
We always saw the hill
With ever shining light.

Flame is mounting higher,
With beacon just ahead,
As we leave the shadows;
Our memories; our dead.

When freedom blazes forth
To spread around the world,
The challenge will be peace,
Its tattered flag unfurled.

The heritage of all
We must again express,
No colour, race, or creed,
Rates share that's more or less.

Each human of this earth
Has place in world estate,
And right to lasting peace
As rulers of our fate.

(September 16, 1944)

Pin Up

Of course it will be nice
To buy a shirt again,
But who can give advice
Of certain where and when?
And, just to prove to some
That buyer never wins;
When the time does come,
They'll add a dozen pins.

Bald Truth

To most men it is plain
Ladies all are more vain --
Or have you seen to date
Lady fair with shiny pate?

Nothing Sacred

They've chased us on the sidewalk,
They've chased us on the road;
They've chased us riding empty,
They've chased us with a load;
They've chased us in the morning,
They've chased us late at night;
They've chased us hit and run, style-
We've had the chance of flight;
They've chased us once too often;
All chivalry is dead
When they run into a house
And hit us while in bed.

[Editor's note: The untitled poem which follows has two versions with slight variations in word order for rhyme.. One begins with the eight lines placed first here. The longer version is typed in a manner reflecting the topic. That typing scheme is preserved here.]

That nasty toothy leer
And tight lipped sneer
Has gone too far at last
Leaving us undone & past
We could give up the pants
With scarcely backward glance
Even letting go of coat & skirt
But now it's got man's shirt.

Said the
        zipper
to the
        button
Your day
        has come
now we
        take over
something
        which leaves
you lower
        than dirt
yes I
        mean we
will now zip up
        man's shirt

Said the
                zipper
to the
                button
your day

has come
now we
take over
something
which leaves
you lower
than dirt.
yes we do
mean we
will now
zip up
men's shirt.

Where riches of the earth abound
Where cowboys on the range are found
Where winters freeze and summers fry
My own sweet land of far off sky.

Where ghosts of bison still do roam
Where streams begin & rivers foam
Where bones of dinosaurs still lie
Oh wondrous land of far off sky.

Where prairie rolls to mountain peaks
Where farmer tills & miner seeks
Where blizzards blow & chinooks sigh
You'll find the land of far off sky.

As far apart as poles away
As far remote as night from day
Are facets of this wondrous land
From frigid peak to jungle stand.

The maharajah flaunts his pomp
To his pachyderms sway & stomp
But turn from jewels & waving
To watch the millions flags clad in rags.

The arid land north from Lahore
And East Bengal where monsoons pour
Are merely fragments of mosaic

What now of colours you would flaunt
Grey shiv'ring skeletons, bare and gaunt?
On naked ghosts of summer past
With rustling shrouds in wintry blast.

Sat high above the clouds
Watched jig-saw shapes
As frozen lakes slid by
While moon peered from murky edge
Pale salute to sun on other side
Then sudsy mix far below
Hid shivering earth from view.

Clouds took on a frozen tumultuous face
As pink sunlight splashes
Caressed the fluffy tips
Then dust cap swept away
To bring a million ghostly lakes
Scattered splashes to congeal
Frigid spots of sweat
From rigid glacial dome of blue
Midget jumbo dangles on a pendulum arc.

Limitless great mother mass
Wet netted covered withered blue
Welded fractures slashed
By sullen grey of watery
Waste falsely promising moist reprieve
To explore afoot such unworldly world
Took people who knew fear
And yet must press on.

In tiny corner of their weak endeavour
Became more gods than people
But many felt unflexing grip
That crushed life force
And claimed its due
From all their Eden warmth & peace
No one skirts awesome might
Unconquered dormant challenge.
Prepared to squeeze slight warmth
That may cling for fleeting seconds
Till swallowed by utter chill of universe
Scarce touched by tiny specks
Of stars that glow greater than humans
Thoughts could ever grasp.

Worn earth patched
With hues of green
And gold and spotted
With eczema of works human
Velvet seams to keep the whole intact.

Headlights stab the dark
Cut green tunnels

Night closes in behind
Then roof flips back,
To expose a million stars
Faint tears in blackest roof.

Majestic giants in green plumed robes
Stand as proud sentinels
Of beautiful countryside
Mauve carpet of the moors
Heather clings to flat
And barren moors.

Frightened red & black topped mushroom homes
Huddle by the steel clad path
Of swift & clacking train.

Brighter tone of new warm brick
Stares glassily at speeding train
Then we break clear for brief stretch
Of fresh green robed land again.

Silver worm of tube
Burrows under city's feet
Breaks forth near edge of busy heart
Blinking in the light.

I searched the town from store to store
Found many gifts there by the score
But still in on store could I find
Exactly what I had in mind.

Made a Christmas wish
Same as for Year New
But repeating wish
Made for year or two.

Simple wish, and yet
Can't see how it can
Ever be fulfilled.

A lovely wreath upon the wall
Heart shape for Christmas and for love
A small and dainty wreath that's all.
Couldn't it be roost for turtle dove?
Behind the skill was love & more.

With beauty of a rose
In most delightful bloom
Her magic always gives
New light to any room.

Each day would start out right
Would really be worthwhile
If it would just begin
With her good morning smile.

No Cream?

What's a slip between friends
When it is one that sends
Now honey it would seem

That you skimmed off my cream
Since milk is spilt & gone
Why sit & worry on
So, hon, you may as well
Just wait & let blood tell.

Delightful to know, pert and pretty
Eyes truly youthful pattern weave
Beauty shines as lights of city
On any clear cool summer eve.

Reserved a bit but open heart
Adorable you must believe
Her fresh charm draws one from the start.

Now, honey child, don't get bored
When I say we can't afford
So many things, not just one.
Which we need for use & function

Don't forget that you and I
Have what money cannot buy
Touch or nod, a sideways glance
Memory tunes at any dance.

This we <u>can</u> afford my dear
Countless thoughts & deeds each year
And a never-ending list
Of love for two, since we kissed.

Though when you ask I am dumb

I do enjoy every crumb
Since each bit of midday treat
Comes with love from you, my sweat.

No matter what a Christmas brings
In fun & gifts and other things
Our love has put them in the shade
A gem that can't be bought or made.

Though fortune smile for us so kind
And a million gifts, at least, we find
The total cannot measure up
To drop of our love's brimming cup.

Our Christmas tree cannot be bare
As long as one star twinkle there
With precious message shining bright
I love you darling, day & night.

Remember when, back a way,
(Yes, it was in month of May.)
You would get a line or two
Of verse I wrote just for you?

Maybe well of words ran dry
Or I didn't even try
Matching song of man & wife
The sparkling verse of our life.

Not a word for birthday fare
To remind you that I care

When our double two comes ‘round
No single rhyme could be found.

Now it’s back, we hope to stay
Not a poem every day
But at least enough to show
Versey hubby’s not so slow.

Without words

Of our teasing verse
This one is the worst
As we find our fourth
Is for us the first.

Though you did expect
That with verse I’d stall
Wasn’t it a shock
With no verse at all?

Blame it on our clime
Even on my cold,
But, it did arrive -
Like it, nine days old?

Early luck was out
Drawing one in four
Doesn’t mean a thing
As we’ll miss no more.

Though there was no rhyme

Once upon our day,
Life together is
Poem light & gay.

Minutes grew to hours, days to months, and then
Years we'd been together passed the two times ten.
Full living that we've shared has made sweet time fly by
Which left no time for words – one good reason why.

Think upon our love, ten thousand dreams ago
When two hearts we pledged at least for life or so
Remember all the verse, poems by the score,
How the flow dried up, and then there were no more.

Reason is so simple, or it would seem to be
That as I explain, I know you will agree
Fate has filled our cup so full of life & love
And give what mere verse never could be above.

Almost a thousand weeks you know
There has been one who loves you so
And tried at least a million ways
To please for seven thousand days.

There is one hope I know we share,
Always & ever as we care,
To be together as beforehand
At least seven thousand twice – or more.

Turned Not Burned

You bring home the bacon
TO please me honey, dear
(That I am off all meat
Is neither there nor here.

I put away my books
And trotted home at noon
While you worked on & on
All through the afternoon.

I even shopped a bit
For odds & ends we need
To keep our pantry stocked
With things on which we feed.

The answer's plain enough
And whom am I to shirk;
When I am here at home,
While you are out at work.

It needs no master mind
To tell the tables turned
So, help yourself my dear
I hope that nothing's burned.

May this year's birthday bring
More of worthwhile pleasure
As we share gift of love
Happiness to treasure. (1975)

She has special magic
Though may not be aware
Always at the ready,
No matter when or where.

There's no need to worry
Her magic will do harm
She has special aura
To captivate & charm.

Here's one she'll always please
With her soft, gentle style
As I fall under her spell
Of her sweet, magic smile.

House Boss

Around our house we're at a loss
When people ask us 'who's the boss?'
But soon we'll have the answer right
Without resort to quarrel of fight.

Gardener's View

Let me have but a plot of land
Where I may freely try my hand
Wooing Nature, in hopes that I
Will find sweet favour in her eye.
I have no wish for far-flung fields,
Or crops of grain with wondrous yields.
I stand on tiny plot each Spring
And am .. by Nature's grace .. the King.

To plant a seed and watch it grow;
This miracle of life I know
And welcome such a worthy toil,
Confirming bond of me and soil.

Who can lay claim to greater deed;
War ace, or one who plucks a weed
To help the plant of seed to grow?
Death or Life ... to reap and sow

Happy Day

Once upon your birthday,
When you were twenty-one
Life began new chapter
Full of love, laughs, and fun.

The years you've added up
Have done you little harm.
Each birthday seems to bring
A little extra charm.

May you carry on
And kick your heels up too
Now and every day
At least 'till ninety-two.
Birthday message for Fred

(dated January, 1980)

Bought a birthday card
Especially for you
Wished you all the best

With added joke or two.

Fancy card's at home
While we are all at sea
Here's a substitute
Hope you'll accept with glee.

Here's to petty, pompous Joe
Pleading for another chance
To guide us through year or so
In erratic national dance

(Dated February 14, 1980, when Joe Clark is Canada's prime minister for six months between Pierre Trudeau's governments.)

Arm Burger

We may think meat is hard to get,
But alley-cat, and no one's pet,
Must surely have more meatless days.
This time it is the man who pays
As pussy, which can mean no harm,
Takes sample – restaurant owner's arm.

NOTES ON SCRAPS OF PAPER

Unfinished writings?

Bits and pieces of Archie's writings are found on scraps of paper of various sizes, colours, and vintages. One or two are typed but most are in Archie's handwriting in ink or pencil

For the most part, there is no indication of dates or contexts for much of this writing.

Some of these writings are one-liner jokes and others are ideas which may have been for elaboration later but later doesn't come in Archie's busy life. There are also a variety of poems never before published.

In arbitrary order, essentially ranging from the smallest to largest pieces of paper, here are the remainder of Archie's writings on scraps.

Couple are standing on front steps as visitors with several children leave. Wife says to husband, "And when they came as newlyweds they only intended to spend a week here."

Couple are sitting in bedroom bundled up in coat and wearing ear muffs. She says to husband, "Why do you think they turned off the heat, if they want us to stay longer?"

In horse race one horse is behind but extra long nose reaches over finishing line. Owner explains to friend: "Just an angle I figured for winning races."

One rabbit to another, "What became of my lucky man's foot?"

Dog sitting up says to owner, "Well, you told me to speak, didn't you?"

I thought that double feature meant an extra chin.

Scene is mountain switchback road with car speeding out into space at a bend. Passenger says, “I’m sure we should have turned here.”

What do you call someone from Ireland who stays out all summer? - Paddy-o-furniture.

Some people don’t like getting up in the morning. Others just lie about it.

Look so good out the morn, just left it out.---

Stranger notices how polite motorists are here. They always honk before they knock you down.

Warning to visitors- When a motorist waves you by it’s no invitation – just a dare.

Cry has changed from “Get a horse!” to “Get a pedestrian.”

In the old days when the world was flat, once you got ahead that was it until you dropped off the edge.

If men’s clothing fashions are sensible, why are there cuffs, collars, and ties?

Now, if you keep going, eventually you are back behind the people you passed.

Knobs on milk bottle tops are for covering over caps. A blind person says they were for holding convenience.

Noticing the new walk and stop lights for pedestrians, one person says to a hurrying companion, "Don't run. It says 'walk'."

People who go crazy on December 25th are Christmas crackers.

The first woman on December 24th is Christmas Eve.

Young African women are jungle bells.

One spaceship rocket pulling another is missile tow.

When Christmas is Sunday it's holly.

What do you call a cat that digs in the sand box? - Sandy Claus.

If you wed several people who are someone's mother - Marry Xmas.

Rip a door opener – Turkey.

Fat on a person at Christmas is plump padding.

Third letter hurried to cover up with soil but we were seen – cranberry sauce.

Sharp tip sofa – Poinsettia.

Five day work week for everyone: Simply divide 365 by 5= 73. Put the extra weeks in summer and have that much more nice weather – maybe.

Holiday idea: Taper off by working half an hour the first day back, one hour the next, and so on. Also, start holidays gradually.

It's becoming obvious that a Russian moon shot with a human crew is imminent. The dual flight of cosmonauts shows this. They send the second cosmonaut to keep tabs on the first to make certain he returns.

It's natural for Russians to be ahead of everyone else in space travel. You can't blame them for wanting to get away from it all.

Children

All of us were children at one time, most of us, anyway. There are some who never grew up and others just revert back.

Our own children are just spirited. Other people's are rude.

Ours are clever. Others are stupid.

In connection with offering items to baby and the one it chooses decides its career: awaken one in the morning to the jingling of coins.

Cereal children

Life is just on bowl of continued story after another these

days.

What I mean is the never ending flow of new breakfast cereals that flow across our breakfast table – sometimes under the table too when some of the unexploded ones suddenly let go with their delayed action.

At that I suppose I'm lucky having just one young fellow gathering boxes of crunchies, hot-shots, and what have you from the shelves of the grocers.

People with half a dozen children must need special rooms for the cereal they buy.

It's not that I object to children having lots of variety, but the insidious way the breakfast food makers foist their food on unsuspecting mothers and fathers.

Junior simply must get the package with the "free bubble gum" inside. The "toasty roasty" pellets aren't really important.

Some cereal boxes have cut-outs on the outside of the box which usually means a cupboard full of cellophane wrapped cereals that my split and fill the room at a moment's notice.

It's not that I object to the young fry getting supersonic ray pistols, miniature frogmen, 3-D pictures of space ships, and all the other modern wonders of our present juvenile world.

But why must they inflict the tons of rustly, raspy cereals on us.

Here's a suggestion. All the parents should form an anti-premium club...

[Editor's note: Perhaps if there were another page to this writing, parents might still revolt against cereal makers who continue to put a "premium" on children.]

Shining example

Have you ever noticed how some people have their shoes shining like new all the time, and others can scuff up and keep their shoes dusty looking at all times?

That's not too bad so long as the two groups don't tangle.

Here's my say tale. I am a dusty-toed advocate and I married into a spit-and-polish family.

Before we get too involved, let me explain that we non-polishers do occasionally give our shoes a bit of a brush. But, perhaps it may be our sensitive souls.

In any case, we can't stand glaring shoe shines. That's why it was such a strain for me in the Air Force. You see, even there a fellow had to pass the odd inspection.

In desperation, I sailed for England. It was better there but you couldn't get away with dull shoes all the time, especially between rain storms.

Then I had a bit of luck. A group of us took off for the tropics and, lucky me, we landed in India.

Here was the perfect spot for the unpolished. In a town of

no paved streets, the dust was so thick they couldn't tell whether you shoes had been polished.

During the monsoon weather, they couldn't see for water.

But that doesn't explain how I get alon. If yg with the spit-and-polish part of our family.

Before we go into that, here's a peculiar result of the dusty and polished mixture. Our little boy insists on having polished shoes at least once a month.

In between times he scuffs in the best tradition of we non-polishers.

Here's how I solve things myself. If you'd ever watched me walking with my wife you would have noticed that I always keep on her left side.

The reason? Well, have a look, (take off shoes one by one and show one polished and the othe not – or, better still – have right half of each shoe polished.

I could carry this idea further with one trouser leg pressed, the other one rumpled and the same with my jacket sleeves. I could be wearing a tie, but with one side of my collar open.

Paint Job

There's no reason why you can't do your own painting. After all, people of all ages carry out painting in one form or another.

Youngsters paint everything in sight, if given a chance. Many women paint themselves.

People paint the town. I won't mention the colour for fear that I am accused of being a "fellow traveller". In fact, I don't even want my copy read between the lines.

Doctors paint the inside of throats. I think there's a horse called a "paint" too.

So, why shouldn't you or I be able to paint a house?

Before you get too far down the list, let me demonstrate the finer points. Brush, yes you need a brush.

A neighbour of mine tried a spray gun one calm day. One of those freak wind storms came up and for three blocks the trees and shrubs turned prematurely white.

Three children in a nearby family got completely coated and the parents phoned their member of parliament.

Apparently they were under the impression that Canada had made an agreement with the U.S. to get around the segregation question by a blanket policy of spraying everyone with white paint.

The matter had been taken up at the United Nations before my neighbour could shut off the paint spray.

Well, we start with a brush. Notice I say start. After half an hour or so, if you paint the way I do, you'll just have to rub yourself back and forth on the house to apply a nice even coat...

...Use white first because it's easier to paint over when you change your mind about the colour.

...Start with more paint than you need. When you stir it you'll probably slop out a quarter of the paint in the tin.

...Let children help. Think of the fun painting on top of a 7 meter ladder with a child clinging to each leg while someone below tells you not to splash the flowerbed.

If the ladder wobbles and you feel yourself slipping, try to drop the paint pail towards the house. In this way, some of the paint will be saved as it splashes on the house.

...After the first flies light on your fresh paint job, settle for the speckled effect, or save money for a stucco job.

Austerity

Simply put, we are buying more from other nations than what we are selling to them. The solution is obvious. We should start consignment selling.

Stockpile our goods in other countries. They pay as they use. Our producers can carry on at full blast, making for full employment.

For funds, we could borrow from other's using stockpiles for security.

Austerity in government means asking for higher taxes in order to spend less.

Although it takes much less time to earn enough money for our wants, our requirements have increased to the point where we work twice as long to obtain a little less than what we'd really like to have.

Doctoring

Ann to doctor – But I thought they now considered colds were caused by weather and climate conditions or emotional disturbances, rather than a virus.

Doctor – Please, after all, I'm the authority.

Sneeze. You tell 'em doctor. I've been a virus since I was – sneeze – high to a sniffle.

Modern times – Instead of a sore throat, people have strep throat. Virus pneumonia becomes Virus X. Old fashioned cold or 'flue are scarcely mentioned any more.

Fall out

You are doubtlessly as confused as I am about the value of fallout shelters and whether there would be enough of anything left even for the survivors.

After extensive study & long cogitation, I have arrived at a solution that is practically fool-proof. But, being an impractical sort of individual, I'm not so sure.

A couple of wars ago (the second big one, as big ones went B.A.B. (before atom bomb) I was honoured with an all-expenses paid trip to India.

Don't ask me what I visited because since they started this Pakistan mumbo jumbo, I can't decide whether it is not East Pakistan or South East India.

After three years of living the life of a rajah (at least that's how the movie makers portray the lush living) I am more qualified that mere natural born inhabitants to give expert opinions of everything oriental.

The solution came one evening as I sat in front of the T.V. watching C.B.C. musical triumph, at times submerged beneath the background rock and roll music of my young son's radio, and reading Time Magazine (should I have said the Victoria Times?), while my wife gave a running commentary on the day's happenings.

From the inner recesses of my ever active mind came the key word "yoga".

The answer was almost too good – but no, it had to be the only solution.

Without going into great detail, (of course I could) it is simply a matter of studying and practicing yoga.

Instead of investing money which I haven't available, to build a shelter which may protect or may become a tomb, I have begun a concentrated study of yoga with special emphasis on – breath control.

Of course I have a natural affinity to breathing, having done it in varying degrees for many years.

Instead of stressing civil defence, the government should arrange show courses in Yoga. Then, if the time should come, a few minutes warning would be ...

[Sorry reader, ending lost. We may never know how yoga could save the world. Perhaps "breath control" is about calming down and not saying anything obnoxious, such as "We declare war."]

IH A UN

Dentists can be human. I have an understanding with mine. There is none of this one-sided conversation that has made so many dentists unpopular.

Most people must be satisfied with an "ugh, guggle" response to even the simplest queries.

I feel far superior to such poor gurglers who haven't learnt how to talk through a mouthful of knuckles and miscellaneous dental tackle.

Once the dentist (who else?) gets me strapped down and the clamps are in place, our dialogue follows this pattern:

"Had any trouble lately?"
"O, othig ew peak of".
"How about that one?" tapping a sensitive molar.
"Ow! A ih oar."
"Hm." The dentist adds the drill to the already overcrowded opening. Then, after my hysterics subside somewhat, "See, it didn't hurt."
"Ih ihn't uht ew ew een."

Comes a lull while the dentist swills out my mouth with a mouthwash that needs no "Spit please" reminder.

More drill activity ensues which leaves a cavity (so my tongue reports) big enough to hide all the paraphernalia, including the dentist's head.

But my tooth doctor is too canny to take such an obvious risk.

Then, the conversation (?) might drift off into world affairs while my dentist uses everything but his feet, (at times I wonder about even that) to pack the cement into the excavation.

"Things look bad in Europe."
"Eh, ay ewer oo."
"We're lucky to be living here instead of over there."
"Ee ewere aw."

But, alas, all this is in the past now. It happens after a particularly long session.

Stumbling exhaustedly along the corridor to the elevator, I collide with someone going the other way.

This person's tongue-tied outburst catches me off balance:

"Eye own't ew ook eh ewr owin?"
"Oh owee erh," I blurt out.

Later, at the hospital, the doctor tells me that some of my teeth have come out through the back of my neck.

Even now there are still knuckle bumps across the back of my neck.

"O ell, ih uhs ave ushig em."

Christmas Shopping Instructions

[The editor adds the title to this three page item, handwritten in pencil.]

Soon the jingle of Christmas bells will replace the jingle, if any, of money in many pockets.

The first steps in the jingle dispensing process is the making up of a list of those eligible for presents.

Naturally, one must make a complete list and enemies should be included for a very good reason.

Imagine the satisfaction of watching someone you particularly dislike sampling chocolates that are well seasoned with soap or red pepper.

Of course, enemies have to be worth the expense of else a cheaper gift is in order.

Those less costly presents could be exploding cigars, stink bombs, black face soap, or some such delightful little surprise package.

Incidentally, don’t forget to add the names of a few friends. No Christmas gift list is complete without them.

Once the list is ready, be sure to wait until the last moment or at least pick an extremely busy time. If you happen to enter an uncrowded store, leave immediately.

After all, who can do Christmas shopping successfully without being jostled or trampled underfoot?

Keep the list where it is difficult to retrieve and always take it out when you find yourself surrounded by a group of parcel laden shoppers.

At such times, try to stand in a narrow passage-way and if possible near a glassware counter.

This gives people passing by an opportunity to do a certain amount of damage with the least trouble.

You'd be surprised at the friendly attitude the victims take under these circumstances.

As yes, if you find time when your are not searching for or replacing the list, buy something.

Never let the sales clerk decide for you. Always insist on looking at the entire stock even when you are merely wondering whether you should make a purchase.

Never hesitate about changing your mind. Clerks do not mind in the least if you change your mind after they have wrapped up your purchase.

Such gestures of thoughtfulness are never out of place.

Pay no attention to sizes. A shirt is a shirt.

Just pick up a pretty multi-coloured creation and if the silly clerk insists that you take some particular size, choose a good big number.

Jim or Pete may be small, but who knows how big his neck might be.

A sure test for ties is to wave one in front of a baby or small child. If the infant becomes hysterical with fear that is the tie to take.

Brightness and variety of colour are both essential in ties.

Do not buy all your gifts at once. They may be doubt regarding some.

It would be sad indeed if you gave a present without receiving one in return. So remember to make certain before you buy.

Never forget the true spirit of giving. Price should not be considered. A good idea, however, is to have some price tags made up and to accidentally leave them with the gifts.

When the receiver sees a ten-dollar price tag on a three-dollar article, the effect is highly satisfying.

Care should be taken too, when passing on last year's white elephants, not to return these to the original sender.

If you follow these instructions carefully, it will serve you right.

Undeposited story

[Here is one of Archie's story ideas that he apparently never follows up on.]

Man puts twelve $500 bills in a safety-deposit box. Later he finds they are gone.

He sues the bank but nothing is proven. The court upholds the man but a higher court reverse the decision. The man dies.

Years later a woman brings three of the bills in and a teller recognizes them by the serial numbers.

The woman has had the bills in her safety-deposit box, thinking they belonged to her mother who shared the box with her.

The man dropped the envelop containing the $500 bills behind a desk in the safety-deposit room and it remained unnoticed for almost a year until the woman picked it up, thinking she had dropped it?

Story angle: Perhaps the woman's mother noticed the man drop the envelop and waited for an opportunity to pick it up. Then she held the money at homemaker

Some definite need for cash is her motive. She is somehow prevented from spending it.

Start story where woman presents bills at bank.

An Epilogue of Guesswork

Archie gets his break a few years after the war ends and he has returned to his pre-war employer.

Archie does become a professional paid writer for radio for several years. He leaves this field by choice.

Most of his adult life he works in accounting. Why?

There are family stories attempting to explain what happened, most coming from Archie's spouse Hazel.

Hazel's stories change over time and reflect both her perspective and her interesting way of telling tales.

Archie often defers to her story-telling because he says it sounds more "dramatic" and "exaggerated".

Without completely accepting Hazel's version of Archie, there are some factors which are less likely to be exaggerations or dramatizations.

Evidently, after depriving young people of most of their 20s due to war, the Canadian government decides to restrict the returning young war veterans to two paths.

One is to accept money for advanced education and the other is to accept money for housing.

In Archie's letters to Hazel he takes part in planning a house, but in his diary writings, he expresses an interest in returning to school to improve his future opportunities.

At various points in his life Archie says he might have studied science without specifying what field or botany.

But in his youngest adult years he is taking writing courses and publishing at least one item, "Worthwhile Memorials".

In later years Hazel says she laments the choice for a house instead of an advanced education.

The correspondence between Archie and Hazel on housing, versus Archie's writing about returning to school, imply that Hazel plays a key role in choosing housing over education.

It would be interesting to find out how many other war returnees made the same choice.

Since the next generation of Canadians included only 10% with university degrees, the choice of housing over education may have been common among returnee parents.

Whatever the origins of Archie's choice, the ups and downs of housing markets, not writing, are the prime financial influence on Archie's family.

But this money cushion does not translate into Archie's return to professional writing.

Another story about abandoning the writing field is one that Archie either originates or repeats.

While writing for radio his work is not credited to him publicly, unlike the rolling credits of television and film.

If this is why Archie switches from writing to accounting at the radio station it is bad timing. The radio station is starting to expand into television when Archie switches.

The switch is entirely voluntary, not a reassignment by the broadcasting company. Archie leaves writing for radio just when his name was about to be shown in TV credits.

If the radio station itself is the problem, does he apply to write for another station? Like other matters, there is no written record of any effort of this kind.

Archie and his family then move to Victoria "on spec" but with the financial backing coming from selling his house.

This does not appear to be a move of choice on Archie's part, despite several uprootings during wartime.

He stays there for more than ten years after being released by the military.

But there are no diary entries to support or refute his feelings about re-rooting in Edmonton.

He does live there from childhood to early adulthood. All his friends and immediate family are there.

The only conflict on written record concerns members of E.T.C. (Eastwood Tennis Club). Apparently at least some members object to the pre-war "clique" running things.

On the positive side, although Archie writes some good things about his visits and the mild winter during his military posting on the west coast of Canada, he does not write that he wants to live there instead of Edmonton.

Yet he and his family suddenly move to Victoria. As Hazel tells the story, their garden is destroyed by an early frost and Hazel says they should move to the milder west coast.

Hazel says that Archie replies he was waiting for her to say that. So at mid-autumn they leave.

It may be unusual timing because the move occurs just after their child starts school, with the same teacher who teaches his parents.

Why would the move not occur before school or at least after Grade One?

The child is young, but like his parents, for most of their lives, he does not know any other home except Edmonton. Like his parents, all his friends and family live there.

This is not a critique of the move or its consequences over the long run for the child. He benefits by developing lifelong skills of adaptability, mobility, and learning.

Although Hazel's version of events are dramatic and exciting, her story also includes a major omission.

Hazel came from a very nuclear family with two immigrant parents. One of them lamented leaving her land of birth and unsuccessfully attempted to return her family there.

Yet Hazel's family left her behind. Her youngest brother died as a young adult. Her second youngest brother moved east and abroad.

Hazel's only remaining sibling in Edmonton, her sister Winnie, married a professor from the Atlantic coast and moved to Victoria.

Hazel's father retired and her parents moved to Victoria too, ostensibly for health reasons.

Apparently Victoria's humid air and year-round growing vegetation was considered better for Hazel's father's lungs than Edmonton's dry air.

Victoria was also well-known for its U.K.-ethnic population, including retirees coming directly from the U.K.

This was an appropriate place for Hazel's mother's nostalgia for her European place of birth.

After a lifetime of solid integration into her family and living in close proximity to it, Hazel was highly motivated to want to leave Edmonton.

Meanwhile, Archie's parents and generations of the rest of his family still lived in Edmonton. Only his oldest brother Gordon died as a young adult, before the war.

The other exception were his three surviving brothers.

Lorne moved to Montréal. Jim returned to live in the U.K. after the war. Wally remained in the military and was posted in Germany.

Of his remaining siblings, only Archie's two sisters, Edna and Helen remained in Edmonton.

The pull of Hazel's family was much stronger. Essentially, Archie and his family moved to Victoria because Hazel missed her family.

Fortunately, there were work opportunities for both Archie and Hazel when they suddenly packed up and moved to Victoria.

Archie's writing indicates that he finds many job opportunities when he and his family arrive in Victoria.

There are no writing opportunities? Victoria has several radio and television stations, as well as newspapers.

Although Archie does not abandon writing, particularly poetry, his potential as a professional writer is lost when he switches back to accounting and leaves Edmonton for Victoria.

This is the only certainty in this epilogue of guesswork.

However, there is also a demonstrable observation to be made after reading Archie's surviving collection of writings.

Throughout Archie's lifetime, various media continue to publish writing of equal and lesser quality than the writing which Archie shows his ability to write from a young age.

Unfortunately, Archie's full potential as a writer will never be known.

APPENDICES

APPENDIX 1. FIVE YEAR DIARY
APPENDIX 2. LIFE
APPENDIX 3. 1944-1945

[The diary writing in these appendices is transcribed word for word. Sometimes the ink used in the handwritten original pages ran soon after the original writing, making a few words illegible. These words could not be transcribed. In the original longer diary pages of Appendix 3, all the sentences are in a single paragraph. Here the single paragraph of each page is separated into smaller paragraphs for ease of reading. Where possible, the paragraphs are organized according to topic or time of day. When the original writing does not lend itself to this approach, the paragraphs are simply created according to length.]

APPENDIX 1

FIVE+ YEAR DIARY

1937

May 1937

[Editor's note: This diary abruptly begins on May 31.]

(first accounting work)
(beside stove – not CRT)

Monday, May 31: Up at 7:10. Bothered with sore throat. Worked up to 6 p.m. typing some of statements. Saw Grads & Tulsa work out. Wrote to O.C. Davis, Big Pine. Bed 11:30.

June 1937

Tuesday, June 1: Up 7:10. Throat still sore. Busy day. Finished at 5:45. Wrote 3rd N.I.A. assignment. Grads 31 Tulsa 23, 5 minutes overtime. Bed 11:00.

Wednesday, June 2: 7:10 Throat better. Dong a great deal of

sneezing. Through work 5:50. Rode home in rain without rain coat. Retired 10:00 reading Maclean's.

Thursday, June 3: Awoke at 7:10. My cold still holding on. Work piling up. Left office 5:55, after shower. Grads 38, Tulsa 29. Jack went alone. My day over 11:00.

Friday, June 4: 7:10 as usual. Cold still sticks. Got day books up to date again. Forgot Duke of Windsor & Mrs. Simpson married yesterday. Work done 6:00. Social Credit School. Give up 11:45.

Saturday, June 5: Made own breakfast. Through work 12:55. Bought new shirt & tie. Sent $8.00 to N.I.A. Got haircut. Tulsa 46, Grads 35. Reserved seat. Complete day 12:00.

Sunday, June 6: Awoke at 12:00. Weekly bath. Cloudy day. Bought Sunday Mirror, Sunday News, Chicago American. Jack didn't come. Mother, Edna, Helen, and I had Revels. Bed 9:45.
Monday, June 7: 7:10 again. Finish 5:40. Final game Grads 27, Tulsa 19. Certainly a relief. Grads showed more of their old form. End of day 11:00.

Tuesday, June 8: 7:10 as usual. Through work at 5:45. Saw "Under Two Flags". Thought I was to meet Jack at show. He claimed I was to call on him. All 11:00.

Wednesday, June 9: Still 7:10. Slow morning. Rain at noon. Left office 5:35. Back to work at 7:00. Ben didn't show up so came home. Retired 10:00.

Thursday, June 10: 7:10 on the dot. Work done 5:35. Went back at 7:00. Quit at 9:00. Cold has not left yet. Jim returns tomorrow morning. Another day 11:30.

Friday, June 11: 7:10. Jim arrived home. Brought me a pen knife. Also a 12 sided English Threepence piece. Saw "Libelled Lady". All over 11:30.

Saturday, June 12: 7:10. Completed work at 12:55. Took books to library. Didn't bring any out. Bought Sunday News, Mirror, Chicago American. Bed 11:15.

Sunday, June 13: 12:00. First swim of the year. From 3 to 5. Dove off low board several times. Off high once. Sun bath but no sun burn. 10:30.

Monday, June 14: 7:10 approximately. Letter from Davis. Work complete for day 5:50. **Did fourth N.I.A. assignment. Hard until I got started.** All today 11:30.

Tuesday, June 15: **Sent entry in contest to P & G**. Had baseball workout at Technical with Social Credit young people from 7 to 9 after work 5:45. 11:15.

Wednesday, June 16: 7:10. Finished work 5:35. Swimming 7:30 to 9:30. Bought 8 swim ticket. Did considerable diving off high. 11:15.
Thursday, June 17: Work done 5:35. Got book Chats on Feature Writing from N.I.A. back to work 7 to 9. Day complete 11:30.

Friday, June 18: 7:10. Left office 5:40. Baseball workout at Tech 7 to 9. Picked up sides as usual. Our side won. Home & through 11:00.

Saturday, June 19: Finished work 12:40. Bought swimming trunks, string shirt, grey flannel pants, Sunday News & Mirror, also Chicago American. Swimming 7 to 9. 11:30.

Sunday, June 20: Nothing much doing. Sat around. Wrote letter to Davis at Big Pine. All had Revels and ice cream. Enough 9:45.

Monday, June 21: Bad cold most likely from Saturday's swimming. Through work 5:40. Had 2 Revels. All for today 11:00.

Tuesday, June 22: 7:15. Cold still bad. Finished work 5:30 sharp. Bought cold drops. Louis knocked out Braddock 8 rounds. Bed 11:00.

Wednesday, June 23: Still coughing considerably. Mr. Glover gave me a letter at 5:30. Finally away at 5:45. Loafed as usual 11:00.

Thursday, June 24: 7:15. My cold about the same. Work over 5:30. Jack & I saw "Polo Joe" and "Isle of Fury" at Avenue [movie theatre]. Shaved. All once more 11:30.

Friday, June 25: 7:15. Continue coughing. Left office 5:40. Had two Revels. Nothing much doing. Finish today 11:00.

Saturday, June 26: 7:15. Work done 12:40. Bought Sunday News & Mirror & Chicago American. Not much to do. Went to bed. 11:30.

Sunday, June 27: 10:00. Swimming until 2:00. Badly sunburned. Golf out in Bay. Sat around reading. Gave up. 10:00.
Monday, June 28: 7:10. Completed day's grind 5:35. Getting hot. Nothing doing after supper. Fifth N.I.A. Assignment. 11:00.

Tuesday, June 29: 7:15. Very hot. Highest [37°C] in the shade, say it was [68°C] in the sun. Work done 5:40. Simmered 'til 11:00.

Wednesday, June 30: 7:15. Work done for day 5:40. Jack & I saw "After The Thin Man". Very good. William Powell & Myrna Loy. Home 12:15.

July 1937

Thursday, July 1: 9:30. Played golf in afternoon. Went swimming after supper. Walked home in rain. 11:00

Friday, July 2: 7:15 Work over 5:35. Letter from Davis. Mr. Glover failed to return in time to pay us. Nothing much until bedtime. Had a Revel. 11:00.

Saturday, July 3: 7:15. Left office 12:35. Sent $10. to N.I.A. Mother left to stay at Dean's house to mind kids. 11:00.
Sunday, July 4,1937: 9:00. Jack arrived at 12:00 to go swimming. Home again about 3:00. After supper Edna bought Revels. Wrote Davis. 10:00.

Monday, July 5: 7:15. Finished work 5:40. Read N.I.A. material. Wally is down at Sarcee. Left here Friday. 10:30.

Tuesday, July 6: 7:15. Worked until 6:15 to get out statements. Not much to do. Cleaned my bicycle chain. Finally retired 11:00.

Wednesday, July 7: 7:15. Fairly busy. Away from office at 5:45. Jack and I went swimming. Played Monopoly. Finished 12:00.

Thursday, July 8: 7:15. Work over 5:50. Played Monopoly. Bob won. Forget it was Jack's 20th birthday until after he had left. Bed 11:30.

Friday, July 9: 7:15. Finished at 5:45. Jack and I went swimming. Low-board taken out for repairs. Had 2 Revels. Bed at 11:30.

Saturday, July 10: 7:15. Through at 12:45. Jack and I saw "A Day at the Races". Fairly good. **Played game of Parcheesi. Added new rules.** 12:00.

Sunday, July 11: 9:00. Swimming with Jack. 8 Swim Ticket used up. Watched them putting up Midway. Reaches almost to the Arena. 12:15.

Monday, July 12: 7:15. Used Jack's bicycle. Work through5:50. Ben on holidays. Jack & I went to exhibition. Met Phyllis in dance pavilion. Bed at 12:30.

Tuesday, July 13: 7:15. Finished work at 5:30. Went to Dean's house where I was entertained for my birthday, by Phyllis, Olive, and Kay Meredith. 1:00.

Wednesday, July 14: Rained steadily all day. Left at 1:15. Went to Dean's for dinner. Al went to Realto [movie theatre], "We have our moments". Supper at Dean's. Phyllis feeling ill. Left 8:30 – all 11:30.

Thursday, July 15: More rain. Took street car to work. Finished by 5:40. Nothing much doing. Finally went to bed 11:30.

Friday, July 16: 7:15. Left office at 5:45. Jack & I went to exhibition. Over fence as usual. Spent about $1.75. Home to bed 1:00.

Saturday, July 17: 7:15. All done. 12:35. Had haircut. Did nothing all afternoon. Went to exhibition. Fence route. Home & bed 1:30.

Sunday, July 18: 11:00. Went swimming with Jack from 12:30 to 2:15. Home to idleness until bed time. All again 11:00.

Monday, July 19: 7:15. Worked until 5:45. Did plenty of nothing all evening. Gave up and retired reading Liberty 11:30.

Tuesday, July 20: 7:15. Work done by 5:45. Jack & I went swimming until 10:00. Home to bed, getting there at last. 11:30.

Wednesday, July 21: 7:15. Through at the office 5:40. Not much to do and plenty of time to do it in. Just skip it. Bed 10:45.

Thursday, July 22: 7:15. Work all through at 5:40. Jack & I went swimming. Back home at about 10:30. Bed 11:00.

Friday, July 23: 7:15. Finished at office by 5:45. Did a great deal of nothing during evening. 10:45.

Saturday, July 24: Completed everything by 12:45. Saw Chrysler demonstration at exhibition grounds. Wasted away another evening. 11:00.

Sunday, July 25,1937: 9:00. Jack arrived 11:30. Didn't go swimming. Washed my bike. Bell brought Gordie up. Had 2 Revels. Shaved. 10:30.

Monday, July 26: 7:15. Worked until 5:40. Jack & I went swimming. Home 10:15. **Did 7th N.I.A. assignment**. Bed 12:00.

Tuesday, July 27: 7:15. Quit on the dot 5:30. **Wrote rough draft of essay for Liberty contest. Trying to write essay for N.I.A. contest.** 9:30.

Wednesday, July 28,1937: All through at 5:30. Nothing much doing. **Started on letter to Sweet Marie, Willards, Ltd**. Finally went to bed 11:30.

Thursday, July 29: 7:15. Left office 5:50. Finished half the statements. **Wrote letter to Sweet Marie**. Bed. 11:00.

Friday, July 30: 7:15. Left office at 5:40. No raincoat so I rode in streetcar. Saw "Old Hutch" & "Kelly the Second" at Avenue [movie theatre]. Bed. 11:45.

Saturday, July 31: 7:15. Didn't get away from office until 1:15. Had my haircut. Jack & I saw "Charlie Chan at the Opera" & "Reunion". 11:30.

August 1937

Sunday, August 1: 10:30. Started eating Fleischman's Yeast. Too cold for swimming, almost like fall. **Jack, Lorne, and I invented new game like Monopoly.** 12:45.

Monday, August 2: 10:30. Still chilly. Jack brought his camera over and took some pictures. **Played new game all evening**. Wrote Davis. 11:00.

Tuesday, August 3: 7:15. Got out of office 5:45. Sent $8 to N.I.A. **Spent evening playing new game**. Will continue where we left off. 11:00.

Wednesday, August 4: Busy day. Left office at 5:50. **Continued new game. Still uncompleted.** Have eaten 12 yeast cakes so far. 11:30.

Thursday, August 5: 7:15. Mailed have the statements. Left office 5:50. Asked Mr. Glover if I could have holidays next week. Shaved. 10:30.

Friday, August 6: 7:15. Finished statements. Out by 5:40. Jack and I went swimming but discovered a gala was being held. **Played new game**. 11:30.

Saturday, August 7: Left office 12:45. Went to Civil Service Picnic with Jack. Saw Laurel & Hardy in "Our relations" also "Human Cargo" at Avenue [movie theatre]. Bed 12:00.

Sunday, August 8: Wiped off bike. Rode out along Highland road. **Trying to solve first 10 names in Liberty's new contest. Got all but one**. 10:30.

Monday, August 9: 9:30. Wally & I went swimming. Went over to Jack's house to hear Mr. Glover sing. He sings well. Home to bed 12:00.

Tuesday, August 10: 10:00. **Made bicycle tour to Fort Saskatchewan to Namao to St. Albert and back home. Took from 10:45 to 3:15. About [77 km.]**. Swimming. 11:30.

Wednesday, August 11: 10:00 swimming with Wally. **Sent away entry to Liberty's Canadian City Contest**. Nothing doing and to bed. 11:15.

[Although titled "May Contest", this item might be the one mentioned August 11.]

It sprawls out in an undecided way. Portions of the country poke through to make the city look patchy. These gaps make Edmonton so indefinite.

One minute you are in the city, then without warning you find yourself in the country.
No, you are in the city.

A strip of country has merely visited you.

To be or not to be. Edmonton cannot make up its mind.

Streets start together. They begin to crowd and finally manage to squeeze three of four of their number out of existence.

Now you have a street; now you have not. Bring on the padded cell.

Edmonton should make another attempt. It is in a hopeless muddle. The planning of Edmonton must have been done at night.

A dizzy collection of indecision is the result.

I give you Edmonton. If you know it you will not accept it even as a gift.

Thursday, August 12: Loafed around. Went for short ride out to the Highlands. Jack & I went swimming. Returned to find Mr. & Mrs. Dean with Berle. 11:00.

Friday, August 13: 11:00. Took Wally to "Wee Willie Winkie" at Capitol [movie theatre]. Went over to Jack's house to hear Russian fliers. They were lost. 12:30.

Saturday, August 14: 9:30 Went down to collect my week's wage. Jack & I bowled 2 games of 5 pins. Saw "Slave Ship" at the Strand [movie theatre]. 12:00.

Sunday, August 15: 12:30. Very windy with a great deal of rain. Jack didn't show up. Wally brought Johnny for supper. Helen came home. 9:30.

Monday, August 16: 7:15. Through work at 5:40. Jack & I went swimming. Rather chilly. Mr. & Mrs. Dean came up again. 11:15.

Tuesday, August 17: 7:15. Finished at 5:50. C. Lennie had my bike at noon so I used Ben's speed demon. Did nothing in the evening. 10:30.

Wednesday, August 18: 7:15. Through work by 5:45. **Wrote article on "The most difficulty thing I have ever had to do" for N.I.A. Only in rough.** 11:00.

Thursday, August 19: 7:15. Used Ben's bike at noon again. **Stayed 'till 6:00 to type article for N.I.A.** Jack & I saw "Three Married Men" & "Wedding Present". 11:30.

Friday, August 20: 7:15. All through at 5:35. Jack, Bob, & I went swimming. Berle went home. Played Lexicon. TO bed 12:00.

Saturday, August 21: 7:15. Left office 12:40. Jack & I had 2 games of 5 pins, then played snooker with Frarey. Rode Jack home on my bike. Played Lexicon. 12:00.

Sunday, August 22: 11:00. Played checkers. Bell came up with the baby & Gordy. She stayed all night. Had chocolate bar. 11:00.

Monday, August 23: 7:15. Left office at 5:50. Had to take parcel to post office. **Did N.I.A. assignment # 9**. Wally came home. 11:00.

Tuesday, August 24: 7:15. Finished work at 5:50. Jack & I went swimming. Rozelle & Irene camp up for the night. Bed once more 11:30.

Wednesday, August 25: 7:15. Work done at 5:40. Blanche visited us. Gordy has been here since Sunday. Jim and Bell are moving. All 11:00.

Thursday, August 26: 7:15. Away from office by 5:45. Read all evening. Others played Lexicon. Bought a deck of cards. Bed 11:30.

Friday, August 27:

Saturday, August 28:

Sunday, August 29: 10:30. Sent yeast labels away for dance book. Wrote Davis. **Wrote about "You can't have everything." Started two minute story for Liberty**. 11:30.

Monday, August 30: 7:15. Through at office 5:45. **Finished two minute story in rough. Tried to get more names in Liberty contest.** 11:30.

Tuesday, August 31: 7:15. Mr. Glover went to Vegreville. Did half the statements. Left 5:40. Read some after supper. 11:00.

September 1937

Wednesday, September 1: 7:15. Finished statements. Did some ledger balance sheets. Worked until 5:45. Nothing much. 12:00.

Thursday, September 2: 7:15. Ben balanced first time. Mailed a few statements. Left office 5:40. Ruth & Edna came up. 11:45.

Friday, September 3: Paid Ben 85¢ for one-third share in an Irish Sweepstakes ticket. Finished mailing statements. Left office at 5:45. Bed 11:00.

Saturday, September 4: 7:15. Left office 12:55. Played snooker with Jack & Ronnie. Bowled 2 games. Jack & I won against Frarey & Ormond. Joined the Y. Had a swim. Home 12:00.

Sunday, September 5: 10:30. Shaved. Jack & Lorne went out to the aerodrome. I cycled out to Beverly. Did nothing in the evening. 11:30.

Monday, September 6: 12:00. Jack & I went out to the aerodrome after I had been to north Edmonton. We went to the Y. Bed 11:45.

Tuesday, September 7: 7:15. Left office at 5:40. **Did N.I.A. assignment # 10**. Read Liberty. Ruth & Edna came up. Complete day 12:00.

Wednesday, September 8: 7:20. Through at 5:45. Jack & I went to the bowling alley for a meeting of the Recreation League. All over 11:15.

Thursday, September 9: 7:20. Left office 5:50. **Back 7:10 to type two minute story for Liberty**. Met Jack & Ronnie at the Y. Played ping pong. Swan. 11:30.

Friday, September 10: 7:17. Finished work at 5:45. Read Liberty.

Had some home made popcorn. **Tried to find some more names in Liberty contest**. 10:30.

Saturday, September 11: 7:17. Left office 12:50. Jack, Wally, Ronnie, & I played two games of snooker. Bowled two games 10 pins. Went to the Y. Got latest Writers' Monthly. All 11:30.

Sunday, September 12: 10:45. Decided to drop latest **Liberty contest**. Read Maclean's. **Could not think of entry for N.I.A. contest**. Shaved. 10:45.

Monday, September 13: 7:17. Ben on holidays. Busy. Left at 5:30. Went to Y for first class. Jack, Tom, Craig, & I bowled a game. Home 12:00.

Tuesday, September 14: 7:17. Succeeded in getting Mr. Glover to back our bowling team under Pilkington's name. Left office 5:30. Finished MacLean's 11:45.

Wednesday, September 15: 7:17. Through at 5:35. Jack & I went to the Y. Played with the basketball. Swam a few minutes. Home to bed 11:30.

Thursday, September 16: 7:17. Left office 5:35. Bowled in Recreation League, 127, 172, 155. Lost three. Only had four players. Finally got home 11:45.

Friday, September 17: 7:17. Through at 5:40. Received letter from Vincent Neece yesterday. Cleaned my generator. So another day. 10:30.

Saturday, September 18: 7:17. Finished 12:30. Mr. Glover rode me up town. Played four games of snooker with Jack, Wall, ' Ormond. Did very little after supper. Read Liberty. 11:15.

Sunday, September 19: 9:30. Wrote letters to Oliver Davis and Vincent Neece. Lay around all afternoon. Evening the same.

10:30.

Monday, September 20: 7:17. Finished 5:40. **Did 11th N.I.A. assignment**. Went to Y. Bowled in Young Peoples Mixed 5 pins – 232, 277, 153. Won 2 games. 12:00.

Tuesday, September 21: 7:17. Through 5:45. Back to office 7:00 until 8:30. Met Jack at bowling alley. Had swim at the Y. Bed 11:30.

Wednesday, September 22: 7:17. Wet, miserable day. Through 5:35. **Worked on N.I.A. monthly contest**. Read Liberty. Nothing more to do. 10:45.

Thursday, September 23: 7:17. Bowling. Won one game. Scores 140, 97, 171. Team beginning to shape up. Home to bed 11:30.

Friday, September 24: 7:17. Through 5:35. Went to Y for a class. Swam a few lengths after. Home to bed finally 11:35.

Saturday, September 25: 7:17. Left office 12:40. Played three games of snooker with Jack & Ormond. Won 2. Got haircut.

Sunday, September 26: 1:00. Jim & Bell came up. Nothing much for me to do. Jimmie to stay with us. So to bed 11:30.
Monday, September 27: 7:16. Through 5:35. Back to Y at 6:30. Bowled 5 pins. Lost three 187, 153, 174. Slipping. Bed 12:00.

Tuesday, September 28: 7:16. Left office 5:40. Back to office 7:00 until 8:00. Went to Y. Won our game in Hit & Miss. Swam a few lengths. Home to bed 12:15.

Wednesday, September 29: 7:15. Through at 5:35. Did some of the statements. Read Liberty. Loafed around all evening. Finally to bed 11:30.

Thursday, September 30: 7:15. Finished at office 5:40. Jack & I bowled in the league, 10 pins. 113, 161, 132. Slipping. Home to bed 12:30.

October 1937

Friday, October 1: 7:15. Letter from Davis. Through work 5:35. Jack & I went to the Y. Took gymnastics. Parallel bar work. Swam. Home & bed 12:15.

Saturday, October 2: 7:17. Finished 12:45. Paid $3.00 more at Y. Returned to office at 2:00 to finish ledger balance sheets. Home 3:30. Bed 12:30.

Sunday, October 3: 12:30. **Drafted in rough another two minute story**. Mother, Edna, & Helen went to Jim & Bell's house. Bed 12:00.

Monday, October 4: 7:15. Through at office 5:45. **Did N.I.A. assignment #12**. Bowled 5 pins. Won one game. Scores 183, 185, 154. 11:25.

Tuesday, October 5: 7:15. Through at 5:50. Class at Y. Did some gymnastics. Swam a few lengths with Ben. Home 12:00.

Wednesday, October 6: 7:15. Through 5:45. Remained at home. Read Liberty. Sent away some Yeast labels for another dance book & ring. 11:30.

Thursday, October 7: 7:15. Through at 5:35. Jack broke his chain on way to the bowling alley. Lost 3 games. Scores 138, 136, 164. Gray beat Clarke in by-election. 12:30.

Friday, October 8: 7:15. Through at 6:00. Went to Y. Swam a few lengths after the class. Home & to bed 11:30.

Saturday, October 9: 7:15. Left office at 12:45. Jack, Ormond, &

I played two games of snooker. Home. Nothing much until bed 12:00.

Sunday, October 10: 1:00. Started scrap book of newspaper clippings. Improved another two minute story. One into the night. 11:38.

Monday, October 11: 10:30. Thanksgiving. Wrote to Davis & also Vincent Neece. Back tire flat. Couldn't find the leak, if any. To bed 11:30.

Tuesday, October 12: 7:15. Left the office at 5:40. Went to Y for a class. Swam a couple of lengths. Home and to bed 11:30.

Wednesday, October 13: 7:15. All through at office at 5:50. Went to meeting of dramatic club at Y. Home early. Bed 10:30.

Thursday, October 14: 7:15. Left office about 5:35. Took two games in ten pins. Scores 109, 123, 120. Have a new player, Bob Hall. 12:00.

Friday, October 15: 7:15. Mr. Glover away since Tuesday, has Quinsy. To Y for class. Missed the basketball. 11:30.

Saturday, October 16: 7:15. Got away about 12:50. Played five games of snooker with Jack, Wally, and Ormond. Got to bed 12:30.

Sunday, October 17: 1:00. Jim & Bell came up. **Couldn't write anything for some reason**. Shaved & retired about 11:15.

Monday, October 18: 7:13. Busy day. Finally through 5:45. **13th N.I.A. assignment**. Bowled 5 pins. Lost 3 games. 185, 110, 183. Down, down, down! 12:00.

Tuesday, October 19: 7:13. Generator stolen. Through at office at 5:45. Dined at the New King Edward Cafe with Speakers' Club.

Took Y class. 12:00.

Wednesday, October 20: 7:13. Through at 5:40. Glover still pick sick with Quinsy. Attended dramatic class. Did some play reading. Home to bed 11:30.

Thursday, October 21: 7:13. Left office 5:45. Bowled 10 pins. Won three. Scores 148, 154, 176. Improving. Finally to bed. 12:30.

Friday, October 22: 7:13. Work done 5:40. Went to Y class. Shaved. Played three games of basketball. Skinned my knee. Home once again. 12:15.

Saturday, October 23: 7:13. Left office at 12:35. Played three games of snooker with Jack, Ormond, & Wally. Bought the usual comics. Retired 12:00.

Sunday, October 24: 11:30. Did a great deal of exactly nothing. Jack stayed for supper. Helen returned from Jim & Bell's place. Bed at 11:30.

Monday, October 25: 7:13. Through by 5:35. Bowled 5 pins. Lost 2. Scores 253, 274, 135. Down, down, & down. Stayed for meeting. 12:00.

Tuesday, October 26: 7:13. Left office about 5:40. Gave autobiography at Spokes club. Weak. Took Y class. Won in Hit & Miss lounge. Home 12:15.

Wednesday, October 27: 7:13. Left office 5:40. Attended meeting of dramatic club. Dad scrapping kitchen walls. Retired around 12:00.

Thursday, October 28: Left office 5:40. Bowled 10 pins. Won one game. Scores 117, 125, 130. Terrible. To bed 12:00.

Friday, October 29: Through about 5:50. Workout at Y. Won in basketball. Home to bed. Finally managed it by 12:00.

Saturday, October 30: Up 7:13 as usual. Left office about 1:00. Bowled a game of 10 pins. 50. Received letter from V. Neece. Bed at 12:00.

Sunday, October 31: 11:30. Snowed a bit but all melted. Wrote Davis & Neece. **Prepared contest for Liberty**. Bed 11:30.

November 1937

Monday, November 1: 7:13. Finally through at 5:45. Won 2 games in 5 pins. Scores 215, 143, 175. Fair. 12:30.

Tuesday, November 2: 7:13. Left office about 5:45. **Gave three minute talk at supper meeting. Subject "Oysters"**. Y class. 12:30.

Wednesday, November 3: 7:13. Through at 5:45. Dramatic club meeting. Gred Valcarrey read play by Barry. All 11:30.

Thursday, November 4: 7:13. Finished about 5:45. Won two games in 10 pins. Scores 136, 108, 127. Terrible. Bed by 12:30.

Friday, November 5: 7:13. Finished at 5:40. Took class at Y. Won game of basketball. Home to bed. About 11:30.

Saturday, November 6: 7:13. Through about 12:45. Played snooker, 3 games. Played Bingo at Avenue [movie theatre]. No luck. Bed 12:30.

Sunday, November 7: 11:30. **Started N.I.A. contest**. Bought Readers' Digest. **Prepared part of speech on "Salt"**. Bed 10:30.

Monday, November 8: 7:13. Work through about 5:45. Bowled 5

pins. Scores 147, 152, 175. Slipping further down. 12:00.

Tuesday, November 9: 7:13. Left office about 5:45. **Spoke on "salt" at dinner club**. Had work out. Just got 2 points in basketball. Bed 12:30.

Wednesday, November 10: 7:13. Left office at 5:40. Trying hard to snow. Rode on street car to Y for Dramatic Club. Future meetings Thursday. 11:30.

Thursday, November 11: 12:30. **Thought over speech for Speakers' club. Wrote a bit on N.I.A. contest**. Played Bingo at Avenue [movie theatre]. Won $1.00. 12:30.

Friday, November 12: 7:13. Heavy snowfall made heavy going. Through about 5:45. Bad cold which I nursed instead of going to Y. 11:00.

Saturday, November 13: 7:13. Left office about 1:00. Didn't have bike. Played three games snooker. Bought spats, rubbers, & underwear. Bingo lost. 12:30.

Sunday, November 14: 11:30. **Wrote part of short short story for Liberty. Did some more on N.I.A. contest**. Saw hockey game E.A.C. 8 Cardinals 5. 10:30.

Monday, November 15: 7:13. Left office about 5:50. Played 5 pins. Won! Acores 141, 171, 175. Terrible. Bowled 135 in 10 pins. 12:15.

Tuesday, November 16: 7:13. Left office 5:50. **Spoke on "Youth's Opportunities in Alberta"**. Workout at Y. **Finished 15th N.I.A. assignment**. Bed 11:45.

Wednesday, November 17: 7:13. Left office about 5:35. **Wrote N.I.A. contest entry in ink**. Played Bingo. Lost. Home to bed 12:15.

Thursday, November 18: 7:13. Through at 5:45. Lost 3 games in 10 pins. Scores 111, 108, 110. Not so good. Rode on streetcar. Bed 12:00.

Friday, November 19: 7:13. Through at 6:00. Went by street car to Y. Lost in basketball. Left for home early. Finally to bed around 11:30.

Saturday, November 20: 7:13. Work over 12:50. Played 3 games snooker. Sore wrist. Saw picture at Avenue [movie theatre] "Wake up & Live". Home to bed 12:45.

Sunday, November 21: 12:00. Saw game at Arena. Cardinals 3 Southside 5. **Began preparation for 3 minute talk**. Wrote Davis. Bed 11:00.

Monday, November 22: 7:13. Left office about 5:45. Played 5 pis. Won 3 games. Scores 211, 149, 183. Slight improvement. Did 16th N.I.A. assignment. Home 12:00.

Tuesday, November 23: 7:13. Finished at office about 5:55. King Ed for supper with club. Y class. Home to bed getting there about 12:30.

Wednesday, November 24: 7:13. Left office at 6:00. **Went to Y for dramatic club meeting. Decided to work on a comedy**. Home to bed 11:20.

Thursday, November 25: 7:13. Left office 5:45. Won 2 games 10 pins. Scores 169, 154. Slight improvement. Sat out last game as we had 7 players. 12:00.

Friday, November 26: 7:20. Through at 5:35. Took class at Y. Won in basketball. Started to use rope vaulting & rings. Home to bed 12:00.

Saturday, November 27: 7:13. Left office about 12:45. Played 3 games snooker. Played Bingo. Lost. Home to find Jim & Bell visiting. 12:30.

Sunday, November 28: 12:15. Saw hockey game. E.A.C. 5 South Side 3. Paper shoved 5-2. **Prepared 3 minute speech for club. Thought of 5 names**. 11:30.

Monday, November 29: 7:13. Complete work about 5:45. Won 2 games 5 pins. Scores 215, 189, 189. Improving. **Did 17th N.I.A. assignment**. Bed 11:45.

Tuesday, November 30: 7:13. Did statements. Left office 5:45. **Improving in speakers' club**. Y at about 9:00. Home to bed around 12:00.

December 1937

Wednesday, December 1: 7:13. Away from office 5:50. Back at 7:00 to work. Left for Y at 8:00 for Dramatics. Only one other member turned up. All 11:00.

Thursday, December 2: 7:13. Out of office around 5:40. Back at 7:00. Finally got new typewriter. Bowled 10 pins at 9:00. Won 2 games 135, 187. Gained 2 pins. 12:30.

Friday, December 3: 7:13. Through about 5:50. To Y for class. Won in basketball. Now in 2nd place in hit & miss. Home to bed. Shaved. 11:45.

Saturday, December 4: 7:13. Left office at 12:50. Played 4 games of snooker. Played Bingo. Glover left for England. Have Glover's portable. Bed 12:30.

Sunday, December 5: 12:30. Wrote letters to Davis & Neece. Saw hockey game. E.A.C. 9 Cardinals 0. **Typed out speech for Tuesday**. 11:00.

Monday, December 6: 7:13. Left office 5:45. Won 2 games in 5 pins. Scores 139, 147, 174. Not so good. Have a new bowler – Margaret Fulton. 12:00.

Tuesday, December 7: Took street car at noon. Cold. Quit 5:45. **Spoke on "Safety Glass" at club**. Won in basketball at Y. Home to bed 11:30.

Wednesday, December 8: Rode streetcar. Lunch downtown - 30°C. Left office 5:40. Blanche & Jimmy to visit us. Stayed home. 10:45.

Thursday, December 9: 7:13. Through work around 5:40. Won 3 games 10 pins. Scores 175, 195, 126. Average up to 140. Home to bed 12:00.

Friday, December 10: Still using streetcar & taking lunch. Work done about 5:45. Went to class at Y. Home 11:45.

Saturday, December 11: 7:13. Left office 12:30. Bought shirt & tie for Wally for Christmas. Played Bingo & lost. Saw "Saratoga" at Avenue [movie theatre]. 12:00.

Sunday, December 12: 12:00. Went to meeting of dramatic club at Y. Only three others there. Planning Minstrel Show. Did 18th N.I.A. 11:45.

Monday, December 13: 7:13. Left office about 5:40. Won 1 game in 5 pins. Scores 163, 138, 99. Terrible. Home to bed. About 12:00.

Tuesday, December 14: 7:13. Left office at 5:30. Last meeting of Spokes Club of year. Named it "Toc S. Club". Had meeting of dramatic club. Bed 12:15.

Wednesday, December 15: 7:13. Through around 5:40. **Typed out short story**. Loafed around the remainder of the evening.

Bed 11:30.

Thursday, December 16: 7:13. Left office about 5:35. Played 10 pins. Won 3. Scores 160, 125, 184. Won 2 games to get in play-offs. 12:15.

Friday, December 17: 7:13. Finished work 5:45. Went to Y for class. Won one game & lost another in basketball. Home 11:30.

Saturday, December 18: Left office 12:40. Did some Christmas shopping. Played Bingo and lost. Home to bed 12:30.

Sunday, December 19: 12:30. Saw hockey game. E.A.C. 3 Safeway 2. **Tried to write short story. No go.** Bed 12:00.

Monday, December 20: 7:13. Left office 5:40. Aunt Nell is sending clothes and other things. Didn't bowl. Bed about 10:30.

Tuesday, December 21: 7:13. Took lunch. Did some Christmas shopping at noon. Got off at 5:00 o'clock to do some more. Jruesdale up from California.

Wednesday, December 22: 7:13. Left office about 5:30. Got barrel of dishes and boxes of clothes and quilts from Aunt Nell. 11:30.

Thursday, December 23: 7:13. Quit work around 5:35. Got paid. Did some shopping before bowling. Lost 2 games. Scores 92, 115, 135. 12:30.

Friday, December 24: 7:13. Left office at 12:30. Completed Christmas shopping. Jack came around. Finally to bed about 12:00.

Saturday, December 25: 10:00. Gifts received were tie, shirt, socks, garters, arm-bands, gloves, two shaving outfits – one from Jack. 12:30.

Sunday, December 26: 12:00 Played the new game, 4-5-6 Pick Up Sticks. Jim, Bell, & family came up. Went to "Follow The Sheel [?]" at Avenue [movie theatre].

Monday, December 27: 12:00. Loafed around. Played few games of Pick Up Sticks. Bed at last at about 12:00.

Tuesday, December 28: 7:30. Took lunch & rode streetcar. Through about 5:40. Brought home mirror I forgot on Christmas. 11:45.

Wednesday, December 29: 7:13. Finished work at 5:40. Continue to ride the streetcars. Loafed around & to bed 11:30.

Thursday, December 30: 7:13. Left office about 5:45. Jack & I visited Bell & Jim. Home to bed about 12:30.

Friday, December 31: 7:13. Quit work about 4:30. Went by myself to Dreamland [movie theatre] to see "Variety Show". Dick Powell. Home 3:00 a.m.

1938

January 1938

Saturday, **January 1**: Up at 2:00. Read copy of Better English. **Did very little all day**. Went to bed at 12:15.

Sunday, January 2: 11:30. Saw hockey game (?) E.A.C. 12 South Side 3. **For some reason am unable to write anything**. Bed around 12:00.

Monday, January 3: 7:13. Rode bike but took lunch. **Starting to read books suggested by NIA.** Finished work 5:40. Dead during evening 12:00.

Tuesday, January 4: 7:13. Took lunch again. Finished work about 15:30. Stayed at home reading Well's Outline of History 12:00.

Wednesday, January 5: 7:15. Lunch once more. Finished work about 5:35. Continued reading Well's book. Bed about 11:30. Thursday, January 6: 7:15. Worked until 5:40. Bought Better English. Bowled 10 pins. Scores 164 & 81. Terrible. 12:00.

Friday, January 7: 7:15. **Got a raise. Now $14.00**. Paid last N.I.A. instalment. Left work at 5:35. Went to Y. Lost in basketball. Got home about 11:00. Bed about 12:00.

Saturday, January 8: Up7:30. Rode street car. Through work 12:30. Won 40¢ in flipping but lost 25¢ again. Saw "Captains Courageous" at Avenue [movie theatre]. Bought three comics. 12:15

Sunday, January 9: 12:00. Saw hockey game. E.A.C. 6, Cardinals 3. Jim, Bell, & family up. Weather has been mild for last week. 11:45.

Monday, January 10: 11:00. Taking Coronation Day. (Extra day allowed because of the Coronation last year.) Bowled 5 pins. Won 3. Scores 158, 147, 174. Rode home in car with Gordy. Bed 12:00.

Tuesday, January 11: 7:15. Finished about 5:35. Club meeting of New K.E. Dramatic Club at Y. Rode home in car with Louis Simms. Bed 11:30.

Wednesday, January 12: 7:15. Took lunch and rode street car as I did yesterday. Worked 5:40. **Did rough draft of minutes of Toc S. Club & started speech.** 11:15.

Thursday, January 13: 7:15. Left office around 5:40. Bowled 10 pins. Won 1. Scores 149, 145. Played game 5 pins & 1 game snooker. Home & bed 12:45.

Friday, January 14: 7:15. Took lunch & rode street car as usual. Left office about 5:35. **Took class at "Y"**. Won basketball 15-2. Bed 11:30.

Saturday, January 15: 7:15. Finally finished about 12:35. Bought comics & Writers' Monthly. It costs only 25¢ now. Bed about 12:15.

Sunday, January 16: 12:15. Shaved. Lent (?) Wally 10¢. Saw hockey game. Cardinals 6 South Side 3. Wrote some "Dinkys" for Liberty. 11:30.

Monday, January 17: 7:20. Finished at 5:35. Bowled 5 pins. 147, 168, 152. Lost 2. Rode home with Irene Johnstone in her father's car. Bed 11:30.

Tuesday, January 18: 7:20. Continue to take lunch. Promptly 5:30. Left Spokes Club (Toc S.) at 9:15. **Received certificate from N.I.A.** Bed about 12:30.

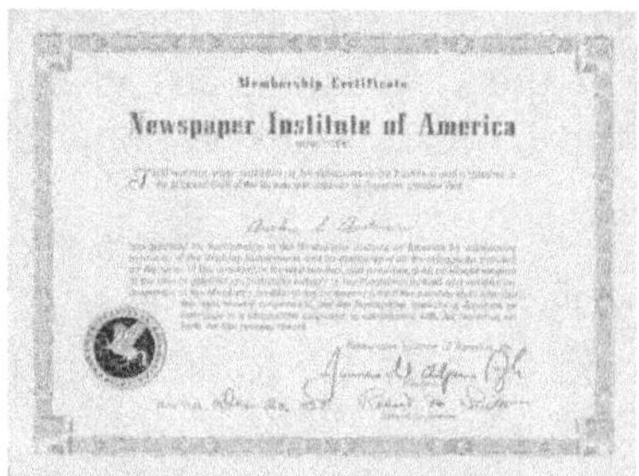
Membership Certificate

Newspaper Institute of America

Wednesday, January 19: 7:20. Left office around 5:35. Spent evening 'catching up'. Went to bed early about 11:30.

Thursday, January 20: 7:20. Work over around 5:35. Lost 3 games in 10 pins. Scores 109, 116. Worse & worse. Bed at

12:00.

Friday, January 21: 7:20. Left office about 5:30. Went to "Y". Lost in basketball. Cold started. Bed about 11:30.

Saturday, January 22: 7:20. Cold getting me down. Finished at 12:30. Bought comics as usual. Read Outline of History. 12:30.

Sunday, January 23: 11:00. Did not go to hockey game. Sneezing a great deal. Score South Side 4-Cardinals 2. Shaved and retired 11:30.

Monday, January 24: 7:05. All finished at 5:30. Cold is worse. Weather becoming more chilly. Did not bowl 5 pins. Bed early 8:30.

Tuesday, January 25: 7:10. Left office 5:30. Did not go to Toc S. Meeting. Read during evening. Cold still hanging on. 9:30.

Wednesday, January 26: 7:15. Tom did not show up all day. No word. Left office at 5:35. Cold not so bad. Weather mild. Bed early again 9:30.

Thursday, January 27: 7:15. Finished at 5:30. Tom still sick. Won 2 games 10 pins. Scores 114, 163, 155. Home to bed 12:30.

Friday, January 28: 7:15. Continue riding street car. Weather colder. **Bought typewriter ribbon**. Quit work about 5:35. Bed at 11:30.

Saturday, January 29: 7:15. Letter from Davis. Left office 12:40. Bought 3 funnies. Played Bingo & lost. **Letter to Newspaper Institute of America (N.I.A.)** also one to Writer's Digest. Bed 12:15.

Sunday, January 30: 1:30. Saw hockey game E.A.C. 7 Cardinals 2. Jack stayed for supper. Wrote Davis. **Prepared speech for**

Toc S. Bed 11:30.

Monday, January 31: 7:15. Bowled 5 pins. Won 3 games. Scores 131, 143, 159. Not so good. Home & to bed about 12:15.

February 1938

Tuesday, February 1: 7:15. Left office about 5:30. **Gave speech on "Why Canada should Fortify" at Toc S. Club.** Y for workout. 12:00.

Wednesday, February 2: 7:15. Continue to take lunch & ride street car. Went back to do footages for stocktaking. Home to bed 11:00.

Thursday, February 3: 7:15. Left office 5:35. Ten pins. Won 1 game. 191, 130, 136. Went to pieces after good start. 12:30.

Friday, February 4. 7:15. Left office about 5:35. Went to Y. Won basketball game 8-4. Home to bed 12:00.

Saturday, February 5: 7:15. Left office 12:30. Got haircut. Played Bingo & lost. Jim & Bell to see us. To bed about 12:30.

Sunday, February 6: 1:00 Hockey game Arena. Cards 5, South Side 4. Read until bed time. Bed about 11:00.

Monday, February 7: 7:15. Left office at 5:35. Won 2 games in 5 pins. Scores 164, 182, 152. Improving. Bed about 12:00.

Tuesday, February 8: 7:15. Left for K.E. at 5:40. No speeches. Another party next door interfered. Went to Y for class. Bed 12:15.

Wednesday, February 9: 7:15. Left office about 5:40. Read in the evening. Went to bed fairly early, about 10:00.

Thursday, February 10: 7:10. Finished work for day at 5:30. Won 1 game in 10 pins. Scores 122, 106. Not so hot. Bed 12:15.

Friday, February 11: 7:10. Through work 5:40. Went to Y for workout. Lost in basketball. Finally home to bed at 12:00.

Saturday, February 12: Completed work at 12:30. Bought new overcoat at Eaton's, $19.50, grey. Won $1 at Bingo. Bed at 12:30.

Sunday, February 13: 12:00. Started story for Writers' Digest Contest. Wrote letter & sent subscription to them also. Retired at 10:15.
Monday, February 14: 7:10. Lost 3 games in 5 pins. Scores – 143, 109, 138. Terrible. Home to bed at about 12:00.

Tuesday, February 15: 7:10. Toc S. Club as usual. Only 5 present. Went to "Y" for workout. Home to retire at 11:30.

Wednesday, February 16: 7:10. Left office at 5:40. Saw "The Emperors' Candlestick" at Avenue [movie theatre]. Played snooker. Bed 11:45.

Thursday, February 17: 7:10. Completed work 5:40. Lost 3 games in 10 pins. Scores 123, 134. Played snooker. Bed 1:00.

Friday, February 18: 7:10. Left office 5:35. Workout at Y. Lost in basketball. Won 2 out of 3 games in volleyball. Bed 12:00.

Saturday, February 19: 7:10. Left office at 12:30. Played 1 game 5 pins. Saw "The Game That Kills" and "It happened in Hollywood" at Empress [movie theatre]. Lost at Bingo 12:45.

Sunday, February 20: 1:00. E.A.C.'s now city champion. Jack stayed for supper. No hockey game today. Work on Liberty contest. Fin to bed at 10:30.

Monday, February 21: 7:10. Won 2 games in 5 pins. Scores 176, 280, 175. Improving. Had 7 players which is strange. Bed at 12:00.

Tuesday, February 22: 7:10. **Won debate against Norman Patterson on Morals of Rising Generation**. Lost in basketball. Home to bed 11:30.

Wednesday, February 23: 7*10. Saw "Laurel & Hardy Out West" & "Ghost Goes West" at Avenue [movie theatre]. Took Wally. Home & bed 12:30.

Thursday, February 24: 7:10. 10 pins as usual. Scores 132, 109, 159. Won 2 games. Played snooker with Graydon & Jack. Bed 12:30.

Friday, February 25: Stayed home instead of going to "Y". **Drafting short story for Writers' Digest**. Bed fairly early at 11:00.

Saturday, February 26: 7:10. Finished at 12:30. Got haircut. Jack & I played Bingo and lost. So to bed at about 12:45.

Sunday, February 27: 11:00. Glover returned from Old Country. Read rather than loafed. Nothing much happening. Snow practically all gone.

Monday, February 28: 7:10. Slightly colder. Hudson Bay Company half torn down, are doing 1/2 at a time. Did not bowl 5 pins. Jack did. 11:15.

March 1938

Tuesday, March 1: 7:10. Rode bike yesterday but streetcar today. **Spoke on over-government at Toc S Club.** Tie game in basketball. Bed 11:30.

Wednesday, March 2: Took Wally to Avenue [movie theatre], "Picadilly Jim". Not bad. Home & to bed at approximately 11:00.

Thursday, March 3: 7:10. Left office about 5:45. No bowling. Tournament Week. **Arranged to buy an Underwood Portable "Universal".** 11:00.

Friday, March 4: 7:10. **Paid $10 down on typewriter. $60 more which includes carrying charge.** Didn't go to "Y". Bed at about 12:30.

Saturday, March 5: 7:10. **Received new Underwood typewriter. Brought wrong one so had them exchange it. Cost 470. including carrying charges.** Played Bingo & lost. E.A.C. 4 Calgary 3. 1:00.

Sunday, March 6: 11:00. **Did considerable typing. Typed out story for Writers' Digest Contest. Also started answer to N.I.A. Contest.** 11:30.

Monday, March 7: 7:10. Weather brighter. **Received $2.00 cheque from Maclean's for item in Parade.** Bowled 5 pins. 159, 109, 194. 11:30.

Tuesday, March 8: Didn't go to Toc. S Club or Y. Read during evening & finally to bed at 11:00.

Wednesday, March 9: Took Wally to "Pick a Star" & "Good old Sook". Played snooker first. Didn't get to bed until 12:30.

Thursday, March 10: 7:10. Lost 3 games in 10 pins. Scores 159, 109, 148. Worse & more of it. Played snooker. Bed 12:45.

Friday, March 11: 7:10. Lost in basketball 19-17. Swam 4 or 5 lengths. Home to bed at approximately 11:30.

Saturday, March 12: 7:15. **Bought a dictionary for 98¢ at Bay**. Good bargain I think. Lost at Bingo. E.A.C. 4 Trail 2. Bed 12:45.

Sunday, March 13: Caught up on some of my reading. Jim, Bell, and family came up. Played games during evening. Bob & Jack over. 12:00.

Monday, March 14: 7:15. Rain last night. Icy streets today. Won game 5 pins 215, 150, 161. E.A.C. 8 Trail 0. Alberta B.C. Champs. Entered 5 pin Tournament. 12:15.

Tuesday, March 15: 7:10. Attended Toc S. Club. Won basketball at "Y" 19-8. Watched 5 pin bowling. Home to find March Writers' Digest. 12:30.

Wednesday, March 16: 7:10. Left off 5:50. Bowled 5 pin tournament team. Total 27 26. My scores 131, 109, 155. Bad. Home and bed at 11:45.

Thursday, March 17: Won 2 games in 10 pins. Scores 143, 202, 140. Improving. Five pin total with handicap 2744. Leading so far. Bed 12:30.

Friday, March 18: Ate supper at Yale. Bowled in singles 5 Pin Tournament 143, 184, 171 with handicap 520. Not even in running. Saw "A Slight Case of Murder". 12:00.

Saturday, March 19: Left office 12:45. Played 2 games snooker with Wally. Now in 3rd place in team event 5 pins. Played Bingo & lost. E.A.C. 7 Saskatoon 3. 1:00.

Sunday, March 20: 8:15. Surprise. Breakfasted at Corona with members of 3 spokes clubs. McNally spoke. **Typed N.I.A. contest entry. Worked on Liberty contest.** 11:15.

Monday, March 21: 7:15. Saskatoon 2 E.A.C Nothing. O.

Kennedy elected in by-election for Federal House. Margin 1,936 votes. Lost 5 pins. 186, 190, 173. 12:00.

Tuesday, March 22: 7:15. Went to speakers club. Went to Drama Festival instead of "Y". Saw Norwood Y people in "The Valiant". Home & bed 1:00.

Wednesday, March 23: E.A.C. 6 Saskatoon 3. Good game Capacity crowd. Took Wally. Two years since I started at Pilkington. Bed 12:15.

Thursday, March 24: Won 3 games in 10 pins. 148, 146, 144. Consistent at least. Weather has been fine all this month. Bed at 12:00.

Friday, March 15: Did not go to Y. Business rather slow. Read during the evening and went to bed at 11:30.

Saturday, March 16: Saw "Singing Marine" at Avenue [movie theatre]. Got $1.60 for coming 3rd in 5 pin team event. Saw game. St. Boniface 7 E.A.C. 3. 12:30.

Sunday, March 27: 11:30. Jim & Bell with family came up. **Played game of writing stories among ourselves**. 12:00.

Monday, March 28: Cold and much snow. Won 2 games 5 pins. 160, 235, 132. Spotty. Home & bed at approximately. 12:30.

Tuesday, March 29: **Spokes Club i.e. Toc S had 1 minute extemporaneous speeches to warm up.** Won basketball at Y. Home to bed again 11:30.

Wednesday, March 30: Weather continues cold but snow has stopped. Took Wally to "That Certain Woman" & "Great Hospital Mystery" at Avenue [movie theatre]. 1:00.

Thursday, March 31: Won 3 games by default from Norsemen.

Scores 122, 168, 147. Home to bed. St. Boniface 8 E.A.C. 3. 12:00.

April 1938

Friday, April1: To "Y" for workout. Won in basketball. Bought ticket for Y Junior game next Friday. Snow it melting. Bed 12:15.

Saturday, April 2: Played Bingo & lost. E.A.C. 3 St. Boniface 1. E.A.C.'s have to win next 2 games. Finally to bed at 12:30.

Sunday, April 3: 12:30. **Typed out speech for Tuesday.** Weather colder with more snow. **Worked on limerick contest.** Bed 11:00.

Monday, April 4: 7:05: Won 3 games in 5 pins. In playoffs 122, 208, 181. St. Boniface 6 E.A.C. 5. E.A.C.'s out. More snow but wet. 12:30.

Tuesday, April 5: Went to Toc S. meeting as usual. Won in basketball at Y. Home to bed once more, about 11:30.

Wednesday, April 6: Took Wally to Avenue [movie theatre] "Mtn. Music". Lost in 5 pin playoff. 139, 181. Terrible. Played snooker. Bed 12:00.

Thursday, April 7: Lost 3 games in 10 pins. 158, 99, 142. Out of running. One week to go. Played snooker. Bed 12:00.

Friday, April 8: Mr Parrett sick in Llyodminster. Saw Comets beat Calgary 60 to 35 at McDougall. Home and bed 11:30.

Saturday, April 9: Weather improving. Saw Deana Durbin in "Mad About Music". A good picture. Lost in Bingo. Home to bed 12:30.

Sunday, April 10: Wakened at 10:30 by Lorne telling me Ben had called to say Mr. Parrett had died. Means a readjustment. **Typed Christmas greetings I am trying to sell**. 11:30.

Monday, April 11: Things rather upset around office. Saw Grads workout at Arena. Were beaten by Boys. Home & bed 11:30.

Tuesday, April 12: Did not go to Y or Toc S. Club Just read in an effort to catch up in this. Bed 11:00.

Wednesday, April 13: Saw show at Avenue [movie theatre]. "Dragerman's Courage" and "Perfect Specimen". Played a game of snooker with Wally. 11:30.

Thursday, April 14: Finished 10 pins by losing 3 games. 136, 145, 130. Not so good. Lost in snooker with Jack & Graydon. 12:45.

Friday, April 15: (Good Friday) Got up about 12:00. Jim & Bell came over & Jimmie with Johnie & June, also Mrs. Schimmerhorn & Blanche. Party for Jimmie's birthday.

Saturday, April 16: J.E. Harrison from Toronto. Will doubtlessly settle things. Lost in Bingo with Wally after snooker game. Bed 12:30.

Sunday, April 17: Up at 11:00. Wrote Davis. **N.I.A. monthly contest* greeting cards & verse I hope to sell.** The day finally ended. 11:00. [See "Life" below, for more.]

Monday, April 18: Not much to do now that bowling is over. Learning Ben's job which I will be taking over. Bed as usual before 12:00.

Tuesday, April 19: Toc "S" club goes on Open Forum. Saw "Snow White" at Capital [movie theatre] with Jack. Bed after 12:00.

Wednesday, April 20: Avenue [movie theatre] with Wally. "Jones Family in Big Business" & also "Midnight Taxi Fair". Home to bed 12:15.

Thursday, April 21: **Loafed during evening instead of trying to write something. Must have lazy spells.** Bed 11:00.

Friday, April 22: Did not go to "Y". It will soon be over for the year. Learning more of Ben's work. Bed 10:30.

Saturday, April 23: Helen's birthday. Bought her shorts & sweater. Got 2 pairs of socks. Helen had a small party, Jean, Rozelle, & Irene. 12:00.

Sunday, April 24: Grads 72, Toronto 28 last night. Up at 1:00. **Typed out rough draft of N.I.A. contest entry**. Bed early at 10:15.

Monday, April 25: **Glover has new V8. Christmas verses returned. Sent them out again. Wrote poem to try poetry field**. 11:00.

Tuesday, April 26: Did not go to Toc S. **Typed out humorous poem & will send it tomorrow. Started Mountie story for pulps**. 10:45.

Wednesday, April 27: Took Wally to Avenue [movie theatre] as usual. Saw "Topper" & "Sofie Lang Goes West". Home to bed by 11:30.

Thursday, April 28: Work seems to be piling up. Trying to learn Ben's job makes me neglect some of my own work. 11:10.

Friday, April 29: Went to "Y". Won 2 games of basketball. Weather rather unsettled. Home to bed at 11:30.

Saturday, April 30: Worked all afternoon writing up statements to learn how. Played Bingo for last time & lost. Bed 12:30.

May 1938

Sunday, May 1: Up about 12:30. **Typing more of Mountie story. Nothing much besides.** Bed at about 10:00.

Monday, May 2: Work increasing. Wet weather. **Writing more of the story**. Bed at about 11:30.

Tuesday, May 3: Went downtown & heard boxing match at Iles where Graydon works. Bowled 2 games. Bed 1:00.

Wednesday, May 4: Still unsettled weather. **Stayed home and typed more of the story**. Bed at 11:30.

Thursday, May 5: **Still writing on my story. Trying some more poetry.** To bed at 11:00 or 11:30.

Friday, May 6: Weather continues cold for this time of year. Ben received a chain letter. This is Tom's first week in the country. 11:00.

Saturday, May 7: Sent out chain letters. Got hair cut. Took Wally to the Avenue [movie theatre] to see "Angel's Holiday". Wasted the evening. 12:00.

Sunday, May 8: Did manage to get up at 12:30. Did not do very much. **Typed some poetry. Parody on Flander's Fields***. 10:30.

[Editor's note: When I'm a child I discover this parody and find it very funny. So I want to read it at an amateur variety show. But Archie says I should not because it might offend war veterans. This makes me think that the parody is written after the 1939-1945 war. I presume it's the product of my dad's experience and satirical impressions of war. Perhaps it's a comment on the 1914-1918 war in the context of the approaching 1939-1945 war, in the sense that if Flander's Fields had been taken to heart there would be less likelihood of the 1939-1945 war. But as Archie often says, writers can write without deliberately including some hidden meaning in their prose. Maybe he was just trying to be funny. With apologies to war veterans, Archie's parody is inserted here below.]

Monday, May 9: **Received my <u>Writers' Digest</u> story and also a poem back. No luck. Will keep trying.** Bed 111:30.

Tuesday, May 10: Warmer. Gordy Ferguson, who started yesterday, should do all right. Work piling up. Grads 40 Chicago 33. 11:15.

Wednesday, May 11: Went to Avenue [movie theatre] with Wally. Played snooker first. Work is still increasing. Gordy is starting to learn. 12:15.

Thursday, May 12: **I am doing more writing now. It seems to be less difficult to do something**. Bed at about 11:30.

Friday, May 13: Went back to the office. Posted the cash so that I will be able to make up the drafts. Ben drove me home. 12:00.

Saturday, May 14: Saw show at the Avenue [movie theatre]. 12:15.

Sunday, May 15: Did get up at 10:30. **Typed out cartoon ideas & sent poetry to the Saturday Evening Post.** Bed before 11:15.

Monday, May 16: Work continues heavy. Left office about 6:00. **Sent story returned by <u>Writers Digest</u> to Black Mask N.I.A. contest.** Bed 11:45.

Tuesday, May 17: Left office 6:15. Back to work from 7:45 to 11:00. Ben drove me home again. Tomorrow I bounce another insurance salesman. 11:45.

Wednesday, May 18: Went to Avenue [movie theatre] as usual. I missed the insurance salesman. Played snooker. Gordy is catching on rather slowly. 12:05.

Thursday, May 19: 10 pin bowling banquet. The team received the huge sum of $2.50. Played snooker afterwards. Bed 12:30.

Friday, May 20: Bought tennis racquet press & balls from Marshall Wells. Joined Eastwood Club. Bob White gave pointers. 11:15.

Saturday, May 21: Played a few sets of tennis with Phyllis Hunter and others. Played Snooker with Jack. Bed 11:30.

Sunday, May 22: Got up about 11:30. Played tennis until about 8:00. Had a lunch in the Community Hall. 10:30.

Monday, May 23: Played a little tennis after supper. Cyril Southall gave me some tips. **Got verse back from Saturday Evening Post**.

Tuesday, May 24: **Sent cartoon ideas to "This Week" yesterday**. Up at 10:30. Not many playing tennis. Played with Given Morgan. Grads 61 Cleveland 38. 11:15.

Wednesday, May 25: Work is continuing to pile up. Gordy still rather slow. Went to Avenue [movie theatre] as usual. Bed 12:00.

Thursday, May 26: Grads won again. Improving in tennis. Jack won a set but I turned around to beat him. 11:30.

Friday, May 27: Paid for my tennis equipment. Total $6.10. Have lost one ball already. Never seem to leave office on time. Bed 11:45.

Saturday, May 28: Bought polo shirt & 2 pairs of socks. Haircut. Saw Deanna Durbin in "100 men & A Girl". Good. Cleveland

44 Grads 36. Bed 12:00.

Sunday, May 29: 11:00. Played tennis. **Sent verse to McLeans**. Hot & dry weather. Relaxed for part of the evening. Bed 11:00.

Monday, May 30: Wrote Davis. Didn't play tennis. Rather windy. Heard game at Dodd's. Grads 61. Cleveland 48. Bed 12:15.

Tuesday, May 31: My first month as a bookkeeper starting. Played a few sets of tennis. Courts in better shape since rain. Bed 11:30.

June 1938

Wednesday, June 1: Back to the office. Did most of the statements. Ben drove me home. Bed at 12:15.

Thursday, June 2: Did not balance at first, $43 out. Back to work. Mr. Glover drove me home at 11:30.

Friday, June 3: Balanced. Played tennis. Introduced to Hazel Brown by Phyllis Hunter. Now getting $17 a week. Paying $7 for board. **No acceptances yet**. Bed 11:00.

Saturday, June 4: Played tennis all afternoon. Saw June Withers in "Holy Terror" & also "Think Fast Mr. Moto". Bed at 12:30.

Sunday, June 5: Up 7:50. Went to Elk Island Park with Jack. John Dennison drove us out. Speakers club picnic. Back by 9:00. Bed 10:15.

Monday, June 6: Continue busy. Played tennis. **Have not done much writing lately. Get a few rejections though.** Bed 11:00.

Tuesday, June 7: Back to the office. Ran into Jack afterwards.

Played snooker with Graydon. Jack sick. Bed 12:30.

Wednesday, June 8: Rainy. Saw "The Good Earth" at the Avenue [movie theatre] with Wally. Home at 9:45. Read until bed time at about 11:00.

Thursday, June 9: King's birthday holiday but not for me. Played tennis after supper. Improving. Home to bed at about 11:30.

Friday, June 10: Typed letter to Saskatchewan government for birth certificate. Typed letter to <u>Esquire</u> as I am sending cartoon ideas. Bed 11:00.

Saturday, June 11: Home at 1:30. Played tennis afternoon and evening. Have new balls I bought yesterday. Bed at about 12:00.

Sunday, June 12: Tennis until it rained in the afternoon. A few sets at night and then to bed around 11:00.

Monday, June 13: Played tennis. Bought pair of $5 shoes at Eaton's. Jack & I took Phyllis Hunter & **Hazel** Brown for a sundae at Elfstroms & then home. First time for me with any girl. Bed 12:30.

Tuesday, June 14: First swim this year. Bought $1 swim ticket. Did not stay long. Air chilly. Home and to bed at about 11:45.

Wednesday, June 15: More tennis playing. Jack & I walked Hazel & Phyllis home again. Getting to be a habit. Bed 12:00.

Thursday, June 16: **Doing drafts**. Have not yet lost interest in tennis. Jack & I walked the two girls home again. 12:30.

Friday, June 17: Jack & I take Hazel & Phyllis to the Avenue [movie theatre] tomorrow. First time we have ever taken girls to show. Saw "Lites of a Bengal Lancer" at Rialto [movie theatre]. Tonight. 12:30.

Saturday, June 18: I asked Hazel at the last moment. Jack pretended to bet the price of the show with Phyllis. Saw them safely home. Bed 12:15.

Sunday, June 19: Wally took my trunks without leave. I had to play tennis instead. Good fun anyway. Bed about 11:30.

Monday, June 20: Phyllis invited us in for a lunch. Jack was shy at first but Hazel worried him in. Finally home at around 12:00.

Tuesday, June 21: Took Hazel swimming. She could not swim but is willing to learn. Met her family. Home to bed 12:15.

Wednesday, June 22: Played tennis as usual. Hazel and Phyllis refused to be treated. Good sports. Took them home. Bed 12:15.

Thursday, June 23: Took Phyllis & Hazel in for pie and drinks. We see them almost every night at the court. 12:00.

Friday, June 24: Jack & I took Phyllis & Hazel to the Avenue [movie theatre] again. Enjoyed ourselves. Home to bed at last at about 12:30.

Saturday, June 25: Invited into Phyllis' after tennis. We seem to be rushing things. Hazel plays the piano well. 12:15.

Sunday, June 26: Swam in the morning. Sunburned. Went to Hazel's house with Phyllis & Jack after tennis. Got home at 12:00.

Monday, June 27: Eastwood Tennis Club Strawberry Social. Took Hazel. She tried to teach me some dancing. First time I ever attempted to dance. I will learn. Bed at about 11:50.

Tuesday, June 28: Gordy & I did the statements. Left my bike at home with a flat. Wally fixed it unasked. He did borrow it, though. 10:30.

Wednesday, June 29: Gordy left for Peace River. I will do the typing until he returns. I get in quite a bit of tennis. Hot.

Thursday, June 30: Did considerable work. Ben leaves tomorrow for the East. That will leave Tom & I. Jack & I walked the girls home.

July 1938

Friday, July 1: 9:30. Went back to finish daybooks for the month. Played tennis in the afternoon & evening.

Saturday, July 2: Worked on statements all afternoon. Invited to Phyllis' house for the evening. Rainy weather coming up.

Sunday, July 3: Back to the office. Finished statements & helped Tom do the footage summary. Weather wet.

Monday, July 4: Did not balance. Back to work & Tom & I finally found the error. The rain continues to oblige.

Tuesday, July 5: Weather cleared up so I played tennis. Gordy back with dislocated shoulder. Nice! I don't think!

Wednesday, July 6: Hazel 21st birthday. We walked about after tennis. Month end work straightening out.

Thursday, July 7: Thursday. Gordy still disabled. I did get Tom to make deposits & check daybooks, though.

Friday, July 8: Jack's 21st birthday. Worked at the office to celebrate. Month end work practically finished.

Saturday, July 9: Hazel held party at the R.A.O.B. Hall. Danced with her friend Marion Brown. Gave Hazel manicure set. 2:30.

Sunday, July 10: Up at 10 o'clock. Took pictures of Hazel, Phyllis, & Jack with my Bullet camera. Treated the girls to milkshakes. Bed 12:00.

Monday, July 11: Gordy back to the typewriter. Work getting straightened out. Played tennis and walked once again.

Tuesday, July 12: Played tennis & attended meeting. Girls did not show up. Probably thought there was a tournament.

Wednesday, July 13: 21 today. The boys bumped me. I treated Tom & Len to a beer. Phyllis fed us watermelon. Got initialled belt from Hazel.

Thursday, July 14: **Went to buy tent on South Side. Worked at office. Talked over Jasper trip with Jack**. Leave on Sunday.

Friday, July 15: Got ready to go to Jasper. Played tennis as usual & walked home with girls. Bed at about 12:00.

Saturday, July 16: Bought the rest of our supplies. Took our tent and bikes to the station. Played tennis & walked girls. Slept at Jack's.

Sunday, July 17: **Saw mountains for the first time. Wonderful. Jasper very pretty nestled in mountains. Settled in up to date auto camp**. Bed.

Monday, July 18: Visited Pyramid Lake. Took snaps of mountain & lake. No cold water yet . Swam. Have seen no bears so far. Sent post cards. Bought watch.

Tuesday, July 19: Went to Maligne Canyon. Beautiful falls. Truly wonderful. Got first drink of cold water. No animals yet.

Wednesday, July 20: Swam at Lake Annette. Saw first bear & a deer. Keen's took us by car to the lake. Insects bad. Good weather.

Thursday, July 21: Visited Mr. Edith Cavel & Angel Glacier. Tough climb but coasted back for [14.5 km.] Got picture of bear.

Friday, July 22: Bothered slightly with arm I skinned yesterday coming down from Cavel. Just loafed. Wrote letter home & one to Hazel. Sent films. Bed 9:30.

Saturday, July 23: Sleep disturbed last night by wind. Windy today. Clouds around mountain peaks. Went to Gheikie & Lake Caledonia. Rained lightly.

Sunday, July 24: Cloudy. Went by truck to Miette. Rained on the way but cleared before long. Pleasant swimming in hot water. Sulphur not too bad. $1^{1/2}$ hours in water.

Monday, July 25: Warm & sunny. Climbed Whistler Mountain. Harder coming down. Came down rocky side on Indian Ridge easily but path remainder of way tiresome. Bear trouble.

Tuesday, July 26: Bear raided us last night taking butter, eggs, milk, shortening, & bacon, about 60¢ worth. Think I heard it but did not investigate. Picked raspberries for supper. No bear tonight.

Wednesday, July 27: Went to Athabaska Falls. A great deal of water in a hurry to get down a rocky incline. Rather large. Biggest we've seen.

Thursday, July 28: Swan at Lake Annette. Still smoky. Has been since Tuesday. Had flat yesterday. Climbed Old Fort Point today. Just [30 metres] or so.

Friday, July 29: Bought souvenirs. Weighed ourselves. Jack gained nearly[3 kilos] & I lost about [half a kilo]. Continues smoky. Met Alf in Jasper. Leaky valve.

Saturday, July 30: Continues cloudy Loafed today. Getting ready to leave. Rained at night. Jack played bear outside the tent. Cold because of the rain.

Sunday, July 31: Up by 6. Packed tent & a fellow carted it to Jasper. Ate dinner at Monceau Cafe. 35¢ Good. Train broke down, one hour late. Home again.

August 1938

Monday, August 1: Played tennis with Jack, Phyllis, & Hazel in afternoon. Showed pictures at Hazel's at night. Philip bothered me talking too much.

Tuesday, August 2: Work & then some. Went back to finish posting. Must have been busy not to have time to do all posting. Will try balance tomorrow.

Wednesday, August 3: Back to office. Balanced first time. A relief Getting work under control. Nights are very chilly now. Took camera to be fixed.

Thursday, August 4: Played in singles tournament against Dic Triscot. Lost 6-2 & 6-1. Jack & I walked with the girls. Gave Hazel a picture of Pyramid Mountain.

Friday, August 5: Rained at night but Jack & I played two sets of tennis. Bought a photo album yesterday. Girls did not show up. Rain possibly the reason.

Saturday, August 6: Developed films at Jack's. Rainy. Printed after supper. We were able to have one or two sets of tennis. Home at 1:00.

Sunday, August 7: Some rain but Jack & I played some tennis. Too much moisture for this time of year. Nights seem very cold too.

Monday, August 8: Rainy. Took Hazel to "Little Miss Broadway" Shirley Temple at Capital [movie theatre]. Lunched. Dropped in at her house. Couldn't escape until 1:00.

Tuesday, August 9: Played tennis. Jack & Phyllis there but not Hazel. Let them go home alone. I went to bed for a change.

Wednesday, August 10: Hazel turned up for tennis but no Phyllis. Jack kindly obliged by helping to escort Hazel home. Rode me home on bicycle.

Thursday, August 11: Phyllis & Hazel both showed up. Escorted them as usual. Have still to pay bills at office. Slow this month.

Friday, August 12: Played tennis until it rained. Let Jack take Phyllis & Hazel home with my raincoat. Bed before 12:00. Surprise.

Saturday, August 13: Had about eight sets. Got my suit from T.A.L. Fleche. Had been measured Tuesday. Rained at night. Jack & I took girls to "Lost Horizon" at Avenue [movie theatre].

Sunday, August 14: Rained. Day spoilt because Hazel's people were to leave for beach and Jack and I had been invited for supper. **Wrote some personal poetry**.

Monday, August 15: Rainy weather. Phoned Hazel but she was busy & I did <u>not</u> get another chance. **Did some typing. Poetry**.

Tuesday, August 16: Horrors. I was supposed to go to Hazel's for supper Sunday. Her folks did go away. Tennis club social at R.A.O.B. Hazel did come.

Wednesday, August 17: Rain. Courts wet. **Typed more poetry**. Miserable weather for August. Hope we get some sunny days.

Thursday, August 18: Composed poem about my failure to keep supper date. Too wet for tennis. Jack came over.

Friday, August 19: Did play tennis. Walked home with girls. They prepared a find lunch. Jack forgot his gloves. We frightened the girls on our return.

Saturday, August 20: Played tennis during afternoon. Helped carry Phyllis' suitcase home as Hazel's family returns tomorrow. Another lunch. Showed poems.

Sunday, August 21: Curses. More rain. **Played tennis with Ken Fleming at night. He is a budding author too.** Bell in hospital. Gordy staying with us. Jim up for awhile.

Monday, August 22: No rain but cloudy. Played tennis. No girls. Jack arried back from Sylvan Lake this morning. Car trouble. Had to hire a car from Leduc.

Tuesday, August 23: Tennis as usual. Walked home with girls. Had a lunch at Phyllis' after leaving Hazel's. Rain. Home after it stopped. 12:00.

Wednesday, August 24: Played tennis with girls. Walked home as usual. Phyllis almost got angry but gave in. Did not get mislaid on way home again.

Thursday, August 25: Considerable posting to do. Gordy practically caught up with daybooks. Tennis with Jack. Typed some poetry. Bed 11:30.

Friday, August 26: Walked with girls to Arena to watch Jack practise against Grads. Phil had to be coaxed. They were both bored. I was too.
Saturday, August 27:

Sunday, August 28:

Monday, August 29: Tennis but no Hazel. Jack went to Arena for practice. Thunder storm cooled things off. Month end nearing.

Tuesday, August 30: Tennis with Hazel. Meeting of E.Y.C. Dance for 17th. $52. in the hole. Jack let me walk Hazel home alone.

Wednesday, August 31: Got Gordy to do daybooks for two days. Wrote up statements until 10:30 or so. Should get done quickly if lucky.

September 1938

Thursday, September 1: Did not balance. Back to work until 11:30. Bill Logan drove me down as he was gong back to work too.

Friday, September 2: Ben found my mistake. Back to work11:30. Cleaned up [illegible] sum, paint sum, & goods [illegible].Just [illegible] 12:30.

Saturday, September 3: Went to Hazel's & she tried to show me a few dance steps. Philip talks as much as ever but is more considerate.

Sunday, September 4: Played rugby at exhibition grounds. Nose-bleed, stiff neck, & sore fingers. Played tennis with Hazel afternoon.

Monday, September 5: Played tennis. Dodds drove me to Leduc in their car (?) Back to play tennis with Hazel in afternoon. Took her to Avenue [movie theatre]. Had to go for her.

Tuesday, September 6: Dark too quickly for tennis. **Typed poem about Philip. Hope he has a sense of humour. I will have to start writing again.**

Wednesday, September 7: Jack & I played tennis. Took 41 tickets each for tennis club dance. Phyllis will not be back for it. **Typed on Jasper Poem**.

Thursday, September 8: Rain. Left bike at office. Went back to work. Gordy had work to clean up. I paid a few bills. Getting busier.

Friday, September 9: Invited Hazel to Capital [movie theatre] "Alexander's Ragtime Bank". **Did more typing on Jasper poem. Thirty verses now. Might be fifty finally.**

Saturday, September 10: Metropolitan Store had a fire. Took Hazel to Capitol [movie theatre]. Magnificent since its renovation. Good, seats, ventilation, and the show was fairly good.

Sunday, September 11: Rugby at exhibition grounds again. No damage. Played tennis with Hazel in afternoon. **More verses on Jasper poem. 38 now**.

Monday, September 12: **Typed more versus on Jasper trip. Up to 45. Nearly finished.** Got cards from Ding & Phyllis both.

Tuesday, September 13: Went back to office but left in time to see show at Avenue [movie theatre]. "Theodora Goes Wild". Very funny. Met Lorne & Jack there.

Wednesday, September 14: Played tennis with Hazel. Watched Jack play Grads. Met Bonny Hunter & learned Phyllis will be back Saturday.

Thursday, September 15: Went back to work because Gordy is behind. Completed drafts. Well up on my work this month.

Friday, September 16: Played a set of tennis. It gets dark quickly. Weather for last week has been very good.

Saturday, September 17: Played a set of tennis. Took Hazel to E.T. Club dance at I.O.O.F. Hall 95 & 112 Ave. Grads 75 Canton 25. Beginning to like dancing.

Sunday, September 18: Played rugby again. Another less serious nose bleed. Tennis in afternoon with Hazel. Phyllis back. Walked Phyllis & Hazel home. Jack missing.

Monday, September 19: Y classes started Monday's this year. Tired easily must be soft. Played volleyball. Declined to bowl 5 pins this year. Grads 79 Canton 52.

Tuesday, September 20: Wrote a "Voice" [invoice] for Tom. My work is well up but Gordy is far behind. Mr. Glover has been away from office.

Wednesday, September 21: Meeting of E.T. Club decided to hold another dance. Oct. 15. Made $17.50 on last one. Heard Grad game at Hazel's. Grads 68 Canton 32.

Thursday, September 22: Played a set of tennis with Jack. We took Phyllis & Hazel to the Avenue [movie theatre]. "Tovarich". God. Met Frarey on way home & got a lift.

Friday, September 23: Completed Jasper poem. Tome liked the "Voice" I did for him. Essay on Jasper & picture album come next.

Saturday, September 24: Tennis in afternoon. Invited to Phyllis' in the evening. Played cards and Jack told ghost stories. Didn't get home 'til about 1:30.

Sunday, September 25: Tennis with Hazel, Phyllis, & Jack. Wrote poetry at night about cartoon ideas I had thought up & had rejected.

Monday, September 26: Class at Y. Lost in basketball 12-17. Swam a few lengths. Intent to swim more this year.

Tuesday, September 27: Hazel, Phyllis, Jack, & I went to Empress [movie theatre]. "Amazing Dr. Clitterhouse" & "Invisible Menace" (First & better) No lunch.

Wednesday, September 28: Went back to office. Dropped in at Avenue [movie theatre] on way home "Alibaba Goes to Town" Eddie Cantor (First & possibly last I'll see of him.)

Thursday, September 29: Have month end work in good shape. Y class. Lost in basketball 7-10. Treated Nick Christophers at coffee shop. Swam again.

Friday, September 30: Did half the statements for a good start. Stopped at about 11:00. Weather getting rather chilly.

October 1938

Saturday, October 1: Finished statements in afternoon but did not balance. Visited Hazel & listened to basketball game. Grads 41 Wichita 27. Hike tomorrow.

Sunday, October 2: Hiked to Capitol Hill & toboggan slide with Bob F. & Ding, Phyllis, Jack, & Hazel. Started 3 o'clock. Home by twelve. Rained as we started home.

Monday, October 3: Still no balances. Back to work again. Checking everything but no luck. Tomorrow will finish all checking.

Tuesday, October 4: Found error at about 5:30. Mistake in balance itself. Had D.B. less in total wrong. Wasted three days for carelessness.

Wednesday, October 5: Took Hazel to Grad game. Grads 33 Wichita 29. Some game. Had reserved ringside seats. Meant to give her program but forgot.

Thursday, October 6: Class at Y. Swam a little afterwards. Lost in basketball. Weather is warm for October. **I don't seem to do much writing**.

Friday, October 7: Took Hazel to Avenue [movie theatre] "True Confession" a scream. Dropped in at her house to find Clem about to leave for a dance with Winnie & another girl.

Saturday, October 8: Jack, Bob F. & I beat Ding, Phyllis, & Hazel in 5 pins. My scores 178, 177, 192. Girls had to treat to lunch. Had tea cups read. Bob & I palms.

Sunday, October 9: Tennis. Jack & I played with Ding & Dot which irked Phyllis & Hazel. Walked down Avenue with them. Took a candid shot.

Monday, October 10: Thanksgiving. Tennis with the girls. Took them to see Ritz Brothers at the Strand [movie theatre]. No lunch. Jack almost broke. Did ride home. Hazel new shoes.

Tuesday, October 11: Finished trading account. Rainy. **Wrote letter for <u>Writers' Digest</u> contest.** Letter to Davis. Tomorrow will crash way into dramatic club. Hazel belongs.

Wednesday, October 12: Crash! (Me coming out.) Dramatic club broke up to go back to St. Faith's [Anglican Church] where they originated from. Hazel losing interest. I miss again. No play for me.

Thursday, October 13: Y for a workout. Lost in basketball again. More swimming. Hope I keep it up this year. **Trying to do more writing**.

Friday, October 14: E. Tennis Club Dance at Alberta Avenue Hall. Phyllis, Hazel, Jack & I, of course Ding & Eddie. Didn't go to bed until about 2 a.m.

Saturday, October 15: Gordy going to leave for a supposedly better job. Took Hazel to "Radio City Revels" at Avenue [movie theatre]. Met Jack & Phyllis. Bed 1:30.

Sunday, October 16: Tennis. Perhaps last this season. Phyllis & Hazel with Jack & I. Ben in hospital having tonsils removed. **Wrote entry to N.I.A. contest. Worked on Jasper essay.**

Monday, October 17: Class at Y. Lost as usual. Swam a few lengths. Dropped in at Rec. but not long. Ron phoned to say he'd be back Tuesday.

Tuesday, October 18: Back to office. Posted all I can ready for drafts. Will be working late often after Gordy leaves. Met Jack on car. He is bowling 5 pins.

Wednesday, October 19: Moving house next to office ready to build addition. Played badminton. Hazel, Phyllis, Jack, Ding, & Bob, and others. A good game once we learn. Warm weather.

Thursday, October 20: Y class. Won in basketball. Jack's first appearance. We went to the Rec & were driven home in one. (Dodd's car).

Friday, October 21: New fellow Wilf Boyce. Phoned Hazel to learn she's in a play & will be busy until Christmas. Back to office until 9. Bed early 10:00.

Saturday, October 22: Called at Hazel's to find Jack & Phyllis awaiting to go bowling. Jack & Phyllis won so Bob & I treated. Hazel had one game 102. Ate at American Dairy Lunch.

Sunday, October 23: Visited Hazel in evening to hear her lines but didn't. Listened to Jack Benny. **Typed on Jasper essay in afternoon**.

Monday, October 24: Weather fine. First meeting Toc S Club. Ben Lange new leader. I'M secretary this week. Workout at Y. Won in basketball.

Tuesday, October 25: Typed daybooks and let Wilf do other things. Back at night to do some posting. Made rough draft of letter to be sent to members of Toc S Club.

Wednesday, October 26: Badminton. Broke Dot Smith's glasses. Had shower. Weather getting cooler but no snow yet.

Thursday, October 27: Class at Y. Worked until 8:00 at office. Met Phyllis on streetcar. Typed circular letter to Toc S members.

Friday, October 28: Arranged to go to Capitol [movie theatre] with Hazel Saturday Worked at office. Trying to get everything read for month-end.

Saturday, October 29: Saw "Carefree". Jack & Phyllis bumped into us at Hazel's afterwards. Hazel went to sleep with Phyllis. We stopped at Phyllis' for awhile.

Sunday, October 30: took Phyllis & Hazel to Macdonald Baptist. Jack did not go. Worked in afternoon. Typed daybooks for all orders priced.

Monday, October 31: Toc S meeting at Y next week. Went back to office after class. Did some of the statements. Left office about 12:00.

November 1938

Tuesday, November 1: Completed statements but did not balance. This was around 11:30. I left Ben & went home hoping he'd find th error.

Wednesday, November 2: He did so I played badminton at Eastwood. Jack drove us in car. Phyllis got huffy & walked home alone.

Thursday, November 3: Class at Y. Back to office first. Month-end almost all finished. Weather colder with snow. **Wrote poem for Philip**.

Friday, November 4: Took Hazel to supper & "You can't take it with you" at Rialto [movie theatre]. Dropped in at her house afterwards. Clem showed up.

Saturday, November 5: Took it easy in the afternoon. Got haircut. Jack called in the evening. Month-end work all complete.

Sunday, November 6: Hazel's for supper. Her parents were out but Philip talked all evening & them Clem dropped in. I waited until he left at 11:30.

Monday, November 7: **Toc S meeting at Y. Told about my Jasper trip**. Class afterwards. Still swimming a few lengths.

Tuesday, November 8: Spent evening at home. Surprise. **Worked on another poem for Philip's paper.** Work at office piling up.

Wednesday, November 9: Hazel went to rehearsal instead of badminton. Phyllis invited Jack & I to her house for pumpkin pie. We stayed until 1:30.

Thursday, November 10: **Up before 7 to type out poem for Philip**. Phoned Hazel & invited her to preview at Rialto [movie theatre]. "That certain age" Deanna Durbin. Met Jack after. Home 3:00.

Friday, November 11: Up at 1:30. Took dancing lesson at Spankie's above Tivoli. **Began another poem for Philip**. Not riding bike. Colder weather.

Saturday, November 12: Bought a felt hot-snap brim hat, first. Took another lesson from June Bond at Spankies. Stayed home for a change.

Sunday, November 13: **Typed three poems for Philip. Stayed home again. Haven't done much typing for a long while.**

Monday, November 14: Took Hazel to Strand [movie theatre] Marx Brothers in "Room Service". Funny but no piano playing or song singing. Wore new hat for first time.

Tuesday, November 15: Had tooth pulled. Worked at office Did not go home for supper but stayed at work until about 9:00. Jack & Ormond at Rec. 3 games of snooker.

Wednesday, November 16: Badminton at Norwood with Phyllis & Hazel. Jack went to Grad banquet. Pretended to have forgotten to invite Hazel to E.T.C. banquet until we said goodnight.

Thursday, November 17: Worked until 7:45. Went to Y for workout. Lost in basketball. Ted Morrisey marking off orders at night now. Addition progressing.

Friday, November 18: Stayed at home for a change. Office work in better shape now. Had another lesson at Spankies. Dancing improving.

Saturday, November 19: Haircut. Eastwood Tennis Club banquet. Took Hazel. Good time. Tried to work in step. I've learned but didn't manage many. Home before 1:30.

Sunday, November 20: **Worked on Jasper essay. Might finish it some day.** Jack over for supper. Weather getting colder. Haven't done any skating yet.

Monday, November 21: Glover & Tom at paint convention in Calgary. Spokes Club – Oil. Tie game in basketball 6-6. Continue to swim a few lengths. Dance lesson.

Tuesday, November 22: Dentist worked on tooth. He packed it & I went back to have it fixed because it ached steadily. Went to bed at 8:30.

Wednesday, November 23: Played badminton. Hazel showed up as rehearsal had been called off. New racquet. Hazel went to Phyllis for night.

Thursday, November 24: Stayed at office. Class at Y. Lost in basketball. Swam a few lengths. Work slackening. Warmer.

Friday, November 25: MacLaurin filled a tooth. Took Helen to Avenue [movie theatre]. "Happy Landing" Sonja Henie. Rather mild weather.

Saturday, November 26: Took Hazel to "There goes my heart" at the Rialto [movie theatre]. Big line-up. We had a discussion about an article I had shown her.

Sunday, November 27: **Worked on Jasper essay & a speech for the Toc S. Typed very little though I did nothing else**. Weather still mild.

Monday, November 28: Toc S meeting. Started one minute extemporaneous talks. Took workout & swam. Went back to office until 11:00.

Tuesday, November 29: Worked late. Went to see "Dracula" & "Frankenstein" with Jack & Ormond. Not very frightening. Weather still very moderate.

Wednesday, November 30: Worked until 7:10. Went to play badminton at Norwood. Hazel at rehearsal. Jack & I had lunch at Phyllis'. Talked & didn't leave until 1:30.

December 1938

Thursday, December 1: Did not balance immediately. Went home about 9:30. Ruth visiting Edna. Managed to get to bed before twelve. (Just.)

Friday, December 2: Balanced. Month end returns nearly completed. Worked through until 9:00. Got new skates from Marshall Wells yesterday $9.50 for $7.10. Dentist finished $6. Two filled, one out.

Saturday, December 3: Dance at Y.W.C.A. Tried out new skates on Macdonald's rink. Enjoyed dance. Dropped into Johnsons afterwards. Home before 2:00.

Sunday, December 4: Up before 2: Went to Phyllis' for supper. Jack, Bob, Ding, Hazel, Grace, & Norman Dodge there. Played games & sang.

Monday, December 5: Month-end returns completed. Toc S club still going strong. Workout. Won in basketball. Swam as usual.

Tuesday, December 6: Took Edna to Avenue [movie theatre]. "Crime school" & "Blondes at Work". Haven't used new skates on big rink yet.

Wednesday, December 7: Badminton. Jack & I played game at Phyllis' after dropping Hazel at her house. Did get away before 12:00. Weather mild.

Thursday, December 8: Wilf & Jack skated on river. I skated with Wally at Avenue Rink. Skates are good. I became tired & hungry.

Friday, December 9: Saw play "Second Childhood" with Phyllis. Hazel one of the main characters. Good. Walked to Hazel's house.

Saturday, December 10: Haircut. Saw "Goldwyn Follies" at Avenue [movie theatre]. Terrible. "Suez" at Capitol [movie theatre] with Hazel. Better. Home shortly after 12. No lunch.

Sunday, December 11: Wasted the day. **Typed out answers to <u>Bulletin</u> [newspaper] contest**. **Typed speech**. Jack & Rozelle for supper.

Monday, December 12: **Spoke about "Christmas Spirit" at Toc S. Club. Meeting of Press Club with Neil Cathbertson & Fred Dambiski.** Met Nick.

Tuesday, December 13: Skated with Jack & Molly at the Avenue Rink. First time I have skated with girl. To Jack's afterwards with Helen.

Wednesday, December 14: Badminton. Late. Met Jack, Phyllis, & Hazel leaving Hazel's. Had lunch at Hazel's afterwards.

Thursday, December 15: Class at Y. Lost in basketball. Swam in pool. Water too cold. Gave me a slight chill.

Friday, December 16: Got new Philco from the Bay to try. Took Hazel to the Avenue [movie theatre]. "On again Off again" & "Jones Family in Paris".

Saturday, December 17: **Banquet of Speakers' Club. Had to debate**. Met Hazel at 10:30. She had been working. Coffee Shop McLeod Building.

Sunday, December 18: Phyllis, Jack, Hazel, & I went to hockey game. Took my cold along. Canadian 6 E.A.C. 5 (surprise) Girls called for us here.

Monday, December 19: No arrangements made for meeting of Toc S, so we ate at the Buffalo Cafe. Took Phyllis & Hazel to Social at E. Tennis Club. No snow yet, mild.

Tuesday, December 20: Have opened charge account at the Bay for Christmas shopping. Wilf & I skate on the river occasionally at noon hour.

Wednesday, December 21: Badminton. Entertained at Phyllis' afterwards. Grace & Norm there also. Left before 12:00.

Thursday, December 22: Stayed at home. Radio programs good. Nearly fell asleep. Work up to date. New office nearly ready.

Friday, December 23: Shopped with Jack at night. Got dresser set for Hazel. Jack got Phyllis Yardley set. Took Hazel for lunch after 10:00.

Saturday, December 24: Went to St. Faith's [Anglican Church] at 11:30 with Jack, Phyllis, & Hazel. Cold with a great deal of snow.

Sunday, December 25: Girls liked gifts. Jack got pen & pencil initialled from Phyllis. I got military brushes, initialed, from Hazel. Went to preview at Capitol [movie theatre] "Dawn Patrol".

Monday, December 26: [-32°C] overnight. Was going skating with Hazel & Winnie. Decided it was too cold. Hope I wasn't expected. Jack for supper. Stayed in all day.

Tuesday, December 27: Jack & I visited Jim & Bell, taking Gordy home. Temperature going down to [-40°C]. [-48°C] overnight. Brrr.

Wednesday, December 28: Entertained at Ding's. Jack, Phyllis, Brian, Mary, Hazel, Bob, & I. Did not get off car at Hazel's. Too cold.

Thursday, December 29: Party at Hazel's. Left after one. Climax when Winnie pushed Phil & front door couldn't take it.

Friday, December 30: Lined up work for month-end. Stayed home. Jack came over. Went to bed before 10:30. Moderating.

Saturday, December 31: Did not balance. Dance at Parliament Buildings.

Party at Phyllis' after. Breakfast at Hazel's. To bed at about 10:00 a.m.

1938 Books:

Swiss Family Robinson by J.D. Wyss. Tales of Wonder &

Outline of History by H.G. Wells. The Castaways by W.W. Jacobs. David Copperfield & Martin Chuzzlewitt by Charles Dickens.

1939

January 1939

Sunday, January 1: Up at 5:00 p.m. In time for supper. Sorted out bills. Will have to budget. Bed at 12:00.

Monday, January 2: Back to office 10:30. No balance. Dropped in at Hazel's on my way home. Typed two pages of matter for Jim. Fifty-five to go.

Tuesday, January 3: Balanced. Took Hazel skating. Went to her house for cocoa afterwards.

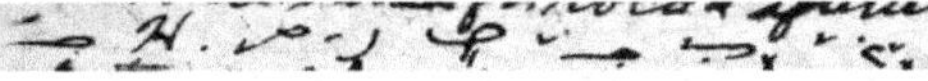

She skates well. Weather not too cold. Weather not too cold.

Wednesday, January 4: Badminton with Phyllis & Hazel. Jack sick – stomach. Had marshmallows & peanuts at Hazel's. Took Phyllis home & slipped on resolution.

Thursday, January 5: Intended to skate. Hockey at Avenue & MacCauley. Just had the walk. Managed to keep resolution but just once.

Friday, January 6: Weather slightly above [-18ºC]. Typed a few pages for Jim. **Started poem on St. John for Philip**. Jack came over for awhile.

Saturday, January 7: Saw "The Young at Heart" at Rialto [movie theatre]. Lunch at the "Log Cabin". Kept resolution after usual hesitation.

Sunday, January 8: Skated at Avenue from 3 to 5. Did not keep resolution. **Typed in evening & prepared speech for Toc S club.**

Monday, January 9: Toc S club first meeting this year. Four present & Ben. Mr Youmans visited informally. Work out but no basketball.

Tuesday, January 10: Skated at Norwood. Improving. resolution twice & nice. Typed after I got home & did not retire until 1:30.

Wednesday, January 11: Badminton. To Phyllis' afterwards. Kept resolution when I took Hazel home. Back to Hunters until 1:30. Later each night.

Thursday, January 12: Skating at Norwood again. Two more for resolution. Work at office in good shape Weather rather mild. Typed until 11:30.

Friday, January 13: Bowled 5 pins for Wilf's team. Scores 118, 159, 158. They went to Camea [?] but I went home. Bed 12:30.

Saturday, January 14: Skating at Avenue. No band Had cocoa at Hazel's. Philip talked a great deal. Resolution upheld but once. Weather chillier.

Sunday, January 15: Slept until 1:00. Typed letter to Davis. **Placed some pictures of Jasper in album. Chose topic for Toc S. Seven minute one**.

Monday, January 16: Toc S club. Only six present. Took class but no basketball. **Typed part of poem on St. John for Philip.**

Tuesday, January 17: Skating at Norwood with Hazel. Resolution once. **Finished poem for Philip. Trying to get story plot**. Weather mild.

Wednesday, January 18: Badminton. Phyllis & Ding not there. Stopped before 10:00. Jack walked with Hazel & I so no resolution. Worse luck.

Thursday, January 19: Stayed home & typed on material for Jim. Supper. I was to attend at Janet Cuthbertson's - postponed. Weather still good.

Friday, January 20: Bowled five pins. Lost three. Scores 114, 133, 117. Weather becoming colder. Paid $8.40 on radio. Debts coming in February.

Saturday, January 21: Dance at YWCA. Managed resolution twice. Dancing improving slightly it seems. Shy, Mary, Bob, Ding, Phyllis, Jack, Hazel, & I.

Sunday, January 22: Skated at Avenue band, my first band. Had supper at Hazel's. Phyllis came over after. Clem too. No resolution.

Monday, January 23: Sleigh-riding party of E.T.C. I was late. Eats & some dancing afterwords. Resolution once. Weather still fine.

Tuesday, January 24: Skating at Norwood. Becoming windy & colder. Resolution once. Home shortly after 11:00 surprise.

Wednesday, January 25: Badminton. Few people present. Heard Fred Allen at Brown's with Phyllis & Jack which made me miss resolution.

Thursday, January 26: Took it easy. Went to bed shortly after 9 but did not sleep until 10:30.

Friday, January 27: Five pins. Lost 3. Scores 154, 114, 69. Played 3-11-33 afterwards. Home after 12. Weather still mild.

Saturday, January 28: Party at Bob Ferrier's. He leaves for R.C.A.F. Sunday. Also Sis & Shy's birthday. Scavenger hunt. Over about 3. Resolution of course. Home 4:00.

Sunday, January 29: Up by 12:00. Took Phyllis to hockey game. Invited to supper. Home after 11:30. Typed voice for Ben. **Did not prepare speech.**

Monday, January 30: Colder, near [-18°C]. Toc S club in social room with other club again. Reg. Rose critic. Back to office 9:30. Left at 11:30 – hot chocolate 12:45.

Tuesday, January 31: Got balance at about 11:00 p.m. Quickest yet. Found mistake I'd made first.

February 1939

Wednesday, February 1: Worked through until time for badminton. Few turning out. No resolution as Jack dragged me away.

Thursday, February 2: Skating with Hazel at Norwood. Cold wind. Edna, Helen, Jean, & Ruth skating too. Nipped fingers. Resolution once. New ski suit.

Friday, February 3: Bowling three by default. Scores 112, 92, 149. Rotten. Jack watched & bowled one game. Month-end cleaned up. A record.

Saturday, February 4: Colder about [-29°C]. Ski train to Banff – Ding, Phyllis, Jack, Hazel, & I. Tried to sleep but not much luck. Resolution five or six times. New mitts.

Sunday, February 5: Phyllis' birthday. Breakfast Calgary. Lunch Mt. Norquay. Temperature [-2°C]. Skated, swam, & hot springs. Mountains more coarse than Jasper. Slept a little return trip.

Resolution seven or eight times.

Monday, February 6: Back at 7:00. Home to change & work at 9:00. Could hardly keep awake. Bed right after supper. No trouble sleeping.

Tuesday, February 7: More awake. Missed streetcar. Had editorial in Y paper, "The News". [Worthwhile Memorials]. Temperature -38°C. Not letting up. Early retiring 8:30.

Wednesday, February 8: No badminton. [-34°C]. Evening at Phlis with Jack, Ding, & Hazel. Walked home with Hazel as usual. Resolution once. Bed before 2:00 a.m.

Thursday, February 9: Typed Voice for Tom. Still around [-34°C]. Paid $5 on typewriter. $5 more. Hudson Bay bill due tomorrow.

Friday, February 10: Bowled. Lost 3. Scores 101, 150, 121. Played 3-11-33, Canada 5, & Duck Pins. Weather continues cold. No skating.

Saturday, February 11: Saw "Trade Winds" with Hazel at Rialto [movie theatre]. Still too cold for skating. Resolution once. Paid bill at Hudson Bay yesterday.

Sunday, February 12: Jack for supper. Went to Hazel's to look at pictures taken on Banff trip. Clem did not show up. Moderating.

Monday, February 13: Toc S club. John Barford guest critic. Back to office afterwards. Temperature around [-18°C]. Girl stenographer Barrett.

Tuesday, February 14: Skating at Norwood with Hazel. Gave her heart-shaped box of chocolates. Dropped in for lunch and missed resolution.

Wednesday, February 15: Badminton with Phyllis & Hazel. Stopped at Hazel's for lunch afterwards. [-12°C]. No resolution possible.

Thursday, February 16: Stayed in for a change. Have tickets for Winter Carnival. Very mild. Just freezing. Almost rained. Bed before 10:00.

Friday, February 17: Whist drive at Ding's. Walked home through wet snow storm. Resolution once. Mary, Shy, Jack, & Phyllis at Ding's too.

Saturday, February 18: Weather colder. Near [-18°C]. Snow & then some. Skated at Avenue but ice not too good. No band. Resolution once.

Sunday, February 19: **Finished Jasper essay, entered N.I.A. contest** & wrote letter to Davis. More snow & temperature around zero yet. 12:00.

Monday, February 20: Toc S only five present. Tie in basketball. Boy hurt & taken to hospital. Typed minutes when I got home. Have debate next week.

Tuesday, February 21: Skating with Hazel at Norwood. Weather fairly warm. Resolution once.

Wednesday, February 22: Badminton with Hazel & Phyllis. 50¢ from now to make up deficit. Hazel stayed at Hunter's as Winnie & Tina in town.

Thursday, February 23: **Caught up on sleep & typing. Finished Jasper essay**. Needs revising of course. Weather very mild.

Friday, February 24: Bowled 5 pins. Lost 3. Scores 177, 133, 188. Improving. Temperature staying up.

Saturday, February 25: Saw Ice Carnival with Hazel. Cold wind. Resolution once. Reserved seats. Typed a little in afternoon.

Sunday, February 26: Have had much snow this week. Hockey game with Jack, Phyllis, & Hazel. Went to Phyllis' after supper. Took Hazel home. Resolution once.

Monday, February 27: Debate at Toc S club. Just five present. Went back to work afterwards until about 11:00. Wilf typed statements.

Tuesday, February 28: Balanced. Wilf came back to type ledger balance sheets. Did not go out for supper. Worked through to 10:30. Balanced.

March 1939

Wednesday, March 1: Sent out statements. Badminton. Ruth & Howard walked home with Hazel & I. Resolution once. Just six turned out for badminton. Cooler.

Thursday, March 2: **Lost in debate "There should be free trade between Canada & the United States" at Y Toc club with Wilf McLean. 150 points to 147.** Basketball. Colder. Snow.

Friday March 3: Stayed home. Stomach slightly upset. Hazel had new hat yesterday. Possible reason. **Brushing up Jasper essay**. Weather cold.

Saturday, March 4: Temperature down to [-35°C]. Took Hazel to Rialto [movie theatre]. "Topper takes a trip". Funnier than "Topper". Resolution once. **Did no typing worse luck**.

Sunday, March 5: Home all day. Up at 12:30. Wrote Bob Ferrier at Trenton. Tried to be humorous. Cold weather holding.

Improved Jasper poem.

Monday, March 6: Debate at Toc S against Y Toc. Norm Patterson & Jack Caldwell won. Played postponed 5 pin games. Won. Scores 203, 178, 175.

Tuesday, March 7: Worked on photograph album. Weather fairly warm. Business slack now as usual. Teaching posting to Will & Gerry.

Wednesday, March 8: Badminton. Next week last time. Hazel's for awhile afterwards. Resolution once. Throat bothering.

Thursday, March 9: Skating at Norwood with Hazel. Not very cold. Resolution once. Developing cold.

Friday, March 10: 5 pins. Won three 156, 127, 190. Sore throat. Weather still moderate.

Saturday, March 11: Went to see "Son of Frankenstein" with Phyllis, Jack, & Hazel. Not very frightening. Resolution once. Cold holding on. Temperature down.

Sunday, March 12: Relapse & worked on photograph album. **Typed Jasper essay over.**

Monday, March 13: Toc S. Bowled in 5 pin tournament team. 144, 214, & 128. Eats at Johnson's afterwards. Weather cold for March.

Tuesday, March 14: Roxy Theatre with Hazel. "Love finds Andy Hardy". Good. Resolution once. Weather still cold. Odd for March.

Wednesday, March 15: Have dictaphone at office. Record voices of different members of staff. Last night of badminton. Eats at Phyllis'. Resolution once.

Thursday, March 16: More dictaphone recordings. Relaxed for a change. Nearly fell asleep listening to [Bing] Crosby. Finally to bed before 11:00.

Friday, March 17: **Stayed in and tried to write & do some work on album. Not very successful.** Bed fairly early again.

Saturday, March 18: Haircut. Saw "Fast & Loose" at Strand [movie theatre]. American Dairy lunch. Weather breaking. Resolution twice for a change.

Sunday, March 19: **Wrote two short short stories. Will submit one to <u>Writer's Digest</u>. Should click some time.** Becoming warmer.

Monday, March 20: Toc S club debate with Y Toc club. They won. Norm Patterson dispute Fred Youman's decision. Snow melting rapidly.

Tuesday, March 21: **Polishing up story for <u>Writer's Digest</u>.** E.A.C. 4 Moose Jaw 1. Jack saw game. Snow practically all gone.

Wednesday, March 22: No badminton. Bowled instead 127, 202, 10. Dutch lunch too. Walked home. Resolution once. **Typed out story for <u>Writer's Digest</u> contest**. Bed 2:30.

Thursday, March 23: Spring weather three years today. Stayed home. Good News of 29 & Crosby. E.A.C. 6 Moose Jaw 0. Hitting stride now.

Friday, March 24: Colder with snow. Won three in 5 pins. 193, 171, 77. Just four players. Will try out bike again on Tuesday. **Sent story to <u>Writer's Digest</u>**.

Saturday, March 25: Took Phyllis & Hazel to Empire [theatre] Opera – The Desert Song. Took Phyllis home first by streetcar.

Walked back with Hazel. Resolution once.

Sunday, March 26: Last night E.A.C. 9 Moose Jaw 2. Had supper at Hazel's. Phyllis cam up afterwards. Took her home so no resolution, although Phyllis suggested Hazel come along.

Monday, March 27: Toc S club. No regular meeting. Ate with supper club & heard speech on Banking. Weather fine & dry. Shower at noon.

Tuesday, March 28: Rode bike to work. General meeting of Eastwood Tennis Club. Elected treasurer. Club $22 down. To be dance on 29th. Resolution once.

Wednesday, March 29: Riding bicycle & coming home for dinner. Warming up. Stayed home. Having trouble with photo album.

Thursday, March 30: Stayed home & relaxed. Have ideas for more stories but am in lazy streak. Weather fairly warm. E.A.C. 6 Brandon 0.

Friday, March 31: Stayed at office. Won three games by default in 5 pins. 218, 170, 133. Girls had to treat us to milk shakes.

April 1939

Saturday, April 1: Hazel & I saw "Pygmalion" at Capital [movie theatre]. Resolution twice. E.A.C. 6 Brandon 0. Two in a row. Worked at office until 6. No balance.

Sunday, April 2: Colder. Snow blowing up. Breakfast at Corona with Speakers clubs. Lymburn spoke. Got balance after two hours. Jim & Bell up.

Monday, April 3: Cold with snow. Streetcar. Considerable work.

Did not leave office until about 16:00 Stayed home. Very windy.

Tuesday, April 4: Listened to hockey game. Brandon 5 E.A.C. 0. Surprise. Game at Winnipeg. Used streetcar.

Wednesday, April 5: Stayed home. Wally showed us how to play contract bridge. Easy. Weather rather cold.

Thursday, April 6: Party at Mary Brown's. E.A.C. 9 Brandon 3. E.A.C. western champions. Party over by 2:00. Driven home. No resolution.

Friday, April 7: Good Friday. Typed a little. Harry Young turned over treasurer's books. Weather warming up again.

Saturday, April 8: Dad's birthday. Took Hazel to "Little Princess" Shirley Temple at Capitol [movie theatre]. Resolution twice. Clem & Tina neared & we walked away.

Sunday, April 9: Meeting of E.T.C. Racqueteer Staff. Phyllis, Jack & I there. Wrote a letter to Bob Ferrier. Snow. Tennis is not far off.

Monday, April 10: Riding bicycle again. Stayed home. Streetcar because of snow. Work increasing. Did some typing. Oshawa 9 E.A.C. 4.

Tuesday, April 11: Bicycle today. **Typed an article for Eastwood paper.**

Wednesday, April 12: Stayed at home. Oshawa 12 E.A.C. 4. Terrible. Games being played in Toronto. **Drafted fantasy story.**

Thursday, April 13: Bicycle still. Work heavy. Weather spring-like. Jimmie's birthday. Jack up. Stayed home all evening.

Friday, April 14: Took Hazel to three one-act plays at Avenue

Community Hall. Heavy rainfall. Soaked. Resolution once. Work piling up again.

Saturday, April 15: Saw "Midnight" at Capitol [movie theatre] with Hazel. E.A.C. 4 Oshawa 1. Improving. Resolution twice. Won pool of $1 on hockey game.

Sunday, April 16: **Jack & I turned out a page each for the E.T.C. paper <u>The Racqueteer</u>**. Did no other work. Sunny but cool wind.

Monday, April 17: Last meeting of Toc S club for year. Listened to speaker at supper club. Oshawa 4 E.A.C. 2 Final.

Tuesday, April 18: Work still heavy. Weather warm. Riding bike. Stayed home after supper. Relaxing for awhile.

Wednesday, April 19: Worked at office until 8:00 doing drafts. Behind this month. Home to relax. Spring weather holding.

Thursday, April 20: Went for walk with Hazel, Anne, & Norman – Jasper East & Flats. Walked all way back. Resolution once.

Friday, April 21: Five pins. Lost 3. Scores 90, 145, 196. E.A.C.'s returned & were paraded. Saw them from streetcar.

Saturday, April 22: Hazel & I saw "Three Smart Girls Grow Up" Deanna Durbin. Best show for some time. Resolution twice after rather long time stalling.

Sunday, April 23: Wrote Davis. Jack & I played at golf out behind his place. **Retyped part of Jasper poem**. Took a few snaps. Warm & bright.

Monday, April 24: Weather still fine. C. Lennie rode my bike home & I took streetcar. Stayed home & took it easy.

Tuesday, April 25: Hazel & I saw "Marie Antoinette" at Avenue [movie theatre]. Fairly good. Resolution twice. Weather getting milder.

Wednesday, April 26: Worked at office after supper. Getting ready for month-end. Very hot for this time of year.

Thursday, April 27: More overtime. Summer heat rather unusual. Work increasing. Will be hectic this month-end.

Friday, April 28: Bowled one game. Had milk shakes at Black Cat. Bowling finished for season. Hot. Tired after hard day.

Saturday, April 29: E.T. Club Dance. Not very large crowd. Gordy with Hazel & I. Stormy weather. Resolution twice after a talk about Phyllis & Jack.

Sunday, April 30: Worked at office from 1 until 7. Fagged out. **Too tired these nights to do any typing.**

May 1939

Monday, May 1: Tennis began. No balance. Walked home with Hazel. Heard Grads 37 St. Louis 25. End of series. Resolution once. Phyllis staying at Brown's.

Tuesday, May 2: Balanced after few hours overtime. No tennis but collected $2 on tennis fees. Considerable work to do.

Wednesday, May 3: walked home with Phyllis & Hazel. Resolution twice after stroll down 96 St. Weather quite warm.

Thursday, May 4: Played tennis until it rained. Did not walk home with girls. Hudson Bay sent up radio but did not take ours to repair.

Friday, May 5: Dance at Camet. C.N. Tennis Club. Broke up at 1:00. Driven home. Resolution twice. Bought blue trench coat at Bay. Rainy.

Saturday, May 6: Showery. Courts too wet for tennis. Danced at Namayo with Phyllis, Alex, & Hazel. Lunch at Selkirk. No resolution.

Sunday, May 7: Played tennis with Jack & others. Windy. Phyllis & Hazel dropped around for the evening but not to play.

Monday, May 8: Saw "Boys Town" at Avenue [movie theatre] with Hazel. Weather cold. Snowed a little but cleared up for evening. Resolution three times.

Tuesday, May 9: Jack came along with Phyllis, Hazel, and I but was snubbed. He rode me home on bicycle afterwards. No resolution.

Wednesday, May 10: Walked home with Hazel. Invited in at Brown's and left about 12 after three or four resolutions. Rather chilly.

Thursday, May 11: Walked home with Hazel after tennis. Work becoming heavier. Behind a few days. Weather improving. Resolution twice.

Friday, May 12: Jack picked Hazel & I up in new car & drove us to her place. No resolutions. **No reply from <u>Writer's Digest</u> yet**.

Saturday, May 13: Saw "The Castles" Astaire & Rogers at Capitol [movie theatre]. Got roller skates. Met Phyllis at Brown's after show. Resolution three times but h\not home until 2:00.

Sunday, May 14: Official opening E.T. Club. Good crowd. Social after six sets. Started at 9:30 in morning. Extremely hot. Sunburned. Did not roller skate.

Monday, May 15: **Story back from <u>Writer's Digest</u>**. Worked at office. Roller skated alone afterwards. Girls too tired. Jim & Bell up.

Tuesday, May 16: Not feeling very well. Bed after supper. Thunder storm with some rain. Did not eat anything all day.

Wednesday, May 17: Ate a little. Played some tennis. Walked home with Hazel. Another thunder storm. Resolution two or three times. Home in drizzle.

Thursday, May 18: Streetcar again. Saw at Strand [movie theatre] "Yes My Darling Daughter" & "Torchy Runs for Mayor" with Hazel. More rain. Resolution four times. Streetcar home in rain.

Friday, May 19: Rain. Missed car. **Studying new magazine <u>Unknown</u> for possibilities of plot I have.** Getting $28 from today but not enough. Will try for more.

Saturday, May 20: More rain. Saw "Doris Jordan's Follies" with Hazel. Fair. Ate at Haigs afterwards. Resolution three or four times.

Sunday, May 21: Dampness prevails. **Wrote some on fantasy story**. Jim & Bell up for visit. No tennis. Did not go out at all.

Monday, May 22: Tried out roller skates again – alone. Skated to 97 Street & back. Rather rough. Weather remains unsettled.

Tuesday, May 23: More rain. Streetcar again. Went to preview at Capitol [movie theatre] "Hardys Ride High" with Hazel. Resolution three or four times afterwards.

Wednesday, May 24: Tennis all afternoon. Lakeview with Phyllis, Alex, & Hazel after supper. Met Jack, Ted, Doc, Shy, May, & Ding. Danced.

Thursday, May 25: Tennis until dark. Did not walk home with Hazel. Tennis fees rather slow. Bob White not cooperating as much as would like.

Friday, May 26: Tennis as usual. Walked home with Hazel. Resolution twice. Work increasing slightly. Gerry leaving for new job.

Saturday, May 27: Saw "Dark Victory" at Capitol [movie theatre]. Resolution four or five times. Haircut. Played a few sets in the afternoon. Rather hot.

Sunday, May 28: Played tennis all day. Walked home with Phyllis & Hazel. Resolution once. Cloudy with wind at times.

Monday, May 29: Worked at office. Month-end coming up Grads 41 Chicago 29. Not much interest. Bed fairly early.

Tuesday, May 30: Worked but back in time to walk home with girls. Tried to teach roller-skating. Resolution once. Fees coming in slowly.

Wednesday, May 31: Worked at office until after ten. Weather cold for this time of year. Grads 36 Chicago 24. City ready for Royalty.

June 1939

Thursday, June 1: Worked until about 7:30. Balanced. Wilf helped a little. Crowds of people in town for Royal Visit.

Friday, June 2: Golf at Prince Rupert 147. Saw King & Queen on Portage Ave. Played some tennis. Saw K & Q leave. Watched fireworks. Resolution once. Legs tired.

Saturday, June 3: Went to Lakeview with E.T.C. Danced until

12:30. Back to city about 2:30 or so. Resolution three or four times. Twenty-six went out to Lakeview. Wilf there too.

Sunday, June 4: Rain almost all day. **Finished page for <u>Racqueteer</u>.** Short day. I got up at 2:30. **Too tired to write anything else**.

Monday, June 5: Rode car as weather threatening. Did very little after supper. Cleaning up month-end work but quite a bit to do yet.

Tuesday, June 6: Still overcast. Rather cold but some people on courts. Month-end fairly well cleaned away. Gerry leaving soon.

Wednesday, June 7: Tennis with the gang once again. Walked home with Hazel. Resolution twice. Rather cool for June. Considerable rain too.

Thursday, June 8: More tennis. Walked home with Phyllis & Hazel. Had cocoa & toast at Hazel's. Resolution twice. Weather improving.

Friday, June 9: Roller skating with Hazel on Portage Avenue. She fell heavily once. Phyllis did not come as she had promised. Gordy [illegible] home with me.

Saturday, June 10: Played a few sets in the afternoon. Saw "Confessions of a Nazi Spy" at Capitol [movie theatre]. At at Log Cabin. Rained a little. Resolution five or six times.

Sunday, June 11: Played at C.N. courts. Hazel with Wilf & Agnes. From three until dark. Walked home with Agnes, Hazel, & Jack Truscott. Resolution once.

Monday, June 12: Meeting E.T.C. Courts rather wet. Played one set. About twenty present. Hazel & Phyllis not out. Club tournament coming up.

Tuesday, June 13: Worked for awhile but home in time for a set of tennis. Weather has not been very warm yet this year.

Wednesday, June 14: Played a little tennis. No swimming yet this year. Too chilly. Work at office piling up.

Thursday, June 15: Walked home with Phyllis & Hazel. Resolution twice. Eleanor rather slow at daybooks.

Friday, June 16: Called in at Phyllis' last night. Bill Tidbury among those present. Tried some dancing. Closing date for tournament. Entered.

Saturday, June 17: Saw "Gracie Allen Murder Case" at Strand [movie theatre]. Baked white cake in afternoon. Lost in singles to Byron Cowell 6-2 & 6-4. Resolution four or five times.

Sunday, June 18: Jack & I beat Jiggs & Ted C. 6-1 & 6-2. Hot. Supper at Brown's. My cake eaten. Tennis afterwards. Resolution twice.

Monday, June 19: Tournament well underway. No matches for me. Played a set or so for fun. Strawberry Social. Jack drove us home.

Tuesday, June 20: Jack & I lost to Clem & Ken 6-3 & 6-2. Hazel & I too. Phyllis & Ted 6-0 & 6-2. Just secondaries for me now. Resolution two or three times.

Wednesday, June 21: Getting work under control. Not enough sleep. Walked home with Phyllis & Hazel after tennis. Resolution three or four times.

Thursday, June 22: Interclub. Played afterwards. Won two sets. Surprise. **Too tired to do any writing. Will try to do some soon. However.**

Friday, June 23: Played a little tennis as usual. Tournament moving along. Should finish soon. I am practically out. Played set with Jiggs.

Saturday, June 24: A few sets. Saw "Invitation to Happiness" at Capitol [movie theatre]. Resolution four or five times. Weather threatening. Last chance in tournament tomorrow.

Sunday, June 25: Up at 9:30. Lost against Ken Price 6-1 & 6-2. Terrible. Rain stopped further play. Still did not get to bed early.

Monday, June 26: Rainy. Did not play tennis. Month-end creeping up. **Tried to write about Royal Visit. Easier listening to radio**. Have a cold.

Tuesday, June 27: Did not play tennis. Interclub. **Tried to type but no success**. Will be busy this month-end. Warm.

Wednesday, June 28: Warmer. Hazel won semi-finals in Ladies Singles Secondaries 11-9, 1-6, 6-4 against Ding. Frarey drove Hazel home.

Thursday, June 29: Worked for awhile but home in time for a set. Walked home with Hazel. Resolution two or three times. Weather warm.

Friday, June 30: Worked some more. Windy. Back in time to ride home with Hazel & gang in Ted's car. Resolution twice. Home 2:00.

July 1939

Saturday, July 1: More work. Did half the statements. Saw "Streets of New York" at Strand [movie theatre]. Ate at Merricks. Gave Hazel **pink mirror** for birthday. Received fountain pen. Resolution six or seven times. 2:00.

Sunday, July 2: **Hazel left for west coast** in morning. Worked but did not balance. Wilf did posting but was not checked. Played two sets tennis. Had drive in Ted's car with Jack.

Monday, July 3: Balanced at about 9:00 p.m. **Home to discuss west coast trip with Jack. Leave on 14th for two weeks**. Still not getting to bed early. Weather warmer.

Tuesday, July 4: Worked late at office trying to get month-end work done. Did not play tennis. Too tired. Can use a vacation.

Wednesday, July 5: Working again for awhile & played a set or so. Sat in Ted Allard's car & ate licorice for awhile. Home to make statement for E.T.C.

Thursday, July 6: Meeting of E.T.C. $50 in hole. Received letter from Hazel. Appropriate since it is her birthday. Work keeping heavy.

Friday, July 7: Had a few sets of tennis. Weather getting warmer. Have not been swimming this year. Getting work cleaned up.

Saturday, July 8: Bought shirts, ties, & socks for west coast trip. Got card from Hazel. Walked home with Phyllis. Work not too bad.

Sunday, July 9: Quite hot. Jack with Olive Quilly beat Dick Triscott & me two sets. Played some in the evening until dark.

Monday, July 10: Hot & then some. Worked through until about 9:30. Got information on west coast trip. Will leave Friday night for two weeks.

Tuesday, July 11: Wind came up to spoil tennis for evening. Will have hike with E.T.C. tomorrow. Cooler but still warm enough.

Wednesday, July 12: E.T.C. went down to Victoria Park for

wiener roast. About 15 attended. Played baseball. Walked home afterwards.

Thursday, July 13: Worked late to clean up work. Met Jack & Fay. Went over to Jim's for two suitcases. Got sport shirt from family.

Friday, July 14: Left at midnight for Calgary, Vancouver, Victoria, & Seattle. Day coach all night rather uncomfortable but not too bad.

Saturday, July 15: Calgary 6:20. Went to Y & left bags. Visited Pilkington's & Institute of Technology. Saw Grandstand performance. Wrote letters & cards.

Sunday, July 16: Up at 6:00. Travelled all day through mountains. One seat only so sleeping well nigh impossible. Mountains & then some.

Monday, July 17: Vancouver. Big. A city. Finally located at a Mrs. Balback 1662 Robson Street. Saw part of Stanley Park, English Bay, & Lion's Gate Bridge.

Tuesday, July 18: Got up at about 1:30. Raining. Saw Empress of Russia. Last night we saw "Stagecoach" at the Colonial [movie theatre]. Lost way last night & today but found ourselves.

Wednesday, July 19: Played tennis on asphalt courts. Rain disturbed second set. Went to New Westminister. Attended sing-song at Stanley Park & saw colourful fountain.

Thursday, July 20: Visited Marine Building, Happy Land, Museum. Dull at first but brightened up. Saw "Susanna of the Mountain" at Strand [movie theatre]. Went to Happy Land in daytime.

Friday, July 21: Stanley Park, Siwash Rock. Also English Bay where heavy waves were breaking. Met Marg Bradley. Sun burned. Saw China Town.

Saturday, July 22: Capilano Canyon & swing bridge, Lion's Gate Bridge. Went to Happy Land. Rod Dipper twice. Display of fireworks. Day bright.

Sunday, July 23: Another fine day. More tennis. Down on beach again & got slightly more burnt. Met Marg Bradley & Jack Hamilton.

Monday, July 24: Over to Victoria. Quiet & peaceful. Saw Crystal Garden Pool. Found room easily. Saw "Alexander's Ragtime Band" at Columbia [movie theatre].

Tuesday, July 25: Visited Butchart Gardens. Seattle after dark. Lights make city look cheerful. Took taxi to Y. Walked around.

Wednesday, July 26: Met two fellows. Took us to Washington Lake. Saw "Captain Fury" & "The Gorilla" at Coliseum [movie theatre]. Saw "Battleship Pennsylvania".

Thursday, July 27: Climbed up Smith Tower 42 stories. Public Library. Saw "Let Freedom Reign" & "Charlie Chan in Honolulu" at State [movie theatre].

Friday, July 28: Princess Marguerite [ferry boat] coming over but Kathleen now. Rough crowd at Vancouver Station. Got in smoker with gang. Not much sleep. Saw fire.

Saturday, July 29: Alberta. Banff & finally Calgary. Too hot. Saw "Man about town" at Capitol [movie theatre]. On our way to Edmonton.

Sunday, July 30: In at 6:25. Frarey met us & drove us home. Slept for awhile & then played some tennis. Some more after supper. No Hazel.

Monday, July 31: Back to office. Wilf did good work. A set of tennis tonight. Rain. Took streetcar to Hazel's. Resolution three or four times.

August 1939

Tuesday, August 1: Picture from Hazel. Gave her perfume treasure chest. Work late at office but home by 10:30. Just part of statements completed.

Wednesday, August 2: Worked late again. Completed statements and balanced first time. Wilf had checked all his own posting.

Thursday, August 3: A great deal of work to be done. Warm weather makes work seem more difficult. Jack & I saw pictures at Hazel's.

Friday, August 4: Played a few sets. Walked home with Hazel and resolution a few times. Still good weather which is strange.

Saturday, August 5: Worked in afternoon. Saw "Magnificent Fraud" at Strand [movie theatre]. Lunch at Log Cabin. Resolution a few times. Weather quite warm.

Sunday, August 6: Swam in early afternoon. Dinner at Brown's. Tennis until supper time. Did nothing but relax in evening.

Monday, August 7: Civic Holiday. Hiked with Hazel to end of ravine & Clover Bar Bridge. Back along tracks. Resolution but once.

Tuesday, August 8: Jack & I went to Brown's silver anniversary. Rather late when we finally left. Played considerable Bingo.

Wednesday, August 9: Work late to try to get things finished before Mr. Glover leaves for two weeks. Warm weather.

Thursday, August 10: More late work. Getting everything cleaned up. Wilf on holidays making more work which is no good.

Friday, August 11: Worked late but Jack drove me home at ten. Cleaned up bills. Mr. Glover going on holidays next week.

Saturday, August 12: Went to Roxy by truck with Phyl Barnes Otto Poatz. Lunched & danced at the Grove & got to bed before 3:00. Resolution twice.

Sunday, August 13: Good weather. Hazel over for supper. Played tennis afterwards. Walked Hazel home. Resolution twice. Met Clem.

Monday, August 14: Meeting E.T.C. Phyl & Ding back from holidays. Hot. Bike has flat. Walked with Phyllis & Hazel. Resolution twice.

Tuesday, August 15: Went roller skating with Hazel. Rain spoilt things & we did not skate very much but were able to try skating together. Resolution twice.

Wednesday, August 16: Time for some tennis. Club finances still poor. Hazel & I walked around afterwards. Weather chilly. Resolution a few times.

Thursday, August 17: Weather has been very dry. My tennis seems to be improving. Was to show Winnie some bookkeeping but company spoilt it. No resolution.

Friday, August 18: Played some tennis. Walked home with Hazel & resolution twice. Mr. Glover has been on holidays a week.

Saturday, August 19: Went to Lakeview with Alf Rands, Winnie, & Hazel in new Plymouth. Resolution two or three times. Alf drove me home.

Sunday, August 20: Played a few sets in afternoon & evening. Jack drove Doc, Ted, & I to White Mud after dark. Helen home yesterday from tonsil operation.

Monday, August 21: Had two wisdom teeth pulled. Bike has another flat. Chillier at nights now. Resolution twice.

Tuesday, August 22: Bike not fixed yet. Played a set or two of tennis. Straightened club books. Typed short piece to try new 35¢ ribbon I got at Eaton's.

Wednesday, August 23: Bike still not fixed. Mr. Glover will be back next week. I left early & played some tennis. Resolution once afterwards.

Thursday, August 24: Not very long to play tennis. Might close in quickly. Never seem to get much sleep these nights.

Friday, August 25: Bike running again. Played some tennis. Walked home with Hazel. Taught Winnie bookkeeping. Resolution few times.

Saturday, August 26: Wiener roast of E.T. Club at Whitemud. Walked along creek with Hazel. Resolution a few times. Jack had car.

Sunday, August 27:

Monday, August 28:

Tuesday, August 29: Blowout. Bought new tire & tube. **Rode out to St. Albert with Doc, Ted, & Jack after tennis.** Began letter to Davis.

Wednesday, August 30: Beginning month-end work. Late work. Weather warm. **Situation tense in Europe. Militia guarding bridges, etc. in Canada.**

Thursday, August 31: More late work after talk with Cy Southall. Half statements written up. **Work not too heavy because of war fear**.

September 1939

Friday, September 1: Balanced almost immediately. **Germany & Poland fighting. England [U.K.] & France expected to declare war soon. No war officially declared between Germany & Poland**. Wrote Davis.

Saturday, September 2: **Finished Racqueteer**. Saw "Star Maker" at Capitol [movie theatre]. Had cake & pop at Hazel's. **Ultimatum given Germany by England [U.K.] & France**. Resolution few times.

Sunday, September 3: **Roused at eight by Extra: England at War!"** Played tennis in afternoon. Hazel wont a set 6-4 in afternoon & 6-2 at night. Good for her.

Monday, September 4: Threatened to rain. Played some tennis in afternoon. Rained slightly after supper. Had to postpone roller skating plans.

Tuesday, September 5: Went back to work to clean up a few things. Expect rush if glass prices go up. No more glass can be promised from England [U.K.] [Pilkington Brothers was a U.K. company.]

Wednesday, September 6: Ben married today. Hazel, Gerry, Eleanor, Wilf, & I attended & went to reception afterwards. Took taxi from office where we picked up present.

Thursday, September 7: Meeting E.T.C. Decided to have dance. Walked home with Hazel. Resolution few times. Nights are getting cooler. Dark too early for tennis.

Friday, September 8: Change in glass price. Worked late. Left office at about 11:30. Sold more glass last few days than usually do in half a month.

Saturday, September 9: Saw "Goodbye Mr. Chips" at Capitol [movie theatre]. Felt rather woozy with a cold. Resolution twice & staggered home.

Sunday, September 10: Worked at office & played tennis afterwards. Showers. Family & Jack went to Elk Island leaving me alone. Did E.T.C. books over. Four years or so.

Monday, September 11: Rained all day. Bad cold. Rode streetcar. Wrote letter to Herman Joselson in Seattle. Kink in back for some reason.

Tuesday, September 12: Weather clearing. Mr. Glover back from East. Worked late. Quite cool. Cold hanging on. **War in Europe not progressing much.**

Wednesday, September 13: Skies clearer. Back to work again. Expect things will slow down soon since all customers have put in supply.

Thursday, September 14: Work quite heavy because of price advance. Sold more glass last few days than we ordinarily do in a month.

Friday, September 15: Worked quite late endeavouring to clean up all work. Typed two daybooks. Mr. Glover still down East.

Saturday, September 16: saw "Beau Geste" at Capitol [movie theatre]. Good. Had lunch at Hazel's. Played Bill Logan beaten 6-8. Improving. Resolution a few times.

Sunday, September 17: Gang went to Cooking Lake for the day. Our rugby team was weak so we prepared the meals. Shy & I paddled canoes back in darkness.

Monday, September 18: Played Rop Rummy at E. Club House. Lost at first but ended up 30¢ ahead. Not bad for the first time.

Tuesday, September 19: Roller skating on Portage. Both improving I think. Resolution. Went almost to the end. **Many soldiers around these nights**.

Wednesday, September 20: Took it easy for a change. **War rages in Europe yet**.

Thursday, September 21: **Roller skating on Portage. Bumped into two soldiers who promptly fell over**. Nights are getting colder. Resolution a few times.

Friday, September 22: Made mistake. Thought Y class was tonight so I just stayed at home & relaxed listening to prize fight & rugby game.

Saturday, September 23: Played rummy at E. Club House. Saw "Each Dawn & Die" at Capitol [movie theatre]. Met Anne & Ken afterwards & ate at Drive Inn. Resolution few times.

Sunday, September 24: **Typed final copy of Jasper essay**. Went to Hazel's for supper. Campbell Playhouse on Sundays. Snow. WE walked party way [illegible].

Monday, September 25: First Y class this season. Won in basketball. Meeting of Toc S & Y Toc. Clubs to decide on this winter's programme. May amalgamate.

Tuesday, September 26: Rained at night. Hazel & I roller skate but went to see "Andy Hardy Gets Spring Fever" at Empire [movie theatre]. Sunny. Met Phyllis & her mother afterwards. Resolution twice.

Wednesday, September 27: More rain. Rode car. Stayed at office until after 8:00. Wrote up some statements. Have to do month-end quickly this month. Hot.

Thursday, September 28: Snow. Rode car. Worked late at office but had workout afterwards. Lost in basketball. Month-end work shaping up rather nicely.

Friday, September 29: Back to work getting month-end work lined up. Weather good 'though nights are getting chillier. **Europe still wars**.

Saturday, September 30: The gang bowled. I lost. Hazel & I went to Namao in Art Hook's car while others went with Jack. We got stung as our party drank.

October 1939

Sunday, October 1: Balanced at 4:30. Relaxed in the evening listening to radio. Will clean up work quickly this month I hope.

Monday, October 2: meeting of Speakers Clubs. Amalgamated. Meetings will be on Thursdays. Workout & basketball win which I lost again.

Tuesday, October 3: Hazel & I roller skated down Portage. Month-end work finished with exception of Y. Outing. Resolution twice.

Wednesday, October 4: Went back to work for awhile to price orders. Business holding up fairly well. Weather keeps quite good. Rained.

Thursday, October 5: Meeting of new speakers' club. Impromptu speeches. Jack Barford critic. Won in basketball afterwards. Hal Richards hurt.

Friday, October 6: Miserable weather. Stayed home & relaxed in the evening. Business holding up although glass stock running very low.

Saturday, October 7: E.T.C. Dance at I.O.O.F. Hall. Made over $20.00. Good time. Hazel rather late & we arrived after nine. Resolution twice afterwards.

Sunday, October 8: Over to Brown's after supper. Took Hazel to see "The Wizard of Oz" at Capitol [movie theatre] preview. Clem & Tina could not get in. Resolution four times. Bed 4:30.

Monday, October 9: **Managed to squeeze out poem about the Royal Visit**. Slept most of day, however. Getting colder. Soon have to look for skiis.

Tuesday, October 10: Windy. Rode streetcar. Quite busy. Stayed home at night & listened to radio. **My writing is being neglected.**

Wednesday, October 11: Streetcar. Balanced E.T.C. books. Made over $25. Not bad. Weather chilly with wet snow. Stayed home & loafed again.

Thursday, October 12: After speakers' meeting went to Jessie Hales for E.T.C. meeting. Snowing wetly. Made about $28 on dance, we know now.

Friday, October 13: Bowled 10 pins. Scores 164 & 147. Played snooker with Jack & Ted Allard afterwards. Ted Cole too. Lost on last shot. Foggy & chilly.

Saturday, October 14: Saw "The Real Glory" at Rialto [movie theatre]. Met Anne, Helen, & friends at American Dairy Lunch. Ken drove us home. Resolution two or three times.

Sunday, October 15: Up around 2:00. Went to Hazel's after

supper. Met Browns. No Clem, strangely enough. Stayed until after 12:00. Resolution twice.

Monday, October 16: Workout at Y. Won in basketball. Jack there. Swam a few lengths. Bob White rode home with us from Y.

Tuesday, October 17: Weather better. Rode bike. Hazel & I went to visit Eleanor Rudolph. Merely talked. Waffles for lunch. After twelve again. Resolution twice.

Wednesday, October 18: Weather fairly warm. Stayed home & **worked on <u>Liberty</u> contest. Lorne's outfit may go East on Monday. War may last for years by present action**.

Thursday, October 19: Streetcar. Speakers' club. Won in basketball. Jack & I went to Rec afterword & Frarey drove us home. Weather mild.

Friday, October 20: Stayed home & put pictures in album. May finish it if I'm not careful. Rode bike. Weather quite good.

Saturday, October 21: The gang bowled 149, 203, 99. Lost by 14 pins. Had to pay. Jack drove nine of us home. Some fun & we made it.

Sunday, October 22: Weather closing in now. Rained lightly at night. Visited Hazel. Clem showed up. Result – left after 1:00. Resolution twice.

Monday, October 23. Snowed all day. **Went to station to see Lorne leave for Kingston with wireless section. Large crowd**. Temperature low.

Tuesday, October 24: More snow. Temperature [12°C]. At Brown's with Eleanor Rudolph & Clarence Cocky. Cards & Chinese Checkers. Resolution three times. 1:30.

Wednesday, October 25: Stayed in office all day. Snow staying. Didn't leave house after supper. Tom Corno called with fruit & candy. Stuffed.

Thursday, October 26: Ben criticized at club. Five minute speech. Missed part of workout. Basketball and swimming. Still chilly.

Friday, October 27: **Packed everything ready to move tomorrow. Just the bed left in room when I finished**. Weather milder.

Saturday, October 28: **Moved**. Saw "The Old Maid" at Capitol [movie theatre]. No lunch. **New house cosy**. Weather moderating. Resolution three or four times.

Sunday, October 29: Had supper at Brown's & listened to radio in the evening. Stayed until about 1:00. Resolution twice. Not too cold.

Monday, October 30: Class at Y quite strenuous. Took gymnastics & played both basketball & volleyball. Got a slight bump on the eye.

Tuesday, October 31: Masquerade party at E.T.C. Hazel gypsy, Jack pirate, & I devil. Fun. Jack walked home with Hazel & I & Phyllis.

November 1939

Wednesday, November 1: Worked through until 10:30. Did not finish statements. Got ride home at diner time in Dodd's car. Chesterfield due today did not come.

Thursday, November 2: Speakers' Club at Y. Back to work. No balance. Forgot time. 1:30 when I left office. Walked home in the fresh air.

Friday, November 3: Hazel & I took Govt. dance at Macdonald Hotel. Ding, two Margs, Doc, Shy, & Jack. Johnson's for lunch. Had to hire taxi.

Saturday, November 4: Jack, Phyllis, & I at Hazel's. Popped corn, played cards & Chinese Checkers. Relaxed in afternoon. No resolution. Chillier.

Sunday, November 5: Jim, Bell, & kids visited. All enjoyed new chesterfield. Jim too it easy. Everyone home for a change. Jack over for awhile.

Monday, November 6: Practised with Jack & Wilf. Workout & gymnastics followed. Swam a few lengths too. Tried some weight-lifting.

Tuesday, November 7: Jack & I sent letters to delinquent E.T.C. members and I tried to balance the books but can't at present.

Wednesday, November 8: Stayed at home. New chief clerk being broken in. Tun. Composed invitation to show Hazel.

Thursday, November 9: Speakers' club and the class afterwards. Won in basketball but did no swimming. Chief clerk Clark, Austin Anderton, & I not chummy.

Friday, November 10: Bowled with the Dodgers. 155 & 126. Had to climb in window when Jack & I returned. Got three ski outfits for Jack, Hazel, & I.

Saturday, November 11: Saw "Hollywood Cavalcade" at Capitol [movie theatre] with Hazel. Played snooker in morning with Frank, Ted, & Jack. Resolution four or five times.

Sunday, November 12: Hazel for supper. Jack & I argued part of the evening. Took Hazel home after twelve. Got back about 1:30. Resolution two or three times.

Monday, November 13: Practised basketball with Jack & Wilf. Took class & lost in basketball. Swam a few lengths. Snow melting rapidly.

Tuesday, November 14: Snow nearly all gone. Work slackening which means we'll soon be taking things fairly easy.

Wednesday, November 15: Have much less work to do. Anderton prices orders and has taken over much of my work. Goody.

Thursday, November 16: **Meeting of Spokes Club & spoke impromptu**. Workout with basketball & swimming finally getting home.

Friday, November 17: Hazel & I visited Eleanor Rudolph again. Played cards & talked. Resolution a few times & so to bed after 12:00.

Saturday, November 18: Ben showed me how to fix ski harness. Finished my pair after he left & will do Jack's tomorrow. Saw "Edith Cavell" at Capitol [movie theatre]. Resolution three or four.

Sunday, November 19: Jim, Bell, & family down. Visited Hazel at night. Heard Orson Wells. Resolution a few times & to bed.

Monday, November 20: No signs of snow. Class at Y as usual. Played some basketball in Hit & Miss, mostly the latter.

Tuesday, November 21: Fixed plates on Hazel's skiis. Haven't boots for her yet so could not install all harness.

Wednesday, November 22: Another night of relaxation. Quite likely I will not have to do any more overtime.

Thursday, November 23: Spokes club meeting. **Spoke about glass. Talked afterwards and missed workout**. Played basketball & swam.

Friday, November 24: Did not go out after supper. Wrote two poems. One about E.T.C. banquet & other about Gordon Brown [Hazel & Philip's brother].

Saturday, November 25: E.T.C. banquet. Down about &6. Good time. Danced about four times with Hazel. Resolution three or four times.

Sunday, November 26: Went to Cooking Lake with Ted, Kerry, Doc, & Jack. Played cards at Rover Den in the evening. Lost 80¢.

Monday, November 27: Ground still bare. Not cold. Barely freezing. Y class. Won in basketball 13-11. Swam a few lengths. Home fairly early.

Tuesday, November 28: Saw "Babes in Arms" at Capitol [movie theatre] with Hazel. Resolution a few times. Snow holding off. Skiis waiting.

Wednesday, November 29: Month-end work will be delayed since daybooks are done on schedule now. Took things easy at night.

Thursday, November 30: Spokes club. Lost in basketball 14-12. Took gymnastics and swam afterwards. Cold trying to beat me.

December 1939

Friday, December 1: Bowled for Dodgers. Scores 127, 170, 175. Won three. Went home afterwards. Am doing no overtime yet. No snow.

Saturday, December 2: Did half statements. Worked until 2:30. Won in bowling competition we staged. Jack drove some of us home.

Sunday, December 3: Relaxed. Read a little & waxed skiis. **Wrote some poetry**. Still waiting for snow but none comes.

Monday, December 4: Stayed home after leaving work at 6:30. Relaxed. Slight cold. Not balanced yet. New system – more fun.

Tuesday, December 5: Balanced at last. Visited Hazel. Eleanor & Clarence did not come but we got along all right. Resolution twice.

Wednesday, December 6: Caught up on some more reading. Month-end returns nearly complete. Soon be able to organize my work.

Thursday, December 7: Heard Judge Hoshing speak instead of spieling ourselves. Y class. Won in basketball. Swam a few lengths. No snow.

Friday, December 8: Stayed at home during the evening & read more of Martin Chuzzlewitt. Listened to radio. Snow not here yet.

Saturday, December 9: Saw "Espionage Agent" at Strand [movie theatre] with Hazel. Had light lunch at her house. Resolution a few times. Home before 2:00.

Sunday, December 10: Fixed shelves in room. Supper at Hazel's. **Wrote humorous article for Gordon**.

Monday, December 11: Class at Y. Won basketball. Small snow flurry but this did not last long enough to cover ground. Office work in good shape.

Tuesday, December 12: Weather still good. Stayed downtown at noon. Trying to do some Christmas shopping. Work at office will soon be easy.

Wednesday, December 13: Took Helen to “Broadway Serenade”- Jeanette Macdonald at Avenue [movie theatre]. Still keep rather late hours.

Thursday, December 14: Spokes club supper at Log Cabin. **Gave stump speech. Terrible**. Won rest as best novice in gymnastics. Jim left for old country.

Friday, December 15: Balanced E.T. Club books. Will be lucky if we break even this year. Read a little. Am taking books from library.

Saturday, December 16: Hazel’s father sick. Possibly gall stones. We merely went downtown for a short while. Had picture taken at Goertz.

Sunday, December 17: Went skating at Horse Shoe Lake with Ted, Doris, Art Hall, & Jack. Lost in hockey scrimmage. Paid for drinks.

Monday, December 18: Went to class at Y. Won in basketball. Did not swim. Weather continues quite mild. Christmas shopping in good shape.

Tuesday, December 19: Saw Mrs. Rice regarding Community League Fees. Listened to radio & finished statements for E.T.C. Socials. Christmas cards ready.

Wednesday, December 20: E.T.C. Raffle. Anderton won ham. Morrissey- turkey. Streets still slippery from yesterday’s ice coating.. Few flakes of snow. Resolution twice.

Thursday, December 21: Speaking clubs met for Christmas party.

Won quiz. Took shower at Y. Got ashtray for present. Gave mechanical toy.

Friday, December 22: Finished Christmas shopping. Stayed home for a change. Not enough snow for skiing yet. Hazel has not got her ski boots yet.

Saturday, December 23: **Gave poem to girls at Harry Taits**. Bowled & lost. Met Hazel afterwards & we all went to Johnsons. Resolution twice.

Sunday, December 24: Hazel came up & we went to church at 11:30. Did not get home until almost 4:00 in the morning. Resolution four times.

Monday, December 25: Gave Hazel twin lamps. Received a watch. O.K. Hazel down to our house again. Weather warm with very little snow. Resolution three times.

Tuesday, December 26: Took have to see Deanna Durbin in "First Love" at Capitol [movie theatre]. Quite good. No lunch. Resolution a few times.

Wednesday, December 27: Party at Brown's. Jack, Ferron family, & me. Broke up after twelve. I washed dishes with Winnie. No resolution.

Thursday, December 28: Went skating with Hazel at Avenue. First time there this year. Weather around [-15°C] to [-12°C]. Resolution three times.

Friday, December 29: Took Hazel to Marshall Wells for ski boots. Jack helped fit them & we thawed out his car. May ski soon if snow comes.

Saturday, December 30: Saw "Mr. Smith Goes To Washington" with Hazel at Rialto [movie theatre]. Good. Had lunch at her house afterwards. Resolution a few times.

Sunday, December 31: Started our for Kepasciwin in Dodd's car with Ding, Joan, King, & Hazel. Broke fan belt before Spruce Grove. Partly fixed it & went on. Engine began to boil.

1940

January 1940

Monday, January 1: Went to "5th Avenue Girl" at Strand [movie theatre] in evening. The boys were at a farm getting water at 12:00. Got to Stony Plain, repaired & started back. [Three to five kilometres] out broke down completely. Spent night on road. Had breakfast in Stony.

Tuesday January 2: Sleepy all day. Month-end rather slow. Snowfall. Tried out skiis. Seem quite good. Worked up a sweat. Jim is in England [U.K.] with troops.

Wednesday, January 3: Visited Hazel & Browns were present. Resolution a few times after we agreed to extend it. Made some new ones but none as good as the original.

Thursday, January 4: No balance. Back to Y class & Spokes club. Impromptu debate. Won in Hit & Miss game. Water in showers chilly.

Friday, January 5: Bowled 10 pins. Won 2. Scores 132, 112, 116. Enough snow to ski now. Went to Frank Hall's house. Lost $1.00 in poker.

Saturday, January 6: Saw "Rulers of the Sea". Skiied in afternoon & first time with harness. Climbed back up hill from golf course. Resolution few times.

Sunday, January 7: Hazel, Jack, & I went skiing. Arrived home 7:30. Hazel had supper at our house. She tries hard. Walked her home & resolution three times.

Monday, January 8: Meeting of E. Com. Club. Bob, Harry, Ken, Jack & I attended. Hot argument. MacCraigs [?] instigators because their daughter mistreated.

Tuesday, January 9: Hazel & I skated at Avenue Rink. Waxed her skiis afterwards. Resolution two or three times. No further snow. Mild.

Wednesday, January 10: Stayed home & read some between loafing. Adjusted my skiis. Marion & Wally came in which delayed my retiring.

Thursday, January 11: Spokes Club meeting. Too late for workout but played volleyball & basketball. Lost in the latter. Home fairly early.

Friday, January 12: Bowled 10 pins. Won 2. Scores 169, 147, 141. Exactly my average. Played cards at home – 500. Still no snow.

Saturday, January 13: Saw "The Amazing Mr. Williams" at Strand [movie theatre].No lunch. Snow at last in good quantity. Resolution three or four times.

Sunday, January 14: Jack, Hazel, & I skied from 12:30 until after 5:00. Twisted ankle. Learnt some stemming. Hazel improving. Supper at her place. Snow.

Monday, January 15: Snowed all day. Ankle sore. Did not go to Y. Stayed home & sorted E.T. Club books. **Too tired to write any letters or work**.

Tuesday, January 16: Cold. [-26°C to -29°C] Tightened &

adjusted plates on Hazel's skis. Played whist for remainder of evening. Resolution a few times.

Wednesday, January 17: More snow & cold. Stayed at home. Loafed instead of working. **Work on poems, etc. slipping badly**.

Thursday, January 18: Spokes Club. **Made one of the best speeches I have ever delivered. Satire on Aggression by Italy, Japan, & Germany.**

Friday, January 19: Stayed home & completed some poetry. Weather becoming slightly milder. El Barrett, our steno has been sick the last two days.

Saturday, January 20: Hazel & I saw "Raffles" at Rialto [movie theatre]. **I committed a grave faux pas. Felt terrible afterwards. Refused to carry out resolution. Hazel quite kind**. Skiing in afternoon.

Sunday, January 21: Skiing from 12:30 until 5:00. Improving. Not too cold. Took streetcar home. Went down through Ravine. Loafed in evening.

Monday, January 22: Steno still absent. Did not go to Y. Read library book. **Typed poems**. **Formed plans for wiping out Saturday rottenness**.

Tuesday, January 23: [-35°C] Saw "Only Angels Have Wings" at Avenue [movie theatre] with Hazel. She was sick yesterday (stomach). She invited me to leap-year dance. No resolution by choice.

Wednesday, January 24: Still around [-29°C] Tom drove me home. Finished library book. El Barrett still sick. Business very slack. Did no work in the evening.

Thursday, January 25: **Spokes Club. Spoke on propaganda**. Basketball. Won. Weather warming. Open Forum next week.

Friday, January 26: Bowled 10 pins. Won two games. Scores 123, 132, & 154. Rather poor. Home immediately afterwards. Waxed skies.

Saturday, January 27: Skied in afternoon. Saw "Another Thin Man" at the Capitol [movie theatre]. Lunch at Brown's. Resolution still suspended.

Sunday, January 28: Did not ski. Hazel & I walked. **Started some more writing at home**. Cold coming. Weather quite mild.

Monday, January 29: Stayed home to look after cold. **Wrote a few lines of verse**. Listened to radio for the most part.

Tuesday, January 30: Was able to do more poetry. Sent question to "Information Please" & another one to man I had intended to sell gags to.

Wednesday, January 31: Bought new shoes & spats. Hazel & I saw "The Firefly" at Rialto [movie theatre] with "Night Hawk". Quite long from 8:30 'til 11:45. No resolution.

February 1940

Thursday, February 1: Spokes Club. Jack absent. Ben was critic. Impromptu speaking. Pick up teams for basketball. Home early.

Friday, February 2: Girls took us to Leap Year Dance at Macdonald. Taxi both ways & lunch at Johnson's. Treated us very well. Balanced almost at sight.

Saturday, February 3: Saw "Gulliver's Travels" at Capitol [movie theatre]. **More poetry**. No more snow. No skiing this weekend.

Jasper Ski Train postponed. No resolution yet.

Sunday, February 4: Had supper at Hazel's. Clem appeared later. **Started to work on Writers' Markets & Methods Talent Test**. Not very cold.

Monday, February 5: Did not go to Y. **Read & wrote some**. Listened to Lux Play "The Young in Heart". Worked on Talent Test. Should have some to E. Com. Meeting.

Tuesday, February 6: Went skating with Hazel at Norwood. Weather fairly warm. Went home not too late. Resolution still suspended.

Wednesday, February 7: **Stayed home to do some writing but did not accomplish a great deal**. Weather remaining warm & no more snow.

Thursday, February 8: Open Forum at Spokes Club. Discussed dissolution of parliament. Won in basketball. Jack not at Y. No swimming.

Friday, February 9: Bowled 10 pins. Won one. Scores 134, 153, & 210. Won pot on last score. First & possibly last time.

Saturday, February 10: Warm weather holding. Saw "Hunchback of Notre Dame" at Capitol [movie theatre]. Lunch at Hazel's. Resolution not allowed again for a while.

Sunday, February 11: Managed some typing. Tweedsmuir died. No snow & not skiing. Bell visited. Wally in on leave. Jack over for a few minutes.

Monday, February 12: Went back to office to write up stock books. Austin drove me home. Just missed Information Please. Weather good.

Tuesday, February 13: **Wrote poetry for girls at Harry Taits**. Bought Valentines Chocolates for Hazel. Some soft snow. Completed test for Writers' Methods.

Wednesday, February 14: Presented Valentines & verses to girls. Skated at Avenue with Hazel. Gave her chocolates. She gave me poem too. Received Valentines & poems from girls, Phyllis, & Ding. Resolution few times for occasion.

Thursday, February 15: Open Forum at Spokes Club. Forgot money but luckily had 10¢ for ride home. Lost in basketball. Have had some snow but wet.

Friday, February 16: **Wrote poem for Phyllis & Ding. Made copies of Leap Year Dance poetry**. Stock rather wrong as usual. Wilf left for table tennis tournament in Calgary.

Saturday, February 17: Saw "The Great Victor Herbert at Capitol [movie theatre]. Fairly good. Resolution a few times to finish off with.

Sunday, February 18: Stayed at home and read Don Quixote. Trying to finish it. It is quite interesting in places, although old words are used.

Monday, February 19: Did not go to the Y. Still reading Don Quixote to finish it before the weekend. Eat lunch at Y now & read more.

Tuesday, February 20: Listened to radio, helped Helen with homework, & read more of Don Quixote. It takes some reading.

Wednesday, February 21: Skating at Norwood with Hazel. Cold. Down to [-29°C] or lower. Feet touched. Resolution two or three times.

Thursday, February 22: **Regular speeches. Mine rather poor**.

Workout. Won in basketball. Forgot money. Found dime in purse for streetcar ride home.

Friday, February 23: Bowled & won three. Scores 174, 164, & 184. Not bad. On top of league by a game. Getting colder but not snowing.

Saturday, February 24: Saw "Glenora Skating Carnival Comedienne". Tale good. Had six encores. Resolution two or three times as usual.

Sunday, February 25: Went to visit Hazel in the evening. Listened to Orson Wells. Resolution a few times. Weather fairly cold but no snow.

Monday, February 26: Stayed home in evening & listened to play instead of going to Y. Weather around [-23°C]. Not too cold.

Tuesday, February 27: Read & listened to radio. **Haven't been able to type anything worthwhile yet. Old trouble of laziness it seems.**

Wednesday, February 28: **Hazel & I saw "Gone with the Wind" at the Capitol [movie theatre]. Best picture I have ever seen**. Resolution a few times.

Thursday, February 29: **Spokes Club had discussion regarding conscription & other important questions of the moment**. Workout. Won in basketball.

March 1940

Friday, March 1: Bowled. Won one. Scores 171, 125, 141. Not so good. Will be in tournament with team next week.

Saturday, March 2: Saw Mae West at Rialto [movie theatre] in

"My Chickadee" with W.C. Fields. **Rank!** Snow fading. Season's skiing over it seems. Resolution twice.

Sunday, March 3: Wrote Lorne & Davis. Weather mild. Snow melting. **Must begin story for Writers' Digest contest soon as last of this month is deadline**. ["as" often used to mean because in Archie's writing.]

Monday, March 4: Telephone Whist at Ding's home. I had high score 186. Beaten by score at some other house. Muddy. Ted Allard drove us home. Resolution twice.

Tuesday, March 5: Barely freezing. Wet heavy snow makes everything sloppy. Lined up books for E.T.C. Balanced. Mistake in posting. Poor daybook figure.

Wednesday, March 6: Weather becoming cooler. Business rather slack. Read library book & listened to radio. **Must write short-short for Writers' Digest soon.**

Thursday, March 7: **Spoke about hobbies**. Club late in breaking up. Missed calisthenics but played hit & miss only to lose. Snow.

Friday, March 8: Bowled in 10 pin tournament. Scores 157, 174, 171. Good but team down & lost. Stopped at Jack's Shoppe with Fay & Jack. Home 1:30.

Saturday, March 9: Haircut. Saw "Blossom Time" at Empire [movie theatre]. Good music. Resolution a few times. Not home until after 2:00.

Sunday, March 10: Skied with Hazel. Perfect 'though snow tin in spots. She is catching on to stem. Brown's for supper. Resolution twice and home before 1. Typed [illegible] Bulletin.

Monday, March 11: Wilf on holidays. **Read & revised Gordon Brown's essay on the English Press**. **Kept me up until after**

one a.m.

Tuesday, March 12: Fairly warm. Snow melting slowly. Finished library books & listened to radio. Bob White phoned about E.T.C. books & I said they would not be ready.

Wednesday, March 13: Lined up E.T.C. books as well as I could but did not close off for year. Consider March 1st proper time. There might be trouble.

Thursday, March 14: **Read poetry at speakers' club**. Workout for a change. Hit & miss. Weather rather indefinite but snow going.

Friday, March 15: Won one game in 10 pins. 140, 113, 190. Came to average approximately. Fay with sore ankle. **Did some work on short-short**.

Saturday, March 16: Saw "At the Balalaika"*. Russian picture Nelson Eddy. Capitol [movie theatre]. Resolution a few times. Finished paying Y fees. Home late – about 2:30.

[*According to the official trailer of this Hollywood musical, one of the main songs is called "At the Balalaika", but the movie is called "Balalaika".]

Sunday, March 17: **Worked on short-short almost all day. "The Light Changes"**. Have to send it in soon for Writers' Digest contest. Wet snow storm in afternoon.

Monday, March 18: **Typed final copy of story for Writers' Digest contest**. I typed daybook. Eleanore on holidays & Wilf not back yet. Wet snow melted soon.

Tuesday, March 19: Completed books for E.T. Club after wasting part of evening. Will not close books until after dance on March 30th.

Wednesday, March 20: E.T. Club annual meeting. Jerry Delane new treasurer. Jack president. I declined. On finance committee. Resolution a few times. $6.81 down.

Thursday, March 21: Considerable snow. **Provincial election Socreds returned. Made political speech at Spoke's club. One of my best efforts**. Watched weight lifters.

Friday, March 22: **Skiing with Jack & Ted Allard. Banged knee after falling on jump at Highlands. Swelled up & I could not bowl 10 pins.**

Saturday, March 23: Four years with Pilkington [today]. Saw "Judge Hardy & Son" at Capitol [movie theatre]. Resolution a few times. Took things easy in afternoon with injured knee bothering slightly.

Sunday, March 24: Hazel for supper. She sent mother a lily. Limped home with her to find Clem & Tina in possession of front door. Resolution twice.

Monday, March 25: Driven home by Vern. Listened to radio programme & read. Marion Macdonald up to visit us. Jimmy staying for a short while.

Tuesday, March 26: Dominion election. [William Lyon Mackenzie] King returned with good majority. Snow staying with us. **Typed copy of a poem**. Knee improving slowly.

Wednesday, March 27: Saw Deanna Durbin "It's a Date" at Rialto [movie theatre]. Considerable snow still on ground. Knee still sore. Resolution twice.

Thursday, March 28: Spokes Club. **Debate on conscription. Lost**. Couldn't workout with knee. Took shower & home to bed or something. Income tax. $2.66.

Friday, March 29: Did not bowl because of knee. Typed a few things instead. **Starting to send out a few poems**. Snow hanging around.

Saturday, March 30: E.T.C. dance at Masonic. Made around $20.00. Knee behaved fairly well. Resolution a few times. New spring coat.

Sunday, March 31: Stayed home to do more typing. Snow not melting very rapidly. Quite cold for this season. **Will write more poems soon**.

April 1940

Monday, April 1: **Thirteen years since we arrived at Edmonton**.* April Fool jokes floating about. Snow still with us. Books not near to balancing stage. [*Archie's family moved to Edmonton in April 1927, i.e. before his 10th birthday. He was 9.]

Tuesday, April 2: El Barrett back from holidays. Did half statements. Will try balance tomorrow. Cold weather and snow not going rapidly.

Wednesday, April 3: Saw "Grapes of Wrath" at Capitol [movie theatre] with Hazel. Resolution a few times afterwards. Had cocoa & doughnuts at her house. Bed 2:00.

Thursday, April 4: **Typed two poems for Helen Speakman last night. Her birthday today**. Spokes Club discussion on helping Y. Shower & home early.

Friday, April 5: Bowled one game- 107. Knee too stiff for more. Won two games. Weather chilly [-13°C] in morning. Some snow left.

Saturday, April 6: Saw "North West Passage" at Capitol [movie theatre]. Weather chilly. Resolution a few times. Knee slowly improving. Will take another week or so.

Sunday, April 7: Checked over E.T.C. books. Will soon turn them over to Jerry Delane. **Typed poem for Helen Speakman & copies of some she had lost.**

Monday, April 8: Office work goes smoothly but no records broken. Unseasonal cold. Temperature down to [-23°C].

Tuesday, April 9: **Typing verse mostly these days. All comes back again. Luck isn't yet**. Cold weather holding.

Wednesday, April 10: **Executive meeting of E.T.C. Drafted new constitution**. Jerry Delane drove us home. Courts will not open until May.

Thursday, April 11: Did not go to Spokes Club meeting. Near end of season. **Typed** & listened to radio at home.

Friday, April 12: Knee not strong enough for bowling. Team won three games to enter playoffs. Weather still keeping chilly.

Saturday, April 13: Jack & I drained water at tennis courts. Saw "His Girl Friday" at Capitol [movie theatre]. No lunch. Resolution a few times. Late as usual.

Sunday, April 14: Supper at Hazel's. Snow. Wet and chilly. Up late. Left Brown's at 12:00. Surprise. Resolution two or three times.

Monday, April 15: Dodgers in 10 pin playoffs. Won two straight without my help. Now advance to finals. May be in the money.

Tuesday, April 16: Listened to radio & **typed a little on fantasy story**. Can't get going yet. Weather springlike at last.

Wednesday, April 17: Knee greatly improved. Warm now. **Typed out poem to send out. Rejects still keeping up. Did some work on fantasy story**.

Thursday, April 18: **Decided to leave Spokes Club**. Helped Hazel oil skiis. Felt rather feverish. Read funnies to her afterwards. Resolution a few times.

Friday, April 19: Bowling playoffs. Won. Now in semi-finals. Did not play. Feeling rather ill. Could eat neither lunch nor supper.

Saturday, April 20: Just managed to get through morning. Flu & cold. Rained steadily. Lay around all afternoon & evening. Stood up Hazel.

Sunday, April 21: More rain. Sick in bed. Hazel called in afternoon & stayed for supper. District a few blocks away badly flooded. Hazel brought some oranges.

Monday, April 22: Still down. Rainy. Hazel called in evening & **I had her read a science fiction story which evidently bored her**. She brought ginger ale.

Tuesday, April 23: Not out of bed yet. Weak. Weather remains cloudy & cool.

Wednesday, April 24: Hazel called in the afternoon. Snowed in morning. Remain in bed. Flu hanging on refuses to release me.

Thursday, April 25: Ben called in the morning. Weather continues disagreeable. Reading considerable. Feeling slightly better.

Friday, April 26: Up at last. Hazel visited in evening. Tom brought my wages. Had lunch when Hazel called. She had tooth pulled yesterday.

Saturday, April 27: Haircut. "Road to Singapore" at Capitol [movie theatre] with Hazel. Resolution a few times afterwards. No lunch. Weather brighter for a change. Weak.

Sunday, April 28: Walked in afternoon with Hazel. Refused to stay for supper. Jack over at our place. Typed a few things. No pep. Well but listless.

Monday, April 29: Back to work. Mr. Glover in Calgary. Weather still unsettled. Bought license for bike. Rode up to see Wellon about auditing E.T.C. books.

Tuesday, April 30: Rode streetcar. Did some typing. Cold catching up to me. Do not seem to be quite well yet. Bed early 10:30.

May 1940

Wednesday, May 1: Began using bike again. Good to get home for dinner. Will not balance quickly as daybooks are behind. Social E.T.C. Resolution twice.

Thursday, May 2: **Stayed at home & typed some. Rejections continue to trickle in from poetry**. Rode bike again. Knee still weak.

Friday, May 3: Walked around with Frank & Jack. Passed Hazel. Played two games of snooker which cost me but 10¢. Slight rain in morning.

Saturday, May 4: Saw "Strange Cargo" at Capitol [movie theatre]. No lunch. Resolution a few times. Slipping slightly back to bad habit which I hope to conquer soon.

Sunday, May 5: Slept late. **Wrote an article I think might be all right**. Worked on photo album. Not so good. A slight rain.

Cough lingering.

Monday, May 6: Ben gave lesson in driving. Roller-skated with Hazel until it rained. Had to borrow coat to get home. Resolution a few times. Cough frequently.

Tuesday, May 7: Sprinkled but I rode bicycle. Ben leaving Pilkingtons next week. **Loafed in evening writing a few lines of poetry**. Bed early 10:45.

Wednesday, May 8: Tennis started. Cloudy. Sprinkled slightly. Hazel had cold & did not play. Won two out of four sets. Rather dusty.

Thursday, May 9: More tennis. Another driving lesson from Ben. Hazel at courts. Walked home with her. Resolution a few times. Weather warmer.

Friday, May 10: Played tennis but no Hazel. My form seems very poor so far. Need more practice perhaps.

Saturday, May 11: Saw "Young Tom Edison" at Capitol [movie theatre] with Hazel. No lunch. Played tennis in afternoon. Dave Greenfield beat me. Resolution few times.

Sunday, May 12: Played tennis with Hazel. Very few around. She is improving. Quite warm. She brought skiis up in afternoon.

Monday, May 13: Rained a little & I thought courts too wet. Took Hazel to "Stanley & Livingston" at Avenue [movie theatre]. Good. Resolution few times.

Tuesday, May 14: Played tennis but no Hazel. Rod bike to & from courts. Tennis not improving yet.

Wednesday, May 15: Played tennis earlier as Hazel called for me. Walked her home. Resolution as usual. Rained a bit.

Thursday, May 16: Asked Glover for raise. He promised to check up & see. Tennis with Hazel. Resolution a few times. Rained lightly.

Friday, May 17: Asked Mr. Glover about Ben's job. He did not know much. C.O.* will have final say. Tennis with Hazel. No resolution. Weather warming.

[*Company Office, headquarters?]

Saturday, May 18: Tennis in afternoon. Saw "Buck Benny Rides Again" at Capitol [movie theatre]. Lunch afterwards. Resolution a few times. Left before 1:00. Up early tomorrow.

Sunday, May 19: Round Robin opening tournament. Won 10 games out of 35. Windy. Hazel came for lunch. Tea at hall. Walked Hazel home. Resolution a few times.

Monday, May 20: **Story from Writers' Digest. Won 71st prize a dictionary. Beginning? First time I ever made anything from my writing.** Tennis & walked Hazel home. No schedule. Left her house at ten. No resolution. Weather fine.

Tuesday, May 21: Weather stays warm. More tennis. Worse than previously. Walked Hazel home. Returned home myself before 10:30. Bed 10:45.

Wednesday, May 22: Another warm day. More like July. Tennis after supper. Walked Hazel home. No resolution. Home before 10:30.

Thursday, May 23: Tennis with Hazel. Weather still perfect. Home early as usual this week. Hazel dug out bathing suit. Jack came & told of Cooking Lake.

Friday, May 24: Gang went to Cooking Lake. Ding, Mary, May, Bradley, Shy's girl, Hazel, Doc, Jack, Ted, King, Shy, & I. Eaten by mosquitoes. I exhibit A. No resolution.

Saturday, May 25: Saw "If I had My Way" at Rialto [movie theatre]. Rather cool. Resolution a few times.

Sunday, May 26: Cloudy & cool. Played tennis afternoon & evening with Hazel. Bell up with new baby.

Monday, May 27: Saw "Pinocchio" with Hazel at Strand [movie theatre]. Enjoyed it. Home fairly early after resolution a few times.

Tuesday, May 28: Played tennis. Arranged own sets & I had a few good sets. A large crowd. Warm weather helped.

Wednesday, May 29: Watched Philip being confirmed at St. Stephen's Church. Weather sultry. Electrical storm kept me late. Resolution few times.

Thursday, May 30: Played tennis. Clouded over. Left Hazel's house early & beat rain home. Weather cooling off.

Friday, May 31: Rained all day. Took lunch. Loafed in evening. Paid on chesterfield. $19 to go. Have $11 in bank now. Not bad.

June 1940

Saturday, June 1: Rainy. No tennis. Saw "Typhoon" at Capitol [movie theatre]. Leg bothered considerably. **Typed jokes in afternoon**. Resolution quite a few times.

Sunday, June 2: Cloudy. Played tennis in afternoon. Hazel for supper. Almost quarrelled. Acted meanly but finally laughed it off. Resolution twice.

Monday, June 3: Played tennis with Hazel. Walked her home & retired before 10:30. Books not balanced yet. Weather unsettled.

Tuesday, June 4: Rained in evening. **Typed a few jokes. Intend to type all collection.** All statements not written up yet. May balance next month.

Wednesday, June 5: A few sets of tennis. Weather warming up. No sign of a balance yet. Walked Hazel home as usual.

Thursday, June 6: Inter club. Played a set or so on one court not used. Won 5 out of 7 sets in inter-club against C.N.R.

Friday, June 7: Hazel gave me new strap for watch which she had taken to have adjusted. Played tennis between rain drops.

Saturday, June 8: Saw "Virginia City" at Capitol [movie theatre]. No lunch. Resolution several times. Finished paying for chesterfield. Might save some money now.

Sunday, June 9: Played some tennis in afternoon. Supper at Brown's. Fooled away evening. Resolution a few times. Rained slightly.

Monday, June 10: Played a few sets. Rained on way home. Arrived at Hazel's rather damp. Resolution once & her father arrived home.

Tuesday, June 11: Inter-club. Played set of mixed before start. Hazel & I won 6-0. Had pop at Jack's with Art, Marg, Mary, & Hazel.

Wednesday, June 12: Learnt Wilf planning to leave. Will mean extra work as Eleanor will take his place.

Thursday, June 13: Clouds still threatening. Wind & rain cuts down some of our tennis. Not very warm yet.

Friday, June 14: Tennis still holds interest. Improving I think. Wilf leaving tomorrow for C.N. Express. Me next (?)

Saturday, June 15: Played some tennis. Saw "The Invisible Man Returns" at Rialto [movie theatre]. No lunch. Resolution a few times.

Sunday, June 16: Jack & I eat Dick Triscott & Jerry Delane 8-10, 12-10, 6-3. Played 110 games that day. Hazel beat Marg Mitchell in singles.

Monday, June 17: Beat Ted Cole 6-2, 6-3 in tournament. Next match hopeless, Ted Allard.

Tuesday, June 18: Inter-club. Did not play tournament. Fooled around afterwards. Tennis improving.

Wednesday, June 19: Lost to Ted Allard 6-0, 6-0. Windy. Hazel & Dot beaten by Ding & Phyllis – three sets.

Thursday, June 20: Jack & I beat Dave & Art Hook in tournament. Will likely play Ted & Frank next.

Friday, June 21: Hazel & I lost in mixed 6-3, 6-3 against Turner & Campbell. Terrible. Weather warm however.

Saturday, June 22: Some tennis in afternoon. Saw "Edison the Man" Spencer Tracy at Capitol [movie theatre]. No lunch. Resolution a few times.

Sunday, June 23: Played tennis with Hazel most of day. Weather good if it will last. Resolution a few times. Home after 12:00.

Monday, June 24: Hot. Played a few sets. Ted drove us part way home. No resolution. Did not leave office until 5:50.

Tuesday, June 25: Too damp for inter-club. Had a few sets however. Weather unsettled again.

Wednesday, June 26: Rained. Took streetcar. Cleared up

afterwards & I played a set or so of tennis.

Thursday, June 27: More rain. No tennis. **Typed some & took it easy. Have done little writing for long time.**

Friday, June 28: More rain. Courts are damp enough now. Loafed at home all evening. Too lazy to get anywhere.

Saturday, June 29: Played some in afternoon. Saw "For Freedom" at Capitol [movie theatre]. No lunch. Resolution a few times. Left before 1:00.

Sunday, June 30: Played tennis. Hazel lost against Masie in tournament. Winnie played afternoon. Resolution a few times.

July 1940

Monday, July 1: Went swimming with Hazel in morning. Sunburnt. Tennis in evening. Resolution a few times. Tired & hot.

Tuesday, July 2: Two days posting to do. Eleanor sick in afternoon. Storm spoilt tennis. **Typed jokes**. Tired so retired at 10:00.

Wednesday, July 3: Rain spoilt tennis again. Jack called in & we discussed Pigeon Lake for most of the evening.

Thursday, July 4: Work accumulating. Eleanor not too ambitious. Tennis as usual with the customary walking. Weather unsettled but no rain.

Friday, July 5: Have not finished month-end yet. Tried balance but no luck. Tennis for awhile. Walked Hazel home as per usual.

Saturday, July 6: Meeting E.T.C. $50 in hole. Resolution letter from Hazel. Appropriate since it is her birthday. Work keeping heavy.

Sunday, July 7: Warm. Played a few sets. Hazel slightly ill so did not play in evening. Typed instead. Thunder storm ended day.

Monday, July 8: Cloudy but no rain. Played a set or so of tennis. Resolution a few times. Office work slightly behind but will catch up this week.

Tuesday, July 9: Played a set or so. Still cloudy & cool. Not July weather. Hazel treated Jack, Doc, & Ted to ice cream. No resolution.

Wednesday, July 10: Beat Art Hall in secondary singles 6-3, 6-1. Courts damp. Remains overcast & chilly. Resolution a number of times. Home at 1:00.

Thursday, July 11: Cleaned up at night but did not warm up. Had two good sets of tennis. Invited Hazel to Exhibition next week.

Friday, July 12: Played tennis but not with Hazel. She had hair done. Rained after dark but briefly. Pedalled home in drizzle. Unsettled.

Saturday, July 13: Rained all day. Saw "Irene" at Capitol [movie theatre]. Received wallet & keytainer from Jack. Hazel gave me her picture & wallet. Resolution a few times. Pyjamas from Lorne.

Sunday, July 14: Rode bicycle with Gordon Brown. Supper at Brown's. Hazel & I went to see midway erection. Resolution a few times. Feel tired.

Monday, July 15: Played set of tennis. Saw "War Savings Stamp" show at Avenue with Hazel. Cloudy day but cleared off. Evening warm & pleasant.

Tuesday, July 16: Cloudy all day. Rained in evening making no tennis. **Typed on story**. **Wally went away again, leave over. (Has been here since Sunday.**)

Wednesday, July 17: Rainy. Saw grandstand performance in arena with Hazel. Muddy on midway. Had number of rides. Potato chips & popcorn ending. Resolution few times. [illegible]

Thursday, July 18: Cleared up in evening. No tennis. Worked on album but unsuccessful. Everyone out leaving me alone. Bed by 10:00.

Friday, July 19: Played a few sets of tennis. Weather hot with no clouds. Saw some of fireworks from courts. Resolution but once strangely enough.

Saturday, July 20: Played horses. Lost $2. Hazel & I went to Exhibition Fun. Rained at 12:00. Resolution a few times. Home after 3:00.

Sunday, July 21: Rainy. Read Gone With The Wind. No tennis although weather cleared up before supper. Jack & Ted left for coast this morning.

Monday, July 22: Tennis with Hazel. Weather unsettled. Walked home with her & buttered bread for their lunches. Resolution a few times.

Tuesday, July 23: Rode bicycle through heavy downpour at noon. Read more of Gone With The Wind. No typing. Too lazy still.

Wednesday, July 24: No rain but cloudy. Had two sets of tennis. No Hazel. Home early to read Gone With The Wind. Office work in good shape.

Thursday, July 25: Walked almost to tennis court before I noticed

Hazel half a block behind. Weather warm but not too hot. No resolution.

Friday, July 26: Tennis with Hazel. Very few around these evenings. Walked her home as usual. Resolution twice. Nights quite cool for this season.

Saturday, July 27: Some tennis in afternoon with Alex Perry. Saw "The Doctor Takes a Wife" at Capitol [movie theatre]. No lunch. Resolution several times. Weather warmer & brighter.

Sunday, July 28: Played some tennis. **Rode out Fort Trail on bicycle with Hazel**. More tennis in evening. Walked around for awhile afterwards. No resolution.

Monday, July 29: Played tennis as usual. Weather becoming better. Jennie Hook lunched with Hazel & me. Played rummy. Resolution twice. Chilly.

Tuesday, July 30: Went to Rev. Naimby's with Hazel & her family & saw films of Eastern Canada, U.S., European trip. Fair. No resolution.

Wednesday, July 31: Played some tennis. Beaten badly by Art Hook 6-1. Bad cold which is queer for this time of year. Resolution a few times. Good weather.

August 1940

Thursday, August 1: Rained in morning. Cleared up for tennis. No Hazel. Had good sets with Walt McIntosh, Mae, & Marg Mitchell. Won a set.

Friday, August 2: Fine weather but cool. Played a set with Jennie & Hazel. Inter-club first. Cold holding tightly. No resolution. Not near to balance yet.

Saturday, August 3: Saw "New Moon" at the Capitol [movie theatre]. No lunch. Cloudy but no rain except in morning. Resolution a few times. Home earlier.

Sunday, August 4: Up at 9:30. Clipped jokes for collection. Tennis in afternoon & supper at Hazel's home. More tennis & resolution number of times.

Monday, August 5: **Hazel & I cycled out to aerodrome & Calder.** She fell & skinned knee. Tennis after supper. Resolution a few times. Weather warm & pleasant.

Tuesday, August 6: **Tried to join 96 Battery N.P.A.M.** [Non-Permanent Active Militia (1867-1940 – Renamed Canadian Army (Reserve) in 1940)] **but found they were overstrength**. Worked an hour. Played snooker at Rec & lost. Hot.

Wednesday, August 7: Worked at office until about 10:00. Rode bike & used new flashlight. Weather hot & I have played no tennis lately. Leave on holidays Saturday.

Thursday, August 8: **Put application in for R.A.F. Will get medical after holidays. Went to armouries again & learned that 92 & 61 Batteries will fill up soon**.

Friday, August 9: Light rainfall in evening. Saw "Marx Brothers at Circus" & "Charlie Chan at Treasure Island" at Avenue [movie theatre] with Hazel. Resolution a few times. Almost freezing.

Saturday, August 10: **Went to Pigeon Lake Sunnyside Cottage Ma-Me-O**. Hazel, Dad, Frank, Ted, & I left at 8:15 & arrived at 9:45. Finally found cottage.

Sunday, August 11: Woke early as I slept in tent with Jack. Rowed across to Ma-Me-O for milk & eggs with Jack & Helen. Slight sunburn in afternoon. Walked with Hazel down to auto camp.

Monday, August 12: Rowed Marian & Helen & tried to catch fish. No chance. Sunbathed & swam with Hazel. Unusual wind storm in evening with [129 kilometre] gale. Large waves.

Tuesday, August 13: Hazel & I rowed across to Crystal Springs & Westerose later – a deserted town. Took five hours. Swam & sunbathed afterwards. Strolled along beach road in evening. Few resolution.

Wednesday, August 14: Went fishing with Helen. No luck. Annoyed because Hazel didn't come. Went on long walk to cool off. Managed it. Clouded over & no swimming. Hazel & I walked out by auto camp. Resolution several times.

Thursday, August 15: Slept in until 9:00. Walked with Hazel in afternoon to get diamond willow. Resolution few times. Weather still cloudy. Had quick dip among large waves [shorthand].

Friday, August 16: Lay on the beach with Hazel until we were both burnt to a crisp. Hard to sleep at night. Resolution few times as usual.

Saturday, August 17: Jack & Bell with Betty & Gordy came for weekend. Breakdown. Arrived at about midnight. Hazel & I stayed up all night. Resolution.

Sunday, August 18: Hazel & I walked along Beach Road as day broke. Back to make breakfast. Slept a few hours in afternoon. Ted broke down so Jack & Bell stayed.

Monday, August 19: Jack & Bell had to take bus which made Jack lose half a day. I asked Hazel [short hand:] . Resolution. She consented. Talked it over.

Tuesday, August 20: Weather treating us well. Hazel & I have good talks & make plans which we hope to see come true.

Wednesday, August 21: Keeping our secret & hope to do so for about two years. Swimming & fish & row. Frank talks. Few resolutions.

Thursday, August 22: I am getting deeper. Feel fatter & certainly have not worried out here. Weather remains good.

Friday, August 23: Weather remains good. Row a bit each day. Keep trying for fish that are not there. Resolution each night now.

Saturday, August 24: **Got Diamond Willow with Hazel. [First Nations man] saw us on reservation & held us up for 25¢. Hazel went to cottage for money**. Resolution at night.

Sunday, August 25: Last day at Sunnyside. Resolution a few times. Dip in big waves with Hazel & Jack. Drove to Mulhurst. I drove back. Improving. Home 10:30.

Monday, August 26: Back to office & stack of work. **Paraded with 61st Battery N.P.A.M. with Fay, Jack, Jim, & Ted. Marching for most part.**

Tuesday, August 27:

Wednesday August 28:

Thursday, August 29: **Arranged for medical with Air Force for Tuesday. Attended N.P.A.M. parade 61st Battery. Given simple medical**. Started letter to Lorne.

Friday, August 30: Work up to date. Corn roast E.T.C. Presentation to Bob & Jessie who are getting married. Resolution a few times. Weather warm & bright.

Saturday, August 31: Haircut. No one at courts so no tennis. Hazel worked late taking stock. Called for her at store 10:30. Walked around town. Few resolutions.

September 1940

Sunday, September 1: **Awoke 8:30 to go on route march. Jack did not call & I did not go**. Swam with Hazel. Sky smoky. Hazel stayed for supper. Resolution few times.

Monday, September 2: Played tennis in morning with Hazel. **Whittled in afternoon**. Stomach misbehaving. At no supper. Hazel stayed for supper. She took me to Avenue [movie theatre] "Destry Rides Again". Resolution.

Tuesday, September 3: Roller skated in evening. Not feeling very good. Got brush wool jacket for Hazel. Too small. Resolution few times. **Take Air Force medical tomorrow**.

Wednesday, September 4: **Hazel came up to help whittle diamond willow**. Jack dropped in. Weather warm but smoky atmosphere from north fires. Resolution few times.

Thursday, September 5: Did not balance. **N.P.A.M. will soon be working on cannons**. Driven by Frarey as usual. Overcast but no rain. Fairly warm.

Friday, September 6: Balanced. Teeth checked by dentist. Appointment next week. Roller skated with Hazel. Weather keeping warm. Had cocoa at her home. Resolution few times.

Saturday, September 7: Ben nearly sold me an insurance policy. Saw "Rhythm on the River" at Capitol [movie theatre]. Lunch at Hazel's. Resolution a few times. Cloudy.

Sunday, September 8: **Tried to repair typewriter**. Hazel over in afternoon. Her house for supper. Took it easy with her afterwards. Read to each other. Resolution number of times.

Monday, September 9: Sunny. **N.P.A.M. rifle drill part of the time. Made legs sore**. **Finally fixed typewriter. Margin release needs adjusting**.

Tuesday, September 10: Fine clear days. Work in good shape. **Hazel came over & we whittled**. Resolution few times.

Wednesday, September 11: Weather holding. Picked out typewriter desk. Roller skated with Hazel. Arranged for insurance policy with Ben. Resolution a few times.

Thursday, September 12: Work up to date. Austen going on holidays next week. **Went to N.P.A.M. Considerable marching. Did not quite get gun drill**.

Friday, September 13: Dentist cleaned my teeth. No fillings nor pullings. Roller skated on Portage with Hazel. Lunch at her place. Resolution several.

Saturday, September 14: Went to library for most of afternoon. Saw "Boys from Syracuse" at Rialto [movie theatre]. Hazel treated. Lunch at her house. Few resolutions.

Sunday, September 15: Remarkably warm & bright. **N.P.A.M. from 10 until 1:00**. Few sets of tennis. Beat Jiggs Real 6-5. Hazel's for supper. Resolution many times.

Monday, September 16: Austen on holidays. **61st N.P.A.M.** Received literature from Book of the Month Club. **No word from Air Force yet**.

Tuesday, September 17: Roller skated with Hazel. Night fairly warm. Read one chapter of M.L. [Married Life?] which we bought. Resolution several times.

Wednesday, September 18: Becoming cooler. Work up to date. **Hazel & I whittled & read M.L.** Marion Macdonald up. Lunched. Resolution twice.

Thursday, September 19: Discovered July balance wrong. Means rechecking. **N.P.A.M. gun laying at last. Rifle drill. Squad drill. Worked on poetry.**

Friday, September 20: Roller skated. Read more of M.L. with Hazel. Educational. Resolution several times. Found one mistake in July sheets.

Saturday, September 21: Hair cut. Found error in July balance. **Told Mr. Glover about Air Force**. Tennis in afternoon. Saw "Young Dr. Kildaire Goes Home" at Strand [movie theatre]. Read more M.L. Many resolution.

Sunday, September 22: Played two sets with Hazel. She came over for supper. Read Leaves of Grass & Memory Hold the Door. Number of resolutions.

Monday, September 23: Chillier fall beginning to tumble. **N.P.A.M. with squad & rifle drill not to forget P.T.** [physical training, later called physical education] **Squeezed out some poetry**.

Tuesday, September 24: Fairly cool. **N.P.A.M. one hour gun-laying & one hour squad drill. Learning more. Finished more poetry. Started another poem.**

Wednesday, September 25: Bell & Jack over. **Hazel helped whittle. Completed another poem. Have two pieces of diamond will nearly finished**. Resolution few times.

Thursday, September 26: **Started more poetry**. Worked on photo album. Roller skated for awhile. Read more of M.L. Tired & sleepy. Resolution many times.

Friday, September 27: H**azel came over to whittle**. Did a bit more on album. **Two pieces diamond willow nearly finished**. No reading. Number of resolutions.

Saturday, September 28: Lost in tennis against Harry Young 6-1, 6-0. Secondary Semi-Finals. Saw "Boom Town" at Capitol [movie theatre]. Lunch at Hazel's. Resolution few times.

Sunday, September 29: **Parade N.P.A.M. 10:00 to 11:00 a.m.** Tennis with Hazel. Two sets in afternoon. Supper at Brown's. Read M.L. & Buchanans' Autobiography. Resolution several.

Monday, September 30: Austen back. Work well lined up. **61st Battery parade. Gun laying & gun drill. Improving**. Driven by Ted Allard. Work on album.

October 1940

Tuesday, October 1: Rain. Soaked twice. Rode streetcar in afternoon. **Hazel whittled with me but not much progress**. Resolution several times.

Wednesday, October 2: Meeting E.T.C. Banquet planned for November 9th. Finances nearly even. Resolution few times. Weather overcast.

Thursday, October 3: Rode streetcar again. **Parade of N.P.A.M**. Walked as Jack had sold car & Ted's not running. Walked home in misty rain.

Friday, October 4: Streetcar again. Read at Hazel's home during evening Memory Hold the Door & Toronto Star. Resolution number of times.

Saturday, October 5: Sore throat. Haircut. Hazel took me to "I Love You Again" at Capitol [movie theatre] with William Powel

& Myrna Loy. Lunch at her house. Few resolutions.

Sunday, October 6: Not up until after 1:30. Ill with head cold. Hazel came for supper & read in evening instead of church. No resolution (cold).

Monday, October 7: **Parade N.P.A.M.** Nights cold now. Rode streetcar to work. Cold settled in chest. **No word from Air Force.**

Tuesday, October 8: Hazel over in evening. **Sandpapered diamond willow. Another one nearly completed.** Cold sticking. Chilly. No resolution. **Completed some poetry**.

Wednesday, October 9: Bills ready to pay. Visited Hazel & read M.L. Also Toronto Star. Hazel has Book of the Month joining gift of Joseph in Egypt.

Thursday, October 10: Streetcar. Cold seems worse. **N.P.A.M. Stood around most of evening. Walked to armouries with Art Hall**. Ted drove us home.

Friday, October 11: Over to Hazel's home. Tena Evans in town. **Had to sit listening which was no fun**. Tired. Didn't wait for other people to retire – simply left.

Saturday, October 12: **Typed jokes in afternoon**. Saw Deanna Durbin in "Spring Parade". Cocoa at Hazel's home afterwards. Resolution few times. No reading.

Sunday, October 13: Up before 12:00. Played tennis in afternoon. Hazel over in evening to be entertained by Jack & family. Few resolutions.

Monday, October 14: Thanksgiving. **Hazel & I picked up racquets & then whittled**. Finished M.L. & few resolutions. **Hazel stayed for supper.& I took her home before N.P.A.M.**

Tuesday, October 15: Took bike but carried lunch. Rained at noon. Cleared up later. Hazel up to read Memory Hold the Door. Resolution a few times. **Typing more jokes**.

Wednesday, October 16: Rode bike. Read funnies & Joseph in Egypt at Hazel's. Resolution a number of times. Becoming colder but no snow yet.

Thursday, October 17: N.P.A.M. 7:30. **Inspection by Griesbach. Sloppy. Squad drill**. Ted ran out of gas. **More typing of jokes. Nearly all "A's".**

Friday, October 18: **Hazel & I whittled** & read Memory Hold the Door. Still riding my bike. Chilly but no snow. Resolution a few times. **War developing more**.

Saturday, October 19: Haircut. Saw Ginger Rogers & Ronald Coleman in "Lucky Partners". Lunch at Hazel's. Her treat tonight. Resolution many times. Weather pleasant.

Sunday, October 20: Typed on fantasy story. Half finished. Supper at Brown's. Read Joseph in Egypt with Hazel. Resolution a few times. Hot for October.

Monday, October 21: Rainy in morning. Thunderstorm in afternoon. **N.P.A.M. Uniforms being issued. Might get mine tomorrow**. **Typed more of story. Soon be finished**.

Tuesday, October 22: **Got uniform & boots in afternoon**. **Brought Hazel down to whittle & admire. Re-varnished another piece of diamond willow**. Resolution several times.

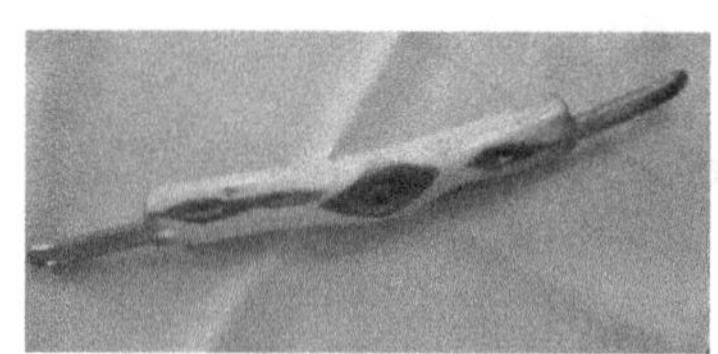

(Apparently, the object in the photo is the only surviving piece of diamond willow that they whittled.)

Wednesday, October 23: Took streetcar. Post up to date. Went over to Hazel's in evening to read Joe [abbreviation for Joseph in Egypt.] Resolution a few times. Weather holding.

Thursday, October 24: Work caught up. Hard to find things to do. **N.P.A.M. Wrote more on fantasy story**. Becoming cooler but not too bad.

Friday, October 25: **Brought Hazel down to whittle & read**. Read Memory Hold the Door. Weather keeping fine. Resolution number of times.

Saturday, October 26: **Finished fantasy story**. Saw "Hired Wife" at Rialto [movie theatre]. No lunch. Resolution many times. Weather changing. Slight rain.

Sunday, October 27: Rainy. **Read over fantasy story**. Worked on box for books. Visited Hazel in evening. **She read fantasy story**. I helped her make lunches. Few resolutions.

Monday, October 28: **N.P.A.M.** Walked as Ted at hockey practice. Riding streetcar. Wet and muddy. No snow yet but chilly.

Tuesday, October 29: **Brought Hazel up to whittle**. Bell called & Jack around. **Fantasy story read to send away**. Resolution a few times. Bed 12:30.

Wednesday, October 30: Got book on juvenile writing from Writers' Digest. Weather clear & cool. Visited at Hazel's Read Joe. Resolution a number of times. Weather good.

Thursday, October 31: **N.P.A.M.** Went to E.T.C. afterwards &

took Hazel home when Hallowe'en party finished. **Uniform only costume**. Resolution few times.

November 1940

Friday, November 1: Hazel ill but better when I went over in evening. Listened to radio. Left before 10:45. Resolution few times. Chilly but no snow.

Saturday, November 2: Bought slippers for Lorne. New photograph album. Saw "North West Mounted Police" at Capitol [movie theatre]. Lunch at Hazel's. Resolution numerous.

Sunday, November 3: **Route out near St. Albert. About [14.5 kilometres] total. Manoeuvres too.** Visited Hazel in evening & read Joe. Philip wanted help on article. Resolution three.

Monday, November 4: Wrote up half statements. **N.P.A.M. lecture & squad drill.** Completed snaps in album for Jasper. Captions only thing left. Bed 12:30.

Tuesday, November 5: **Hazel came up to whittle & read**. Cold with flurries of snow. Raw wind. No balance. Resolution several times & bed before 12:00.

Wednesday, November 6: [-15ºC] N.P.A.M. with squad drill & lecture. Cold walking home. No balance yet. Eleanor away which helped.

Thursday, November 7: Balanced. Visited Hazel. Her mother ill so cooking was order of evening. Read Toronto Star. Cold so no resolution. Weather chilling.

Friday, November 8: Cold worse. Staggered through day & tried to type in evening. Bed finally at 10:00. Nearly burnt by thermogene I put on.

Saturday, November 9: Slept in afternoon. E.T.C. banquet. Took Hazel in taxi. Bought her corsage.

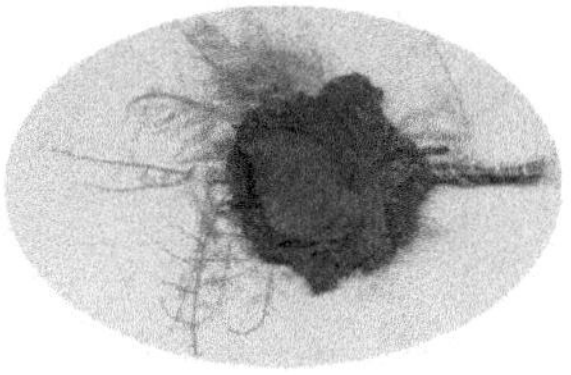

(Dried & kept until 2015)

Good time. No resolution afterwards. Cold improving.

Sunday, November 10: Weather colder. Called for Hazel & brought her for supper. Bell & children up. Took Hazel home after 12:00. No resolution.

Monday, November 11: [-32°C] Parade we intended to attend cancelled. Typed & arranged photo album. Hazel took me to Avenue [movie theatre]. Resolution several times.

Tuesday, November 12: Still cold. Visited Hazel & read Joe. Helped her make lunches. Have three albums now. Resolution number of times.

Wednesday, November 13: **N.P.A.M. rifle drill & lecture on gas**. Walked down & Ted drove us home. Mild. Around freezing.

Thursday, November 14: Snow melting. Cooler at night. Brought Hazel up to read. John [author of Memory Hold the Door] half finished. Resolution a few times. Bed 12:45.

Friday, November 15: Read Joe & Toronto Star at Hazel's home. Weather quite mild. Snow disappearing. Resolution considerable number of times.

Saturday, November 16: Wrote two poems. Saw "Strike Up the

Band" Mickey Rooney & Judy Garland at Capitol [movie theatre]. Resolution as usual. Left earlier than usual.

Sunday, November 17: Slept 'til 1:30. Went to Brown's for supper. Read some of Joe. Resolution number of times. Windy with some snow.

Monday, November 18: **N.P.A.M. lecture, physical training, & squad drill**. Weather fairly good. Not too cold. **Received poems back**.

Tuesday, November 19: **Typed out poem in evening**. No Hazel as she had to work overtime. Stealing my stuff. Bed early.

Wednesday, November 20: **N.P.A.M.** Jack had to bowl instead. **Physical training, drill, & lecture. Nearly 10:20 before we quit**. **Typed poem for Hazel**.

Thursday, November 21: Went skating at Avenue. Not too cold. Cocoa & toast afterwards. Resolution to top things.

Friday, November 22: Hazel over to read John. **Finished two poems today. Must be poetry week.** Weather fairly cold Resolution several.

Saturday, November 23: **Typed part of story <u>Conquest of Size</u>.** Went to "Carmen" at Empire [movie theatre].

Sunday, November 24: Some typing in afternoon. Visited Hazel in evening. Read Joseph. Resolution several times. Fairly cold.

Monday, November 25: **N.P.A.M. physical training, squad drill, & lecture**. Colder but not any more snow. **Typed on <u>Conquest of Size</u> & sent cartoon ideas away.**

Tuesday, November 26: Temperature dropped to [-20.5°C] by evening. Skated at Avenue with Hazel. Lunch & resolution at her house.

Wednesday, November 27: Mercury climbed up again. Snowed heavily. **N.P.A.M. lecture, physical training, & battle drill**. Invited to free show at Empress [movie theatre] tomorrow.

Thursday, November 28: **Treated to show at Empress [movie theatre] "Ramparts we Watch". N.P.A.M.** Home to find Hazel over. Took her home after we had lunch.

Friday, November 29: Work caught up. More snow. Visited Hazel in evening. Read funnies. Visited Phyllis in hospital first. Resolution few times.

Saturday, November 30: Saw "Arise My Lover" at Capitol [movie theatre]. Colvert & Ray Milland. Skiing for first time. Jack & Frank. Lunch at Hazel's. Number of resolutions 12:30.

December 1940

Sunday, December 1: Slept late. **Typed five more pages of story**. Brown's for supper. Winnie home with friend. Left before 11:00. Resolution but once.

Monday, December 2: **Received "Conquest of Size" summary back from Unknown. N.P.A.M. typed more pages of this story. Sending summary out again to <u>Astonishing</u>.**

Tuesday, December 3: All statements written up. Hazel & lead [?] John. Mild [-3°C]. Found another item for <u>Maclean's</u>. Resolution once.

Wednesday, December 4: Balanced. Sold a book of raffle tickets. **N.P.A.M. no physical training- lecture & squad drill.** Mild weather. **Typed remainder of story**.

Thursday, December 5: Read Joe & Toronto Star with Hazel. Mild weather holding. Developing sore throat. Resolution several times.

Friday, December 6: Read more of John in evening. Work well in hand. Cold starting to get me. Some resolution & bed early.

Saturday, December 7: **Typed two poems**. Haircut. Went to Edmonton School Boys Band in which Philip plays trombone at Empire [theatre]. No resolution. Late again.

Sunday, December 8: Hazel up for supper. Rained in morning. Icy. Cold in control. Read John. Took Hazel home early. No resolution.

Monday, December 9: **N.P.A.M. Did not take physical training because of cold**. Received Writers' Digest. Weather keeps warm.

Tuesday, December 10: Hazel & I invited Anne & Ken McLennan. Entertained. Ken drove us home. Getting colder. Hazel gave me nose drops. No resolution.

Wednesday, December 11: Bought three presents. [-26°C] **N.P.A.M. No physical training. Lecture & rifle drill**. **Typed letter to go with story. Sending it out for third time**.

Thursday, December 12: Went to Hazel's. Read Joe & Toronto Star. Cold still with me. Temperature from [-23°C] to [-16°C] or [-17°C].

Friday, December 13: Skated at Norwood Rink with Hazel. Warmer. Resolution a few times. Cocoa at Hazel's home after skating.

Saturday, December 14: Waxed skiis. Saw "The Bluebird" at Avenue [movie theatre] & The Jones family in "As Young as You Feel". Resolution several times.

Sunday, December 15: Hazel & I left house at 12:00 noon. Skied all afternoon. Home at six. Hazel had supper at our place. Bell up. Resolution several times.

Monday, December 16: **N.P.A.M. lecture on possibility of unit disbanding. Not much physical training**. Driven by Ted as usual. Temperature around [-18°C].

Tuesday, December 17: Hazel had to attend concert for her girl's class. I addressed Christmas cards. Jack over. **Wrote letter to Major Vereker re: N.P.A.M.**

Wednesday, December 18: **N.P.A.M**. Went to E.T.C. raffle draw. Hazel won ham. Picked her own number. Art Hall & Phyllis walked part way.

Thursday, December 19: Hazel up to visit. Read but little. No more snow. Streets rather icy but weather fairly warm.

Friday, December 20: To see Hazel in evening. Decorated front room. Resolution several times. Weather quite mild.

Saturday, December 21: Haircut. Finished Christmas cards for mailing. Saw "A Dispatch From Reuters" E.G. Robinson at Capitol [movie theatre]. Few resolutions.

Sunday, December 22: Decorated some of dining room. Brown's for supper. Left early for a change. Bed before eleven. No sleep 'til after twelve.

Monday, December 23: N.P.A.M. Received pay & greatcoats. Called for Hazel at Taits in Ted's car. Refreshments at Cecil's. No resolution. Jimmie up to visit.

Tuesday, December 24: Hazel & I went to Garneau Theatre. Supper at Log Cabin first. Returned to go to St. Faith's for Christmas Eve service. Home about 3:00 a.m.

Wednesday, December 25: Cedar chest to Hazel. Boudoir doll & Eau de Cologne. She gave me writing desk. Two cards each. Brought Hazel over in evening. Took her home & left before 4:00.

Thursday, December 26: Up at 2:00. Visited Brown's after supper. Nairnky [?] there too. Resolution few times. Played geography game & Bingo. Bed 1:30.

Friday, December 27: Visited Hazel in evening. Read Toronto Star & Joe. Not getting much colder. Slight fog. Resolution few times.

Saturday, December 28: Loafed in afternoon. Saw Jack Benny & Fred Allen in "Love Thy Neighbor" at Capitol [movie theatre]. No lunch. Several resolutions.

Sunday, December 29: **Did not go on route march called for today. Wrote some poetry**. Visited Hazel in evening. Misses Francis there. Resolution few times.

Monday, December 30: **61st lecture & battery Foot Drill**. More snow. Jack at E.T.C. meeting. Bought tickets for Capitol [movie theatre] preview tomorrow.

Tuesday, December 31: Visited Hunters for a short while. Brought Hazel back home before going to Capitol [movie theatre] Frolic, "Tin Pan Alley". Resolution at theatre. Several times afterwards.

1941

January 1941

Wednesday, January 1: Bed 4:30. Up 2:00. Hazel & I skated at Avenue. Sorted bills in afternoon. Wrote letter to Book of The

Month Club. Resolution many times.

Thursday, January 2: Party at Carter's. Brown family & Currey's present. Quiz & geography games. Did not walk home with Hazel. [-23°C]

Friday, January 3: Statements completed. Party at Hazel's home. Curreys & Mr. Carter there. [-30.5°C] Resolution number of times. Left before family retired.

Saturday, January 4: Started day by falling downstairs to landing. Bruised back. Saw Marx Brothers "Go West" at Strand [movie theatre]. Lunch at Hazel's. Resolution several times.

Sunday, January 5: Up at 2:00. Hazel & Jack over for supper. Wasted evening playing games & listening to radio. Read a few pages of John. Several resolutions.

Monday, January 6: **61st lecture, physical training, battery foot drill. Jack's last night. He leaves January 9th for Brandon**. [-33°C] & moving down. Bed 11:00.

Tuesday, January 7: [-34°C] at first but became milder. Read Joe & Toronto Star at Hazel's. Resolution number of times. Chilly in Brown's front room.

Wednesday, January 8: [-29°C] Rise finally to about [-20°C]. **61st. Given hat badge**. Walked. Ted at hockey game. Jack leaving tomorrow.

Thursday, January 9: Keeping around [-23°C]. Saw Jack off at C.N. Destination Brandon. Hazel & I got to station just in time. Resolution several.

Friday, January 10: Mild [0.5°C]. Brought Hazel to our house. Finished Memory Hold the Door by John Buchanan. Number of resolutions. Rise in temperature makes me drowsy.

Saturday, January 11: Tried out shorthand. Might try R.C.A.F. as clerk. Saw "Lillian Russell" at Princess [movie theatre]. Good Lunch at Hazel's. Many resolutions.

Sunday, January 12: **Finished a poem**. Brown's for supper. Their radio broken. Read Joe. Helped with dishes & lunches. Several resolutions.

Monday, January 13: Received two more books from Book of Month Club. **61st parade. Battery & squad drill. No lectures nor physical training**. Ted still chauffeuring. **Tested my typing. Crossed 44 & 42.** [words per minute?]

Tuesday, January 14: Weather keeping steady. Read Joe with Hazel at her house. Resolution several times. Broke new resolution. **Will see Air Force again soon**.

Wednesday, January 15: A bit chillier. Not much work at office. **61st lecture, physical training, & battery drill. Tested typing speed. Approximately 40.**

Thursday, January 16: [-29°C] Hazel over to help with shorthand & reading. Glass top for desk. Finished poem but not typed out yet. Resolution several.

Friday, January 17: Visited Hazel. She helped with shorthand again. Read Toronto Star. Readers' Digest. Read from Book of The Month Club. Several resolutions.

Saturday, January 18: Wrote letters to Lorne & Jack in afternoon. Saw "The Long Voyage Home" at Rialto [movie theatre]. No lunch. Resolution several times.

Sunday, January 19: Left house for skiing with Hazel at 1:00 p.m. Back at 6:00. Supper at our house. Read one chapter Trelawney Resolution few times.

Monday, January 20: **61st parade from 7:00 to 11:00. Rather tiring**. Temperature keeping around [-9°C] More snow.

Tuesday, January 21: Cool but still above [-18°C]. Light snowfall. Practised shorthand at Hazel's home. Read four pages of Joe. Resolution once. Bed at 11:00.

Wednesday, January 22: **Received letter from R.C.A.F. 61st four hour parade. Walked to armouries with Frarey**. Ride home with Macallum. [-23°C]

Thursday, January 23: [-30.5°C] by night. **Told by R.C.A.F. that as I had shorthand & typing would be called soon**. Read Toronto Star at Hazel's. Few resolutions.

Friday, January 24: [-34°C] in morning. [-29°C] by night but cold winds. Hazel up to read **Trelawney**. Sent her home on street car. Bed 11:30.

Saturday, January 25: Saw "Second Chorus" at Capitol [movie theatre] with Fred Astaire & Paulette Goddard. Met Wally & Marion. Wally home on leave. Resolution several times.

Sunday, January 26: Up by 10:30. **Typed poetry**. **Parade of 61st. Rifle practice & gun drill. Dismissed before 5:00 p.m**. **Wrote article for Liberty. Sending out poem & stories**. Bed 10:00.

Monday, January 27: 61st 7:00 until 11:00. Temperature up to [-4°C] or [-1°C]. **Sent out poems, stories, & article**. Bed 11:30.

Tuesday, January 28: Temperature up to [10°C]. Read Joe at Hazel's. Tried shorthand but too weary for much. Typing speed 50 words per minute for 5 minutes. Resolution many times.

Wednesday, January 29: 61st four hour parade (almost) 7 to 10:35. Last long parade. In future only once a week – Wednesday. Wally left again.

Thursday, January 30: Still mild. Skated at Norwood with Hazel. Cocoa & toast. Two new Book of The Month books for Hazel. Many times for resolution. 1:00.

Friday, January 31: Found Barbara Watt (Franklin) when I called to see Hazel. She went out for awhile. Read funnies. Resolution some.

February 1941

Saturday, February 1: Haircut. Saw "Bitter Sweet" at Capitol [movie theatre] – Nelson Eddy & Jeanette Macdonald. No lunch.

Sunday, February 2: Typed part of story. Supper at Brown's. Read some in evening. Hazel has two new books. Resolution few times. Slipped on new resolution.

Monday, February 3: **Called up by R.C.A.F. Passed X-ray. Leave for Brandon Friday**. Hazel over in evening. **Looked over poetry**. Wrote to Wally. Resolution several times.

Tuesday, February 4: Visited Hazel. **Winding up everything before I leave**. Stayed quite late. **Can't count on much sleep**.

Wednesday, February 5: **Discharge from 61st**. Supper at Dodds. Hazel & I visited Hunters. **Window shopped for rings**. Resolution few times.

Thursday, February 6: Supper at Brown's. **Hazel & I got rings at Irving & Lacey. Told Mr. Brown we are engaged. He seemed quite agreeable**. Resolution many times.

Friday, February 7: **Rode Red & White for farewell. Rechecked in morning. Ticket afternoon. Left 9:05. Large crowd at station. Hazel & I had short ride when train shunting.**

Saturday, February 8: **Saw Wally in Saskatoon where we stopped for few minutes. Brandon two hours late. 5:30. Checked at "C" Squadron & had supper. Met Jack & looked around.**

Sunday, February 9: Loafed in Recreation room in afternoon. Met Fred Youmans. Wrote Hazel & mother (dropped note to them yesterday) United Church in evening (St. Pauls).

Monday, February 10: Went through Records & Pay Office. Assigned $20 for present time. Got first three knocks. [vaccinations] C.B. for 36 hours. [confined to base?] Both arms sore.

Tuesday, February 11: Ronnie, Jack, and I saw "The Howards of Virginia" at Strand [movie theatre]. Move our bunks every day. Front of first room & we leave.

Wednesday, February 12: Saw movie in arena. "Mad Miss Manton". Jack & I together. Had shower. No uniform yet. Weather chilly.

Thursday, February 13: Stayed in during evening & wrote letters. Now in first bunk & will move to main Depot tomorrow. Took shower.

Friday, February 14: Moved from "C" Squadron to "B". (same as Jack now) Received two valentines & chocolate Valentine from Hazel. Letter too. Pay day $10 advance. Didn't go to Valentine dance.

Saturday, February 15: Loafed in morning until called down to Trades Test Office for typing. Finished 12:00. Wrote a few letters. Three letters received.

Sunday, February 16: Wrote some more letters during day. Went to church in evening. St. Paul's United. Y peoples social afterwards. Hiccup trouble cured.

Monday, February 17: Worked in Trades Test Office. Wrote Phyllis & Ding in evening. Temperature down to [-29°C]. Mailed letter to Hazel.

Tuesday, February 18: Got issue all but kit bags today. Had my second knock for tetanus. C.B. tonight & tomorrow.

Wednesday, February 19: Loafed, read, **wrote poetry** & letters. **Discovered I will work in Trade Test Office until further notice**. Should be easy.

Thursday, February 20: Back to work. Rather easy. Cut first stencil & helped Gordon Pickering run off copies. Show in arena last night. Jack & I saw it. Wrote Wally.

Friday, February 21: Busy in morning but slack rest of day. Cold holding on – most in head. Jack left for Rivers yesterday. Hot shower & bed.

Saturday, February 22: Worked until 2:15 in afternoon. Went to post office to mail letter for Hazel. Bought Silvo.

Sunday, February 23: Took snaps at post office with Chuck & John. Had hot chocolate afterwards. Went to St. Paul's in evening.

Monday, February 24: Worked in morning but had third "knock" in afternoon. More painful than first two. Wrote letters in evening.

Tuesday, February 25: C.B. so I wrote five letters. Got one from Hazel & one from Jack. Drowsy from "knock" so retired early.

Wednesday, February 26: Worked fairly hard. Saw Y show on arena floor "State of Midnight" with Ginger Rogers & William

Powell.

Thursday, February 27: Letter from Hazel. Received in afternoon – mailed yesterday. Mailed one to her for Saturday. Plenty of typing today.

Friday, February 28: Paid $17.30. Drafted for MacDonald. Caught 4 o'clock train & reached Portage la Prairie at 7:00. Ate supper at Olies & saw Ritz Brothers. Train 12:15.

March 1941

Saturday, March 1: Arrived #3 B & G School at 1:00 a.m. Up at 8:30, ate, & went through Records. Put to work at Stores Office. Through at 5:30.

Sunday, March 2: Worked until 12:00. Wrote to Hazel & sent handkerchief. Played cribbage with Hub Cunningham i afternoon. **Two poems for Hazel**.

Monday, March 3: Worked hard all day & at night from 7:00 to 9:30. **Too tired to worry about the hole I am in**. Wrote some to Hazel.

Tuesday, March 4: **Getting to like it here**. Show at Y recreation hall. Crummy but it did pass the time. Plenty of shorthand letters.

Wednesday, March 5: Worked fairly hard. Weather moderating. No mail through yet. Back after supper. **Writing story**.

Thursday, March 6: Food not much better but station is not officially opened so this it to be expected. Received six letters. Four from Hazel.

Friday, March 7: Fairey Aircraft coming in. Another show - "Swing That Cheer". Better than first. Two letters & Toronto Star from Hazel.

Saturday, March 8: Was to get weekend pass to Winnipeg. Station quarantined so I wrote Hazel & Jack. Received Bulletin from Hazel.

Sunday, March 9: Day off but I worked for Canty, drafting up new system he is going to start. Through before 3:00 & back to letter-writing.

Monday, March 10: Conditions improving. Official opening today but we are still under quarantine. Plenty of work for me these days.

Tuesday, March 11: Show at Y - "Swing That Cheer"*. Took Dick Test today & will have result tomorrow. No more late work so far. Weather warmer. [*same as March 7]

Wednesday, March 12: Passed test as "negative" will be able to leave camp on passes now. Pool system in operation. First day off 19th.

Thursday, March 13: Received parcel from Hazel. Show postponed so I showered and wrote & read. Time passing fairly rapidly.

Friday, March 14: Canty wanted me to work late but I reminded him of show & escaped. Boris Karloff in "Night Key". Large screen & better sound.

Saturday, March 15: Blizzard made lights blink at night. Men lost on Lake Manitoba. Saturday tight & wrote Hazel. Frank Naher [?] shared cake from home.

Sunday, March 16: No work in morning as heating unit in hangar not operating. Heat – so work – in afternoon. Wrote mother & carried on Hazel's letter.

Monday, March 17: Two parcels. One from home & one from Hazel. Opened first but saved other. Wrote a few letters. Snowing.

Tuesday, March 18: Canty didn't come in until 4:30. Wanted me to work late but I declined 0 show "They Made her a Spy" - Sally Eilers.

Wednesday, March 19: 24 hour leave. Portage where I wrote & had my tunic altered. Saw "Hudson's Bay" in evening at Playhouse [movie theatre]. Bus back.

Thursday, March 20: Enough work to keep busy. At 17:15 Canty said we would work with no leave for six days. Boys annoyed. Three letters & Toronto Star.

Friday, March 21: A letter from Hazel. Show – Charlie McCarthy & W.C. Fields in "You can't cheat an honest man". Wet snow taking us back to winter.

Saturday, March 22: Food improving. Walked (I mean rode) to MacDonald last night for M.O. to London Life. Stayed in tonight writing Hazel & reading her letter.

Sunday, March 23: Snow melting again. Kept busy all day. Read more of Toronto Star & finished letters to Hazel & Mrs. Brown. Wrote Dad yesterday.

Monday, March 24: Weather chilly with snow. Quarantined for the morning but free by 15:00 hours. Not much work to do, though.

Tuesday, March 25: First Aeroplane ride – 25 minutes. Circled Portage La Prairie – from No. 3 B & G. Attended meeting at office and got away at 22:15. Annoyed.

Wednesday, March 26: Went to Orderly Room at 19:00 hours &

Wonacott told me some of procedure. Wrote & read remainder of evening.

Thursday, March 27: Last night's snow brought more mud. Slow day. Letter & Bulletin from Hazel.

Friday, March 28: Show - "Code of the Streets". Letter & Toronto Star from Hazel. Pay day - $10.30. Studying notes on clerking for Trade Test.

Saturday, March 29: Meals rather poor today. Mud drying up. Letter from Hazel. Wrote to her & studied for Trade Test.

Sunday, March 30: Fairly easy day & food suited me. Read more of DeShaw's notes for Trade Test. Clear & bright with less mud.

Monday, March 31: Cleaning up for spring. Getting set for 24 hour leave in Winnipeg. Lined up few articles – razor etc. I am taking.

April 1941

Tuesday, April 1: Rain in morning. Cleared up later. Missed bus but rid in truck to Portage. Snow storm. Arrived Winnipeg 9:30. Tom Cotter took me home.

Wednesday, April 2: Got to bed at 2:00. Up at 9:30. Went to Rotary Club. Luncheon with Tom. Stayed in & wrote Hazel in afternoon. A good leave thanks to Tom & Eleanor.

Thursday, April 3: Up on time after 1:30 retiring. Given Trade Test and managed to pass for "C" Grouping. Questions easy. Snow melted again. Spring(?)

Friday, April 4: Moved to No 9 Barrack Block tomorrow. Camp drying up. Show - "Freshman Year" not too bad – seemed familiar. Wrote a few lines.

Saturday, April 5: Told Good Friday a holiday & my days off are Saturday & Sunday. Moved into No. 9 Barrack Block. Wrote Wally, T. Cotter, & Hazel.

Sunday, April 6: Wet snow turning to rain which kept up all day. Worked steadily. Food improving – butter on the table now.

Monday, April 7: Mist & rain. New uniform. Letter from Hazel & one from mother & dad. Must be spring this time. Enough work.

Tuesday, April 8: Less rain but mud thick. Toronto Star & parcel from Hazel. Water shut off after 8:00 p.m. Managed to shave first. Ate peppermints from Hazel.

Wednesday, April 9: No rain. Clearing. Letters – Ted Allard & Hazel. Shower. Finally got laundry back. Missed being hooked for duty at MacDonald. Good supper.

Thursday, April 10: Fairly slow day until late afternoon. Got ride to Portage & another lift to Winnipeg. Rode streetcar to Cotters.

Friday, April 11: Rain in morning but cleared later & ended fairly pleasant. Loafed around house reading & writing. Didn't retire until 12:30.

Saturday, April 12: Up at 9:30. Took trousers to be altered. Tom drove me around in afternoon. Warm & bright. Saw "Road to Zanzibar" with Tom in evening.

Sunday, April 13: Not up until 11:00. Loafed most of day. Walked around for an hour or so. Bus to Portage & taxi to MacDonald. Bed at 1:00.

Monday, April 14: Little work in morning. Left some over at

17:15. Ate chocolate cake from Bell. Two letters from Hazel. Got new tunic back.

Tuesday, April 15: Bright & clear. Snapped plane. Worked at office instead of taking Duty Watch. Considerable work last few days.

Wednesday, April 16: Another warm day. Almost had to scrub mess hall floor but went back to work instead. More snaps of planes.

Thursday, April 17: No late work. No letter from Hazel. Caught up on Toronto Star reading – new one arrived today. Bright but not as warm.

Friday, April 18: Snowed but cleared up. Cold & wintry. Saw "Lady's' From Kentucky" - Y show. Showered but didn't shine or polish. Letter from Hazel.

Saturday, April 19: Clear & warm. Not much work. Catching up on reading. Supper best so far. Throat sore all day. Got snaps back – good.

Sunday, April 20: Almost a holiday. Started at 9:00. Through by 4:45. An easy day and all meals were above average. Cold wind.

Monday, April 21: Check from 6st. Letters from Hazel, Mother, & Jim. Wrote Davis & Jack. Worked steadily all day. Some left for tomorrow. Warmer.

Tuesday, April 22: Wet snow which finally cleared away. Didn't see show "Damsel in Distress" but got ready for 48 instead. Tetanus knock -showered.

Wednesday, April 23: Clear warm day. Got through work at 5:00 o'clock & caught bus. Portage bus late. P.M.C. insel (?) salesman. No room Cotters – stayed at Y.

Thursday, April 24: Lunched with Tom at one o'clock. Bought broach for Hazel. Stayed at Cotters again. Uniform altered. Rained in afternoon but cleared up after.

Friday, April 25: Mailed cake tin to Bell. Bright but chilly. Got "Wings" broach for Hazel. Tom went to armouries so I walked to bus depot. Slept on bus.

Saturday, April 26: Bright & warm. Plenty of work left. Received Easter Egg from Hazel – sent April 12th. Toronto Star arrived too.

Sunday, April 27: Extremely warm – near [27°C]. Got summer uniform & underwear. Work hour or so at office for Duty Watch. Canty away.

Monday, April 28: Cloudy with rain off & on all day. Warm, though & mud not too bad. Duty Watch.

Tuesday, April 29: Cloud & chilly. Pay day at 18:15. Show afterwards "Stage Door" - Adolphe Manjou, Ginger Rogers, Kay Hepburn. Good. Work slow.

Wednesday, April 30: Cleared up & ended bright & warm. No work first but too much in afternoon. Letter from Hazel. Wrote Molly Dodds & finished letter to Hazel.

May 1941

Thursday, May 1: Work plentiful. An hour's dull in afternoon. Short thunderstorm after supper. Writing Hazel & reading Star most of evening.

Friday, May 2: July in May weather keeps up. Saw shorts of Hopalong Cassidy in "Borderland" but didn't wait for feature. Took shower.

Saturday, May 3: Warm weather keeps coming. Not more than five or six men in bunkhouse after supper. Work is steady – too much so.

Sunday, May 4: Still hot. Got buttons & eagles for summer uniform. Dafoe draft known – not going. Joed to scrub mess hall at night.

Monday, May 5: Thunderstorm cooled off heat slightly. "AC" & "C" Group coming through. Took shower. Went back to work from 6 to 7.

Tuesday, May 6: Went to Portage on first day of 48. Visited Island Park & snapped few pictures. Back to camp & saw shorts only of Hopalong Cassidy.

Wednesday, May 7: Stayed in camp & loafed. Wet & snowy. Dafoe draft left. Dave Fraser & Archie Morrison with draft.

Thursday, May 8: Cold & frosty. Wore great coat. New sergeant major tough. Not much work to clean up at office.

Friday, May 9: Weather warming up again. Saw Peg O My Darling -fair. Work easy. Food steadily improving.

Saturday, May 10: Warm & bright. Not much work in afternoon but stayed to type two letters for Canty. Parcel from Hazel – Good.

Sunday, May 11: Breakfast at Snack Shop. Hot. Hitch-hiked Gladstone and back. Had to walk a few [kilometres]. Showered me afterwards.

Monday, May 12: Cloudy but fairly warm. Not much work. Letter from Hazel. Wrote Mr. Glover & Bell. Sent Writer's Digest to Hazel.

Tuesday, May 13: Worked overtime at office but I don't know why. Rain & mud again. Fairly warm, though. Work until 21:00.

Wednesday, May 14: Moved to Barrack Block #11. Began to rain at noon. Close to drill hall work now.

Thursday, May 15: Weather clearing but cool & cloudy with some mud left. Muster parade – one nail only allowed per man for clothes hanging.

Friday, May 16: Worked in D & R section typing R.P.O.'s. Wrote Hazel in evening -received letter from her & also from Bell.

Saturday, May 17: 48. Went to Portage. Photo taken but not so good. Saw "One night in South America" Don Ameche, Alice Faye. Saw crashed plane.

Sunday, May 18: Hitch-hiked to Gladstone & met Ross Prosser. Went to farm – Claytons. Sweltering. Driven back in Morton's car – Manitoba M.L.A.

Monday, May 19: Cooler. Not much work. Ryan Troupe put on stage show. Letter from Hazel. Lent camera for snaps of show.

Tuesday, May 20: Little work in morning but plenty in afternoon. Dance in camp – among those not present. New cupboards for [illegible, perhaps for clothing to make up for lack of hooks].

Wednesday, May 21: Not much work during day. Windy. Went back to work until 9:30. No mail.

Thursday, May 22: Almost freezing cold. New fatigue shoes. Letter Hazel – snaps from Portage & photo I had taken on Friday. Showered.

Friday, May 23: Weather warming. Wing parade. Stood for an hour. Whew. Letter Wilf Boyce. Feverish with cold trying to get me.

Saturday, May 24: By myself in office all day. No work so I read & enjoyed me. Wrote a few personal letters. Warm & pleasant.

Sunday, May 25: Cowan back but I did no work. Finished reading Digest. Weather warm but getting windy. Wrote a few more letters.

Monday, May 26: Clouded over & chilly with wind but no rain. Letter from Hazel – good. Very little work to do at office.

Tuesday, May 27: Drizzle rain & muddy before night time. Saw Cecil Rhodes “Empire Builder”. Head cold since Friday. Sore throat too.

Wednesday, May 28: More drizzle & more work. New filing cabinet for office. Letter Hazel. Cold improving. Took shower. Finished poem for Hazel.

Thursday, May 29: Rain carries on. More work in the office these days but I still have time to sit around. Still writing letters.

Friday, May 30: Rain slackening. Told of parade at Portage Monday. Saw “The Invisible Man Returns”, again. Reading up-to-date.

Saturday, May 31: Last lap. Rainy in morning as I went to Portage & had picture taken. Saw “Men of Boy’s Town”. Letter from Hazel. Read and wrote in evening.

June 1941

Sunday, June 1: Chilly but broken clouds. Wrote Hazel in morning & read Digest. **Tried to write story but no luck**. Read & wrote more.

Monday, June 2: Sprinkled all day. Parade in Portage in evening – no rain there. Saw “Sea Wolf” at Elite [movie theatre] with Price. Bed at 1:00.

Tuesday, June 3: Physical training but I was excused. Still cloudy but no rain. Saw “Love Affair” - Irene Dunne & Charles Boyer. Letter Hazel.

Wednesday, June 4: Began clear but clouded over. Letter & story from Hazel. Finished reading June Digest. Finished letter for Hazel. Shower & bed.

Thursday, June 5: Rained until noon & then clouds began to thin out. Saw cartoon of show “Three Sweet Girls Grow Up”. Wrote Hazel. No mail.

Friday, June 6: Cold – almost like winter. Liberties only mail. Mail to come to Barrack blocks now. Work heavier.

Saturday, June 7: Cleared up – ended warm & bright. Hitched to & from Portage. Saw “Dr. Kildare’s Crisis” at Playhouse [movie theatre]. Back before 12:00.

Sunday, June 8: Clear & warm. Read & wrote in morning. Sampled cake from mother. Read Star novel. Wrote Wilf Boyce & Hazel.

Monday, June 9: Cloudy but no rain. Another parade at Portage. Opening baseball game of the season. Not back until 22:00 hours.

Tuesday, June 10: Rainy in morning. Got issue raincoat. Rain stopped. More gravel on roads. Letter & Star from Hazel. Wrote Hazel. Saw shorts of “King of the Damned”.

Wednesday, June 11: No rain but cloudy. Worked hard in afternoon. Letter Hazel & Jack. Wrote Tom Cotter & Hazel.

Intend to go to Winnipeg this week.

Thursday, June 12: Cloudy but no rain. Worked steadily all day. Airmail letter Hazel & newspaper about Jack being killed in plane crash.

Friday, June 13: Finally cleared up. Late finishing work. Portage for photos. On to Gladstone, car stopping at camp for luggage. Prossers.

Saturday, June 14: Not up until 9:30. Warm & pleasant. Helped Ross fix Golf Links' mower. Walked by White Mud River in afternoon. Loafed evening.

Sunday, June 15: Another warm day. Went to Clayton's farm with Ross & his wife – supper there. Back after nine. Bus to camp at 11:30.

Monday, June 16: Hot & sticky. D.R.O. said fatigues could be worn from tomorrow on. Shower for me.

Tuesday, June 17: Hot, even in fatigues. Cooled off after supper with thunderstorm – near cloudburst. Letter from Hazel. Didn't go to show.

Wednesday, June 18: Work piling up but no night work. Weather warm & clear. Kit inspection postponed to Friday.

Thursday, June 19: Short march before work in morning. Given lecture by fire chief instead of drill in afternoon. Not much lessening of work.

Friday, June 20: Kit inspection. Saw "They Drive By Night" George Raft, Humphrey Bogart, Ida Lupino, & Anne Sheridan. Good.

Saturday, June 21: Still warm & bright. Letter, Star, & parcel from Hazel. Didn't go to Portage as I planned. Showed & sampled parcel.

Sunday, June 22: More perfect weather. Afternoon off. Loafed, read, & wrote Hazel. Wrote Wally, then Ross Prosser & Tom Cotter.

Monday, June 23: More heat. Letters from Hazel & mother. Showered & tried to keep cool in evening. Trade Test Officer coming.

Tuesday, June 24: Trade Test Officer here. Hotter & hot. Work rather slack these days. Showered again. Wrote Hazel. No mail.

Wednesday, June 25: Still hot. Trade Test. Flight Wonacott helped & I was given "B" Group on his recommendation. Move to Orderly Room.

Thursday, June 26: First day in Orderly Room easy. Killed time most of day. Hot yet tried to storm but didn't.

Friday, June 27: More heat & not much work. Letter from Davis. 48 begins tomorrow night. Two killed crash, first fatal one.

Saturday, June 28: Keeping hot. Missed but but caught one at corner. Arrived in Winnipeg shortly after nine. Tom & Eleanore entertaining. Bed 1:30.

Sunday, June 29: Slept late – no rain but cloudy & cool. Took a drive out to a ferry in Tom's new Ford. Bed by 12:00 this time.

Monday, June 30: Rainy & cloudy. Bought purse & cushion cover for Hazel. Almost cold out. Cleared off in evening. Bet at camp 1:30.

July 1941

Tuesday, July 1: Clear but chilly. Worked in C.R. in afternoon. Helped make up mail. Letter from Hazel. Didn't see show. Writing Hazel instead.

Wednesday, July 2: Warmer. Duty Watch. S.P. in Mess Hall. Letters from Ross, Wilf, & Hazel. Had lunch after S.P. duty. Bed 11:30.

Thursday, July 3: Drill in afternoon. Enough work to keep me busy. S.P. at Guard House this time. Read most of time. Bed 11:30.

Friday, July 4: Warm & bright. Busy for a change. Saw Minstrel Show. Thunder storm during night woke me. Parcel from Mother.

Saturday, July 5: Worked in Accounts for awhile. Warm weather still. Star & letter from Hazel. Wrote mother & Ross Prosser. Hazel as usual.

Sunday, July 6: Afternoon off. Loafed & read. Watched gunners at [about 23 metres] range. Wrote Hazel. Ate ginger cookies & nuts from home.

Monday, July 7: Keeping warm. Letter from Hazel. Leave for August through. Wrote Hazel. Showered me. Five months in service.

Tuesday, July 8: Worked on Evidence for Court Martial case. "Saw Mother Casey's Chickens". Thunder storm during show but stopped when picture finished.

Wednesday, July 9: Warm & pleasant. Birthday presents – handkerchief from Edna. Shirt and peppermint patties from mother. Letter from Hazel. Showered & wrote Hazel.

Thursday, July 10: Cold but warmed up as day advanced. Hitching not too good to Gladstone but finally got there at ten o'clock. Bed early.

Friday, July 11: Up 5:20. Ross & I went to Clear Lake. Swam & canoed. Down winding road on way back. Slightly sun-burned. Bed early at 11 o'clock.

Saturday, July 12: Up at 10. Swam in White Mud River in afternoon – perfect day with clear sky. Back by bus at 10:30. Bed by 12:00.

Sunday, July 13: Half day off. Clear & warm. Milk dispenser in Mess. Opened gifts from Hazel – identification bracelet & slippers. Remuster to "B" Group in D.R.O. effective July 1st.

Monday, July 14: Work still light. Weather keeps good. Duty Watch mess hall but nothing to do as work already done. Letter from Hazel.

Tuesday, July 15: Weather holds. S.P. at Guard Room for Duty Watch. Finished before 23:00. Wrote Hazel. Began to rain after lights-out.

Wednesday, July 16: Rain. Cleared off in morning & ended warm. Letter from Hazel. Another Schick Test. Wrote to Hazel most of evening.

Thursday, July 17: Thunderstorm before reveille. Rain & sun alternated all day. Sun won finally. Spent evening reading and writing to Hazel.

Friday, July 18: Blue sky day. Joed for funeral parade of Sgt. Thorardson. MacDonald & I saw "I Wanted Wings" afterwards.

Saturday, July 19: Hot. Worked at W & B in afternoon – shorthand & typing. Letter from Hazel. Wrote Hazel during evening. Tired.

Sunday, July 20: Hotter. Worked at Accounts. First knock for Diphtheria. Quit work before 16:00 hours. Wrote Hazel.

Monday, July 21: Arm slightly swollen after "knock". Letter Hazel. Warm or almost hot. Taken from C.B. to Orderly Room again.

Tuesday, July 22: Weather keeps warm & pleasant. Worked in Orderly Room again. Took one hour's drill. Hot.

Wednesday, July 23: Went to Portage in the morning. Had summer uniform pants shortened. Back to camp in afternoon. Letter from Hazel.

Thursday, July 24: Stayed around camp. Sun-bathed in morning. Played horse-shoes with Price in evening. Wrote Hazel. Lights out 10:30 again.

Friday, July 25: Another warm day. Lights out back to 11:00 again. Saw "College Swing". Clouded over and thunder storm during night.

Saturday, July 26: Cloudy & rain but warm. Bought new suitcase & picked up picture of myself. Saw Dr. Kildare Vil. [?] People".

Sunday, July 27: Unsettled but no rain. Played horseshoes in afternoon. Wrote Hazel & read Digest. Showered me. Rained during night.

Monday, July 28: Began rainy but cleared up. New system Duty Watch all this week. Mopped mess hall & finished before 20:00.

Tuesday, July 29: Letter to Hazel. Hot & bright. Duty Watch S.P. at mess hall. Had lunch after 23:00 hours. Busy in C.R.

Wednesday, July 30: Dull but only few rain spots. On Court of Inquiry all day. Paid $24.28. Letters Edna & Hazel. Mess hall for Duty Watch.

Thursday, July 31: Warm. Duty Watch mopping mess hall. Worked in C.R. Wrote Hazel. One hour drill as usual.

August 1941

Friday, August 1: Up 05:30. Back to office for Duty Watch. A hot day. Working in C.R. Finally letter to Hazel.

Saturday, August 2: Worked Equipment Section in morning, then Orderly Room & C.R. in afternoon. Star & letter from Hazel. Worked office for Duty Watch – Warm.

Sunday, August 3: Worked Equipment section morning. Back to Orderly Room & C.R. Worked at night for Duty Watch & wrote Hazel. Shower.

Monday, August 4: Still hot. Had foot bath for athlete's foot – potassium permanganate. Mouth wash powder for ulcers. No letter from Hazel.

Tuesday, August 5: Hot all day. Saw "Bringing Up Baby" with Cary Grant & Katherine Hepburn. One fellow fainted from heat.

Wednesday, August 6: Slight sprinkle but cleared in afternoon. Typing statements for Accounts. Another foot bath. Finished last letter to Hazel before leave.

Thursday, August 7: Went back to work in C.R. after supper. Everything packed ready for leave. Last letter from Hazel before we meet.

Friday, August 8: Stopped work at noon & took kit & spare

clothes to Barrack Warden. Sent large suitcase in by M.T. Went to Portage at 17:00 hours. Left by C.N. with Minty – air conditioned car.

Saturday, August 9: Left Minty at Saskatoon. Relaxed in Tourist Coach. Reached Edmonton at 8:15. Saw Hazel first. Strolled for awhile. Resolution quite a few times.

Sunday, August 10: Visited Brown's. Played set of tennis in afternoon. Hazel staying at our home all week. Catching up on our resolutions. Weather good.

Monday, August 11: Not up until afternoon. Visited Pilkingtons & Harry Tait's. Hazel & I enjoyed us in the evening. Resolution making up for last six months.

Tuesday, August 12: Loafed part of the day. Went to Hazel's for supper & stayed all night. Slept with Philip. Read Star funnies.

Wednesday, August 13: Up at 7 & to the East End Swimming Pool. Stayed around park until three or so. Back to Brown's & then home for us. Bed.

Thursday, August 14: Stayed home in morning. Up town in afternoon. Visited Pilkingtons & then saw "One Night in Lisbon" at Capitol [movie theatre]. Resolution many times.

Friday, August 15: Stayed around home & read with Hazel. Sprinkled slightly. Visited Dodds in evening. Storm so Hazel & I didn't go to her home. More resolutions.

Saturday, August 16: Took Jimmy home. Saw Winnie. Said goodbye to Mr. Brown at store. Rained in afternoon. Taxi late but rain late too – after 10:30. Met two airmen on train.

Sunday, August 17: Unsettled all day. Reached Portage at 6:15. Drizzle. To camp by Alonsa bus at 8 o'clock. Got blankets &

pillow at guardhouse.

Monday, August 18: Slept in until 06:50. Orange only for breakfast. Worked in C.R. fairly steadily. Clear & warm. Wrote Hazel. Camp not too good after leave.

Tuesday, August 19: In C.R. regularly. Saw "Sea Devils" with Vic McLagen, Preston Foster, & Ida Lupino. One hour's drill as usual. Warm day.

Wednesday, August 20: Working on outgoing mail. Wrote Hazel. Getting back into routine again. Morning chilly but day warms up quickly.

Thursday, August 21: More heavy in C.R. Letter from Hazel. Showered me. One hour drill with no break. W & B tomorrow.

Friday, August 22: W & B all day. Through before 17:00 hours. Up to Gladstone to stay with Ross over weekend. Hitched ride.

Saturday, August 23: Slept late. Finished letter to Hazel. Loafed around reading most of day. Weather unsettled & rather cool.

Sunday, August 24: Slept until nearly 10:00. Loafed & read Digest. Rainy. Left after supper as lift offered. Sun came out but cold. Letter from Hazel.

Monday, August 25: Almost winter-like. At W & B old building – some shorthand but work easy. Duty Watch but no Joe. No letter from Hazel.

Tuesday, August 26: Still chilly. Moved to new W & B. Building. Two letters from Hazel. Not much work. Wrote Hazel as usual. No Joe Duty Watch.

Wednesday, August 27:

Thursday, August 28:

Friday, August 29: Weather still rather cool. Paid $15.00. Still no Joe for Duty Watch. Put in letter for transfer to Lethbridge.

Saturday, August 30: Unsettled with rain & sun taking turns. Missed Joe on Duty Watch. Letter & Star from Hazel. Rain at night.

Sunday, August 31: Warm & pleasant. Completed week with no Joe's on Duty Watch. Took snaps around camp. Wrote Hazel.

September 1941

Monday, September 1: Started dull but warmed up. Thunder storm ended day but kept hot. Letter from Hazel. Wrote her, Wilf, & Edna.

Tuesday, September 2: Mixture cloud & sky. Last Diphtheria knock. Chilly wind but day fairly pleasant. Not much work in W & B.

Wednesday, September 3: Rainy all day. Worked hard in afternoon. Letter from Hazel. Finished letter to her. Dampness making barracks chilly.

Thursday, September 4: Rain keeps pouring. Drill didn't last usual hour. Work not very heavy. Letter from Mother. Wrote Hazel of course.

Friday, September 5: Not as much rain. Parcel (unopened) from mother with pyjamas. Left to Winnipeg in Sammy Beggs car. Arrived around 8. Bed 10.

Saturday, September 6: Sunny day. Up town most of day. Saw Bob Hope & Dorothy Lamour in "Caught in The Drift". Read

Digest in evening. Bed 11:00.

Sunday, September 7: Dull. Stayed in house all day reading & writing. Eleanor sewed props on my uniform. Bed before eleven, setting alarm for 04:30.

Monday, September 8: Back in C.R. Parcel from mother – new pyjamas & shirt. Letter & Star from Hazel. Saturday letter waiting for me too.

Tuesday, September 9: Weather clearing. Musketry instruction in morning. Much work in C.R. Late finishing. Sky clear by sunset. Wrote Hazel as usual.

Wednesday, September 10: Bright & warm. Work fairly slack in C.R. Letter from Hazel. Finished one to her. Ban on postings now lifted. Showered me.

Thursday, September 11: Work fairly easy now. Reading notes borrowed from Gillingham. Weather stays fairly warm. Keep up letters to Hazel.

Friday, September 12: Plenty of work. Finished letter for Hazel. Studied Gillingham's notes. Showered me. In bed before 10. Wrote Molly Dodds.

Saturday, September 13: Day started & ended clear with clouds in between. In charge of C.R. Finished at 17:15 hours. Letter & Star from Hazel.

Sunday, September 14: Slept in until 19:00. Clouds cleared during day. Two sets tennis with Dave Fayfe (corporal) – 6-3, 6-1.

Monday, September 15: Wire about living at Portage instead of camp. Overflow from Brandon coming here. Rain but cleared up again. Letter from Hazel.

Tuesday, September 16: Warm & clear. Latest news 500 men coming to No. 3. No postings for Lethbridge. C.R. work running smoothly.

Wednesday, September 17: Clear & warm. Letter from Hazel. Taking work easily. 75 men came in after supper. Still no news about a move to Lethbridge.

Thursday, September 18: Postings to Lethbridge but no clerks yet. As hot as summer today. Excused from one hour drill. Work fairly heavy in C.R. Wrote Hazel as usual.

Friday, September 19: More summer weather. Stood-in on Duty Watch fro Jack Campbell. Joed for fire crew. Slept in No. 5 Hangar. Given late meal.

Saturday, September 20: Wet & chilly. Went to Portage in evening. Saw "The Mummy's Hand" & "Alibi" - fairly good. Back on early bus before lights out.

Sunday, September 21: Stayed in bed until 09:00. Still damp & dismal. Read letter from Hazel. Showered to finish off day. Wrote Hazel as usual.

Monday, September 22: Weather clearing. Letter from Hazel. Wrote her, Ross, & Phyllis. Enjoying work in C.R. - not posting yet.

Tuesday, September 23: Clear at first but clouded over. Had one hour drill. C.R. work in good shape. Spent most of evening writing Hazel.

Wednesday, September 24: Rainy. Letter from Hazel. Weather chilly – fall here. Work fairly light in C.R. with four of us to keep things caught up.

Thursday, September 25: Overcast & cool but no rain. Showered

& climbed into bed early. Wrote Hazel. No more word on posting to Lethbridge.

Friday, September 26: Began rainy. Stayed cloudy all day. Decided not to go to Gladstone. Star from Hazel. Letter from Edna. Wrote Hazel as usual.

Saturday, September 27: Up in time for breakfast. Clear & frosty. Bill Hooker & I went to Portage in afternoon. Saw "Life Begins for Any Hardy". Wrote Hazel at night.

Sunday, September 28: Up before 07:30. Took things easy, writing Hazel in morning. Vaudeville show at night. One of the best we've had here. Parcel from Hazel.

Monday, September 29: Hazel's letter as usual. Weather still unsettled but no snow. No Joe for Duty Watch. Postings coming but nothing for me – yet.

Tuesday, September 30: Warmer but cloudy. Ed (?) Price left for physical training course at St. Thomas. Old crowd breaking up. Another no Joe night & 22:00 roll call.

October 1941

Wednesday, October 1: Slight mist cleared before noon. Hazel's letter on time. Another No Joe night. Showered & wrote Hazel. Disappearing cake & nuts in parcel.

Thursday, October 2: Weather still unsettled & cool. Another Joeless Duty Watch night. No postings to Lethbridge for clerks yet. Saw "TransAtlantic Tunnel" - Richard Dix.

Friday, October 3: Helped Deshaw send signal on teletype after supper instead of going on Duty Watch. No snow yet but cold enough.

Saturday, October 4: Fairly busy but cleaned up work. Letter from Hazel on time. No Joe again on Duty Watch. Cloudy.

Sunday, October 5: Not much to do. Fairly warm day. Wrote Hazel at office in afternoon. No Joe & excused from 22:00 hours roll call.

Monday, October 6: Letter from Hazel. Won $4 on World Series Pool. [U.S. national baseball championship] Sight drizzle during day. No snow yet but it tried hard in morning.

Tuesday, October 5: Sulky grey day. Saw “Swingtime” with Fred Astaire and Ginger Rogers. Had seen before but still enjoyed it.

Wednesday, October 6: Weather keeps chilly & cloudy. Letter from Hazel as usual. Showered me. Wrote to Hazel most of evening.

Thursday, October 9: Weather improving. Showered me & got ready to visit Ross for weekend. Work at office fairly heavy.

Friday, October 10: Clearing. Hitchhiked to Prosser’s after supper. Letters from mother & Hazel. Work as heavy as ever. Bed around eleven.

Saturday, October 11: Perfect blue sky. Wrote Hazel most of time. Went with Ross to farm to pick up pliers he had misplaced.

Sunday, October 12: Perfect blue sky day. Slept until ten. Loafed most of day. Took bus back at 23:00 hours. Hazel letter waiting. Bunk made by DeShaw.

Monday, October 13: Hazel’s letter & my writing used up spare time. Cloudy but cleared after awhile. Indian summer must be here.

Tuesday, October 14: Became involved in work & didn’t go on

pay parade in afternoon. Fine clear weather keeps things pleasant enough.

Wednesday, October 15: Paid in morning. ($15.00) Letter from Hazel on time. C.R. work keeps up but not too much to do these days.

Thursday, October 16: Skipped the one hour drill in morning to work. Nothing exciting. Listened to radio & wrote Hazel in evening.

Friday, October 17: Work in C.R. in good shape. Indian summer weather carries on. Wrote Hazel most of evening.

Saturday, October 18: Bright & clear. Worked on Inspector General's Report. 24 hour pass cancelled. Stood to [?] for Dencose & Joed for Officers' Mess. Got away at 1:30.

Sunday, October 19: Up at 07:00. Worked all day on Inspector General's Report. No time for writing until evening. Sun still in control.

Monday, October 20: Hazel's letter started week well. Bright & clear again. Spent evening writing Hazel. Find work fairly easy these days.

Tuesday, October 21: 48s cancelled for next week. Watch stopped. Hair spring seems to be out of line. But sun still shines on. Saw "Two for Breakfast".

Wednesday, October 22: Usual letter from Hazel. Days are still blue-sky style. Work is fairly easy with few bumps. Will ask Flight about leave tomorrow. Concert featuring Baranoff – violinist.

Thursday, October 23: Parcel from mother. Letters from Phyllis Hunter & Mollie Dodds. Indian summer keeps things warm.

C.R. work going smoothly.

Friday, October 24: Keeps clear & warm. Extra time on my leave okayed. Letter from Hazel – also Star. Received 48 hour pass after all. Stayed on station.

Saturday, October 25: Left camp around 11:00 hours. Hitched to Portage & Winnipeg. Bought one of those books. Thumbed back to Portage by 19:00. Saw “Knockout” & “Officer & A Lady”. Lift back to No. 3 M.T. panel truck.

Sunday, October 26: Tried to snow. Below freezing. Loafed & wrote Hazel during day. Slept in & missed breakfast. Showered to finish off day.

Monday, October 27: Moved from C.R. to Orderly Room (worse luck). Wintry weather. Splinter in left hand stopped work for day. M.O. carved wood out. No Joe on Duty Watch. Two letters from Hazel. One delayed Saturday one.

Tuesday, October 28: Keeps cold [-10.5°C]. Work easy in Orderly Room. Back after supper to clean up for I.G. Took nine letters from Adjutant – finished 21:00 hours.

Wednesday, October 29: Worked late typing for Inspector General. First snow. Missed first Duty Watch parade so no Joe. Visited Hazel as usual.

Thursday, October 30: Joe for Duty Watch was to pick up chairs after show. Saw “Underground” - Jeffry Lynn. Not much time for writing to Hazel. Snow remains. Paid $22 – [illegible] over on hours.

Friday, October 31: Work slack. Repaired typewriter to fill in during morning. Rushed last part of day. Usual telegram at night took nearly1 1/2 hours.

November 1941

Saturday, November 1: Snow disappearing. Typed D.R.O. Joed for Officers' Mess dance. Letter & wedding invitation from Hazel. Bed at 03:30 Sunday morning. Warmer.

Sunday, November 2: Up 11:00 hours. Rainy. Typed on D.R.O. in afternoon but stopped early. No Joe for Duty Watch & excused 22:00 hours roll call.

Monday, November 3: Letter from Hazel didn't arrive. More snow. Not much work around office. Stood to for Gillingham but no Joe. He got roll of film from Portage.

Tuesday, November 4: Letter from Hazel. Supper at Henwoods. Intended to hunt for rooms but didn't make it. Back on early bus before lights out.

Wednesday, November 5: Very little work to do. Letter from Hazel. Most of snow gone. Addresses of place in Portage given to me by Henwood. Showered. Wrote Hazel in evening.

Thursday, November 6: Still loafing around Orderly Room. Wrote Hazel. Showered & sorted laundry in evening. Keeps cloudy & chilly. Winter must be here for keeps.

Friday, November 7: Worked at W. & B. Ordered winter hat & new boots at clothing stores. Got props [propellers] for greatcoat. Bart Krause & I met Edna Baxter from Neepawa on bus. Mix-up with greatcoats but finally got right one. Played rummy until 02:00.

Saturday, November 8: Not up until 10:00 hours. Went downtown in afternoon. Bought Digest & writing pads. Loafed in evening. Bed slightly after 23:00 hours. Cold weather.

Sunday, November 9: Not up until 11:00. Loafed most of day.

Tom & Eleanore out for supper. Left on early bus at 6:00. Wandered around country – Alonsa line.

Monday, November 10: Worked on Occupational History forms. Went to Equipment Section in afternoon. Two clerks posted overseas. Weather cloudy but fairly warm. Letter Hazel.

Tuesday, November 11: Still on O.H. forms. Observed two minutes silence [Armistice Day – later Remembrance Day]. Day felt sulky. Not overworked. New clerks make work easier than ever.

Wednesday, November 12: Letter from Hazel on time. O.H. forms keep me looking busy. Doug Dorsay chief assistant. Showered me. Started letter to mother. Clear sky.

Thursday, November 13: Keeps fine though chilly. Fairly busy all day. Overseas postings took Jack Hooper. Stand-to for Henwood. But no Joe.

Friday, November 14: Received book from Hazel. Cold developing – worse luck. O. History forms keeping me busy. Snow nearly gone again.

Saturday, November 15: Kept busy until 17:15. Made final arrangements for rooms in Portage. Letter from Hazel on time. Rode back with police run before 23:00.

Sunday, November 16: More snow. Stayed in bed until 11:00. Cold nearly knocked me over. Read book Hazel sent. Wrote last letter before we meet. Showered me in morning.

Monday, November 17: Not up until 06:45. Hazel's letter & Star today's mail. Told the gang I'm getting married Saturday. Read in evening as no letters to write.

Tuesday, November 18: Wet snow. Cold developing – for the wedding I suppose. Had throat spray at hospital.

[November 19 to 28 mistakenly dated 1942.]

Wednesday, November 19: Took evening local for Edmonton. Had berth so that I would be well rested. Snowy with blizzards.

Thursday, November 20: Breakfast at Saskatoon & on to Edmonton. Hazel met me alone at the station. Spent night at my house.

Friday, November 21: Made final arrangements & got marriage license. Hazel bought me signet ring & we picked up wedding ring.

Saturday, November 22: got pendant for Hazel & finished all details. Wally best man – St. Faiths Church. Picture at Blythes. Spent night at S [illegible] Hotel.

[In error, the entries suddenly change to 1942, but it remains 1941.]

Sunday, November 23: Visited our families & went back to Corona for our second night. Rather late when we retired.

Monday, November 24: Went to my home & family saw us off on train. Had lower berth & porter to remove superfluous confetti.

Tuesday, November 25: Day passed rapidly. Stopped at Portage to mail letter to Mrs. Guinn. Winnipeg at suppertime. Stayed at Marlboro [Hotel].

Wednesday, November 26: Up in afternoon. Got knives & forks. Supper at Cotter's. Left on night train for Portage. Stayed at Mayfair [Hotel].

Thursday, November 27: Bought electric stove & moved into rooms at Guinn's. Had our first supper together in new home.

Friday, November 28: Shopped for groceries & organized things. Unpacked some of our luggage. Freight hadn't arrived.

[Saturday, November 29 & Sunday, November 30 have no entries.]

December 1941

[Entries start again on December 5, but continue from Friday, November 29 and 1941 returns.]

Friday, December 5: Hazel phoned to tell me things had been sent express instead of freight. $10.80 to pay practically flattened us and threw things out of line.

[No entries from Saturday, December 6 to Tuesday, December 7. Diary resumes.]

Wednesday, December 10: First Duty Watch since Hazel & I married. Rather strange to be sleeping alone. Barracks felt stuffy & bunk hard.

Thursday, December 11: Second day of Duty Watch. Telephone Hazel each night as well as at noon. Bunk still rather uncomfortable.

[No entries from Friday, December 12 to Monday, December 15. Diary resumes.]

Tuesday, December 16: Major nicked 33 of us for being late on parade. Given rifle drill after supper. Finally home at 21:00 hours.

[No entries from Wednesday, December 17 to Wednesday, December 24. Diary continues but dated 1942 in error.]

Thursday, December 25: Invited to Guinn's for Christmas Dinner. Chatted with Mrs. Guinn afterwards. Didn't leave the house all day.

[No entry on Friday, December 26.]

Saturday, December 27: Bill Hocker for supper. Helped Hazel prepare meal. Entertained Bill until nearly midnight. Our first supper guest.

[No entries from Sunday, December 28 to Tuesday, December 30. Diary continues.]

Wednesday, December 31: Given holiday for New Years. No cheque so Hazel & I stayed at home though Deshaw offered to finance us.

1942

January 1942

Thursday, January 1: Promoted to Corporal in D.R.O. effective January 4, 1942. Visited Wonnacott – woo-woo & stayed for supper with Fairburns. Left early as Major & wife got us.

[No entries from Friday, January 2 to Sunday, January 4. Diary continues.]

Monday, January 5: Went to Elite [movie theatre] with Ed Deshaw & Betty Kennedy to see “Shining Victory”. Invited them for lunch afterwards. Enjoyed us.

[No entries from Tuesday, January 6 to Friday, January 9. Diary continues.]

Saturday, January 10: Hazel & I saw “A Yank in the R.A.F.” at Playhouse [movie theatre]. My skates arrived from home. Throat sore. Bought horehound.

Sunday, January 11: Throat worse. Couldn’t talk very much. 24, so I was able to stay in bed until the afternoon.

[No entries from Monday, January 12 to Wednesday, January 14. Diary continues.]

Thursday, January 15: Brought home ice cream as surprise but it nearly melted in clothes closet. Had to put it in the refrigerator.

Friday, January 16: Hazel made chocolate. Good. (Hazel please note in case you read this.) Nearly as good as I could do myself.

[No entry on Saturday, January 17. Diary continues.]

Sunday, January 18: Hazel & I went to English Church. First time since we were married. Church quite beautiful inside.

[No entries from Monday, January 19 to Tuesday, January 20. Diary continues.]

Wednesday, January 21: Duty Watch. Hazel & Betty came to dance. Hazel & I together most of evening so we had a near perfect time.

[No entries from Thursday, January 22 to Tuesday, January 27. Diary continues.]

Wednesday, January 28: Hazel & I went skating at arena. Skates dull but we made out all right. Dorothy Guinn with us. Snow.

[No entries on Thursday, January 29. Diary continues.]

Friday, January 30: Saw "Birth of the Blues" at Playhouse [movie theatre] – Bing Crosby. Dragged at times. Met Wonacotts – were entertained as we entertained them at lunch in our rooms.

Saturday, January 31: 48. Up at 1:00 after working first around 07:00. Shovelled snow from sidewalk. Experimented with waffles. Fell asleep in evening.

February 1942

Sunday, February 1: Church in morning. Made chocolate pancakes – good. Maple syrup. Rather quiet day.

Monday, February 2: Still doing Doug's & my own (?) work in Orderly Room. Padgett's remuster should soon be through.

Tuesday, February 3: Posting come through for Bella Bella B.C. Hazel upset but managed to cheer her up. May be a chance for cancellation.

Wednesday, February 4: No further word from Ottawa. Doing parade states [stats?] along with other work. **Could be a dream we'll wake up from soon.**

Thursday, February 5: Still no reply. Will start with clearances if no word tomorrow. Getting everything packed at Portage.

Friday, February 6: Posting stands. Clearances finished in morning. Left MacDonald in afternoon. Bernice & Millie kissed me goodbye. Hazel & I finished packing – ready to go.

Saturday, February 7: Left for Edmonton. Had enough meal tickets for Hazel & I to eat in diner- class. Couldn't change upper at Saskatoon so Hazel & I in Upper 14 – fun.

Sunday, February 8: Hazel's people met us. Went up to my house later & then to St. Faith's Church. Dinner at Hazel's & then my house for supper & sleeping.

Monday, February 9: wally leaving for Trois Rivières. Went to see Pilkingtons & Harry Taits. Had baggage delivered. Saw "Sergeant York" at the Capitol [movie theatre].

Tuesday, February 10: Went downtown again. Saw Mr. Glover. Didn't manage anything we had planned. Supper at my house.

Slept at Brown's.

Wednesday, February 11: Left for Vancouver. Not much snow until we passed Jasper. Clouds in way of mountains. Wrote Hazel at night in Upper 14.

Thursday, February 12: Taken to Jericho Beach from C.N. Station. Visited Aunt Nell at Caroline Courts. Aunt Mary appeared. Had supper & back to camp.

Friday, February 13: Had lunch with Aunt Nell but back to Jericho Beach for Trans. Warrant. Sent Valentines & letter to Hazel. Left on Catola at 10:50.

Saturday, February 14: Stayed up late watching ship load & unload at ports. Crossed open sea during night but I was in bed. We are well fed.

Sunday, February 15: Arrived at Bella Bella 12:00 hours. Didn't work in afternoon. Rounded up baggage & found bunk in "A" Barracks.

Monday, February 16: Worked in Orderly Room but did very little. Saw "Red Lights Ahead" in mess hall. Rather old & not too good.

Tuesday, February 17: Wrote mother. **Issued rifle & 20 rounds**. Turned out 22:00 hours & warned there might be an alarm. Slept in shirt & underwear. All clear.

Wednesday, February 18: Still working in C.R. Bright & clear for a change. Bella Bella still stands. Japanese mustn't be able to find us. Wrote Hazel. **Given lecture on use of rifles.**

Thursday, February 19: C.O.'s inspection at 13:30 hours. Drilled afterwards. **Toured station with Adjutant. Learned the positions of all defence posts**.

Friday, February 20: Received letter & Valentine from Hazel. Also Valentine from Winnie. Duty Clerk at Orderly Room. Wrote gang at MacDonald.

Saturday, February 21: Up at 8:30 as I didn't have to report until 10:00. Worked steadily & finished around 18:00 hours. Wrote Hazel. Showered me.

Sunday, February 22: Up 08:30 as no one works until 10:00 on Sunday. Two letters from Hazel, one from Book Of The Month club & Christmas card from Ben Lange. Meeting in mess hall. C.O. spoke. Show "Two for Breakfast", but didn't stay as I saw it before.

Monday, February 23: Started at Operations. Merely learning so no work. May get Joed if I'm not careful – all same Equipment Section MacDonald. Practice Alarm. I stood guard at Operations.

Tuesday, February 24: Barrack fatigue until 10:00. Swept & mopped floor. Still at Operations. Clear & warm again. Wrote & read during evening as usual.

Wednesday, February 25: Not overworked in Operations. Rushed awhile in afternoon. Began raining after supper. Saw shorts of picture show. Haircut by camp barber.

Thursday, February 26: Rain keeps up with wet snow. Still at Operations – worse luck. No parades – but no future. Wrote Hazel as usual.

Friday, February 27: More rain but smoke gone. **Paid $20.76.** Letter from Hazel. Gave Dorfman **$2 for Bella Bella pennant.** Read & wrote during evening. Showered me.

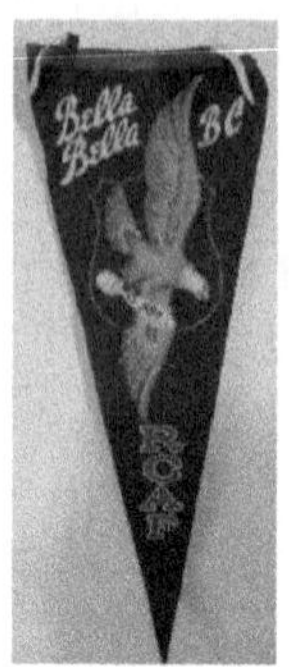

Saturday, February 28: Rain keeps falling. Wrote letters most of day. Worked until 21:00 hours. **Started short short for Writers' Digest contest**. Arranged shifts. I start at 23:59 Sunday.

March 1942

Sunday, March 1: Off duty all day. Read & wrote letters most of time. Rain keeps falling. Boat late - not until 17:00 hours. Went down to see. Saw show "Stolen Sweets". Slept Operations night shift.

Monday, March 2: Up at 07:15. Few spots of snow. Clear & bright again but at noon hail & rain. Letter from Aunt Nell. Letter & parcel from Hazel. Windy and rainy at night. Wrote Hazel. Showered.

Tuesday, March 3: Bleak & wet again. Spoke to F/O Gant & wrote letter to C.O. On Duty at 17:00 hours. Some trouble but Flt Sgt Louis helped. **Wrote Hazel. Wrote another poem for her – back in form.**

Wednesday, March 4: Rain still in control. Letter to C.O. not yet typed by Orderly Room. Fairly busy during evening. **Have started daily exercises**. On duty at 17:00.

Thursday, March 5: Sky trying to win day ended clear. Tom back at 18:00 hours. On duty at midnight. Snack at mess hall in evening. No work during night.

Friday, March 6: Rain again. Tom & I walked to Bella Bella & had lift back with Duty Run on crash boat. Two letters & magazines from Hazel. Read magazine & **worked on short short**.

Saturday, March 7: Began cloudy & no rain. On duty at 17:00 hours. Wrote Hazel & read <u>Astonishing Magazine</u>. Tom slept at office too.

Sunday, March 8: Two letters & <u>Toronto Star</u> from Hazel. More rain – no let up. Last night in Cypher Room. Back to Orderly Room tomorrow. C.R. I think and hope two new W.O.G.s helping Tome.

Monday, March 9: Cleared up – no rain all day. Worked in Orderly Room. Helping around Records easy. Wrote Hazel & Helen in evening.

Tuesday, March 10: Worked Records in morning. C.R. in afternoon. After supper break at O. Room until 20:30 with Jim Watt. Rained most of day. Cleared at night. Wrote Hazel.

Wednesday, March 11: Started clear but ended wet with some snow & hail. Worked in C.R. all day. Wrote Hazel. Saw "It's Pop Who Pays". Showered me before bed.

Thursday, March 12: Work getting organized in C.R. Day started fairly well but ended wet with snow. Joe for unloading beer kegs & cases. Lunch at mess hall afterwards. Cheese & biscuits.

Friday, March 13: Clear & no rain all day. Mail in so busy at C.R. Two letters from Hazel, one from Ben Lange, Ed Deshaw, and Mother. Joe for picking up paper after supper. Soon finished.

Wrote Hazel as usual.

Saturday, March 14: Bright & clear again. Outgoing mail not great. Paid $10. Went back after supper to send out a few letters. Showered me & wrote Hazel.

Sunday, March 15: Rain & clouds once more. Barrack Joe so no work in morning. Two letters from Hazel. One from Ross Prosser. Parcel from Hazel. Concert & show at official opening of Recreation Hall. Didn't stay for Vernon & Irene [illegible].

Monday, March 16: Rain still in charge. C.R. work slack. Wrote Hazel in evening. 48 to Ocean Falls tomorrow. Duty Watch starting. Week at a time but I'm not on until next Monday.

Tuesday, March 17: Worked hard at C.R. morning. Unsettled – rainy. Over to Ocean Falls on Charles Todd. Arrived 11:30 after leaving Bella Bella to stay for 48. Wrote Hazel. Gerry on night duty.

Wednesday, March 18: Overcast & drizzling. Walk around in afternoon. Saw "Road Show" in evening. Wrote Hazel for finale. Not to bed until after 0:00. Ben McKee, Sgt W.A.G. at Gerry's with me.

Thursday, March 19: Up around 10:15. Rain keeps falling. Gerry made our breakfast. Walked over to swimming pool. Bowled 5 pins – 59, 144, 87, & 207. Wrote Hazel. Boat returning at 21:00 hours. Arrived Bella Bella at 00:45.

Friday, March 20: Mail in & Work at C.R. heavy. Two letters from Hazel. Cloudy & wet as ever. Adjutant back from leave.

Saturday, March 21: Snow to start spring. Worked late on outgoing mail. Wrote Hazel as usual. Not cold but wet & sloppy slush.

Sunday, March 22: Ground covered with snow. Letter from Hazel & Norm Davis. Saw show "There Goes My Heart" again after work in office – overtime.

Monday, March 23: Cleared a bit. Snow nearly all gone. Joed for setting up benches for concert in recreation hall. Rifle drill for an hour. Wrote Hazel instead of seeing camp concert.

Tuesday, March 24: Outgoing mail fairly light. Finished off easily at 17:00. Joed for canteen bottle picking & floor mopping. One hour drill after supper.

Wednesday, March 25: Not much to do. Jim Watts on 48. Drill at night 18:30. Picked up sticks & paper on Duty Watch. Rainy.

Thursday, March 26: C.O.'s parade in morning. Not too stiff. Joe for bottle picking up on Duty Watch. No drill tonight for change. Cloudy but no rain.

Friday, March 27: Almost perfect day with blue skies. Two letters from Hazel. Joed as runner in Wireless Section. Visit with Hazel cut short. Received web equipment in afternoon.

Saturday, March 28: Rain again but only a few sprinkles. Worked hard on outgoing mail. No Joe on Duty Watch. Read Star & wrote Hazel during evening. M.O. woke everyone in morning.

Sunday, March 29: Fairly bright. Two letters from Hazel. No Joe on Duty Watch. Work not too heavy in C.R. Wrote Hazel during evening as usual.

Monday, March 30: Told of high officials visiting. Prepared for inspection but none came. Clear & bright again. Ready for 48 at Ocean Falls.

Tuesday, March 31: Another bright day. Left on Charles Todd at 13:15 & reached Ocean Falls at 16:35. Stayed at Colsons with

Ernest Lousley (?). Walked around in evening & retired early.

April 1942

Wednesday, April 1: Hiked around Claire Mange Mountain with Ernie. Saw "Western Union" with Colsons in evening. Played double solitaire with Mrs. Colson until around 02:00. Lunch before bed.

Thursday, April 2: Up around 11:30. Another pleasant day. Stayed in to write Hazel & read. Left for Bella Bella at 21:00. Back at camp at 23:59.

Friday, April 3: Clear & bright. Two letters & Star from Hazel. Wrote & read during evening. Showered me. Laundry cost $1.46. this time. Sgt Bouchard & Corporal Leigh leaving soon.

Saturday, April 4: Another clear day. Jim on 48. Got parcel. Easter egg from Hazel. Kept busy in C.R. on both outgoing & incoming mail. Finished around 17:30. Read & wrote Hazel.

Sunday, April 5: Perfect blue again. Rushed with mail. Two letters from Hazel. One from Edna. Bulletin from Hazel. Had defence manoeuvres in afternoon. Wrote Hazel.

Monday, April 6: Warm & bright again. May get Joed out of hooks as wire sent to Ottawa asking for Corporal Steno. No Joe on Duty Watch. Drill for $1^{1/2}$ hours. Wrote Hazel.

Tuesday, April 7: Rain part of day but cleared in evening. Practice alarm. Fun – almost. Busy in C.R. No Joe on Duty Watch. Wrote Hazel & read.

Wednesday, April 8: Cloudy but no rain. Had Adjutant cancel wire asking for corporal for 9 (BR). Rehearsal for I.G. [Inspector General] parade in evening. No Joe on Duty Watch. Wrote Hazel.

Thursday, April 9: Put in name for drill test. Some rain but not heavy. I.G. arrived at 17:00 hours. Only Joe for paper picking. Assembled web – fun.

Friday, April 10: Rained all night. Mail two letters, parcel, & Star from Hazel. Work quite heavy. I.G. inspection in afternoon. No Duty Watch – surprise.

Saturday, April 11: I.G. looked over C.R. & seemed satisfied. Through at 17:30 hours as outgoing mail late. Shortage of clerks makes things tough.

Sunday, April 12: Two more letters from Hazel. Weather cloudy but no rain. Trying to get hooks but no luck so far. Wrote Hazel in evening. No Joe.

Monday, April 13: Jim & I working on Flight Lieutenant Gauthier but no luck for hooks yet. Adjutant stubborn. C.O. away but may help when he returns.

Tuesday, April 14: George Neal & Ricard in hospital made more work for rest of us. Dave Carmichael leaving tomorrow – fun. Last chance to try for hooks. I get drill test at 15:00 hours tomorrow.

Wednesday, April 15: Cloudy with few spots of rain. Took drill test from three to five & back at 6 until 7:30 – fun. Passed with mark of 82.12% - not bad. Duty Clerk until 10 o'clock.

Thursday, April 16: Ricard back to help in Orderly Room. Promotion to Corporal in D.R.O. effective 1-4-42. At last I've started. **Voted on conscription plebiscite**. Wrote Hazel in evening. Rain most of day.

Friday, April 17: Sewed hooks on last night. Work keeps coming with no help in sight. Rain is not letting up. Wrote Hazel.

Saturday, April 18: More rain. Duty Clerk at night. Wrote Hazel part of time. Showered. Quite a struggle to get all mail out on time.

Sunday, April 19: Showery. Two letters from Hazel. One from Frank Hal & Aunt Nell. Camera from Hazel. Wrote Hazel in evening instead of seeing show.

Monday, April 20: Unsettled. More rain. Called back in evening by Adjutant to take shorthand on Bella Bella beginning. Interesting. Wrote Hazel as usual.

Tuesday, April 21: Rainy most of day. Got mail out on time. Duty Clerk at night. **Wrote article for Station Paper**. Managed only one letter to Hazel. Showered me.

Wednesday, April 22: More rain. Married five months. Wrote Hazel in evening. Yearly Tetanus knock -right on time. Arm slightly sore.

Thursday, April 23: Rain keeps falling. Mail in early. Two letters from Hazel. Eight new clerks arrived. Pressure should let up now.

Friday, April 24: rain almost stopped. New fellows in way for most of the time. Zipped through out going mail. Jim Watt went on 48. Duty Clerk. Typed letter for Adjutant.

Saturday, April 25: Cleared up for a day. Joed to help clear water mains after supper on Duty Watch. Smoker but I didn't attend.

Sunday, April 26: Back to rain once more. Two letters from Hazel. Wrote in evening & read Toronto Star novel.

Monday, April 27: Clear day for a change. Didn't work me too hard. Read Star novel & wrote Hazel in evening. Still no 48 in sight.

Tuesday, April 28: Managed to get mail out on time. Duty Clerk at night. Adjutant kept me busy. He & I agreeing more often now.

Wednesday, April 29: Keeps cloudy. Work fairly slow. C.R. shaping up but needs more organizing. Denny Wey helps a bit.

Thursday, April 30: Joe for barrack cleaning but missed C.O.'s parade. Rainy. Mail came in. Two letters, Star, & magazine from Hazel. Worked after supper on mail & Daily Diary for Adjutant.

May 1942

Friday, May 1: More rain. Busy with outgoing mail. Went back after supper to finish. Daily Diary for Adjutant. Through at 21:30. Paid $16.38.

Saturday, May 2: Rainy again. Work fairly heavy. Duty Clerk. Didn't get time to write Hazel. More clerks but I have more work.

Sunday, May 3: Had some help from Wey with incoming mail. Two letters from Hazel. Star also. Cloudy & unsettled.

Monday, May 4: Work in fairly good shape although Wey not helping much as he has other work. Cloudy & rainy as usual.

Tuesday, May 5: Cleared slightly with no rain. Left Wey in charge & took Charles Todd at 13:15. Arrived around 16:30 Ocean Falls. Went to Colsons.

Wednesday, May 6: Up around 11:30. Went along Farm Road. **Climbed up mountain side, slipped [7.6 metres] or so & lost fountain pen. Lost identification bracelet at night in another climb**. Saw "Remember the Day".

Thursday, May 7: Up before 12:00. Swam at Ocean Falls pool. Trouble with Kozak on way back. Visited Brennans before leaving. Back around midnight.

Friday, May 8: Work piled up as Wey taken for work by Adjutant. Fired 20 rounds with 3.06. Duty Clerk. A great deal to do – filing. Two letters from Hazel. One from Lorne.

Saturday, May 9: Sent more mail out. Showery. Starting to get C.R. work under control after lapse during 48.

Sunday, May 10: Cloudy but cleared off. Two letters from Hazel. Wrote her in evening. Work getting under control. Incoming mail not too heavy.

Monday, May 11: Sun came back. Walked with George Neal in evening & found a few sea shells. Wrote Hazel at first before we walked.

Tuesday, May 12: Kept busy with mail. Cloudy but no rain. Read & wrote Hazel in evening. Max Thomas back from operation.

Wednesday, May 13: Almost sunny. Work in good shape. Haircut. Duty Clerk but wrote Hazel most of evening. Showered me.

Thursday, May 14: Warm & bright. C.O.'s parade in morning. Not much work. Mail in afternoon. Two letters from Hazel. Walked to Bella Bella Store for stamps.

Friday, May 15: Outgoing mail kept me from sitting around. Few clouds and no rain. Wrote Hazel & read in evening.

Saturday, May 16: Sent out more mail as boat not in until evening. Duty Clerk but wrote Hazel most of time. Weather improving.

Sunday, May 17: Pleasant – almost summer. Two letters & Star from Hazel. Letter from Jim. Mail kept me working. Saw "Hold that Ghost" - Abbott & Costello.

Monday, May 18: Cloudy but rain not steady. Worked on filing. Wrote Hazel in evening. Showered me before bed.

Tuesday, May 19: Rain again. Mail kept me busy all day. Sent letter Station paper & Writers' Digest to Hazel. Read & wrote during evening.

Wednesday, May 20: More rain but not all day. Work not very heavy. Duty Clerk at night. Wrote Hazel & typed for Dorfman. Alert expected but didn't come.

Thursday, May 21: Rainy & unsettled. C.O.'s parade washed out. Mail in middle of afternoon. Two letters from Hazel. Wrote during evening.

Friday, May 22: Cloudy but showing signs of clearing. Busy with incoming & outgoing mail. Wrote Hazel during evening.

Saturday, May 23: **Posted overseas**. Clouds broken – almost hot. Dashed around getting clearances. Missed sports day. Watched dance in evening before Cardona arrived 22:30.

Sunday, May 24: Cloudy but not much rain. Loafed on deck most of day with Matt Allen, John Dickson, & Carl Walstrom.

Monday, May 25: Reached Vancouver about 05:30. Drizzle & misty. Wired Hazel. Stayed at Matt Allen's home & entertained by him & sister Marie. Train at 19:15 hours.

Tuesday, May 26: Spent day watching lower part of mountains. Clouds low & rain all the way. Surprise – Hazel at station alone. D & D – three. [meaning?]

Wednesday, May 27: Hazel & I up before 12:30. (Staying at Anderson Senior's.) Bella Bella rain tagged along. Snowed in afternoon. Supper at Merricks.

Thursday, May 28: Snow for variety. Didn't visit Bell. Clearing p.m. Went to Hazel's for suitcase & pack. Loafed in afternoon. Up at 12. Bed.

Friday, May 29: Up by 10:15. Packed & got ready. Just made 12:10 C.P.R. for Calgary. Pleasant trip. Calgary 6:35. Dinner at White Lunch Cafeteria. Registered at Empire Hotel 9th Avenue. Had bats (?)– early to bed.

Saturday, May 30: Up at 11:45 at Bank of Montreal. Wife Hazel useful for $60 share. Capitol [movie theatre] Abbott & Costello. Lunch at Eaton's. Bowness Park at 9 – miniature golf. Dancing fun. Had haircut & shoe shine. Hazel [illegible]. Ate between 1 & 2 a.m. on 8th Avenue. Bed late – fun.

[Archie & Hazel don't know if this is the last time they will see each other. War rages overseas.]

[End of five-year diary containing entries from six years: 1937 to 1942. The story concludes in Archway: Six Year Book of Dreams.]

APPENDIX 2

LIFE

These page of handwriting describe Archie's personal life and work experience at Pilkington Brothers, a U.K. glass company in Edmonton, Alberta, while attempting to become a writer instead of an employee.

This is perhaps Archie's first employment after completing his formal schooling. He makes passing reference to his former colleagues in Archway: Six Year Book of Dreams.

The work setting of "Life" becomes apparent on page two of the original work, where Archie writes "at P.B.(C) L." which is an abbreviation for the company name, with (Canada) in parenthesis indicating that this is a non-Canadian company with offices in Canada. The L. is for Limited.

For one reason or another, Archie chooses not to spell out the names of his co-workers and friends, instead using only their initials.

Anyone with access to the employee information of the time could easily discover the full names of the people Archie mentions.

However, the abbreviated names of co-workers and friends can be discovered by looking into Archie's five year diary of 1938 to 1942.

Not knowing the names takes nothing from this narrative of a very young Archie who wants to write about his life and on-the-job personal experiences.

Archie writes:

April 17

Before leaving on his usual trip to the country last week, G.F. Parrett's car ran out of gas in the subway. First time such a thing ever happened.

The following Saturday he ran out of gas himself. Too bad.

Friends asking about his death seemed merely anxious to establish the fact that they had known him. Strange, most people are like that.

Applicants for his job on Monday 11th, and he had only died Saturday. One of the position seekers claimed to be a good friend of Parrett.

He certainly proved himself a liar.

Mr. Glover loves to flourish his vocabulary. Writing C.O. about Parrett he slung in a few such as "demise" and "he failed to rally". (He got that from the doctor I'll bet.)

Found it very depressing having to explain to others over the telephone about Parrett.

J.E. Harrison from C.O. detests smokers and there is a no smoking sign in the warehouse.

Smokers in the office and warehouse took their final puffs before Harrison arrived Saturday morning. (Of course they can quit "any time they want to".)

As he got out of the car we noticed a man who just left had carefully deposited a butt in the middle of the floor. Horrors.
TG quickly kicked it under the safe, making everything O.K.

The worst “bromide” at Pilkington Brothers (Canada) is HTM, his favourite saying being “How are things percolating?”

People never seem to tire of these worn out expressions and yet the wonder why I sometimes lose patience and treat them with abruptness.

Today I did considerable writing but could not get started on Friday. No doubt my “lazy streak” is submerged only occasionally.

I should do as much as possible at times like this to prepare for my slack times which leave me with plenty to do and yet leave me unable to do it.

I often wonder if I could teach myself to work at almost any time?

May 10

I consider the new position I am taking over rather difficult. I wonder what I will think a year from now?

Gordy Ferguson, the new man taking my place, seems to take things too easily at times. I wonder. He has just been with us two days but he is rather free and easy with everyone.

Perhaps he is not as tactful as he could be. If he can do the work, though, I should not complain.

I am still not certain as to whether or not I want to take Ben’s place. One of my faults seems to be lack of confidence.

Another rejection. Will I ever become a writer? I should try harder. I put things off too much.

Mr. Glover told me to leave envelopes with letters I left for him to sign because I neglected to do so last night.

This is the second time since I started at Pilkington Brothers (Canada) Ltd. that he has nearly scolded me.

I dislike his methods. He never actually reprimands me openly but tells his troubles to other members of the staff.

I would prefer a tongue-lashing from him. Then I would know exactly where I stand.

Mr. Glover and I have little in common. Three times since February, when driving me up town in his car he has begun a conversation with practically the same words:

"Well, are you still bowling?"

I endeavour to answer interestedly, if not enthusiastically. Peculiar how we usually try to appear interested when in reality we are bored.

Frankness would pay sometimes.

June 8

It was quite a thrill when I finally got the books balanced. We work until 6:00 or later practically every night. Perhaps things will ease up soon. Gordy is catching up slowly.

My new work is easier in certain phases.

Rejections continue. A first acceptance will be an event.

Tennis occupies much of my spare time now. Writing has for the time being taken a back seat. I'll have to get back to the typewriter again.

June 14

Yesterday was the first time I ever treated a girl. Jack and I took Phyllis., Hazel, and H.D. to Elfstroms for a sundae.

I was with Hazel. She chose a walnut sundae. It was 20¢ compared with the banana split chosen by Phyllis.

That mean something, though it does not seem very likely. I prefer Phyllis to Hazel at the present time. Maybe Hazel is better though.

First appearances are sometimes deceiving. We shall see. This may mean my start to association with girls.

Hazel did spring to my defence (all in fun of course) when Jack and Phyllis turned on me. I imagine she thinks I'm all right.

On the other hand, she may merely have been testing, using me to experiment on. I'll know someday. I hope.

Hazel is not beautiful but I like her.

Jack and I mentioned that we were going swimming on Tuesday for the first time this year. Hazel does not swim but she said she had not been swimming this year either.

She said so twice. Very much like a hint if you ask me.

Perhaps I judge wrongly. I did not rise to the bait, however, if that is what it was.

I am inclined to be rather contrary and I don't like people trying to make up my mind for me.

Otherwise I might have asked her to come along. Next time maybe. I hope there is a next time.

Gordy is struggling on but does not seem to be catching up. If business slacks off this summer all will be well. If not________?

I was in the same position myself, I believe, but I struggled through, catching up before Christmas. We shall see what happens.

Developments should come soon to make things more interesting.

I am the youngest of the four of us, we who gathered at Elfstrom's.

Phyllis is the oldest. Her birthday is in February, I think. Hazel's is on July 6th. Jack's is on July 8th. Of course I am July 13th, I'm told.

We are all 21 this year. Coincident. An agreeable one though Phyllis writes poetry and reads detective stories. Hazel reads Reader's Digest. She has a diary.

I did not tell them I have one (and this too) but I'll let Hazel know sometime.

June 28

Yesterday I tried to dance at the Eastwood Tennis Club (E.T.C.) Strawberry Social. Hazel, who I took, was patient with me. I will enjoy dancing once I learn.

Joining the ETC was a fortunate thing for me. I do not think Hazel is pretty and yet I like her all right. She is easy to get along with.

Jack, Phyllis, Hazel, and I should have some very good times together. Jack and I walk home with them practically every night.

We did each other a lot. The girls enjoy it. Phyllis pretends she is angry. Hazel just takes it all in fun.

I have entered a new phase in my life. Rather nice so far. Thank you ETC.

September 11

Back again. Peculiar how one's taste changes. I discovered I like Hazel better than Phyllis but I can't decide how much I do like Hazel.

At times I almost dislike her. Her family gets me down, too.

I haven't even made up my mind whether I like her enough to kiss.

G.F. has not caught up yet and treats the matter lightly.

I like to get my balance. Each month seems new and different. I am getting tired of my job though.

If I don't write more stories soon I'll be in a rut. Tennis is practically finished so I should settle down.

My entire life may be changed by this summer's happenings. Wonder where I would have been if I hadn't started tennis?

Jack might have been in a different position too. I think he likes Phyllis a great deal although he may be unable to analyse his feelings just as I can't.

This winter may reveal a great deal.

October 4

Our hike, (Phyllis, Hazel, B.F., Jack, and I) was a success. We went past Capitol Hill after getting a lift in Dodd's Car(?) to 142 Street.

I ate bean sandwiches using buns while the rest had canned sausage with their beans.

Had a large fire which we lounged around afterwards.

Hazel and I walked to the toboggan slide. It looked good, dips and all. We climbed up.

She slipped so, naturally I held her hand the rest of the way up and down. She sometimes seems as shy as I.

Back at the fire we sat around for a time. I had to ask Hazel to put her head on my chest (not directly of course),

She had been resting her head on a box and I suggested she try a softer resting place. I knew she wished to do so but I admired her for waiting for me to take the lead.

I started a bit of mental mud-slinging which made her angry (this couldn't have been pre-arranged) and she stood up herself for awhile.

Both of us threw quite a few words around.

Finally with the help of B. ('R' is correct) F. I turned her over my knee and gave her a lusty smack or so (this had been planned but mad our act seem better and more natural).

We toasted marshmallows later and Hazel put on a good show. I wondered at times if she wasn't really angry.

Tramping back through the dark we went single file with hands on the shoulders of the person in front. Hazel did not object to my placing my hands on her shoulders.

We walked from the top of the hill through a drizzle, with my raincoat in the knapsack (Lorne's).

Treated the girls and boys to pop at the streetcar line store. B.F. wished to pay part but I insisted, mainly because he had purchased some chocolate bars on the way out.

Sat with Hazel on the way back and she almost forgot she should be angry with me.

Off the streetcar at her place she broke down and told Phyllis and Jack that we were friends once more. We put on a good act, I think.

Saturday afternoon I tried to balance the books. No luck. Back on Monday. Still much of nothing. By Tuesday, 5:30 I had checked all posting.

Going over the balance again, I discovered that I had made an error in taking off the total of DB's less Cr. Notes.

I was slightly put out but glad I'd found my error. It gives one a rather frustrated feeling to find that after checking all one's work (wasting almost three days) that the mistake should have been detected immediately.

I suppose I'll live and learn, or at least live.

October 9

I think Hazel likes me a great deal. About two weeks ago I had said I would be at her house on Saturday night if I got my work finished.

I arrived rather late to find H.O. asking her out somewhere. She had refused, using my date as an excuse although she did not know whether or not I would come.

She has refused C.S. or K.S. a number of times too, preferring my company although he could show her a better time.

Jack, Bob F. and I beat Ding, Phyllis, and Hazel in five-pins on Saturday. We spotted them 150 pins a game too. The penalty was lunch, on them.

We stuck them for 50¢ each. Jack raised the ante to 55¢,

Tea cup reading for the others and palm reading for Bob and me. Discovered that we are all a little superstitious.

Walked from Hazel's after shaking her people. She was sleeping at Phyllis' that night. Didn't offer to take her arm. Both waiting for the other to make the first move.

Are we shy. I believe she was slightly put out.

Tennis today. Jack and I played singles while Hazel and Phyllis played with Ding and Dot the tongue-tied girl.

The next set Jack and I played with Ding and Dot, which irked Hazel and Phyllis, I don't think. I took a candid shot of Hazel and Phyllis as they left the court.

Jack and I walked down the Avenue with them and Hazel started shining up to Jack to compensate for my red-head teasing.

I don't seem to have enough nerve to kiss Hazel goodnight. I think she'd like it.

I invited myself to join her dramatic club and I've promised myself to give it all I've got. We'll see. Hope the other members of the club don't think I'm intruding.

Hazel told me they'd invited her back to the dramatic club. I took the cue and said I'd like to join. She thought it would be O.K. Nice planning on her part.

I'm trying to do some more writing. Poetry is all right but I think I can become a successful writer if I snap out of my lazy habits and start writing.

October 12

Did manage to write a letter for Writers Digest Contest.

Many things happened yesterday. I feel like a heel but Hazel apologized or perhaps I should say "because" she apologized for something that was really my fault.

After tennis I asked her if she would care to see the show at the Avenue. She said "No." she'd rather see something else.

I knew she referred to a certain concert but I felt in a mean mood, so I refuse to take the cue. I pretended to be slightly put out. I did not feel happy.

I walked away, saying goodbye to everyone though.

I couldn't make up my mind whether or not I should go down to her place that night and ask her to go to the concert.

In the midst of my worrying Jack returned to say Hazel was very upset, thinking she'd hurt my feelings. He suggested I take both Phil and Hazel to the concert.

I agreed and told him to relay my decision, mentioning I'd been kidding about the show.

Jack thought he might have to practise basketball but he didn't so we both called on Phil.

We did not say anything until it was too late to go to the concert. My fault.

When we did get to Hazel's I ducked out of sight, mainly because I wasn't sure how she would take it.

Phil and Jack told Hazel's mother they'd come to take Hazel to the show.

I popped up when Hazel appeared. She agreed to go, declaring she did not want to go to the concert.

Hazel's mother kidded me about being to late to take Hazel to the concert. Although she was joking I felt very small.

Luckily it was too dark to see my face plainly. Bet it was red.

Hazel was very penitent and insisted in abjectly begging forgiveness. I had to change the subject. I felt small enough to crawl under a snake's stomach.

Hazel would not choose a show to see. We all strung along to the Strand to see the Ritz Brothers in "Straight Place & Show". Mother says I was laughing in my sleep.

I summed up enough courage to put my arm around Hazel in the show. I think the show pepped her up some.

She was wearing new tight shoes which seemed to be hurting her but she didn't complain. She mentioned that they hurt but did not seem to be seeking sympathy.

I arranged to accompany her to the first meeting of her dramatic club. I think I could make an actor – such conceit.

I talked by her gate half an hour at least but did not discover how to kiss her goodnight.

All the time, too, I kept mentally kicking myself for my former meanness.

I thought about it all day but couldn't arrive at anything definite. I did my work right too.

Now I know Hazel does care for me but I'm still indefinite. I do like her a great deal, more so when I'm trying to say goodnight.

The moon has something to do with it – maybe.

Hazel is a good sport and can take it. I wonder if I can take it? I hope so but I'll always envy her stand last night.

She didn't realize though that I would and should have apologized. Maybe she is out to get her man, and I'm it.

October 16

The Dramatic Club idea has exploded. The club is going back to the Anglican Young People (AYP) which is where it came from.

Hazel doesn't like the AYP nor does she fancy the part she has in the play that they are going to produce.

There is a vacancy in the play but I don't think I want it unless

Hazel keeps on.

Another ETC Dance on Friday at the A.A. Hall. Jack, Phyllis, Hazel, and I went.

I did not pass up a single dance but had to leave Hazel sitting out because I danced with other girls and the boys did some sitting out of their own.

At one time I had to divide my time between Phyllis, Ding, and Hazel Jack and Bob had dropped across the street for a game of billiards. Nice people.

I enjoyed myself although I did bump into quite a few couples.

Not many there. Lucky if we break even.

Spent more time without accomplishing anything in the goodnight line. Maybe I'm afraid of starting something I may not be able to finish.

Took Hazel to the Avenue Saturday night. She had a new hat with a veil and I forgot to tell her how much I liked it. It did look very becoming.

Jack interrupted my goodnight efforts by dragging me away.

Gordy gave notice. He is leaving next Saturday for a higher paying job in Imperial Oil – West End.

His work is certainly behind which may be a contributing factor. If he can't take it, this is the best thing for us all.

He has had quite a number of different jobs. Maybe he is the type that can't be satisfied.

What a time to quit. I see myself doing considerable overtime the remainder of the year.

It'll be good experience. I'll appreciate how easy my job is when we break in a new fellow. My work is fairly easy now.
I almost refused to take it on at first but I learnt that it is best not to hesitate because a job seems difficult at first.

I'm breaking out of my lethargy, I hope. I managed to grind out an entry to the current National Institute of Authors Contest. Also I got in some work on the Jasper essay.

Hazel is going to do a little bowling and will try badminton this Wednesday. I hope I'm not dragged back into the bowling racket. I will play badminton.

October 18

E.F.G. tried to pump me regarding Gordy's reason for leaving. He thought perhaps the latter was fed up – couldn't take it.

I refused to comment saying I thought Gordy was leaving simply because prospects at Imperial Oil looked brighter.

T.G. did some order pricing but quit immediately upon Ben's return. Gordy is catching up slowly. I don't think he'll be caught up when he leaves.

He arrives just before 8:30 now and takes his full $1^{1/2}$ hours for lunch. He seems in a happy frame of mind too.

At the time Gordy started with us, J.D. had said it was a good place to work.

I met J.D. tonight and mentioned he had met Gordy and had referred to Gordy's changing of employment. J.D. said Imperial Oil was a good place to work.

Gordy remarked that J.D. had told him the same thing about another firm. E.F.G. was right too. Gordy must be fed up.

He is an only child and must have been pampered. Consequently he takes the easiest way out when the work piles up.

I am either selfish or else I care for Hazel. Tonight, coming home with Jack, we saw K.S. get off the car at Spruce. No one will play for his tennis cup.

I thought that queer and said so. He lives on Alberta Avenue by 80th Street. When Jack said K.S. might be going to visit Hazel's home I started.

A nervous tingle went through me. It does this when something upsets me. I felt jealous.

I think K.S. did go with Hazel at one time through he is considerably older.

I'm practically decided to kiss Hazel goodnight tomorrow after badminton. We'll see. She seemed to expect one tonight but I disappointed her.

October 19

I didn't kiss her. After badminton Jack and I paid for Phyllis and Hazel. The rent for the gym was $3. There were ten players, making it 30¢ a person.

They objected and insisted on paying us. We struggled but finally gave up. I like Hazel more for her action and she was pleased that I let her have her own way.

Although Gordy is learning he has agreed to return nights to try to catch up a slight amount. He could refuse but he evidently wishes to leave a good impression if possible.

Friday, October 21

New man in today, Wilf Boyce (Baldy). He's slow in basketball but I'll know about his work fairly soon. G.F. tried to teach Wilf everything in one afternoon which just confused him.

I got Wilf To add day books and he did them correctly. A good start.

Back to work. H.T.M. and B.L. back too. E.F.G. dropped in.

I'm in a peculiar state. On my way to the office I laughed two or three times for no reason. Now I feel gloomy.

Hazel is in a play. Not the one she had a part in originally. It will occupy her time for about two months.

I don't think I could crash it but I'd like to despite the fact there's a great deal of work to be done in the office. I'll try my luck tomorrow night when I see Hazel.

I confused her on the telephone by asking if the play practises would effect Saturday nights. When she said no I didn't make a date but let the matter drop.

She will expect me tomorrow, I hope.

Saturday October 22

Jack and Phyllis were waiting when I arrived at Hazel's. We went bowling with them and also Bob and Ding.

Pairing off Hazel and I were low. She received a 50 pin

handicap. She's improving. One score was 102. I bowled poorly or we might have won.

Fed ourselves at the American Dairy Lunch. Wasted over half an hour trying to make up my mind but didn't.

Another couple stopped nearby and cut things short or I might have changed my goodnight.

October 23

Went to Hazel's to hear her lines in the play. She began showing me other plays and things she'd taken part in.

Then Jack Benny came on. I didn't hear her lines. Her family were all home and I felt that I was intruding. No more Sunday night visits.

October 25

Started Toc '8' Club last night for this season. I became enthused and we decided to make members turn out or remove themselves. Ben Lang is the new leader.

We gave our autobiographies to give Ben a chance to size up the members. Mine was not so good.

W.B. may take awhile to learn things. I did the day books today and went back to post some tonight. This month-end will be a busy one.

H.T.M. will talk for hours if anyone will listen. I made the mistake of starting a discussion at 5:30. I left the office at about 6:05 and only by walking out on him.

Arranged to play badminton tomorrow night. Phoned Hazel and she'll be playing too.

October 30

I broke Dot Smith's glasses playing badminton but did not offer to replace them.

Went to Capitol on Saturday. Met Phyllis and Jack afterwards. We went into Phyllis' house and sat around after the show.

Girls asked us to take them to church. Jack refused but I gave in.

We went to the Macdonald Baptist. A small number were in attendance. I gained nothing. After the service we stopped at Hazel's. All went well until C.S. appeared.

Friday, November 11

Had supper at Hazel's last Sunday. Her parents were invited out and had to go. Philip talked and talked. I tried not to look bored.

The climax was C.S.'s surprise appearance. Hazel had to ask him to sing. I outstayed C.S. although I had to wait until 11:30.

Hazel had a rehearsal and did not play badminton. I flirted with R.S. Phyllis invited Jack and I to her place for pumpkin pie at about 111:00. I got Jack away at 1:30.

I had decided to let Hazel go her own way the remainder of the week because she had not come for badminton, but I broke down and invited her to a preview.

When I mentioned how late I'd been at Phyllis' she did not believe me at first. Before we left for the preview C.S. turned up.

He wasn't there when we got back at 2:30. We went to Jack's alone, after the show.

Yesterday I went to see a dentist. This was after I'd made three false starts. I also made arrangements to take dancing lessons.

Today I got up about 1:30 and went down for my lesson at 3:00. At 50¢ a time, I'm not sure whether it is worth it. We'll see. I have another lesson tomorrow.

Friday, November 25,1938

Must be growing up. Bought a felt hat. Have just become accustomed to it now, two weeks later.

Made Hazel rather jealous last week at badminton. Had fun with R.S. This week Hazel had a rehearsal but it was called off and she came up to watch the badminton.

Or was it R.S. and me?

Couldn't apply much of my dancing at E.T.C. At the banquet though I did manage a few steps.

That Jasper essay comes but slowly. May finish it by next summer. I must try to curb my engines.

Discovered the dentist is not a bad fellow. Had a tooth extracted and one filled but it didn't hurt. I am almost disappointed.

He did make one ache by packing it but that was merely a temporary measure. It's O.K. now.

I know that Hazel prefers my company because she is jealous

when R.S. and I have fun together.

Brother Wally is weak and I might have to be firm. He has lifted some of my money.

I have not seen him for a week but I will try to confront him soon to straighten out matters. If I could remove him from his present companions that might help.

I am glad he was not present when I discovered my loss. I may not have been able to control myself. I should not have kept tempting him once he took some.

I must do some more writing.

APPENDIX 3

1944-1945

(June 20, 1944 – August 6, 1945)

[On Friday August 25 Archie explains the missing dates of this diary. His kit disappears on a train bound for Delhi. His diary up to then is in the kit. Fortunately, letters of Archway: Six Year Book Of Dreams fill in many blanks. But, as the following entries show, not all the details are included in the letters. So the missing diary notes are a great loss.]

Tuesday June 20: Reached Chittagong at 06:30. Transport slow but arrived at billet in time for wash before breakfast. Back in room with Chas Bishop.

Considerable mail to read & more came in evening. **No word of commission**. Saw Vosper who wished to send me to Cox's Bazar while I waited. Not in favour.

Learnt I am to be posted to Comilla once I become a P/ O. After calling at P. Staff took the rest of the day off.

Wednesday June 21: Saw Vosper again & he suggested Wing instead of Cox's but I wasn't keen. Had details for 39/43 Star & Volunteer Medal entered in paybook.

Went sick with sore ears & given drop treatment. P. Staff wrote letter to Delhi. Saw Vosper again in afternoon & he decided I should go on "C" shift here – good idea.

Macdougall brought gen. that our commissions would date from time we reported as officers.

Only aircrew get back dating.

Saw "Heaven Can Wait" at Palace [movie theatre]. Don Ameche as old man in Hades.

Thursday June 22: Had an easy day. Wrote reams for Hazel. No more rain after yesterday's downpour but cloudy.

Commission is waiting confirmation from Air Minister & our London H.Q.

Mark for pre-commission course only 67. That represents my attitude as I couldn't take it seriously.

Talked & strolled with Pete Guise. Saw "Heaven Can Wait". Last night's picture was "Sahara" with Humphrey Bogart. Nearly midnight before bed.

Friday June 23: Overslept & had to go to the Anglo for Bombay Toast [similar to French toast], fruit salad, cake, and fresh lime in lieu of breakfast.

Continued writing to Hazel in afternoon.

No word on yesterday's letter to the C.O. re my lost kit Have written (Wed.) letter to Reeves at Bagaichi too as he may have clue.

Almost late on 18:30 shift. Working with Ben Littlewood. So little work that I wrote a letter to Hazel – suits me. Hot & sticky but not unbearable.

Saturday June 24: Up for breakfast. Wrote Hazel all morning. Fairly busy on afternoon shift but not overworked. Mail from Hazel.

Social in Officer's Mess but didn't bother as I knew how it would develop. Continued writing to Hazel instead. Usual sticky heat but managed to survive.

Bed fairly early to prepare for early rising. No trouble getting to sleep these nights.

Sunday June 25: No trouble in rousing me at 06:30. Kept a steady pace all morning. Light rainfall & more splashes after tiffin [light midday meal in U.K. India vocabulary].

Read in mess & then started airgraph for Hazel. Papers from Canadian Region. Completed airgraph after dinner & started this diary. Wrote Hazel as usual.

Watch slow but other fellows on shift called me on time. Hot & sticky as usual. Took writing on night shift with me.

Monday June 26: Not much to do so I wrote Hazel during night. Finally fell asleep but not for long. During the day it was cool & pleasant but sleep came only in spasms.

Rose around 17:00 for shower & breakfast, I mean dinner. Read paper for awhile & then returned to billet for writing to Hazel.

Saw "Black Panther" at Lion [movie theatre]. Must have been serial put together for one picture. Infinite in its appeal.

Tuesday June 27: Up for breakfast. Did little more than write Hazel during the day. Sunbathed for a short period after tiffin.

Not exceptionally warm these days. Slight rain sprinkles but not very long or heavy.

Wrote airletter for Hazel. Shift not too heavy. Evening shift slowly but soon struck a steady pace which wasn't slackened until midnight.

Some extra work though everything out of shape to prevent us clearing.

Wednesday June 28: A scramble necessary to get breakfast. Sat on balcony during morning, writing.

Slight over exposure made shoulders, arms, legs, & chest pink but not badly burnt. Busy afternoon shift. Birthday card, 279 & 280. [Numbers of letters received from Hazel to date.]

Read & then wrote Hazel for remainder of evening.

Learnt that **Cushing from the Topa course ad arrived her as a P/O. There must be something holding back my commission.**

Thursday June 29: Awoke easily at 06:30. Hot & sticky even in the morning. Scarcely a break as I worked alone. Relaxed in the afternoon.

Wrote airgraph to Hazel as usual & also airletter to Lorne. Completed airgraph after dinner & wrote ordinary letter to Hazel.

Started a letter to Bill [Alexander] but had to take it on night shift with me. Gradually getting correspondence under control but a stack remains.

Friday June 30: Not overworked during the night. Completed letter for Bill & started airgraph to Mother. Paid 45 chips. Took shoes for repair.

Awoke in afternoon to have cake, fruit salad, & lime. Airgraph 106 from Hazel.

After dinner event to Lion [movie theatre] with Bill Peel & Bill Hodgekinson to see “Once Upon A Honeymoon” with Ginger Rogers & Cary Grant. Old but a laugh a minute. Not in bed until midnight.

Saturday, July 1: Up for breakfast. Sent cable for Hazel’s birthday after writing Mother. Bought shorts & coat hangers.

In the afternoon I went to the Palace [movie theatre] with Sattcliffe & saw “For Whom The Bell Tolls”. Gary Cooper & Ingrid Bergman were both good.

Late in evening shift. So little to do. I wrote a letter for Hazel. Slackest period I can remember.

Called at mess where it was free night for corporals. Had cheese sandwich.

Sunday July 2: Watch stopped but woke early enough for breakfast. Cloudy all day with no chance of sunbathing.

Wrote Hazel in morning & at work. Airgraph 107 total mail. Not much work. Watched football match.

Wrote Hazel all evening to complete two letters & an airletter for her in one day – good. Sticky in the evening but day warm & pleasant. Not up to last year's heat.

Monday July 3: Watch stopped again but I woke up at 06:00 for shower & shave. Easy morning. **Letter from Howrad L.P.O. confirming kit not found**.

Wrote airletter for Mother. Lingered in mess after tiffin. Called at Stores but could get nothing. Completed letter for Mother after dinner & wrote usual airgraph for Hazel.

Rained in afternoon but sun shone long enough for me to enjoy some. Wrote Hazel after dinner until time for night shift. Called at Stores but got nothing.

Tuesday July 4: Work spotty which gave no chance for sleep. Wrote airletter for Ben Lange & started one for Winnie. Slept well during the day.

Started book, The Citadel. After dinner went to Lion [movie theatre] with Bills Peel & Hodgekinson. "The Big Street" was one of Damon Runyon's which I had read.

Good entertainment although the other lads couldn't understand parts. Back at billet around 23:30. Read the book under Charlie came in for bed.

Wednesday July 5: Up early enough for breakfast. Cloudy at first but soon cleared. Read, finished airletter for Winnie & wrote Hazel.

Haircut after tiffin & then went on search for writing pad but not very successful. Bought some peppermints & antiseptic which turned out to be liquid soap. No mail.

Not too busy in evening. Finished letter for Hazel & wrote this. **No word on commission yet but expect word before long.**

Thursday July 6: Read for awhile after breakfast & then wrote Hazel. Not much time for writing in the afternoon as work kept fairly steady.

Charlie Bishop posted to Delhi & will leave in a few days. Read & wrote in the evening. Hot & sticky as usual. Didn't get to bed until nearly 23:00.

Seldom get more than fresh lime from Anglo these days as mess provides good meals.

Friday July 7: Awake at 06:00 to read before water came on. Easy morning & I managed to write to Hazel. At tiffin started to feel off colour.

Relaxed & read book all afternoon. Skipped dinner. Feverish & stomach upset. Wrote ordinary letter & airgraph for Hazel.

After a short rest was able to struggle across to the office. It appears to be a recurrence of last year's trouble.

Saturday July 8: Struggled through the night & even wrote an airletter to Tom Goodwin. No breakfast before climbing into bed. Sleep disturbed twice.

Airgraph 108 from Hazel. Tried a few bites at dinner. Wrote Hazel all evening but felt rather shaky.

W/O Sells told me that there had been an answer to the

letter about my commission saying that confirmation was awaited from R.C.A.F. H.Q.

Sunday July 9: Went sick but M.O. merely prescribed bismuth soda to settle stomach.

Read a Digest for a time, worked on this & wrote Hazel. Health improved during the day & **I was able to do considerable writing**.

On shift finished letter to Hazel & started one for Alexander.

Letter from Howard Reeve to say he knew nothing of my kit but referred me to the Army W.O. who stayed on the train to Lahore.

Monday July 10**:** Practically normal. Charley Bishop left for Delhi. Gave room a thorough cleaning. Sat in sun to finish Bill's letter.

Started airletter for Louis Hodge & finished it in evening. Letter 281, 2, 3, & 4 from Hazel. Not a busy shift but enough to do.

Wrote airmail for Hazel in evening but couldn't get organize for regular writing. Not in bed until after 23:00.

Tuesday July 11: Orderly Sgt. Heavy rain but intermittently. Wrote Hazel during morning between spots of work.

George Sutherland has taken Chas. place in the room. Wrote Hazel after tiffin. Completed letter after dinner &

wrote airgraph.

Cooler than usual because of the rain. Interrupted by different fellows calling during the evening. Read Digest just before going on shift.

Wednesday July 12: Scarcely any work all night. Wrote a letter to Norm Shrubb & then slept awhile. Left to take sick parade at 06:30. Slept fairly well during the day.

Dashed to Palace [movie theatre] after dinner to see Betty Hutton & Eddie Bracken in "Miracle of Morgan's Creek". Goofy and good entertainment.

Sat around for awhile afterwards & then started a letter for Hazel. Bed around 23:00.

Thursday July 13: My 27th birthday. Wrote Hazel in the morning. Cloudy with rain spasms all day. Paid 10 chips [illegible, maybe dhoti] allowance.

Wrote Hazel ordinary & airletter during the afternoon. Rain splashed hardest when I went to mess for dinner. Slack evening shift so I wrote Hazel further & tried poetry.

Not feeling too good & some diarrhea. Monsoons seem to be here in full force.

Friday July 14th: More rain. Ate no breakfast. Paid 65 chips. Lay on charpoy [light bedstead], reading & sleeping during morning. Managed a few lines for Hazel.

Not particularly busy in afternoon. More rain to keep the temperature down. Read & wrote during the evening.

Bigger gaps between mail these days – blame it on the second front. Stomach still unsettled but seems to be returning to normal.

Saturday July 15: No trouble in rising early. Spare moments for writing Hazel in morning.

Sun bathed in afternoon & wrote an airgraph to Mrs. Brown as well as the regular one for Hazel. Wrote Hazel between chats in the evening.

Fell asleep just before midnight but roused myself in time for going on shift. Rain didn't bother then. Worst part of year seems over.

Sunday July 16: Wrote a letter for Hazel & read but didn't sleep during the night. Rained fairly steadily. Slept in short snatches all day but couldn't settle.

Borrowed a book from Norm Addison. **Restless after dinner & couldn't get any writing done**.

Saw "Du Barry Was A Lady" at Palace [movie theatre]. Red Skeleton, Lucille Ball, & Gene Kelly did their best but I wasn't particularly impressed.

There isn't the same zest seeing pictures alone.

Monday July 17: Just early enough for breakfast. Kept reading Captain Moonlight until after tiffin. Rain spotty.

Wrote Hazel regular letter & started airmail which was completed during evening shift. Not a great volume of work. **Was able to do considerable writing**.

Called at Anglo after midnight for fresh line & cake. Haven't had more than a fruit salad outside the mess for months.

Tuesday July 18: Just got up in time for breakfast. Wrote Hazel, read, & got slightly sunburnt in the morning. Fresh lime from Anglo. Not busy during afternoon.

Some rain but not a great deal. Had an argument with F/O Maslin & shook him by my firm stand. Didn't wait for mess meeting after dinner.

Wrote Hazel. Cake, fruit salad, & fresh lime from Anglo. Warm but not too sticky.

Wednesday July 19: No trouble awakening for morning shift. Some rain before tiffin. Work extremely light. Able to write Hazel & sit around most of the time.

After tiffin started airgraph for Hazel. Rained heavily towards dinner time & later in the evening for awhile.

Went to early house at Palace [movie theatre] to see Monty Wooley & Gracie Fields in "Holy Matrimony". Back before rain began.

Nothing at mess but Anglo chico brought cake, fruit salad, & fresh lime. Wrote Hazel started letter to "Red" Davis.

Thursday July 20: Practically no work all night. Completed letter for Davis & read Edgar Wallace book Green Rust. Rained most of night.

No trouble getting to sleep in morning. Letters 285 & 286

from Hazel.

Went to Palace [movie theatre] at 18:00. "No Time For Love" starred Claudette Colbert & Fred MacMurray. Funny & well worth the walk.

Caught in heavy rain afterwards. Read, ate can of corn, fresh lime, & fruit salad. Wrote Hazel for finale.

Friday July 21: Early enough for breakfast. Rain most of the day. Read & wrote Hazel in the morning. Airletter & more ordinary writing for Hazel after tiffin.

Room nearly afloat from roof leak. Called at Stores but shoes not repaired yet – must be making a new pair.

Saw C.C. who read letter from Air Ministry saying they were awaiting word from R.C.A.F. Overseas H.Q.

Wrote airletter for Mother & ordinary letter to Hazel on evening shift. Fresh lime & cake from Anglo.

Saturday July 22: Almost missed breakfast but managed to scramble around. "Tom" Sawyer brought snaps for me – seven duplicates (14 prints) at 4/6.

Read Digest & wrote Hazel in morning. Rain still splatters. Time for some reading & writing on afternoon shift at first but eventually became busy.

Read & wrote Hazel during evening. Rain eased until 22:00 when it poured heavily. Fresh lime, cake, & custard from Anglo.

Sunday, July 23: Plenty of sky showing & bright all morning. Up early enough. After a short reading break, work poured steadily.

A.O.C. visited but I wasn't particularly interested. Mail, 287 & airgraph 109 from Hazel. Wrote Hazel in afternoon & sunbathed.

Completed airgraph for Hazel after dinner & wrote to her most of evening. Warm & sticky. Took reading & writing material when I went on night shift.

Monday July 24: Scarcely a break all night. Toward the end I was able to read Digest & write Hazel. Hit bed in a hurry & didn't stir until 16:00.

After dinner went to "Syncopation" at the Lion [movie theatre] for first show. Afterwards bought paper & envelopes.

At O.K. Cafe had cocoa, egg fritter, & fresh lime. Wrote Hazel for a time, completing airmail & continuing with regular writing until after 23:00.

Tuesday July 25: Easily in time for breakfast. Splashes all day but no heavy rain. Mail in afternoon – letter & paper from Bill. 264 & 265 from Hazel.

Wrote to Hazel most of the day. Started an airletter before dinner & evening shift.

Not much time to spare during evening but completed airletter for Hazel.

Brown, our typist, got me a glass of cocoa & I had cheese & biscuit from George Sutherland. No cafe visit.

Wednesday July 26: Awoke easily in time for breakfast. Clouds & showers foiled my sunbathing plans.

Bought pad of orange coloured paper for two chips – air mail type but to be used for letters to Hazel. Wrote Hazel part of morning.

Started letter for Lorne on shift but didn't get it finished until evening. Kept fairly busy. Sticky at first after dinner but no rain. Wrote Hazel.

Cocoa & "chocolate" cake at O.K. before going to bed.

Thursday July 27: Awake at 06:00 but not up immediately. Steady work all morning with little help. Started airgraph for Hazel after tiffin. Sunbathing but no burn.

Airletter from Mums (U.K.9 with Wally's address. Wrote him in evening before finishing airgraph for Hazel. Rain foiled my plan to visit O.K.

Wrote Hazel regular letter before midnight & night shift. Sticky indoor but cool enough outside.

Friday July 28: Considerable number of messages[?] left by previous watch but Ben & I cleared before 03:00. Couldn't keep awake & had to take an hour's rest.

Read <u>Last Train From Berlin</u> & wrote Hazel. Paid 65 chips. Shoes condemned so got a new pair – too big. Couldn't settle during day & started reading after 15:00.

MacDougall visited. No gen.

After dinner caught in rain on way to Lion [movie theatre] & "Unexpected Uncle" Ann Shirley & Chas James Craig Cob... (illegible).

At O.K. had two cocoa, chocolate cake, & Bombay toast. Wrote Hazel. Her 288 & 100 arrived.

Saturday July 29: Wrote Hazel most of morning & read in between writing. After tiffin more reading & airletter for Hazel. Light rainfall. Atmosphere fairly sticky.

Had trouble at work & couldn't get clear to read or write. Sent photos to Mother & Mums.

News seems to indicate an early end to the war. Went to Anglo after midnight for a couple of fresh limes. Don't call there often these days.

Sunday July 30: Just in time for breakfast. Cloudy but no rain in morning. Walked downtown afterwards for soap at 6. Wrote this & letter for Hazel.

Spotty afternoon, busier towards end. Read in evening & wrote Hazel. George Sutherland got chair & table from mess. Called at O.K. for two cake & two cocoa.

Mess bill 17/12. Warm & sticky as usual but had no trouble to sleep before 23:00.

Monday July 31: Mist drizzle when I arose. Rain off & on during morning. Not too busy. Read Last Train From Berlin & finished it after tiffin.

Magazine from Bill. Sunbathed when sky cleared overhead. From dinner called at station library. Wrote airgraph & ordinary letter for Hazel during evening.

No visit to or from cafe. Slightly sticky but not too warm. No more rain after morning showers. Low thick clouds plentiful.

Tuesday August 1: Light traffic but clear at 04:30. Wrote Hazel. Fell asleep trying to read Darwin's <u>The Descent of Man</u>.

Disturbed twice during day – once when rain came in window. Sole came off one shoe so started wearing new, too large, service issue.

Met Equipment Corporal who said I could have free issue on Saturday.

Rain delayed after dinner but reached Palace [movie theatre] in time for first show. "North Atlantic Crossing" - Humphrey Bogart.

[illegible due to ink – maybe Bowl ...] & two glasses of cocoa at O.K. Wrote Hazel. Hot.

Wednesday August 2: Heavy rain when I rose for breakfast. Rain off & on during morning.

Read & wrote Hazel after re-arranging bed & table. More reading & writing in afternoon. Airletter from Edna & 289 from Hazel.

Cleared enough for sunbathing. Started airmail for Hazel &

completed it on evening shift.

Slack time & I read most of the shift until work became heavier towards midnight. Didn't bother calling at the Anglo.

Thursday August 3: Cloudy but no rain at first. **De-bugged bed with candle flame & read Darwin book**.

Wrote Hazel. Slack enough to finish reading book in afternoon. Clouds cleared away.

Name in D.R.O. so see Accts. - probably about my balance. Letter & papers from Bill. Tour of service set [?] but not answered yet.

Read for awhile after dinner & then wrote Hazel. Hot & sticky.

Shoes served for two chips by travelling "moochi". A bundle of <u>Liberty</u> magazines from Jim Kennedy.

Friday August 4: Broken cloud but not rain. Fairly easy morning. Sunbathed & started airgraph for Hazel in afternoon. Read for awhile.

Completed airgraph for dinner. Chatted with Wally Workman on scientific lines. Wrote ordinary letter to Hazel.

Excessively hot & sticky all evening. Sweated so much from sunbathing I had to hose myself in cold water.

Bombay toast & fresh lime from Anglo before going on midnight shift.

Saturday August 5: Work in small batches all night but was able to read H.G. Wells Rights Of Man. No writing. Sprinkles scarcely dampened going to & from breakfast.

Call at Stores for re-kitting. Supplied with most essentials. Slept in snatches. Heavy rain in afternoon but stopped for dinner. At library discovered it was closed.

Rain splashed on return to billet. Wrote this & then to Hazel after reading Curry & Rice.

Went to Palace [movie theatre] with Pete Guise - “Phantom of The Opera” Nelson Eddy. Music good but picture poor. Cake & lime at Anglo.

Sunday August 6: Up for breakfast. Exchanged shoes. Took shirts & shorts to camp durzi [tailor]. No rain until just after tiffin. Wrote Hazel & read in morning.

When rain stopped walked downtown to buy anniversary card for Hazel. Could find no dictionary. Read & wrote Hazel as rain turned on and off.

During evening shift able to change books at library for Religion Without Revelation by Julian Huxley.

Completed airletter for Hazel & wrote ordinary letter until work became heavy.

Monday August 7: Cloudy with intermittent showers. **War news particularly good**. Read for a time & wrote Hazel. Addressed an airletter for Mums but got no further.

No rain in afternoon. Read Curry & Rice between work spasms. Heat increased after diner. Walked around town but still no dictionary. Read afterwards & wrote Hazel.

Damp with sweat. Called at O.K. for two chocolate cake, two cocoa, & Bombay toast. Completed Curry & Rice before going to sleep.

Tuesday August 8: Orderly Sgt. Didn't get to work until after 08:30. Some rain during morning. Last O. Officer at tiffin. Letter from Mums who has been ill.

Read in afternoon & started airgraph for Hazel to finish it after dinner. At O.K. had two chocolate cake & two cocoa. Chatted with a corporal I met there.

Slight rain sprinkles. Read after dinner & wrote Hazel before & after O.K. visit. No rain as we went across to work at midnight.

Wednesday August 9: Light work. Able to complete Religion Without Revelation. Started airletter for Mum. Left at 06:30 for windup of O. Joe. In bed around 08:00.

Slept fairly well. Rainy day. Letters 290 & 91 from Hazel.

After dinner saw first show at Palace [movie theatre] "Standing Room Only" Paulette Goddard, Fred McMurray & Edward Arnold. Funny & good.

O.K. afterwards for cocoa & Bombay toast. **No writing but tried Liberty crossword.**

Thursday August 10: Up fairly early for breakfast. Cloudy with rain on & off at intervals. Walked to Co-op for cakes. Read Liberty & wrote Hazel before tiffin.

Finished airletter for Mum. Wrote Hazel again in afternoon. Letters 292, 293, & 294 from Hazel. So busy in evening, scarcely time to read mail.

Rain poured steadily but eased at midnight to make trip to billet fairly dry except for puddles.

Friday August 11: Almost forgot to get up. Cloudy but no rain at first. Paid 65 chips. Getting four airletter forms now. Wrote Hazel.

Afternoon extremely busy with few spare moments. Called at station library after dinner to get Twice Seven by Aldous Huxley.

At O.K. had two cocoa, biscuits, & chocolate cake. Wound up evening with letter for Hazel. Some rain as I slid under my net & during night.

Saturday August 12: Early for breakfast & morning shift. Clouds soon cleared away. Easy morning. Airgraph 112 from Hazel.

Read, sunbathed, & started airgraph for Hazel in afternoon. Went to first house of "Princess O'Rourke" Olivia Dehaviland & Robert Cummings. Good & funny.

Two cocoa & biscuits at O.K. Completed airgraph & wrote Hazel ordinary style before night shift. Night hot & sticky with no rain for cooling.

Sunday August 13: Not overworked. Wrote Hazel & Bill. Read a Liberty & did its crossword. Finally fell asleep sitting up. Completed crossword in bed after breakfast.

Slept fairly well during day. Read in mess for awhile in evening. Completed letter for Bill - then read library book until time for bed.

Remains too warm & sticky for comfort. **News continues to improve**. Sylvan Lake card from Edna.

Monday August 14: Just up in time for breakfast. Read for awhile but writing to Hazel interrupted by fellows coming in for a discussion. Have a bottle of lemon squash.

Read, wrote Hazel & sunbathed during afternoon. Got half through an airletter for Hazel during evening. Not too busy but atmosphere oppressive.

Corrick brought some cookies for a snack – good. Counted about [five litres] of water that I drank during the day.

Tuesday August 15: After breakfast read & wrote an airletter for Hazel but made small progress. Bought cookies from nearby bakery.

Hot & sticky in afternoon & worse at night. Not particularly busy. **Heard of landings in South France**.

Chatted with Norm Addison part of evening, completed

airletter for Hazel & wrote an ordinary letter. Most uncomfortable day for months.

Wednesday August 16: Work spasmodic. Read part of a short story in between times. Had biscuits as mid-morning snack. Clear in afternoon.

Forty-five minutes of sunbathe & more reading. Half airgraph to Hazel before dinner.

Early show at Palace [movie theatre] "Girl Crazy" - Mickey Rooney & Judy Garland. Good but sound poor.

Hot. Cookies to munch as I watched. Time for remainder of 'graph & part of ordinary letter before midnight. Fresh lime from Anglo.

Thursday August 17: Easy night. Did cockeyed crossword & fell asleep over book. Rested well during the day although I woke several times.

War in Europe must be nearing an end. After dinner read Liberty & book, Twice Seven.

Tried to sort out poetry which had blotted in my pocket from too much sweating. Finally gave up & rewrote what I could.

Read myself to sleep well after 23:00. Rain during night.

Friday August 18: Easily made breakfast. Read & wrote Hazel during morning. More of same after tiffin. Resumed during afternoon but stopped before dinner time.

Got some atta [eggless whole wheat Indian cookies] cookies at bakery to eat on shift – good. Slack greater part of evening but had to clean up leftovers first.

Read Liberty & argued with our mechanic most of time. No more rain but still cloudy when we left office.

Saturday August 19: As usual, slipped under breakfast deadline. Read & wrote Hazel during the morning.

Easy afternoon shift with Norm. Addison assisting as he is now on same shift. Read part of the time.

After dinner completed verse & airmail for Hazel. Her 295 arrived. Got cookies for Norm & self at bakery. Not as good as atta ones but passable.

Up until after 23:00 finishing airmail. Had vitamin "c" tablet – issue.

Sunday August 20: Cloudy all day but no rain until evening. Simple matter keeping clear as work extremely light. Ate cookies & drank lemon squash.

Accidentally put hand on fan but escaped with slight scratch. Sunbathed nearly an hour after tiffin. Tan developing well.

Started 'graph for Hazel but not completed until nearly 21:00. After dinner read first. Onion sandwiches from Anglo & own lemon squash.

Norm visited but writing not disturbed. George leaves tomorrow. Rain several times during evening.

Monday August 21: Slack all night but only took short nap. Norm not feeling well slept all night. Read a Liberty & worked crossword.

Rain after sunrise but stopped before 08:00. Had to read myself to sleep. After dinner read & did crossword.

Went to Lion [movie theatre] with Bill P., Bill H., & Norm. Saw "Journey Through Fear" - Joseph Cotten. Too long-winded.

Bill Peel in room with me now. At Anglo had onion sandwiches & fresh lime. Short shower but stopped for us to reach billet dry.

Tuesday August 22: Just rolled out in time for breakfast. Read, did crossword, & started airletter for Hazel. Rained during noon hour but waited until it stopped.

Called at S.S.Q. but not due for any "knocks". Sunbathed for an our & completed airletter for Hazel. Letter from Mother & 296, 7, & 8 from Hazel.

Had haircut by same travelling napi. First part of shift so slack was able to change library book for an Edgar Wallace thriller & Madame Curie.

Started letter for Wally & wrote Hazel. At Anglo had onion sandwich & fresh lime.

Wednesday August 23: Under the line again for breakfast. Read The Day of Uniting after tiffin & never paused until the last page was reached. Cloudy & sticky hot.

Completed airletter for Wally after tiffin during shift. Not too busy at first but work gradually increased.

Rain latter part of afternoon stopped until I got to the billet & then continued with flashes of lightening all evening. Read Madame Curie & wrote Hazel. Stickier than ever.

Thursday August 24: Some work but kept clear easily all morning. Norm & I tried crossword during spare moments. Cloudy all day but didn't start raining until after 16:00.

Read & started airgraph for Hazel. Early dinner.

Rode in jeep to Palace [movie theatre] with Bill H. & Norm A. for first show. Rosalind Russel & Brian Oherne in "What A Woman". Good & funny.

Soaked on return trip. Bought cookies. Completed 'graph & wrote Hazel ordinary letter. Fresh lime from Anglo.

Friday August 25: Rain continued greater part of night to make the day fresh & cool. Norm slept but I had little to do. Wrote airletter for Mother, read & tried a crossword.

Didn't get groggy as usual & never slept. Hung around mess after breakfast until time for pay. 70 chips. Slept well with one break as 12:00. Intermittent rain in evening.

Read for awhile. Changed mind about going to pictures. Wrote airmail for Hazel instead.

Chico brought custard, fresh lime, & onion sandwiches. Wrote on account – surprise.

[Added pages from longer, more detailed supplementary diary writings of the same date.]

[Today] I got the brainwave to make up for lost time on this travelling commentary on things as they affect me.

Though much has happened since April 5th, I am still without my original kit and the many pages of these ramblings.

I still won't let my mind dwell on the loss as there was so much that can never be replaced.

The oddest part is that someone does know about my belongings if I could only make the correct contact.

Almost a year ago I was selling myself on the commission idea & now I'm wondering what is taking R.C.A.F. H.Q. so long to agree to something that has passed everyone else up the scale.

I should hate to have gone through that Upper Topa course only to be turned down because of no vacancy or something of that nature.

Despite the fact that there has been such a time lapse, I still feel a certain nervous tension bottled up inside ready for uncorking.

Even though I may never show it outwardly, the notification of my promotion will set me up to pre-Brandon keenness. It will be as if they offered me the chance to begin all over again.

The disappointment of a refusal would bother me more

than I try to pretend.

But, I expect to be a P/O soon. I must be due for a move as everything is running so smoothly & I'm even getting mail through quickly.

Then, there has been that free issue from Stores with the latest good luck of getting a room mate (Bill Peel) who is quiet & intelligent enough to refrain from stupid remarks & questions.

I've also discovered a bakery where the Frontier Cafe once was. The bakery sells fairly good cookies cheaply.

All these small items are just as I want them. I know that there is sure to be a change any week now.

The writing table in the billet with its overhead light extension is just another item that I'll probably be missing soon.

In the meantime, monsoon continues and we are having a good share of hot & sticky evenings to wear us down.

Apparently, an unsympathetic M.O. was all that I needed last month.

A crab stomach sent me scurrying to see him but I became so annoyed at his attitude that I recovered with minimum treatment.

On the second occasion I recovered in a couple of days without seeing the M.O.

Perhaps it was a good idea as I might have spent 8 or 10 days in dock which isn't a good idea.

Today is almost finished as I begin this paragraph. I've been reading Madam Curie and it has begun to have its effect already.

Ambitious ideas are dancing in my head & I even took time for this in an attempt to give it another twirl.

I'm certain that Madame Curie's story was at least partly responsible for my completing a poem tonight so that an airmail could be sent for Hazel.

All I have to do is pull hard on the oars as this latest wave of ambition lifts me high. Once again I have that feeling of being on the threshold of my destiny.

I know there is a contribution I must make to progress but the way isn't clear. Apparently, my writing is at least the wedge.

But, I have an idea there is something more important ahead.

Nothing more than several cups of real cocoa for breakfast this morning set me to dreaming of a future that should come soon.

Little items such as good food will be appreciated more than I thought possible two years ago.

Saturday August 26: Clouds not quite solid. No rain at first. After breakfast called at Stores for clothing parade to get socks, bush shirt, & two pairs of slacks.

Latter of good quality. Read book on Madame Curie, sent dhobi [a person who washes clothing & linen], **copied poetry into small book** & wrote to Hazel.

Sunbathed after tiffin & wrote more for Hazel. On evening shift not much to do. Tried a crossword & started airletter for Hazel. Relieving shift slightly late.

Sunday August 27: Rain falling heavily when I first awoke. Eased by the time I went to breakfast. Called at Stores to learn I couldn't have sheets tomorrow.

Read Madame Curie, shaved & wrote few lines on airletter for Hazel. Weather cleared in afternoon. Slack but couldn't complete airletter for Hazel until after dinner.

Worked crossword for awhile. Still taking vitamin pills. Bill Alexander sent letter to say he is recovering from jaundice. Read & wrote Hazel in evening. Hot. Some rain.

[Added pages from longer, more detailed supplementary diary writings of the same date.]

As I stocked up with more kit yesterday, I began to appreciate the delay there has been in my commissioning – almost as if it had been planned for my benefit.

In the afternoon I enquired about sheets but they put me off until this morning when I was told to return tomorrow.

Stores seem incapable of operating any other way. It is lucky I'm patient.

A long period of sunbathing yesterday made little difference in my colouring although I have acquired a good layer of tan since I started.

I've been tangling with crosswords again but shouldn't get too interested in those master time wasters.

So far I've been able to keep up with the volume of air mail for Hazel which is amazing considering this is little more than reminiscing & chin propping.

But, I'm sure I write what she most wants to read which is all that matters.

The day started with such a rousing downpour that an ordinary conversation was impossible.

In keeping with Indian peculiarities, the water in the mains was not turned on until after 08:00. The man who turns it on must sleep in every rainy morning.

Rain has a habit of pouring hardest at meal times & then stopping after everyone has been soaked.

I paused today & walked to the mess when the water cried off.

Madame Curie still holds me & I'm sure they story of her lift will have a certain affect on mine.

To read of such a worker makes me wonder how I could be so lazy. I need a prod, but I feel that once I pass a certain point I'll astonish myself – I hope.

For some time now I've been bothered with headaches as if some malignant disease were trying to knock me down. Of course, it may be that my imagination is too active.

Most of the time I feel keen & alive.

A common condition in this part of the country is to start the day feeling fairly well, rise to a point of vigorous healthfulness, and then tumble down to a soggy, bloated finale as you drag yourself into bed.

This is never consistent though. Tonight I'm in a neutral state that only the oppressive stickiness keeps from a better feeling.

My insides are slightly tender but that's not unusual with some of the food I use for stuffing.

However, the vitamin "d" together with the vitamin "c" pills should help me to at least hold my own.

A letter from Bill Alexander tells that he is recovering from jaundice. He will never be the same until he gets to healthier climes.

The M.O.s don't seem to appreciate what Bengal has done to Bill's constitution. Even in lost weight there is much he needs to recover.

In the next room there are regular card sessions of fellows who show little consideration for others.

When Bill Peel was in the same room, they gave him little opportunity for sleep on the day after a night watch.

Although the wall acts as a baffle, I am still disturbed at times.

Monday August 28: Cloudy with some rain in morning & afternoon. Easy shift but worked crossword instead of writing. Called at Equipment but received no sheets.

I lost patience as it was the third time I had called about them.

Read in mess after tiffin. Bill Hodgkinson leaving for Bombay soon as tour ex. Started airgraph in afternoon but spent some time rehanging clothes after line broke.

First house at Palace [movie theatre] "Thousands Cheer" Gene Kelly & Kathryn Grayson. Good despite galaxy of stars for padding.

Onion sandwiches & fresh lime from Anglo. Completed airgraph.

Tuesday August 29: One of the quietest night shifts yet. Norm slept as usual. Read <u>Madame Curie</u> & **wrote on travel account**.

Nodded once or twice but didn't sleep. Awoke once during the day to find note from MacDougall asking me to phone him.

He merely wanted to check on get, if any. Called at library to find it closed. Borrowed net from Norm, as mine damp from dhobi.

Pete Guise & I saw "The Hound of the Baskervilles" at

Lion [movie theatre]. Fair. Had chips, poached eggs, cake, & lime at Anglo.

[Added pages from longer, more detailed supplementary diary writings of the same date.]

Just over the half way line of a night shift and also beyond head nodding stage – almost. I usually fall asleep over a book or some writing during these all night sessions.

As with the previous night shift, there is a certain chill in the air which the fan adds to.

The cloudy, damp days seem to squeeze out the heat at intervals and give refreshing respites.

Yesterday morning I made my third successive trip to Stores to enquire regarding issue of sheets.

When they told me I'd have to come back at another time, I called the farce off & fumed out of the section.

It spoilt my morning to have such a culmination to the efforts for a kit I didn't get.

This Equipment Section has never given me complete satisfaction on anything.

It is as if they deliberately schemed, a fantastic idea, to make things awkward for me.

One advantage of being an officer is that I'll buy my own clothes & not give Stores more than a passing thought.

My afternoon was disrupted by the news of Bill

Hodgkinson's notification to get ready for Worli [?] & the boat.

I captured some of his excitement & could scarcely settle to write the customary airgraph for Hazel.

His mind must be a turmoil of emotions. After three years in this country, to know that he will soon be seeing his wife again must be an exhilarating experience.

I know it will make me so unsettled when my turn comes that I'll describe mental circles.

Bill's repatriation renews my hope for that commission but things will have to happen quickly if I am to leaver here this month.

Less than three days remain but there is still that chance while August remains.

At the Palace [movie theatre] I saw "Thousands Cheer" with Bill H., Norm A., & Tom Swayer & was agreeably surprised to find it several notches above the standard star heavy production.

The confinement of all the star "twins" to one part of the picture give the film a chance that others of this type lacked.

Besides the actors holding up the plot were sufficiently strong to carry the picture without the top flight aid injected.

Kathryn Grayson has a satisfying warble while Gene Kelly

did a good job aside from a trapeze act which was probably dubbed in by an expert serialist.

The airgraph which has started out on an even keel developed into a gag writer's nightmare which should at least brighten a few minutes for Hazel.

I have an idea that the screwier I write the better as far as morale is concerned. In future I'll try to make it louder as funnier.

Onion sandwiches from the Anglo gave me a chance to munch into memories even though the vehicle was such an unreasonable facsimile.

Most of the rain has been confined to the night recently with a resulting fresh, cool start for the day.

With the summer on its way out, I shouldn't mind remaining here until next year.

The only objection I have is that by staying put so long I'm missing the broader view of India which I wish to have if possible.

Wednesday August 30: Cloudy & unsettled all day. Bought dictionary at Pen Hospital after breakfast for three chips.

Loafed away morning & afternoon & wrote only few lines to Hazel. Rained as I went to dinner & when I came back at midnight.

Slack shift. 299 & extra letter ex Calgary from Hazel.

Changed books at library for Jocasta's Crime & Edgar Wallace book, The Book of All Power.

Jock Murray brought us cheese sandwiches while Brown got jam tarts. Wet returning to billet.

[Added pages from longer, more detailed supplementary diary writings of the same date.]

Yesterday I almost got excited about nothing. Around noon I awoke & was still trying to settle back when Bill Peel came in from work.

He brought a note from Vosper which instructed me to phone MacDougall during the day.

As I knew he had probably just returned from leave, I presumed he merely wanted to check on the latest gen.

On the other hand, came the hop that he had news for me.

However, I submerged such an illogical impulse by reminding myself that any notification must of necessity come through Group first.

Still, I slept with visions of postings & P/O bars floating through my dreams.

Despite the anticipation of what might be, I didn't hurry that evening and reached the guardroom at 18:00.

There was the usual trouble making connections but Mac's voice finally answered. As I had reasoned, he was just back from the hills, but I felt slightly let down anyway.

He wanted to know if there was anything new before getting his C.O. to send a hastener.

If we don't have some action soon, the war will be over – not that it will break my heart to miss a commission on that account.

My restless mood struck me again & I sabotaged the evening. The first pretext I used for wasting time was in arranging the "missie" net [mosquito net?].

Mine had returned in slightly damp condition as weather didn't give the dhobi a chance.

Norm Addison had a small one which I borrowed & used by adding strings to the corners. This allowed it to hang low enough for proper tucking.

And it all helped batter away time.

Next I turned to a picture & chased to the Anglo to catch Pete Guise. We saw "The Hound Of The Baskervilles".

Although it was supposed to be a thriller, my mind was in a flippant state & horror rolled off without penetrating.

It is odd how I must be in the proper mood for such films to bother me.

My imagination is too vivid for me to dwell comfortably on eerie tales so I prefer to laugh them into their proper place.

An upsetting factor was the presence of Charlie Morgan & Fred Lambert. We met them at the show & they conferred on us the dubious honour of their company.

Perhaps I'm a mental snob but such a combination leaves me cold. Charlie isn't too bad alone. But when he joins forces with Fred the result is often devastating.

After the seasoning I received under George Sutherland's care, I am able to take almost everybody, no matter how boring, with a calmness.

Either I ignore them & think about something else with a blank look of patient tolerance or else I seek to tie them in knots with cross-talk.

I used both methods last night but was ready to kick holes in the ceiling before final release at midnight.

Pete & I had no capes so we walked through a light drizzle while the other two trailed behind & made no offer to share their coats - no imagination.

But I enjoy walking in such a rain with its cool freshness that almost wafts me back home.

For no good reason, I stopped at the Anglo for chips, two poached eggs, two fresh limes, & a slice of cake – the first time I've eaten like that before bed for months.

I could have escaped to bed then but I sat until the others had finished their nattering. Why do I always act so politely & indulge such hypocrisy?

But, I suppose there aren't many people who don't involve themselves in that manner occasionally.

With me, there has to be an explosion for steam letting at intervals and, at such times, I doubt if my sarcasm could be matched.

Yet these outbursts must surprise people accustomed to my usual easy manner & apparent tolerance.

Today, I was scarcely once removed from a dead loss. I stored a poem I'm trying to finish & worked out anagrams for Norm's crossword most of the morning.

There was a preliminary stroll as I called at the Pen Hospital & asked, without hope of success, for a dictionary.

I was shaken when a small one, similar to my old one but with a light blue pasteboard cover, was produced.

Three chips was expensive but I wanted a dictionary so there could be no argument.

Maybe I'm screwy, but **a dictionary does things to me & I feel like a child with a new toy. I loafed through it for some time before putting it down after I returned to the [building?]**

It seems to give me a power that is lacking & impossible without such a book. As if I had the key to the universe.

Any book has a certain attraction for me but those of knowledge more so & a dictionary is in a class of its own.

Although I wasn't hungry, I still called at the corner bakery for a dozen cookies.

While I loafed out the rest of the morning, I munched with scarcely a pause until the last crumb had vanished.

Any I missed, a horde of ants carried off after many dashings & circlings that had no apparent reason.

I experimented by moving a crumb a [couple of millimetres] or so from where ant found it and the only way the ant could re-establish contact was by racing in ever increasing circles until it bumped into the morsel again.

Several times I repeated the mover & not once did the ant go directly to the new location. They must be either stupid or else extremely short sighted.

I dallied in the mess after tiffin with newspaper excuse for wasting time.

At the billet I lay down to concentrate on the poem but kept dosing until I finally gave up the pretence & had a short nap.

Towards the end, I stirred myself to write Hazel but even that was of short duration as the water came on early to send me scurrying to shower.

The rain made up its mind just as I finished polishing my shoes for dinner. And, as it so often happens, the drops slackened once I was at the mess.

But that was too late to keep my pant legs dry. These monsoon capes are all the same size, which is too small for me.

From my knees down, the rain has free play. So I often arrive with trousers well adrip.

Little Angelo was at the gate as I left for dinner & she gave me the customary smack on the back.

Could be she has fallen for me fatal charm if I remember earlier experiences where young gals tried to hide their feelings by hitting me.

I don't realize my power over women & wee gals.

It is just as well I'm reserved & also a one [woman] man. (Hazel please note.)

In one of the two letters from Hazel, there was a newspaper picture of Wally instructing a private on the M.G. in Italy.

Even though his face was hidden in shadow, it pleased to see him so sturdy & fit looking.

Despite his weakness of character, I have a soft spot for him & I am proud of any accomplishments he has.

I have faith in his ultimate success & will always try to help even if he doesn't progress well.

Probably this is the "older brother" complex which makes me feel obliged to watch over him. I'll probably be more considerate with everyone when I return home.

Thursday August 31:Fairly early rising. Cloudy but didn't rain until near end of morning. Wash place basha collapsed during night – fun.

Walked around town to get iodine. [114 ml cost 1/8] & caramels [227 g cost 1/12] & then read for awhile. Wrote this & then to Hazel. Shaved before tiffin.

Not too strenuous an afternoon. Airgraph 115 from Hazel. Airletters from Wally & Louis Hodge. Letter from M.K. about bookkeeping course.

Wrote Hazel & read after dinner. Two Bombay toast & fresh lime from Anglo.

[Added pages from longer, more detailed supplementary diary writings of the same date.]

The event of the morning could be the collapse of the roof on our wash place lean – though oddly enough, the noise didn't disturb anyone during the night when things fell apart.

It cut off my passage to the lavatory, but Bill Hodgkinson blasted a hole to make everyone happy.

He had to break the one remaining wall which was still intact. I wonder if he would have done that under ordinary circumstances.

Since he is about to leave, Bill isn't concerned over such details as he once might have been.

It is a "bless 'em all" attitude for him from now until he leaves Bombay.

The feeling must be wonderful when you know India will soon be no more than a memory – lead me to it.

Prices in some commodities have steadily risen during my stay in these parts. When I bought some caramels this morning I had a graphic proof of this.

At one time I bought them at Dean's for 2/4 a [half kilo] but today the price was [3/8] over 50% in 20 months isn't good in any language, even during a war.

Today continued the spasm of monsoon weather though rain confined itself to one short sharp downpour just before tiffin.

My past must be catching up as a letter (addressed to Cpl. Anderson) from the Canadian Region in U.K. popped up in today's mail.

They are curious about the bookkeeping course I started two years ago.

Now that the book is not around, I want to carry on with that course. I should get it organized eventually.

Mail was more assorted than usual today with Hazel's airgraph & airletter from Wally & Louis Hodge.

The only snag is that I'm slipping behind with correspondence again. I'll have to rattle out answers quickly.

This afternoon I was almost annoyed at Norm.

Probably it started when I had to do a couple of messages while instructions for a procedure which was new to us were being given.

I was slightly put out but had learnt the vital parts of the procedure before the interruption came so I recovered quickly.

Then, a football match started & Norm deserted. I had no trouble keeping clear but the idea of him neglecting work rankled.

Occasionally, I wouldn't mind, but he sees all games played while we are on shift & only helps if work becomes heavy.

Perhaps I'm too conscientious, but I could not turn my back while a message was to be done, especially if it might mean leaving something for the following shift.

I could never condone neglect of work.

Pity the poor fellow working under me as I would drive hard but I'd set the pace too.

While there is a job to be done I must keep to it and a loafer rouses my ire & contempt.

So long as I continue in that manner, I need never fear censure for slackness.

I am certain too, that I get a keen sense of satisfaction from jobs done than the "good enough to get by", individuals.

[There is no entry for September 1, but the added pages do include a long, detailed supplementary diary writings for this date.]

Friday September 1: This month has a sodden start and it was too wet for satisfactory washing in the morning.

Until the roof over our wash house is replaced it will be awkward to wash by the tap during rainy days.

I must have looked silly dashing out under a cape to get water from the tap while rain poured full out.

Although there was but a light sprinkle when we headed for the mess, we took the partially covered route through the cookhouse gate & past the main barrack block.

Despite the time I've spent here, I never considered going that way before.

The habit of going around is so strong I automatically go that way without bothering to consider other possibilities.

That is probably why some inventions take so long & then seem obvious when perfected.

People get so accustomed to one method that they take it for granted & only accidentally bump into certain improvements.

With August went any faith, if any, in that Calcutta fortune teller who said I'd get my promotion & go to New Delhi in that month.

Now that it is over, I realize that I was counting on his prediction but its failure to materialize doesn't really bother – mainly because I know that such things are .01% knowledge & 99.99% familiarity with human nature.

Fortune tellers endeavour to tell people what they wish to hear.

[There is no entry for September 1, but the added pages do include a long, detailed supplementary diary writings for this date.]

Saturday September 2: and near the end of a night shift. I was asleep several times but wouldn't let myself acknowledge the fact as I tried to keep reading.

Brown bored me twice – at least. He is the type who tries to turn any conversation into an endless dialogue.

Whether you continue listening or not he rambles on as if people are hanging breathless on every word I wonder if deliberate rudeness would make him realize I'm not interested.

Even when I turn away in the middle of his discourses, he goes on & on.

Another cute trick is that of giving high points of the news sheet as he reads, although he must know I prefer to read for myself.

Some type – He fell asleep at his billet last night & the D.R. had to wake him around 01:00 or he might never have shown up for this watch.

Yesterday afternoon I carried on the usual time waste trying to write the regular airgraph for Hazel.

The hours slip away before I realize it no matter how hard I try to get something done on that afternoon before a night shift.

Cloudy weather with some rain prevented sunbathing but time dissipated itself rapidly just the same with nothing to show at the end of the afternoon.

In a search for candy, I called at the R.A.F. Club in the evening to get some P.K., a cake of lifebuoy & a large tube of Forhan's toothpaste.

This latter was what must be a 50¢ tube for 1/9, less than the actual price. I never thought such a thing could happen out here, even in a canteen.

Tins of grapefruit were on sale at 1/14 which isn't unreasonable. I'll be sampling some one of these days.

Norm Addison was interested when I told him so we might – might - get together & split a few tins.

Competition was heavy as Norm popped in & out during the evening to interfere with my writing.

To cap things, a fellow named Tennant who I met on the Secunderbad refresher course came looking for a bed & I offered mine.

He showed his gratitude by chatting & preventing me from writing.

Another diversion came as the Anglo chico, Yogis, brought marmalade & toast. - a new item that has been added & good too.

Despite all this, I finished the airgraph & started an airmail for Hazel. **A poem had been half done but this provided the spark for completion.**

That seems to be the answer if a poem won't come clear. I start a letter & write what I have of the verse. The rest son comes. It shows what I can do.

Bill Hodgkinson was around for final goodbyes. He has been extremely nervous lately – more than his usual jumpy nervousness.

An extra tin box he had was given to me backsheesh [gratuity] as he had issued with it from Stores & couldn't charge me.

I am gradually getting all the trimmings. Lucky I hesitated before buying another box for myself. I seem to accidentally do many things just right.

Sunday September 3: Loafed away morning. Some rain. Couldn't settle to anything.

At tiffin an aerograph from Edna shook me as she congratulated on my commission. Jim had written home to say it was through. They must be slow in these parts.

Evening shift began quietly but soon developed into a mad rush as everything came at once & Norm was doing other work.

Clear fresh night. Called at Anglo to find they had closed for night.

[Added pages from longer, more detailed supplementary diary writings of the same date.]

If I ever wanted to murder someone or felt the urge to dabble in mass slaughter, yesterday was the time.

Around 10:00. as I strove to settle for sleep, tow of the Security boys began tuning operations on their motorcycle.

This consisted in racing the engine & then letting it die down only to repeat the process.

A steady noise might have been bearable but the ebb & flow irritated me almost beyond endurance.

Just as I was preparing to break out to a rash & began searching for a heavy blunt object for the massacre, they pushed off & left me in peace.

It was close, but they'll never know what an escape they'd had – maybe.

From then I had a smoother time although it took half an hour to overcome a patch of wakefulness.

That evening a restless spirit moved & I couldn't sit down to read let alone write.

These periods are probably a form of homesickness as a picture show is about the only remedy. But, last night my luck was out.

I went to the Lion [movie theatre] before 18:30 but drew a blank as I had seen "Sgt. York".

Not in the mood for returning to the billet, I wandered around.

Monday September 4: Up fairly early for breakfast. Read but did little else during morning. Too cloudy for sunbathing until nearly noon.

Wrote a few lines to Hazel. Fairly busy afternoon shift. Read for awhile after dinner & wrote Hazel many pages.

Anglo chico brought two marmalade on toast, two Bombay toast, & fresh lime.

Told Vosper of my letter from Edna but he had nothing helpful to suggest.

Around 23:00 when I climbed under my net. Sleep always seems to come easy these nights.

Tuesday September 5: Norm woke me but no need for dashing as I was Orderly Sgt. Didn't meet the O. Officer until 09:00.

Letters 300, 301, & 302 from Hazel. Between work & O. Officer, had no spare time in morning. Couldn't even finish reading mail.

Started airgraph for Hazel & sunbathed an hour after tiffin. Had flag lowering ceremony at 18:00. Read & completed airgraph in evening.

At R.A.F. Club got tin of grapefruit (1/14), chiclets, & toffee, also toothbrush (1/-). Met another Canadian. At Anglo had toast & fresh lime.

Clear moonlight but sticky hot indoors.

Wednesday, September 6: Kept going fairly steadily until 04:00. Brought this up to date & nodded over letter for

Hazel.

Groggy as I left at 6:30. Sleep during day no problem. Letter from Mum. Up around 17:00.

Went to Palace [movie theatre] directly after dinner. Hot indoors but cool enough outside. Saw Joan Crawford & Fred MacMurray in “Above Suspicion”. Good.

Talked to Pete at billet & then went to O.K. for two egg fritters & two glasses of cocoa. Didn’t write anything afterwards but went to bed around 23:00.

Thursday September 7: Up fairly early. Day started clear with clouds around horizon. Sat on balcony to get shoulder scorched during morning.

Wrote Hazel in afternoon & started airletter for her. On evening shift changed library books for Penguin Island, Anatole France, & The Outcast – Winwood Reade.

Busiest I’ve been for many months.

Unable to do anything about commission but must wait until it comes through.

No time for finishing airletter to Hazel. Didn’t bother calling at Anglo after midnight. Cool outdoors but sticky inside.

Friday September 8: Up early to go on pay parade. Sunny most of day & no rain.

Letter from Canada Post Corporation asking for present

address. Paid 65 chips.

Wrote an airletter but didn't complete it until after tiffin on shift. Worked crossword.

Nothing to do for two hours but fairly busy towards end S/[illegible] Cooper bothering again – grr.

Mess bill for Sept. 17 chips. Fresh lime from Anglo after dinner. Wrote letter concerning Bookkeeping course. Two Bombay toast & fresh lime for finale.

Read for awhile, but did not write to Hazel.

Saturday September 8: Airgraph from Mrs. Brown. Early rising for morning. Cool & pleasant most of day. Slight drizzle in morning.

Not particularly busy but kept myself occupied most of shift.

Read & started airgraph for Hazel in afternoon. Dhobi allowance of 8 chips. Went to Palace [movie theatre] early but no room.

Discovered "Heaven Can Wait" at Lion [movie theatre] so returned to billet. Toffee & grapefruit (1/14) at R.A.F. Club.

Norm visited to interrupt reading & writing of The Outcast. Onion sandwiches & fresh lime from Anglo.

Not too warm. Early on shift as watch fast. Everything seemed clear when we took over.

Sunday September 9: Airgraph 116 from Hazel. Occasional messages during night. Able to read & write considerable. Norm slept through as usual.

Rain after dawn but not for long. Flurry of work cut short letter to Hazel. Sleep broken in middle of day but had my share of shuteye.

Early dinner & to Palace [movie theatre] with Norm. Sprinkles dampened us but only slightly.

Rita Hayworth & Gene Kelly in "Cover Girl#. Good entertainment but not an outstanding picture.

O.K. Cafe for egg fritter & two glasses of cocoa. Saw "Major" Morley in mess to ask him to check for my kit at Lahore. Wrote Hazel.

Monday September 11: In time for shower & breakfast. Had rained during night. Cloudy & warm. Read & wrote Hazel during the morning.

After tiffin sunbathed, worked on a crossword, & started a poem for Hazel. Letter for Jim scarcely commenced, spoilt by ink running and had to be scrapped.

Evening shift too busy for writing as I am still on my own. Wally Workman replacing Norm Allison who is on leave. Hot & sticky all evening.

Called at O.K. after midnight for Vimto. Wasted no time climbing into bed. Sleep comes easy these nights.

Tuesday September 12: Light sprinkles soon stopped. Read Saturday Evening Post in mess after breakfast. Read more of Penguin Island & wrote this. Wrote Hazel.

Busiest afternoon shift for many months – on my own which didn't help. Issue of ration chocolate (American K) – fairly good too.

Worked on crossword & did little else. Joe Eves back – talked for a time & spoilt any chance I had for writing. Fresh lime from Anglo.

Tubby Heaton back for awhile & on same shift. Sticky hot. Hoping for hill party at Shillong if I don't leave soon.

Wednesday September 13: No trouble in awakening early. Clear with few clouds all day. Hot & sticky as usual. Left on my own all morning despite total of five on shift. Letter303 & airgraphs 117, 118 from Hazel.

Sunbathed an hour. Wrote half airgraph for Hazel. Early house at Lion [movie theatre] Jack Benny in "The Meanest Man In The World". Good for laughs but rather short.

Completed airgraph & called at O.K. for cocoa, Bombay Toast, & peanut brittle. Brought this up to date. Hot as ever with scarcely a breath indoors.

Cool enough we walked to office.

Thursday September 14: Busy at first but tapered off although little time to spare all night. Wally Workman & Heaton slept while Drysdale & I carried the shift.

Had few minutes to read but fell asleep over book. Clear, bright day. Broken sleep but didn't get up until 17:00. Cloudy with thunder & lightning.

Rushed through dinner to get to Palace [movie theatre] for first house "The Phantom Lady" - Franchet Tone, Ello Raines, & Alan Curtis. Good murder mystery.

Clear sky afterwards. Two fresh lime from Anglo. Sweat dripped. Read for a time & wrote this. Fruit salad & cake with fresh lime.

McDougall called to say his unit had letter claiming ground commissions suspended.

Friday September 15: Early using for Battle of Britain parade [?] Filmy clouds but bright morning. Hot & sticky.

Bought writing pad (two chips) & envelopes. Read & wrote Hazel all morning. Finished airletter for Hazel after tiffin & worked on crossword.

Scarcely a break during shift. Drysdale helped for awhile but had work of his own. Wally Workman Joe for typing as Brown on leave.

Called at Anglo afterwards for fresh lime & poached eggs on toast. It must be Tubby Heaton's influence that makes me eat between meals.

Saturday September 16: Able to get breakfast easily. Cloudy as if thunderstorm brewing. Slightly sticky. Worked on crossword & wrote Hazel.

Storm never developed. Work fairly heavy all afternoon but Drysdale helped at times. Had cake for snack.

Tried a crossword after dinner & then used most of evening to write poem & airmail for Hazel. Warm & sticky as usual. Fresh lime from Anglo didn't cool much.

In order to complete letter for Hazel, had to stay up later than usual. Felt groggy for awhile but recovered.

Sunday September 17: Clear & fresh when I rose early for morning shift. Not a great deal to do but kept occupied by usual morning preliminaries.

Letter from Tom Goodwin told me of the death of both Mr. Dodds & Alec. Their family has taken a beating this war.

Struggled with a crossword & lay in the sun for an hour. Began airgraph & cooled off with three fresh limes & bowls of water over me.

Interruptions during evening made it difficult to finish airgraph for Hazel. Started airmail for Jim.

Anglo chico brought fresh lime, cake, & fruit salad. Fairly hot but breeze.

Monday September 18: Ran into a stack of work which took until 02:00 to clear, with Drysdale's help. Not much after that but kept awake.

Slept well during the day with scarcely an interruption.

Early dinner to get to Lion [movie theatre] for first house. Saw a "Marsie" [?] picture "Cash & Carry". Anne Southern & George Murphy. Entertaining but not brilliant.

Called at R.A.F. Club for cocoa, peas, & chips – also chiclets. Talked with Jack Shegog [?] & ended up in Anglo for fresh lime, cake, & fruit salad.

Chatted with some of the boys until bed time.

Tuesday September 19: Rolled out for breakfast. Filmy clouds. Read Wings Abroad & tried a crossword. Wrote Hazel.

Rained for an hour or so at noon but cleared again. Cool breeze in afternoon. Worked crossword & wrote Hazel. Started airletter but had to finish it on evening shift.

Some rain during evening & night. Busy at first but work finally slacked off to leave me clear before midnight. Called at Anglo for fresh lime, cake, & fruit salad - slipping back into that old habit of night snacks.

Wednesday September 20: Almost slept beyond breakfast time but Bill called me. Tried crossword & then wrote Hazel.

Drizzle most of the morning & continued through afternoon. Just enough work to make time move quickly. Airletter from Wally.

Gen. Sheet & Reader's Digest from District H.Q. Ahead of a downpour returning to billet. Completed letter for Hazel. Copied poems into book. Wrote Louis Hodge.

Chatted with boys below & ate omelette with chips & fresh lime from Anglo. Couldn't get to sleep until late.

Thursday September 21: Almost slept in but awoke just in time. Unsettled but cleared by noon. Enough to keep me working most of the morning.

Sunbathed an hour & started airgraph for Hazel. Shower before dinner & some rain during evening. Still hot and sticky.

Library closed so books remained unchanged. Toe sore as I cut out ingrown nail. Completed airgraph for Hazel & chatted with Pet fresh out of cock from foot rot.

Airgraph 119 from Hazel. Next might bring commission gen. Chips, omelette, & fresh lime at Anglo before night shift.

Friday September 22: Rough night with a trickle of work keeping me from writing. Paid 70 chips. Sleep was easy & lasted until after 17:00.

Drinking party in billet as Ron Coulson leaving on Sunday. Couldn't settle to writing. Went to Lion [movie theatre] with Bill Peel, Pete, & Chas. Morgan to see "Escape" - John Payne (?) & Norma Shearer.

Pre-war story of Germany. Not too bad.

Called at the Anglo afterwards for two Bombay toast, two fresh lime, fruit salad, & cake. Waited until party broke up at 01:00 before trying sleep.

Night close, hot and sticky.

Saturday September 23: Nearly missed breakfast. Strolled around town all morning. Had parcel made up for Mum & bought to filigree silver broaches for Hazel.

Spent rest of morning trying to find something else for Hazel but had no luck. Hot & sunny until afternoon when thunderclouds gathered.

Read & wrote after tiffin. Called around for parcel & brought sandwich biscuits. Busy enough during the evening. Paused for fresh lime only at Anglo.

Hot & sticky as ever during evening.

Sunday September 24: Struggled up for breakfast. Worked on crossword & read library book Fact & Faith by J.B.S. Haldane.

Afternoon shift one steady slug but finished clear. Started poem for Hazel & completed it during evening to include in airmail.

Sticky to an uncomfortable degree. Went to Anglo for fresh lime & two Bombay toast.

Bob Drayson who went on Topa course after I, told me his commission was through. Mac & I must be definitely on the outside.

Two Bombay toast & fresh lime.

Monday September 25: No trouble getting up to clear sky

day. Enough to do all morning but not overworked.

Good mail day – post card from Mrs. Brown, parcel & letters 304, 5, 7, 6 8 from Hazel. Read letters & ate humbugs greater part of afternoon.

Completed letter & airgraph for Hazel after dinner. At Anglo with Wally Workman. Had chip potatoes, fresh lime, & chocolate drink from package sent by Hazel.

Took parcel for “Mum” on shift for censoring. Hotter & stickier than usual.

Tuesday September 26: Considerable work on hand. No clear until after 04:30. Rain cooled the air for awhile. Read a few pages. Chocolate drink for breakfast.

Slept well during the day. Early dinner & a trip to the Palace [movie theatre] Olson & Johnson in “Crazy House”. Goofy & good but not on level of “Hellzapoppin”.

Strolled around afterwards. Chatted with different fellows at billet. Rain ended day. Light trouble but electrician made temporary repairs.

Anglo for poached eggs on friend bread, three fresh limes, & chocolate drink.

Wednesday September 27: Woke up early but dozed until nearly 08:00. Read after breakfast & then took Mum’s parcel to post office.

Walked through town & bazaar remainder of morning but nothing worth buying for Hazel. Read after tiffin & wrote airletter for Hazel.

Nothing to do at first but gradually worked into high gear during evening. Called at Anglo afterwards for poached eggs on toast & fresh lime.

Warm enough but not as bad as usual.

Tuesday September 28: No trouble getting up. For some reason, have been given cocoa at breakfast for past two mornings.

Read in mess & then read book. Wrote Hazel. Shaved before tiffin. Rain fell heavily just before I went to mess. Easy afternoon.

Able to help Drysdale for awhile. Heavy downpour at dinner time dwindled to an all evening drizzle. Airgraph from Hazel.

Nothing on commission.

Tried crossword for a time. Heat made me feel groggy but cool fresh breeze finally helped. Wrote Hazel. Sleep didn't come quickly. Airgraph 120 from Hazel.

Friday September 29: Nearly got up late as watch half an hour slow. Easy morning. Warm & slightly sticky. Completed airgraph for Hazel, read, & tried crossword in afternoon.

Short shower & many broken clouds. Started letter for Bill Alexander. Paused to clip a cover girl who reminded me of Hazel, but soon back to billet after dinner.

Completed letter for Bill & started airletter for Mother. Pete Guise chatted for a time. At Anglo had chips & omelette, toast, fruit salad, cake, lime, & own chocolate drink.

Saturday September 30: Easy night. Toast from Sigs at 03:00. Helped Wally on a message. Completed letter for Mother. Wrote Hazel. Dozed for a short time.

Slept well during the day. Walked around town with Joe Eves & Bill Peel. Too crowded & pictures not worth seeing.

Stopped at R.A.F. Club for cocoa & poached eggs on toast. Wrote Hazel for a while. Fresh lime & fruit salad from Anglo.

Bright moonlight made strolling pleasant. Letter from Bill Alexander to tell that Fredianni now has commission.

Sunday October 1: Cloudy but hot. Up around 07:00 Bill & Joe going on leave. Walked downtown to get linen table cloths & walnut carved box for parcel to Hazel.

Packed it in tin from parcel Hazel had sent to me. Norm Addison & Kettleborough back from leave. Wrote poem for Hazel & incorporated it in airmail letter.

Evening started slack but rushed before the end. Hot sticky atmosphere as usual wasn't too helpful. Unable to shake up Anglo so no snack.

Monday October 2: Awake before 07:00. Broken clouds but hot & clear.

Got parcel for Hazel from durzi. Took it on shift for censoring after I had got customs declaration form for it.

Sent cable to Hazel & then wrote to her for remainder of morning.

Oppressively hot afternoon. Norm Addison back on same shift. Not too busy. Stuffed myself at dinner, especially on cheese & biscuits.

Wrote airletter for Hazel during evening. Had poached eggs on toast at Anglo – also fresh lime. Later than usual retiring.

Tuesday October 3: Awake early but no rush as Orderly Joe. Bright but some clouds. First O.O. away but found a substitute.

Worked crossword with Norm as morning slack. Wrote greater part of airgraph for Hazel after tiffin. Flag lowering simple & quick.

309 from Hazel but no mention of commission.

Completed 'graph & sorted dhobi after dinner. Mailed parcel for Hazel in afternoon.

Wrote ordinary letter for Hazel. Warm & sticky but no worse than usual. Anglo for poached eggs on toast. Bombay toast fresh lime & on chocolate drink.

Wednesday October 14: One of the slackest nights yet. Norm slept on & off but I had little to do.

Wrote an airletter for Wally. Sigs supplied toast. Left at 06:30 for shower & sick parade. Quickly asleep after breakfast. Just woke up once around 13:00.

Early dinner. "More the Merrier" at Palace [movie theatre] but one I had seen. Lion [movie theatre] "Bomber's Moon" didn't appeal from 6 as seats.

At R.A.F. Club had cocoa & bought chiclets. New watch strap for a chip. Read & wrote Hazel. Close & hot – whew!

Thursday October 5: Watch stopped. Apparently balance wheel spindle off true – according to Shegog.

Wrote Hazel in morning & prepared kit for hill party. Read Digest. Discovered minimum kit to be taken. Borrowed small case from Norm Addison. [?] & bed roll bus.

Hot during day & sticky in evening shift. Library closed so left books with Wally Workman. Work heavy at first but cleared away eventually & finished airletter to Hazel.

Called at Anglo afterwards for poached eggs on toast, chips, fresh lime, & own chocolate drink – last of these from Hazel.

Friday October 6 Up fairly early despite fact that watch not going to give time check. Bright & warm but fleecy clouds. Paid 65 chips.

Called at Sick Quarters for hill party first aid box. Read Digest & wrote this. Fruit salad, fresh lime, & cake from Anglo.

Pain in back – must have bruised a rib when I fell on Friday.

An airgraph completed for Hazel but dated tomorrow. Paid for two weeks in advance in afternoon.

Letters 310, 311, & 312 from Hazel. Train left promptly at 16:40.

Vosper "panicked" but treated him rough. Able to curl up for some sleep.

Saturday October 7: Train late to miss connections at Kulawa [?}. Had to wait from 10:00 to 14:00. At Sylhet [?] after 17:00.

Rain added to complications. Went to transit camp which wasn't too good. No lights in basha. Electrical storm continued most of night.

Had enough to eat during train trip as ration packs contained cheese & chocolate.

Also able to buy "pomaleau"[*] (Burmese oranges) which are almost like grapefruit but some are pink inside. [Sounds like pomelo in Spanish. At this point in his life, Archie is unfamiliar with pink grapefruit?]

Open air pictures at transit camp but rain spoilt that. In bed before 20:00 hours.

Sunday October 8: Up early around 06:00. Watch not running. Rain at first but eventually ran out of it on trip up.

Our Gharry ran out of gas which caused several hours delay. Usual poached eggs & toast at halfway house. Also had small green oranges.

Around 14:00 when we reached Shillong. Put in C.1. Two other Canadians there.

After dinner walked to Soldier's Club with "Paddy" (Cpl) Howe. Had cake & lime squash. Saw "What's Cookin'" - Andrews Sisters at Garrison [movie theatre].

Back & in bed fairly early.

Monday, October 9: Chilly in morning. Attended usual C.O.'s talk. Had haircut. After tiffin, clear & warm. Called at camp cinema to see Bette Davis & Claude Raines in "Mr. Skeffington". Good but heavy.

Read & wrote this evening. Ate bacsheesh chocolate I had scrounged from ration pack. Did not go out after dinner – too chilly for K.D. & I have no blue.

Early to bed but charpoy uncomfortable. Also bearer didn't put enough blankets on top. Feels like fall weather at home.

Tuesday October 10: Went to town in American Liberty Wagon. Saw Tubby Heaton at Assam Industries. Handed in watch for repairs. To cost 8 chips.

Back to Assam for more cocoa. Walked back by Soldier's Club. No film at the camp & ones outside did not appeal. Read & loafed away afternoon.

Nothing doing in evening as I read & talked with the boys. Charpoy exercises fairly early but same trouble getting sleep organized.

Bed seems too short for full stretch & chill air doesn't help any.

Wednesday October 11: Just made breakfast deadline as usual. Cocoa for a surprise. Strolled to town for shaving brush & to look over souvenirs for Hazel.

Also got garters for stockings. Yesterday I bought lace dinner set at 29 Rs for Hazel. Had a couple of squashes by Kelvin Cinema & bought toffee.

Saw "Janie" at camp cinema – Joyce Reynolds, Edward Arnold, & Anne Harding. Andy Hardy in reverse & good for laughs.

Every morning so far clear & bright with clouds later. Started to write in evening but Cochrane & another fellow talked me dizzy.

Thursday October 12: Usual breakfast. Bright & sunny. Sat in sun to write this. Hiked to town after tiffin.

Ended up at Kelvin [movie theatre] – George Formby in "It Turned Out Nice Again". Badly cast but funny spots remained.

Rode back in U.S. Liberty Wagon. Airgraph written for Hazel in the morning. Started airmail after dinner but couldn't complete verse.

Distraction as two Yank Sgts came in with beer to teach the boys pinochle. Not noisy but I couldn't concentrate. Arranged my bed so that I didn't have to curl up & kept warm all night by using sweater.

Friday October 13: Slept so well almost forgot to get up. Clouds didn't stop sun's warmth.

Called at Soldier's Club for hot bath but had to wait half the morning. Worth the wait.

Went to town on Liberty Wagon after tiffin but watch not ready. Wandered around all afternoon. Had cheese sandwiches at Morrello's.

Reached Soldier's Club ahead of rain. Had dinner three – salad, vegetable turnover, chocolate blanc mange, & cake. A few drops on way to camp but didn't bother me.

Bought some candy. Read a mystery story all evening & did not write. Warmer.

Saturday October 14: Me early to climb around the hills. Lost hat in process. Back before tiffin to complete airmail for Hazel.

Went to town for watch. New cap cost 6/8. Tried New China but couldn't even get eggs. Too much line-up at B.O.R.'s Club. Dinner at mess.

Called at library but didn't get a book. Managed to get into camp cinema. "Hail The Conquering Hero" Eddie Bracken & Ella Raines. Funny but broke down in middle.

Read Fiesta by Ernest Hemingway. Screwy. Almost too warm in bed for a change – surprise.

Sunday October 15: Cloudy but no rain in morning. Continued reading of Fiesta but didn't find it until afternoon. Cold sniffles. Ticket for tonight's concert.

Wrote airletter for Hazel & started airgraph but didn't complete the latter before tie for the concert.

Several of cast in show were sick but a good performance was presented after a "corny" start. Called at the mess afterwards for cheese sandwich.

Nights are not so cold although I still use all the blankets – four on top & two under. Week of leave gone.

Monday October 16: Loafed away most of morning but completed airgraph for mailing to Hazel. Caught Liberty run to town after tiffin.

Didn't care for picture at Kelvin [movie theatre]. Saw "Paris After Dark" at Garrison [movie theatre]. Watch running fast. Had snack at B.O.R.'s Club – salad & trifle.

Returned to camp for dinner. Stood in line for an hour & a half to see B.E.S.A. Show - "Stand Easy". Good entertainment without too much smut.

Went to bed feeling rather bloated. The double feed for dinner must have been responsible. Broken clouds. Light shower in afternoon soon over.

Tuesday October 17: Just made breakfast deadline. Cloudy

but no rain in morning. Slightly chilly. Went to town on Liberty run with Sgt. Lewis.

Took watch in for adjustment. Hairspring in a tangle.

Letter from “Red” Davis & airgraph from Mother. 313 from Hazel.

Relaxed in afternoon & started airmail for Hazel. Learnt from her that Edna’s commission gen. a false alarm. Mac. must have been right. Went to camp cinema after dinner to see “Slightly Dangerous” - Lana Turner & Robert Young.

Sgt. Lewis was with me. Crawled into bed after the picture.

Wednesday October 18: Up fairly early. Cloudy again with sun breaking through occasionally.

Wrote poem in airmail for Hazel but decided to add a verse which took part of afternoon. Few sprinkles. Played a few games of solitaire waiting for poetry inspiration.

Copied all poetry completed into small notebook. Wrote Hazel ordinary style but not for long. Queued up at camp cinema early but picture postponed.

Had canned peaches & milk before going back. Had fairly good seats with Sgt Lewis. Music soundtrack bad.

Baseball short bored & Andrews Sisters amused - “Moonlight & Cactus”. Comedy Andy Clyde. Hung around bar until after 23:30.

Thursday October 19: Broken clouds. Some rain in

afternoon. Lewis & I went to Soldier's Club for hot bath. Couldn't book for Kelvin. Transport both ways.

Paper clippings from Wally. Played solitaire most of afternoon & started airletter for Hazel. Nothing doing in evening but completed airletter for Hazel.

Dance on in camp which meant no cinema. Loafed & played solitaire most of evening. Fire in fireplace added to lazy atmosphere.

Bed fairly easy. Getting accustomed to chilly air at night & sweater not needed.

Friday October 20: Drifted through morning but stirred me after tiffin to see "Wintertime" - Sonja Henie – at Garrison [movie theatre] with Lewis.

Called at B.O.R.'s Club afterwards for dinner – salad & pineapple dish suited me. Had to wait for rain to stop but got back to camp by 18:00.

Nothing to do during evening. Started airgraph for Hazel but an informal gathering around the fire cramped my style.

Went with Lewis to scrounge fuel & buy cheese sandwiches at mess. Gave up writing eventually & went to bed. Make little progress in letter-writing.

Saturday October 21: Lazy morning. Broken clouds. Bob, Jake, & Lewis started hill climb just before tiffin.

Waited until after meal & then climbed up from where Tubby Heaton left off last year. A hot job but cooled after reaching top in an hour.

Back to B.O.R.'s Club for dinner. Reached camp just after others. Lewis & I went to camp cinema - "Dragon Seed" with Katherine Hepburn.

A good picture of Japanese – Chinese war. Lasted three full hours. Too late for sandwiches but had squash in mess before bed.

Sunday October 22: Bright & pleasant. Wrote more of airgraph I started on Friday. Played solitaire part of time. Dashed to town in afternoon with Lewis.

Kelvin [movie theatre] booked up for "Holiday Inn". Strolled around but paused at Morrella's for cake. Dinner at camp. Finally completed airgraph in evening.

Refused to play bridge with the boys but they found a fourth & carried on until after midnight.

Lewis & I got squash cheese sandwiches at mess. Toasted bread to give more pep to sandwiches. Climbed in fairly early but card players kept me awake.

Monday October 23: Up fairly early. Bright & fairly clear. Only broken clouds.

Considerable chasing around during morning. In charge of 30 returning to "Chitters". Early tiffin & off to quick start around noon.

Long wait at halfway house. Baggage late but in time for train at 18:15. Too crowded for sleep. Sweltering at first but cooled after dark.

During night had to hug myself to keep warm. Thick mist settled to make the air chilly enough for blanket but didn't bother undoing bed roll.

Lewis seemed to be able to sleep but position too cramped for me.

Tuesday October 24: Train on time and transport came promptly. At billet before 11:30. Bill on duty so called at office for key as Norm Addison in dock.

Mail 314 to 319 & airgraphs 121, 2, & 3. MacLeans, Digest, & letter from Gordon Taylor, an R.A.F. boy who met Brown family.

Airletter from Louis Hodge in afternoon. He is heading back here.

Almost had row with Bottomley who insisted I start at midnight. He is going to check on commission.

Slept through sunny afternoon & read mail. Attended mess meeting & spoke to Kennedy about get together of Canadians at R.A.F. Club on November 1st.

Managed letter-airgraph to Hazel before midnight. Sticky.

Wednesday October 25: Slack night. Warm at first. Wrote second page to Hazel's airgraph. Slept for about three hours.

Stomach pains bothered for a while. Was going sick but

changed my mind.

Read after breakfast but soon fell asleep. Awake around 15:00 when MacDougall called but no fresh news. He is posted to Delhi.

Our case is supposed to be under consideration.

Read in mess after dinner. Received issue of six Christmas airgraphs. Sorted out mail. At Anglo had poached eggs on toast, chips, Bombay toast, & fresh lime.

Thursday October 25: Up fairly early for sick parade. Sore throat. Loafed & wrote poem for Hazel. Finished airletter started night before.

Read & wrote airmail to Hazel after tiffin. Took dhobi to Bombay Laundry as regular dhobi has become slack.

Some work left from previous shift. Hot and sticky as usual. Technical hitch caused things to accumulate. Slugged full out but couldn't get things under control by midnight.

Jack Shegog with me. Shift I'm on now seems the best of all. Being on with Bill Peel makes sleep easier too.

Friday October 27: Up for breakfast & gargle at sick quarters. Bright & sunny but not hot in morning. Brought this up to date. Finished regular letter for Hazel.

Afternoon Shift started slowly but gradually stepped up. Time out for cake, & gargle from sick quarters. Became hot & sticky after with stack of work.

Entered poetry in book after dinner. Still warm & close. Wrote Hazel for a while. From Anglo had poached eggs on toast, chips, & fresh lime as chico came around.

Sleep comes quickly.

Saturday October 28: Early rising but no rush as Orderly Sgt – a frame up which I plan to query. Went sick for foot rot & never reached office until nearly 10:00.

Fairly easy morning. O. Officer was once a FlSgt here. He didn't insist on much running about. Wrote half airgraph for Hazel in afternoon.

After treatment, flag lowering quick & simple. Airgraph finished after dinner but read in mess first. Started anniversary poem to go with roses I've planned for Hazel

Poached eggs on toast, fruit salad, & fresh lime at Anglo. Wrote this & ordinary letter for Hazel.

Sunday October 29: Busy most of night but took time out for sleep. Cheese & biscuits for a snack during the shift. Left early to windup O.S. duties.

Had foot treatment after breakfast but in bed by 10:00. Two letters 320, 321 from Hazel. Early dinner after picking up dhobi at Bombay Laundry.

Went to first house of "This is The Army". Not a remarkable picture. In 12as seats.

At Anglo had scrambled eggs on toast, fruit salad, cake, fresh lime. Chat with "Taff" Rees kept me from getting any writing done. Bed before midnight.

First tangerines of season at dinner. First alert too during dinner.

Monday October 30: Not up early than necessary for breakfast. Cloudy & dull.

Strolled around town but only bought writing pad as towels & face cloths too dear. (latter 12 as).

Struggled with poetry all afternoon & started airmail for Hazel.

Rain squeezed a few drops but not enough to lay the dust.

One of the hardest shifts this season. A break in the middle but work so heavy towards end both Jack, Shegog, & I couldn't handle it.

Felt completely exhausted by midnight. I haven't the staying power any longer – Bengalitis.

Tuesday October 31: Up fairly early. Cloudy & ground wet from night rain. Usual all at S.Q. [?] for foot treatment. Rot clearing away but gradually.

Wrote Hazel. Work in spurts during afternoon. Picked up 322 from Hazel on way back from treatment. So & sticky for a while I was gasping. Pleasant outdoors.

Finished poem for airmail to Hazel during evening. Slightly sticky (I mean the atmosphere.) No snack for a change – surprise.

Last night of summer giving all it can. Late to bed as airmail took time for windup.

Wednesday November 1: Surprised myself by awakening early. Cool & misty. Officially first day of winter. Warm but not unpleasant during day.

Airgraph 124 from Hazel. Wrote most of airgraph for Hazel in afternoon.

Went to meeting of Canadians at R.A.F. Club. Seventeen appeared, five of us from Edmonton but I knew none of them.

Got book, socks, & handkerchiefs. Had cheese & egg sandwiches with fresh lime. Didn't accomplish must but good to talk with the boys for a change.

Baseball slated for Sunday. MacDougall ready to leave. Wrote Hazel for a while. Mess dance.

Thursday November 2.

Slept well but woke once to find MacDougall had called & left note to say he was leaving for Delhi on Saturday.

As Kennedy & his gang are leaving for the 'drome soon, I expect to go below with advance too.

Wrote for a while after dinner but did not complete airletter for Hazel.

Mess bill to end of November paid at noon. 21/4-

Friday November 3: No trouble getting up early. Had to pull on a blanket during the night. Cloudy but bright warm morning. Paid 70 chips.

Five airletter forms for Christmas. Completed airletter for Hazel & started airmail to Edna. Correspondence in terrible shape.

Read & completed airmail in afternoon. Evening shift started fairly slowly but the bottom fell out after 20:30. Couldn't do anything about it as work mounted.

Saturday November 4: Cloudy & cool which helped me to get up for sick parade. Had feet check & another four days treatment recommended.

Also gargle as throat doesn't seem right.

Borrowed 629 camera from Roper to use film Hazel sent but too dull in morning.

Read Can gen book & loafed. Wrote Hazel. Busy afternoon but had time out for treatment & gargle. Got P.K. [?] writing pads (8 as) & soap (5 as) from mobile canteen.

Sorted out papers & wrote Hazel after dinner. Have good supply of vitamin pills. Fruit salad, cake, & fresh lime at Anglo.

Sunday November 5: Unsettled but warm during day. Blitzed all work in sight on morning shift besides taking time out for treatment.

FltLt Bottomly shook me by pausing to call it a good show.

Wrote part of airgraph to Hazel after reading in mess. Took snaps with film sent in camera borrowed from Roper.

Went to first house at Lion [movie theatre] Abbott & Costello in "Who Done It". Funny despite slashes.

Completed airgraph & wrote poetry. Poached eggs on toast, fruit salad, & fresh lime at Anglo. Chilly towards midnight. Had sandwiches made from tin of cheese.

Monday November 6: Not much to do but keep slugging until 05:00. Slept a short while, Cool but not too chilly. Slept soundly during day but woke up once.

Warm & bright.

Letter 323 from Hazel. Spent all evening completing poem & writing airmail for Hazel. Want it to reach her for the 22nd.

Almost chilly towards midnight. Using blanket every night now. At Anglo had fruit salad & fresh lime.

Had letter ready for night shift to take on for me Sleep well these nights.

Tuesday November 7: Bright & sunny but not too warm. Had treatment as usual. Strolled around town with "Lofty". Kettlebow & Bill Peel.

Went to Co-op & circled around, ending at Y Coffee House for Vimto & cocoa nut candy. Copied latest poetry into notebook.

Exchanged gym shoes & put name down for sheets. Wrote Hazel airletter & ordinary during afternoon.

Easy evening shift. Lunched on biscuits I had bought during morning. Almost too chilly. One blanket just right.

Wednesday November 8: Just up early enough for sick parade. Almost too cool for shorts. Bright & clear. Given 21 days treatment for feet.

Wrote ordinary letter to Hazel. Afternoon started slack but fairly busy before the end.

Told I was going down below with others on 18th. Talked with Humphries part of evening. Fresh lime from Anglo. Wrote Hazel for awhile.

Went to Anglo with Jack Shegog for fruit salad, toast, & fresh lime.

A chill in the air made blanket feel welcome as I crawled under.

Thursday November 9: Early rising brought shivers before sun came up for clear warm day. Slack morning.

Called at Orderly Room after tiffin to confirm 16 chips (2 mos.) dhobi money for me tomorrow.

Airgraph 125 from Hazel? Others later were anniversary cards, 324, 5,6,7, & 8. Started airgraph in afternoon but didn’t complete it until evening.

Feet healing up well now.

Wrote ordinary letter for Hazel. At Anglo had poached eggs & chips. A nip in the air these evenings. Probably a cooler winter than usual is ahead. Suits me.

Friday November 10: Work trickled in until nearly 05:00. Slept for an hour or so. Using oil stoves for warmth. Sleep came quickly.

Up at noon for tiffin & to collect 16 chips& dhobi allowance. Got extra blanket from Stores in case I can't take & cold nights.

Dozed during afternoon. Early dinner before going to first house at Palace [movie theatre] "Lifeboat" – Tallulah Bankhead & Wm. Bendix. Good though grim in spots.

Cool & pleasant night. Chatted around billet. Wrote airletter for Hazel. Hot lime, poached eggs, toast, & chips at Anglo.

Saturday November 11: Pleasant & warm as usual. Went dental sick. May get trip to Calcutta to visit R.C.A.F. Dental. I hope.

Loafed away most of morning. Wrote Hazel & Bill Alexander. Drinking hot fresh lime these days. Bought eight oranges for a chip. Fruit not so good yet.

Evening shift gradually grew heavier.

Hot cocoa & toast from O.K. as runner went over. Snack of biscuits & cheese from mess. Jack starting on day tomorrow to prepare for move down below.

Sunday November 12: Rolled out in time for breakfast. Clear & bright. Had film taken from camera by Photo Section next door.

Jack Shegog fixed camera winder which was jammed.

Finished letter to Bill & chatted with Jack & "Lofty" Kettleboro. Bill && I worked together on afternoon shift.

Cake & cocoa from O.K. Not very busy. Wrote Hazel after dinner. Chair broken so I sat on bed. Toast & hot fresh lime from Anglo.

Bill & I split a tin of cheese when I gave up for day.

Monday November 13: Bright brisk &. early for morning shift. Not overworked. Letter & parcel from Hazel (sent Aug. 8)

Started regular airgraph. Wrote more on it after dinner but finally went to Lion [movie theatre] with Bill & Charlie Morgan – George Sanders in "They Came to Blow Up America".

Fairly good but not too exciting.

Completed airgraph before going to Anglo for omelette, chips, & toast with hot chocolate from parcel.

Air chilly but didn't bother taking sweater on shift. No word about dental treatment yet but expect to have an argument over it.

Tuesday November 14: Slugged for most of night. Had

cheese sandwich for lunch. Took an hour time out for nap at 06:00.

Managed to clear everything. Bill took dhobi to Bombay for me. Slept soundly but felt groggy when I got up at 17:00.

Developed film had three misses.

Went to Palace [movie theatre] with Charlie & Bill – "Song of Russia" – Robert Taylor & Susan Peters. Good with music to match.

Too late for lunch so let it go at nothing. One blanket just right these nights.

Wednesday November 15: Roused me early enough but didn’t hurry. Clear, bright, & almost chilly. Brought this up to date.

Wrote Hazel for remainder of morning. Spent entire afternoon writing airmail & poem for it. Letter from Helen – good, too.

May not go below until the 20th. Worked steadily all evening but not pressed. Air decidedly cool as we walked back to billet.

Days take all morning to warm up now. Temperature will probably be lower down south. No word on Calcutta dental trip.

Thursday November 16: Easily beat breakfast deadline. Spent morning wrapping souvenir S.E.A.C.’s after I showed Bill how.

Took shoes to Batas for stitching as camp moochi too slow. Wrote Hazel & this before tiffin.

Warm for a while during afternoon. Work steady but not too heavy. Spoke to Bottomley about dental date at Calcutta but he turned both thumbs down.

I'm due to go below on Monday but Bill leaves on Saturday. Collected dhobi on way from mess. (Refund of 6/8 missing)

Wrote Hazel. Cheese (own tin) omelette, toast, & fruit salad with hot chocolate from Anglo.

Friday November 17: Up early but no rush as I reported sick so I didn't come until 09;30. Nealy [?] prescribed inhalations for [?]aches.

Not much work. Sent cable to Hazel after tiffin. Bill cleared kit & chorpoy out. Pay 55 chips as Victory Loan deduction starting.

Wrote air letter & usual airgraph for Hazel. Missed lunch as Anglo closed earlier than I expected. Sending Souvenir S.E.A.C.'s to everyone I know, almost.

Cool, clear evening but didn't need sweater. Bill came on shift to sleep as leaving early in morning.

Saturday November 18: Except for an hour I took off for shuteye, busy practically all night. Had hot chocolate & Roper brought cheese pasties from cookhouse.

Slept soundly during day as P/O Phillips brought camp bed which he bought for me (22 chips & good) but I couldn't be roused. Got up to look it over around 13:00.

Letters 329, 330, & 331 from Hazel. Went to town for bedspreads for parcel to Hazel. Packed heavy kit afterwards.

At Anglo had poached eggs on toast, chips, fruit salad, hot fresh lime, & hot chocolate from parcel. Wrapped up spreads & lace from Shillong.

Sunday November 19: Bright & sunny. Warm. Early for breakfast. Had parcel sewed up & censored only to find it overweight. Had to remove the spread.

(Spreads 18 chips each & lace 29.)

Finally had it o.k. & left it for Unit Post Office to send (2/12). Helped Charley Morgan load our heavy kit as gharry came around.

Wrote Hazel until tiffin time. Went to town for mirror (1/12), pillow (12 as), and mattress (6/-). Have everything ready for pushing off tomorrow.

Norm Addison going home on medical grounds. Fairly busy shift. Had hot chocolate while Roper brought me a cheese sandwich. Sorted out small kit before bed.

Monday November 20: Jack Hunter called me at 06:30. Chilly. Soon ready & had breakfast before 08:00. Usual waiting but started at 09:15.

Stopped at canteen by Dohazari for eggs & chips with squash. Got P.K. & Dr. West's tooth brush (1/6). Dustiest ride I have ever had.

Reached "Shalimar" around 16:00. Pretty but grim. Gharry with heavy kit broke down at Chiringa but arrived in time for bed making around 22:00.

Eating with airmen. Getting a kick out of the whole thing. Wrote this & to Hazel. Day warm & didn't cool quickly.

Tuesday November 21: Up fairly early but bed too comfortable for easy rising. Put on duty when we reported at office. Off at 13:00.

Night watch starts at 22:00. Nothing organized. Hot but not too sticky. Wrote airgraph for Hazel by candlelight during evening but nattering room mates made the gong slow.

Mosquitoes buzzed for awhile. Had a slice of bread before going on shift & took water bottle with me.

Time before midnight went remarkably fast. Cools off much slower in these parts – probably the altitude.

Wednesday November 22: Night did not lag at any time. Head down for over an hour. Small flurry of work towards end of watch.

Bright clear day as usual & too warm for successful sleeping. Besides, the other boys in our basha clumped around & talked too loudly.

Up before 16:00 for a wash. Showers are to be laid on soon.

Two letters, 332 &333 from Hazel. Wrote this & letter for Hazel by candlelight. Started airletter but finally gave up & climbed under.

Tried Toddy with cold water but not too good.

Thursday November 23: Woke fairly early but didn't get up right away. Bright & cool at first. Sorted out things around billet.

Borrowed shovel to cut steps to dirt washing platform. Hot work. Completed airletter for Hazel before noon. Wrote ordinary style to Hazel in afternoon.

Christmas airletters to Mums & Mrs. Brown. Watch running fast – hairspring must be tangled again.

Fairly easy shift from 17:30 to 22:00. Roper brought me an egg sandwich from the YASB [?] Canteen (Arakenteen) [?] Found chilly early. Not too warm with one blanket.

Friday November 24: Awake early but not certain of time as watch galloping. Chilly most of day despite clear skies.

Completed airletter for Mrs. Brown. Wrote Hazel regular letter & started airmail. Back & shoulders slightly sunburnt. Easy afternoon. Hot showers ready for tomorrow.

Had Toddy drink using tin of evaporated milk – good. Lamp filled – fairly bright. Airgraph 126 from Hazel. Letter from Bill – letter & Christmas card from Edna.

Had to wear sweater for warmth after dark. Almost completed airmail & poetry for Hazel but Lee & Chalmers interrupted. Two blankets on bed.

Saturday November 25: Up early without using watch as it continues to speed. Wore shirt as orders say we must. Not a great deal in during morning. Bright & warm all day.

Completed airmail & started airgraphs for Hazel in afternoon. Hot shower & good.

Continued airgraph after dinner. Nights close in quickly after 18:00. Went to Arakanteen with Fred Lambert. Had lemon squash & chocolate cake.

Took cake back for night watch. Pleasant moonlight but chilly. Wrote ordinary letter to Hazel after completing airgraph.

A[?] but seemed to be a false alarm. Took blanket as well as sweater on shift. Power down & stacks of work.

Sunday November 26: Coldest night I've experienced down here. Could do little with work as power too low. Cake for lunch.

Fell asleep over message but didn't lie down. Warmed up fairly quickly in morning. Slept well all morning but talk disturbed later.

Hot shower before dinner. Feel groggy. Wrote Hazel most of evening. Fred brought cake from canteen. Wrote Christmas airletter to Mother.

Not quite so cool but chilly enough. Seem to have more spare time, probably because no cafes or shows handy.

Sleep comes easy.

Monday November 27: Up in time for breakfast. Warm & bright. Wrote Hazel during morning. More writing in afternoon. Christmas airletters to Jim, Wally, & Lorne.

Hot shower. Three Reader's Digests from Bill Alexander. Watch on the run again. Will have to wait until I go to Calcutta for repairs.

Easy evening shift but chilly once sun went down. Roper brought me two slices of cake as we went off shift.

Straight to bed as air too frigid for anything else. Two blankets scarcely enough. Will have to try three.

Tuesday November 28: Awake early but just out in time for breakfast. Not too warm. Copied poetry in notebook & started new poem.

Wrote Christmas airletter for Hazel. Warm enough during afternoon. Not much to do.

Saw F/Lt Bottomley who said I could go to Calcutta (Surprise) after the first when five new sergeants are expected.

Wrote an airletter to Mrs. Claridge (Christmas type) & wrote Hazel. Not quite so cool as usual. Three blankets were used & I felt just right.

Fairly early to bed after boys brought me some cheese as they drank beer. Airletter to Hazel.

Wednesday November 29: Up early enough without knowing correct time. Not too chilly. Spotty morning but busy towards end. Bright & warm.

Dhobi back in afternoon. Started airgraph for Hazel. Cakes from char wallah. Hot shower.

Reg Corrick brought me a tin of salt as he had some sent to him. Completed airgraph after dinner. Chill started fairly early.

Wrote ordinary style & then started airmail under tomorrow's date. Fred had cheese & bread to share with me. Took cocoa on shift at 22:00. Busy from the start.

Thursday November 30: No time out all night but didn't feel sleepy. Had three slices of chocolate cake with cheese, bread, & cheese. Army Cpl. Brought me cocoa.

Blanket lungi [loincloth] style kept me reasonably warm. Not even sleepy at end of shift. Hit the bed hard around 10:00 & not up until after 16:00. Slightly groggy.

Sleep disturbed once or twice. Heated water for cocoa after dinner. Wrote Hazel but Corrick upset things as he visited. Couldn't finish airmail as planned.

Not in bed until fairly late. Still chilly …

Friday December 1: Just up early enough for breakfast. Haircut from camp napi. [?] Sat in sun & wrote to Hazel. Cakes from char wallah. Carried on with airmail.

Mess meeting at 13:30. Opening mess tomorrow. Turned in

plates & irons after dinner 8 as a day. Hot shower as usual. Completed airmail.

Busy shift but did not strain myself. Had to wear sweater for warmth before end of shift. Roper brought sandwiches but fish style which left me lunchless.

Climbed into bed right after work. Full moon. Used sweaters for warmth.

Saturday December 2: Not up too early as mess handy. Poor service. Chilly enough for sweater at first. Wrote Hazel for awhile.

Pay parade at 10:00 but not on time – paid 55 chips. Had hot cocoa with Darby as Fred Lambert boiled water for tea. Cakes from char wallah.

Fairly easy shift at first but grew heavier towards the end. No oil for lamp. Read & wrote by candlelight. Joe for Mess Caterer this month – worse luck.

Bill Peel called to chat & borrow candles. Watch going all right again. Bed fairly early.

Sunday December 3: Not too early rising but there for morning shift. Fairly busy. Wrote ordinary & started airgraph for Hazel.

Sunbathed. Jack Shegog gave me some oil for lamp. Airgraph finally completed but disturbed by boys killing last of the beer.

Had "Slim" Harris bring cake from canteen. Took his jacket

as well as sweater & blanket on shift. A stack of work from the beginning & the pace never slackened as I blasted ahead.

Army boys worked with us for awhile.

Monday December 4: Paused long enough for four pieces of spice cake with cheese & cocoa from own tin – taste of chlorine too strong.

No time out for sleep. Colder than ever. Highest total for work so far. [illegible]

Slept heavily but not well during day. Usual afternoon disturbance. Groggy at first but strolled to canteen after dinner & felt better.

Had cake with lemon squash & brought two pieces away. Wrote this & then to Hazel. Continued on until bed time. An Ensa Show in camp but didn't bother going to it.

Tuesday December 5: Rolled out in time for breakfast. Got tin of water from pump but it collapsed on way back. Chatted with cook regarding water missing.

Spread bedding in [?] for morning. Read Reader's Digest. Wrote Hazel for awhile. Spent most of afternoon writing poetry.

Started airletter but stopped for shower. Kept steady pace all evening. Not as chilly as usual. Christmas card, 334, & 335 from Hazel.

After work completed airletter for early mailing in the

morning. Roper didn't bring anything to eat.

Whoops – here I go again to-

Friday June 1, 1945 – and this is the last sea lap before Canada. Breathes [? smeared ink] there a man is due for a personal test next week.

I wonder. Excitement seems to be bottled up inside waiting for the corkscrew. I don't think the top will blow off until Hazel & I get together.

At the moment it is simmering down inside.

The "Louis Pasteur" won't bring as pleasant memories as the "Sterling & Capetown Castle", but it is that boat which has been rolling on since I boarded the "Letitin" on the 15th of June, 1942.

D. 9 with its mess decks and hammocks brings me back to the starting point in more ways than the obvious one.

If it weren't for the boys playing at being men upsetting things at first, I should have no disagreeable thoughts on the subject.
Little do many of these youngsters realize that this is but the first shock the outside world has to give.

Most of them have done a good job but there comes a time when cowboys & Indians must be put aside for the give and take of everyday life.

I can see the gap between myself and this crowd of school

boys who traded pens for swords too quickly for real tempering of their souls or whatever it is that forms the nucleus of a person.

I hope that most of them are able to withstand the inevitable strain which comes from slowing down from high speed living that can't consider a future more remote than days or even hours.

In the final reckoning, their weight is bound to tip the scales heavily either for advancement or retrogression.

Hitler's evil will take more strange and almost unrecognizable forms for centuries. Perhaps that's why I could not enter into the festive spirit of V.E. Day [Victory in Europe]

Few people seemed to realize the full implication of the cessation of hostilities in Europe, not the least of which is that a bitter struggle is still ahead in the Far East.

Reconstruction alone will be the full time job for our generation.

And how important it is that we build solidly and with an eye to a future that can be truly worth the savage destruction to world progress.

If our struggles were in vain then surely chaos is the least of evils that will pour forth to wreck evolution's train which has climbed so slowly & painfully to its present significant level that promised such green pastures.

Fate seems scheduled to dangle me just so close to the fire.

My recall as Group was about to depart for Akyab [Burma] and points south came only soon enough as my very being might have shrivelled had I gone on through Burma.

Yet, at the time, I considered it no more than a reprieve. Shalimar was rough but the season favoured me there.

My sort of luck appears to soften the roughest bumps but allows me to sail near enough to feel the blast that devours less fortunate people.

Then, the chota monsoon came to remind that I was escaping when I headed for Chittagong & release from an existence that hope for a real future alone had kept me moving on and laughing away despair which often threatened to engulf me.

Only now is it safe to allow myself to think how close I ran to utter desolation during those blank days when the end of wait was obscured.

Realization has come slowly but my real personality is gradually shaking itself free as [kilometres] diminish and home looms close.

Calcutta & the subsequent troop train journey to Bombay remain as a blur in my memory.

I recall the false sadness which pricked as Chittagong was left behind for the last time.

The ferry seemed no better or worse than usual but that part of the trip to & from Calcutta always was a restful interlude.

It was there were I picked up (probably vice versa) “Smitty”, the fellow who couldn’t make up his mind to be Scotch or Canadian.

And to think that I never met his “Anglo” wife from Karachi. Sea-sickness on her part or his own illness [illegible] ship – perhaps.

Re-union with Bert Taylor at Calcutta was a fitting piece to add as I collected up the bits.

And there was the memorable meeting with “Red” Swain who had swollen to almost unrecognizable proportions from his sojourn in Bangalore.

All these have slipped well back in memory lane. For the moment Bert & I are still together but even that association is on the last grains as the parting edges daily nearer.

Next month all this will have grown dim in its turn as Hazel & I strive to close the gap which we feel has been no more than physical.

Yet, every event, (no matter how insignificant) during the

past three years will have some greater or lesser effect upon everything we do.

That final bout with the R.A.F. in which Bert punched while I stood by encouraging & suggesting will be worth the odd chuckle as I remember or recount to others.

Thoughts of the Capetown Castle will always include the “Second Class” passages the R.C.A.F. sergeants insisted upon to the extent of having confirmation radioed from Bombay as we steamed west.

Though I wasn’t aware of it at the time, that was to be the last “luxury” passage on a trooper.

[There are no entries dated June 2 to 4.]

Tuesday June 5: Still the “dream” continues but the awakening is breathtakingly near.

Saturday almost set me on my ear but I received my sea legs issue in time to prevent a double meal count.

I went to the galley with a gang for our breakfast and the lengthy wait too near a bouncing prow didn’t help my stomach which had had no encouragement since the previous evening at 17:30.
A solid basis of mush and break with jam supplied the necessary ballast. But try to convince some poor sailors that food is their only hope – Live and -

My ideas on commissioning took a beating when the trail led home.

Yet how many people will believe that I turned thumbs

down the braid after all the cost?

If nothing else is definite, I do know that reunion with Hazel comes ahead of all other considerations.

Yet, who would seriously ponder on a proposition which stipulated a year in the S.W. Pacific.

Now I'm debating whether it is advisable to go on record concerning the whole affair.

Much depends on whether an immediate discharge is preferred.

My use to the service is at an end as far as I am concerned. A week from today I should hold most of the answers.

Perhaps I'm slipping, but the box of chocolate bars, which I bought as my ration shortly after coming aboard, remains intact.

It can't be the food as there are many deficiencies in my diet.

Possibly the inward excitement & anticipation of much (especially fresh milk) that is to come in the meal department.

And even at that, food will be a minor item.

Shows to go how service life has dulled my sense of living.

But I'm all set to polish away existence film and push aside meaningless days for "todays" which once seemed vague unattainable tomorrows.

With future at my elbow, I dare not think beyond the moment lest the mirage fade into empty dreams.

That is why I feel that I might bubble over when Hazel & I really stand together with no limit to our happiness possibilities.

We shall see, together.

Between checkers and cribbage Bert Taylor & I have laid the hours behind us as quickly as the seconds allowed.

He tries to act tough & cynical but is a good friend if on your side.

The way he voluntarily goes for grub & helps clean the pans makes me suspect we have more in common than I ever thought possible.

Bert an idealist – I wonder.

To understand a person is the path that leads to friendship under circumstances which often appear utterly impossible with no speck of common ground visible.

First impressions must repeatedly spoil what could be mutually beneficial associations.

At one time I felt that Bert had nothing which appealed to my mind.

His example will make me pause before discarding even

the most unprepossessing acquaintanceship that comes to me in future.

[There are no entries dated June 6 to July 23.]

Tuesday July 24: I've just been in Penhold (2T.S.U.) since yesterday but it could be years – what a set-up & I do mean mess.

There is an office for me but no work (& no hope for any) to go with it – worse luck.

The boys in Sigs, Sgt Melrose, LAC Turner, & W.O. Barber (i/c) seem friendly enough but that doesn't make it any easier to loaf.

If nothing definite on discharge is forthcoming by the middle of August, I'll have to try writing my way out – I hope.

Wednesday July 25: Worse & more of it. Never have so many done so little & there seems to be worse ahead.

Already I've been turning over several schemes in my head but maybe something will turn up soon.

Thursday July 26: I'm getting in the groove in a way or perhaps it's a state of resignation.

The 48 for this weekend is definite enough & I should even be able to skip the C.O.'s parade Friday afternoon.

I scraped up enough energy to write Bill Alexander & Jim since yesterday – that is progress.

A Sgt Thomas returned from extended 48 yesterday. I don't care for him but he will probably improve with acquaintance.

He was at B.B. [Bella Bella] when I was there but I can't remember him.

Last night I was ambitious enough to wash my shirt & socks. The laundry tubs in the barracks are just right.

Thursday July 26: My luck held again, but only just. I had practically given up the S.O.P. idea for Sylvan when I found the driver of one of the cars & he had room for one next week.

The oddest part of it all is that the fellow in question sleeps in a room opposite my bunk. Shows to go.

Today's D.R.O. held out new hope as it set forth how employers can claim men through Industrial Sel. & Rel. Committees.

If I can get Pilkington's to play for time, that should settle things quickly. Of course I intend to try for something better but my discharge comes first.

[There are no entries for July 27 to 30.]

Tuesday July 31 & 2 T.S.U. still has a firm grip. I even did two messages yesterday. Home before 17:00 on Friday.

Came to Sylvan Sunday with Hazel, Winnie, their folks, & Ferrons. Cottage Buena Vista near 9th St. Rain dampened things but all went to concert at Varsity Hall.

Too much jive for my taste. Orchestra the whole show with one or two skit exceptions.

Wet & cold Monday but got lift as arranged. Changed to blue at camp. Besides messages, straightened files in own office. Apparently work comes in only over weekend.

Hazel & I saw “Our Hearts Were Young & Gay” at local theatre. Funny.

I took a beating on sleep angle again but set alarm 3/4 hour later as F/S. Marks picked me up at 07:15.

Although Hazel & I sleep in living room as does Winnie, we do get together each day which is the important part.

Dragged around most of day reading Digest. Played horseshoes with Sgt. Melrose. He is a plump, likeable fellow.

I can’t expect to be popular in Sigs as I sit around watching them do the little there is.

Although it is still fall like, the skies are beginning to clear again.

Made out monthly return to surprise W01 Barber as I’m sure he thinks I intend to do as little as possible & only that when told.

At long last, my mind seems to be settling down towards post-war plans.

The best bet would of course be to get into Civil Service in my present job but that may not be possible.

Another plan is to take my C.A. if I can get to Varsity for training.

Opportunities seem to be good for the person who has ability.

Once again I'm wondering what my position will be a year from now. It would be interesting to know some things in advance.

This waiting is the worst thing possible for anyone with my lazy tendencies. It will be harder than ever to discipline myself for real work again.

But, it should be refreshing at first, especially since I'll be able to go home every night.

That seems like a wonderful dream now but it won't be long before I begin to take such things for granted once more – maybe.

[There are no entries for August 1 to 5.]

Monday August 6: The morning after a wonderful week which reached a high point when Hazel & I danced 19 out of 20 twirls at Sylvan Lake Varsity Hall.

I surprised both of us by being almost good which is quiet a feat after three years layoff. That dance smoothed out many things.

Before we started, I wondered if it could be the same.

Once we got into the swing, it was better than ever and the evening slid by quickly & pleasantly – a perfect ending for the week.

Another goodbye yesterday with the tables turned as it was the first time Hazel left while I stayed behind.

My luck was in as I got a quick hitch back to camp.

At least someone is making progress. Henry Benton's discharge came through at last. If I get mine this week everything will be well.

Our good weather has returned just in time to be too late for the holiday week. Perhaps it will be right for discharge leave, even though I might get only 10 days as Henry has.

These goodbyes are wearing although we can take the repeated partings since we know that this is the last lap.

We'll surely stay close together in future & not let anything separate us fro the rest of our time.

An important world item is the announcement of atomic bombs being in use now, the first dropped on Japan yesterday.

END OF DIARY

VOLUMES FROM MYTHBREAKER

Terrian Journals series:

A Sketch of Terrian History
Terrian Journals' How To Make The Nation
Full Employment: Not Fulfilling
Terrian
Terrian Journals: Living as a Newcomer
Middle Earth Journals
Rediscovery Journals
Fukurokuju No Kasumi Journals
Sabbatical Journals
Departure Journals
Adventuredate Unknown Journals
Away Team Journals
Searching For South Journals
Terrian Journals for the Misguided
Terrian Journals' N.S.R.: Not Spying, ...Really!
TJ JNG: Terrian Journals' Jokes Nobody Gets
Terrian Journals First Anthology
Terrian Journals Second Anthology

Archway series:

Archway: Six Year Book of Dreams
Archway: Lifetime Rhyme
Archway's Valentine Love
Archway's Garden Rhymes
Archway's Christmas New Years Rhymes
Archway: Life Before Dreams

Additional Titles:
Language Learning Secrets

www.ingramcontent.com/pod-product-compliance
Lightning Source LLC
Chambersburg PA
CBHW060603100726
47907CB00006B/1496